Olympia

EX. LIB.

£5-00

TRAV

'4412

Ludwig Drees

OLYMPIA

Gods, Artists and Athletes

Pall Mall Press   London

Published by the Pall Mall Press, Ltd.
5 Cromwell Place, London S.W. 7
First published in Great Britain 1968
© 1967 Verlag W. Kohlhammer GmbH, Stuttgart
English translation by Gerald Onn
© English translation 1968 Pall Mall Press, London
Printed in Germany

SBN 269 67015 7

ontents

Introduction   7

I The Sanctuary

  1. The Sanctity of Olympia   11
  2. The Cult of the Olympian Gods   21
  3. Ritual Games in the Sanctuary   26
  4. The Great Festival of Zeus   33

II The Games

  5. The Competitors   41
  6. The Spectators   56
  7. The Sequence of Events   66
  8. The Stadium and Hippodrome   87
  9. The Fame of the Victor   101

III The Art

  10. The Buildings in the Sanctuary   111
  11. The Statues in the Sacred Grove   130
  12. The Zeus of Phidias   145

Epilogue: Olympia's Downfall   154

Bibliography   163

Notes   167

List of Illustrations   179

Index   185

Introduction

The Power of Olympia in Ancient Times

'Olympia has been renowned throughout the ages for its oracle of Olympian Zeus; but even if there were no oracle the fame of the sanctuary would be no less, because of the festival and the Olympic contests.'[1] These words were written by the Greek geographer Strabo, a contemporary of Augustus.

Zeus was the focal point of the sanctuary and the peoples of Greece flocked to Olympia to make their pilgrimage. Eventually tens of thousands were making the quadrennial trip to the sanctuary and the Olympic games became the most popular of all the pan-Hellenic assemblies.[2] But, splendid though the games were, the victor's prize remained simply a wreath of wild olive. In 480 BC, when the Persians were preparing for the battle of Thermopylae, they were told by a group of deserters that their adversaries were watching the Olympic games, at which athletes competed for an olive wreath. Tigranes, one of the Persian officers, wondered aloud in the presence of King Xerxes at 'men who compete with one another for no material reward, but only for honour'.[3]

The Olympic victor received the highest honour, for he was crowned in the temple of Zeus, where he stood face to face with Phidias's great statue. The impression created by this work was so overpowering that it was regarded as one of the seven wonders of the world. At the ceremony the victor communed with the god, who was the author of his victory; he was placed on a level with the god.[4] Pindar, the poet of the Greek athletes, testifies to this:

Verily great is his fame,

Upon whom thy bright honour waiteth.[5]

The Olympic Revival in Modern Times

Olympia did not survive the ancient world. But since the Renaissance the English, French and Germans have considered the possibility of excavating the site and the stadium. The first attempt was the French Morea expedition of 1829, which partially excavated the temple of Zeus, recovering and transferring to the Louvre fragments of the Hercules metopes. But the man who really brought ancient Olympia to life was Ernst Curtius. In 1874 he concluded a treaty on behalf of the German Reich with the government of Greece, whereby Germany undertook to bear the cost of a new expedition and to grant Greece possession of all new finds, a novel provision at that time. Curtius set to work in 1875 and within six years had excavated the whole altis.

The second phase of Olympic exploration began just before the First World War when Wilhelm Dörpfeld undertook a series of deep excavations in order to throw light on the early history of the altis. He continued his work after the war and succeeded in penetrating to the prehistoric levels in the sanctuary, which he dated to the beginning of the second millennium BC.

The third phase began in 1936, following the Berlin Olympics, when a large-scale German expedition was mounted to continue the classical and prehistoric explorations and to excavate the stadium and the hippodrome. Apart from the interruption during the Second World War this expedition has been working in Olympia ever since. From the winter of 1937 onwards it has been led by Emil Kunze, who first excavated and then rebuilt the stadium as it was in late classical times.

A Frenchman, Baron Pierre de Coubertin, revived the ancient games, and the modern Olympics were first held in Athens in 1896. Then came Paris (1900), St. Louis (1904), London (1908), Stockholm (1912), Antwerp (1920), Paris (1924), Amsterdam (1928), Los Angeles (1932), Berlin (1936), London (1948), Helsinki (1952), Melbourne (1956), Rome (1960) and Tokio (1964). In 1968 the games were in Mexico City and in 1972 they are scheduled to be held in Munich.[6]

To establish a link between the ancient and the modern games the torch relay was instituted in 1936. In 1964 the first stage of this ceremony was held in the restored ancient stadium. In the altis a 'priestess' kindled the Olympic flame from the light of the sun, then entered the stadium and handed her torch to the 'sacral king' of the new Olympiad. He passed it to the leader of a team of runners, who then carried it through the stadium, away from the altis and into the grove dedicated to Coubertin. There the runner lit the urn on the modern altar, which continued to burn for the duration of the games. From this urn the Olympic flame was borne by relays of runners to its new temporary home.

Coubertin died in 1937 and his heart was interred in a stele near the altar. Coubertin's successor was Carl Diem who died in 1962. Diem introduced the torch relay, contributed and raised funds for the excavation of the stadium[7] and fulfilled one of Coubertin's last wishes by founding an international Olympic Academy. This institution, which is situated in Olympia itself, has provided annual courses of instruction on all aspects of the Olympic games since the official opening of the stadium on June 22, 1961. In order to preserve the Olympic idea the academy is now erecting buildings and sports grounds near the ancient stadium and the grove of Baron de Coubertin.[8]

If justice is to be done to the phenomenon of ancient Olympia the subject has to be approached both chronologically and in depth. The Greek Olympic games were rooted in prehistoric cults; they entered their historical period with the official inauguration of the festival in 776 BC and then continued for a further 1168 years until they were dissolved in AD 393. The author has already published a work on the historical development of the games in 1962.[9] In this present work he has tried to describe the abundant variety of the cult, the contests and the art of Olympia and to recreate the religious, athletic and artistic synthesis which existed in that period of Greek history.

Part One

The Sanctuary

Chapter One

The Sanctity of Olympia

1. Olympia's Geographical Situation

Olympia lies in the north-western part of the Peloponnese about fifteen kilometres from the mouth of the Alpheus, the largest river in the peninsula. Flowing down from the mountains of Arcadia the sacred river passes through fertile foothills, where vines and olive trees abound, before discharging into the Ionian Sea. The most important place on its lower course, in ancient times, was Pisa, the political centre of the district and the town commanding the sanctuary of Olympia, which was situated some six stades (1.15 kilometres) down river from this royal residence and was occasionally referred to by the same name.[1]

About sixty kilometres north of the Alpheus there is another river, the Peneus, which also flows westwards and forms the main artery of the district of Elis, which was settled by the Epei in pre-Dorian times. The district is aptly named for the word Elis means 'valley-land' and the whole of this lowland plain is broken only by ridges of low hills. Even in the southern part of the territory towards the Alpheus there is no natural barrier of any consequence, so that when the northern invaders descended on the Epei they had little difficulty in subjugating them and subsequently extending their political dominion from Elis to the river Alpheus and even beyond it. This then led to wars with the Pisatans, the inhabitants of the district of Pisa, and since in early Hellenic times politics and religion were inseparable, the Olympic sanctuary also figured in this struggle between the two lowland territories.

The Eleans, who conquered Elis, first invaded the ancient Mycenaean world (under a legendary leader, King Oxylus) during the twelfth century BC in the course of the Dorian migration. The Pisatans and the Epei, on the other hand, both belonged to the collective of immigrant tribes referred to by Homer as the Achaeans, who began their conquest of Greece early in the second millennium BC and subsequently came under the influence of the Minoan civilisation which was centred on Crete. Consequently the religious beliefs of the older tribes were very different from those of the invaders.

After the Eleans and the other peoples from north-western Greece who had accompanied the Dorians on their migration had settled in their new homes Olympia lay on the frontier between the old and the new tribes. The Alpheus separated Elis with its predominantly Elean population from the southern territory of Triphylia where the older tribes, whose roots lay in early, and in some cases pre-Hellenic, times, had succeeded by and large in holding their own against the overextended offensive of the northern invaders. Meanwhile, to the east of Olympia, the Achaeans had sought refuge in the mountainous terrain of Arcadia.

The ultimate victors in this fluctuating battle were the Eleans, who eventually subdued the district of Pisa and gained control of the sanctuary of Olympia, which had previously been held by the Achaeans.[2]

Because Olympia was a sacred place the Eleans tried to establish their own gods there. With the proceeds from their war booty they were able to build the great temple to Olympian Zeus and commission Phidias to create a votive statue. Pausanias tells us that both the temple and the statue of Zeus were built from the spoils taken from Pisa, which the Eleans razed to the ground.[3]

2. The Sacred Character of Olympia

In Olympia, as in all the other sanctuaries of ancient Greece, the actual site—a level terrace set in the 'most beautiful parkland in Greece'[4]—was itself held sacred.[5] Washed on three of its sides by the waters of the Cladeus and Alpheus, and cut off from the hinterland by a steep hill, this enclosed precinct with its plane trees and wild olives was possessed of divine power: '...the Eleusinian mysteries and Olympic games seem to exhibit more than anything else the divine purpose. And the sacred grove of Zeus they had from ancient times called *altis*, slightly changing the Greek word for grove.'[6] The principal landmark of the district is the Hill of Cronus, which is 122.6 metres high. In the south its wooded slopes rise up abruptly from the altis while on its farther face it is separated from the northern heights by a saddle. The Hill of Cronus forms the spur of a chain of hills which in classical times was called the 'Olympian mountains'.[7]

From the south-western face of the Hill of Cronus a low wedge of rock juts out into the altis. In this rock there was once a cleft, in which the earth goddess Gē had an oracle.[8] The cleft has since been filled up as a result of earth tremors and its position cannot now be established, although when the tertiary layers of the hill were cut into in 1930 in the course of construction work on the new road, a fissure in the rock was revealed which could have been connected with the ancient cleft.[9] To the mind of an ancient Greek this cleft was charged with divine power. The mysterious *mana*, which he hoped to acquire from dreams dreamt in sacred places, was manifested here. A priestess then interpreted the dreams induced in the sleeping pilgrims by the forces emanating from the earth and so the oracle of Gē was established.

Presumably the name Olympia came into being at the same time, for the Hill of Cronus had not always been named after the father of the gods. According to Pindar it was Theban Hercules who first called this hill after Cronus.[10] Previously, he says, it had had no name.

But this conical hill is so conspicuous that it seems scarcely likely that it would have remained unnamed over such a long period, for we must remember that the altis was already inhabited before the Dorian migration. Since the Hill of Cronus forms the spur of the 'Olympian mountains' it would perhaps not be unreasonable to assume that it was originally called 'Olympos', a pre-Hellenic word which probably meant mountain. Mount Olympus in northern Thessaly was not the only mountain to bear this name. The Greek mainland, the islands and Asia Minor among them could boast another fourteen peaks, not all of them particularly lofty, which were called Olympus.[11]

Since the cleft of Gē was situated on the spur of the 'Olympian mountains' it is quite possible that the goddess of this sacred place was called 'Olympian Gē', or 'Gē on Olympia', or simply by her epithet 'Olympia'.[12] In that case, the famous sanctuary would have taken its name from the cult; thus the goddess would have been named after the mountain and the sanctuary after the goddess. The sacred character of Olympia, like that of Delphi, was grounded in the cleft. From this it would follow that the earth goddess Gē was the oldest goddess at the sanctuaries of both Delphi and Olympia.

3. Cult Continuity in the Sanctuary

Once the sacred character of Olympia had been recognised, it survived all migrations and became a focal point for the religious desires and needs of the conquerors. Thus the sanctuary acquired cult continuity and with it a history, which we are able to determine by isolating the individual cults which were superimposed one upon the other in the course of time.

The fact that the sanctuary survived for such a remarkably long period was due no doubt to the general belief that the land belonged to the gods.[13] Consequently, far from driving out the resident gods, the new conquerors paid them homage. Having done so, of course, they then proceeded to set up their own gods as well, who, as the gods of the victors, naturally claimed pride of place in the divine hierarchy at Olympia.

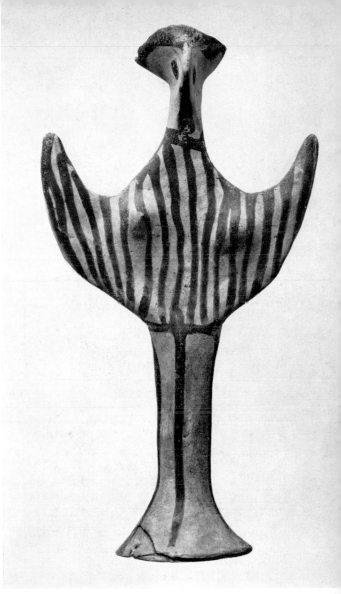

2a. Cult of the earth mother and divine child: small clay figure from Mycenae.

2b. Cult of the moon goddess: clay figure of goddess (Hera?) from Tiryns with crescent-shaped body and arms.

According to legend
Pelops won his bride
Hippodamia in a
chariot-race.

3a. Pelops's four-horse chario

3b. Pelops and Hippodamia.

The Cult of Gē, the Earth Goddess

Even before the Dorian migration a number of fertility cults arose in Olympia, all of which were centred on the cult of the earth goddess Gē. 'And at what is called Gaeum there is an altar to Earth, this too made of ashes: and they say there was an oracle of Earth earlier still. And at the place called Stomium [the opening of the cleft] there is an altar to Themis.'[14] The conception of Themis as the goddess of justice is a late innovation. Originally she was a daughter of Gē, whose laws she enforced.

In Delphi the earth oracle spoke through the mouth of Pythia, and in the sacred precinct of the gaeum in Olympia a woman doubtless also acted as medium until such time as the office of seer passed to Olympian Zeus. Although Gē was deprived of her function by Zeus she retained an outward mark of her original rank, for of the four altars of ash in Olympia one was hers, the others being dedicated to Zeus, Hera and Hestia. The worship of the earth and its regenerative forces marked the beginning of myth among the peoples of ancient Greece.

The Cult of the Earth Mother Ilithyia

Whereas in the chthonic cult of Gē men worshipped the mysterious *mana* emanating from caves and clefts in the earth, in the myth of the 'tellus mater', the earth mother with the divine child, they gave expression to their awareness of the vegetable world. This myth symbolised the process whereby the vegetation emerged from the womb of mother nature and returned to it again each year. No father figure was involved for none was needed.

When the divine child returned to the earth it was transformed into a snake. Pausanias has described the origin of the cult of Ilithyia and her 'snake-son' Sosipolis: 'And it is said that when the Arcadians invaded Elis...and the people of Elis were drawn up in battle array against them, a woman came to the generals of Elis with a baby boy at her breast, saying that she was the mother of the boy and offering him, according to a dream she had had, to help the people

of Elis. And the authorities, crediting the woman's tale, put the child in front of the army...The Arcadians commenced the attack and the child was changed into a snake; the Arcadians then...began to flee, and the people of Elis...won a notable victory; and [they] called the god Sosipolis ['the saviour of the city']. And [at the spot] where the snake appeared to glide off after the battle they built a temple and resolved to worship it and Ilithyia jointly, for they thought it was she who had brought the child into the world.'[15]

This incident is supposed to have taken place at the battle fought between the Arcadians and the Eleans in the altis in the year 364 BC. But the story must be considerably older than this, for it clearly belongs to the period of mythical thought. Ilithyia's name is moreover pre-Hellenic. In historical times her aid was invoked as a midwife but here, in the myth, she is mother nature herself, for it is she who gives birth to the child.

Sosipolis symbolises the earth's vegetation. In winter, when the plants withdraw into the womb of mother earth, the divine child is pictured as a snake, which means that Sosipolis was a chthonic deity. Within the Aegean sphere in ancient times the snake was regarded as a sacred animal, for, like the plants, it concealed itself in the earth in winter, where it shed its skin and then returned transfigured in the spring. It also brought great blessings, for in Olympia the divine child transformed itself into a snake and saved the Eleans, thus appearing as a beneficent being and acquiring its name of Sosipolis, the saviour of the city.

Ilithyia and Sosipolis were worshipped in two separate rooms of the same temple, which was situated on the side of the Hill of Cronus but whose exact position has not yet been discovered. Pausanias has described the ritual observances of the cult: 'At the north end of Mount Cronus, between the treasuries and the mountain, there is a temple of Ilithyia, in which Sosipolis, the tutelary deity of the people of Elis, is honoured...the old priestess of Sosipolis also performs the holy rites according to the custom of the people of Elis, brings lustral water to the goddess and sets before her cakes kneaded with honey.

13

The altar of Ilithyia is in the vestibule of the temple; inside Sosipolis is honoured and no one save the priestess...may enter his sanctuary.... The maidens and women, who reside in the temple of Ilithyia sing songs to Sosipolis and burn incense to him but are not accustomed to pour libations of wine in his honour. And their most binding oath is by Sosipolis.'[16] A live snake was probably kept in the inner sanctum of the temple as a sacred animal.

The child Zeus on Crete forms a parallel to the snake-child Sosipolis. He, too, was well-disposed towards mortals and also appeared to them in the form of a snake.[17] But the Olympic cult was not an imitation of the Cretan cult, for Pausanias tells us that Sosipolis was a daemon indigenous to Elis and his mother was referred to as the Olympic Ilithyia. The myth of the benevolent earth mother and her saviour-child was widespread throughout the whole of the Aegean in ancient times and was preserved in a number of places in the new Olympian religion.

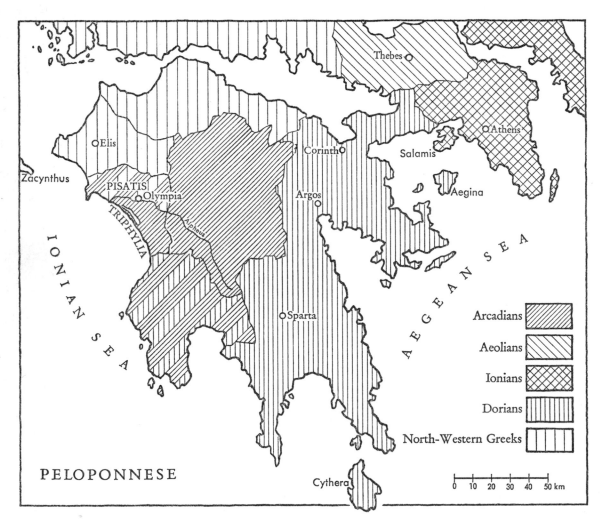

Map of the Peloponnese. For an explanation see page 183 below.

The Cult of the Fertility Gods, Pelops and Hippodamia

When the art of agriculture was carried to Greece from the fertile lands of the Near East as part of the general dissemination of western Asian culture it was accompanied by agrarian cults which had developed from the vegetation rites of earlier times. In Neolithic times man had abandoned his passive attitude to the world; he had learnt to cultivate wild plants and tame wild animals and no longer depended for his food on the random gifts of nature. He had become extremely self-assured, so much so that he worshipped the work of his own hands as divine: the bull was sacred to the cattle breeder; nature, which provided the fruits of the fields, was sacred to the crop farmer. In the course of time these agrarian cults produced their own myth. The annual event of the sowing, which fructified the womb of mother earth, led to the conception of the sacred marriage between mother earth—or the Magna Mater, the 'great mother', as she was now called—and her divine son, the seed corn; after the sacred marriage of the sowing the seed grew to its full height and then died at harvest time, only to be reborn in the following year when the whole process was re-enacted. The cycle of the birth, marriage and death of the agrarian god was celebrated with a special liturgy of its own.

Agriculture soon spread throughout the whole of Greece, bringing prosperity and with it an increase in the population. The early Greek immigrants called the male deity of this agrarian religion Zeus and gave him the laudatory epithet of Pelops, which may be construed as 'the one who produces an abundance', *i.e.*, an abundance of the fruits of the earth. In later mythology Pelops is represented as a king of either Phrygia or Lydia who conquered Greece by force of arms.

In Argolis Zeus-Pelops married the indigenous earth mother, who was later given the Greek name of Hera by the early Hellenes. The word Hera actually means 'year', but in this particular context it signifies the 'year of vegetation', for Hera was the goddess of vegetation. As Pelops's wife she also became the tutelary goddess of the fruits of the earth.

When the first Greeks conquered their new territory shortly after 2000 BC they found this vegetation cult already in existence. Their own gods, who had assumed no specific character and simply represented the elemental forces of nature, either wilted in the face of this fertility ritual or else developed into strange heteromorphic figures such as Poseidon. Meanwhile Argolis became the centre of the great Mycenaean kingdom described by Homer. The lords of Mycenae embraced the existing cult and adopted Pelops as the patron god of their kingdom and the founder of their dynasty, thus furnishing the Atreids with a divine ancestor, an attribute which was, of course, common to all great civilisations in ancient times.

At first Hera had to fight Poseidon for the religious rights in Argolis, her own homeland. But she overcame him and, since Poseidon had been conceived as a horse, she received the laudatory epithet of Hippodamia ('the one who has subdued the horse'). The native goddess Hera then joined Zeus-Pelops as the patron goddess of Mycenae, whereupon the cult of this divine couple spread throughout the whole of the Peloponnese peninsula and even beyond its borders.

It also established itself in Olympia, where Pelops was regarded as an intruder but where, according to myth, the Magna Mater Hippodamia was a native goddess, a daughter of Oenomaus, king of Pisa and consequently of Olympia. Legend has it that Pelops defeated Oenomaus in a chariot-race and so won his daughter's hand. Oenomaus means 'wine-bibber' and was no doubt one of the epithets accorded to Dionysus, the god of wine, whose name was first recorded on a Mycenaean clay tablet. Hippodamia's original name must have been Physcoa who, in historical times, was said to have been Dionysus's lover and was honoured as a heroine in Olympia with a ritual dance.

In view of its regal character the Mycenaean cult introduced into Olympia doubtless appealed most to the nobles of Pisa, for chariot-racing and palaces were the prerogatives of the aristocracy.

15

The Cult of the Grain Mother Demeter and the 'God of the Olives' Iasius-Hercules

Following the introduction of agriculture the peoples of the Aegean were assured of continuous supplies of three basic commodities: bread, wine and oil. As a result, special cults gradually developed in Minoan Crete, all of which were derived from the universal fertility cult of Neolithic times but which proceeded to evolve their own individual conceptions of the Magna Mater and her partner.

The cultivated olive was bred from the wild olive tree, which was to acquire such great significance for Olympia, where the victors in the games were crowned with wreaths woven from its branches. The god honoured by this usage was Hercules. According to ancient legend he first came to Olympia from Mount Ida in Crete. In later myths he is credited with four brothers, one of whom was called Iasius, although this may in fact have been the original name of Cretan Hercules himself. In Olympia these five brothers (who were known as the five Dactyli) made a litter of olive branches on which to sleep. Subsequently Hercules staged a race with his brothers which he called the Olympic foot-race and in which the victor was crowned with a wreath of wild olive.

It is possible that the peoples of the Minoan civilisation on Crete succeeded in cultivating the wild olive and that subsequently this tree cult spread from Crete to the mainland and so to Olympia. But there is another version of the legend which attributes this achievement to Attica, for the Athenians claimed that it was their patron, the goddess Athene, who first brought the olive tree to Greece.

The cult of the grain mother Demeter certainly came from Crete. In the Homeric hymn to Demeter the goddess describes herself as a slave who was taken as booty and transported from Crete to Greece. Her low social position, the tyranny of the mighty to which she was subject and the sorrow inflicted on her by the rape of her daughter Persephone raise this simple grain mother to the level of a pre-Christian 'mater dolorosa' who espoused the cause of suffering humanity, holding out the promise of deliverance and a future life. Her cult was probably particularly widespread among the workers and slaves in the Minoan, Mycenaean and Hellenic world. In Crete the grain mother Demeter lay with her lover Iasion in a thrice-ploughed field, a sacred marriage of the agrarian cult. Now, we have already seen that Iasius was in Olympia, where he slept on a litter of wild olive branches. But Demeter was also worshipped in Olympia, where she received the epithet Chamyne, which means a 'litter', or 'couch on the ground'. And so there are cogent reasons for assuming that Iasion and Iasius were one and the same person, that the Olympic Iasius was in fact the original marriage partner of Cretan Demeter. From this it would follow that the litter of wild olive branches was actually a nuptial couch, and that the reference to the Dactyli sleeping on this litter was an allusion to the nuptials of Demeter and her lover Iasius. There is a specific association between the ploughed field and the olive tree because in Greece in ancient times grain and olives were grown in the same field, just as they are today.

The sanctuaries of Demeter were always situated outside the towns with which they were associated. This was equally true of her sanctuary in Olympia, whose exact site has yet to be discovered but which would certainly have been placed outside the sacred grove. We know nothing of the liturgy for the Olympic Demeter, from which we may reasonably assume that hers was a secret cult like the mysteries of Eleusis.

Zeus Takes Over the Altis

With the collapse of Mycenae shortly after 1200 BC and the intrusion of the Dorians and north-western Greeks Olympia underwent a profound change. The victorious god of the Dorians and Eleans forced his way into the ancient sanctuary on the Alpheus.

Zeus allowed the resident deities whom he had conquered to retain possession of the Hill of Cronus and its base while he established himself in the midst of the plane trees and wild olives of the altis. That Zeus should have been worshipped in a sacred grove was in keeping with Dorian custom for he already

4. Funeral scene depicting chariot-race in honour of
Patroclus. Originally, similar races were staged annually
at Olympia to celebrate the anniversary of Pelops's death.

5. The lord of the altis:
Zeus as a warrior.

possessed the famous grove of Dodona in the far north of Greece. The great northern god took possession of Olympia by hurling a thunderbolt into the altis from the summit of the mighty, cloud-capped Mount Olympus in Thessaly, where he sat enthroned.

Places struck by thunderbolts were sacred; they were called *enelysia*[18] and were dedicated to Zeus Kataibates, who strikes with thunder and lightning. These sacred places were always enclosed to mark them off from their surroundings. This was also done in Olympia and the spot where Zeus's thunderbolt had struck was the most sacred place in the altis. An altar was erected there to Zeus Kataibates and the whole precinct was fenced in;[19] in the immediate vicinity of this *enelysion* was the great altar to Olympian Zeus, at which daily sacrifices were made.

The victorious Eleans, who occupied the territory of Elis with its low hills and broad valleys as far south as the Alpheus, paid special tribute to Zeus.[20] As their foremost god he succeeded to the religious offices of the deities who had preceded him. He annexed the oracle of the earth goddess Gē; he slew Iasius with a thunderbolt and took the grain mother Demeter, the goddess of the poor and the slaves, as his lover, who then bore him Persephone. The fact that this child was a daughter and not a son is a measure of the change which had taken place in the agrarian cult. Hera, the former patron goddess of Mycenae, he took as his wife. Although at first sight this would appear to constitute promotion, in actual fact by this marriage Hera lost her former significance as the Magna Mater, who was superordinate to her male partner in the sphere of the fertility cults. As the wife of divine Zeus she was even deprived of her fertility, for she was simply a companion to her husband and not the mother of his children.

Hera, the Magna Mater, then separated out from Hera, the wife of mighty Zeus, and continued to exist as a divine being in her own right, albeit at a less exalted level, under her old name of Hippodamia. But the victorious god of Mount Olympus laid sole claim to the name of Zeus, which means 'God', thus depriving Pelops of his original rank and reducing him to the status of a hero, a demi-god.

The Cult of the Heroes

The new tribes did not understand the cults practised by their vanquished opponents. To their way of thinking a god who was born and died each year was no god at all, for he was demonstrably mortal. And so, although the ancient agrarian gods of the Minoan and Mycenaean era continued to exist, they were reduced to the ranks of the demi-gods or heroes.

Pelops was given a grave within the altis consisting of a natural mound surmounted by an artificial tumulus, which was between thirty-one and thirty-four metres in diameter and was surrounded by a circular stone wall. Later this circular installation was refashioned and acquired a polygonal shape. Pausanias has described it: 'Within the Altis there is a separate grove to Pelops...who is as highly honoured among the heroes at Olympia as Zeus is among the gods. This grove is surrounded by a stone wall and contains trees and statues. The entrance... [to the Pelopium] is from the west.'[21] The excavations have shown that the old Pelopium, which goes back to about 1100 BC, was a cenotaph.[22] In view of the development of the cult this could scarcely have been otherwise. Pelops's wife was of course regarded as a heroine. She, too,

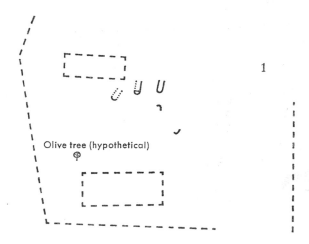

Olive tree (hypothetical)

1

Fig. 1: The altis in the Bronze Age (beginning of 2nd millennium BC).

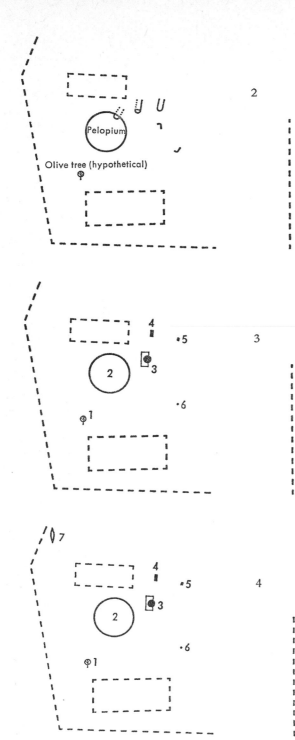

was given a grave, a circular mound the same size as her husband's, whose site, however, has not yet been discovered.

Once a year ritual celebrations were held in honour of the heroes at the graves of Pelops and Hippodamia. The rites were doubtless performed at nightfall, this being the normal custom in Greek hero-worship: sacrificial victims were slaughtered, burnt offerings were made, libations were poured and a solemn dirge was chanted. The liturgy at Hippodamia's grave was performed by the women who celebrated the feast of Hera, which had been inaugurated by Hippodamia. Once a year these women were allowed to enter the enclosure, where they also performed a special dance for the dead heroine.[23]

At the obsequies in honour of Pelops a black ram was sacrificed, the choice of colour symbolising night and death. The blood of the ram was poured into a hole in the funeral mound while the animal's flesh was burnt on a pyre of white poplar. Apart from the woodcutter, who was given the neck of the ram for having supplied the wood, nobody was allowed to partake of the flesh of the victim, for there could be no communion between the living and the dead. Anybody who did so was rendered impure and was forbidden to enter the temple of Zeus.[24] The fact that Zeus-Pelops was displaced by Olympian Zeus did not disrupt the continuity of the religious rites: the wood of the white poplar remained obligatory[25] for the burnt offerings to the Olympian god, and the Eleans continued to make a preliminary sacrifice to Pelops before sacrificing to Zeus.[26]

Fig. 2: The altis in Mycenaean times (late 2nd millennium BC).

Fig. 3: The altis in protogeometric times (11th and 10th centuries BC). The figures refer to: 1 Olive tree, 2 Pelopium, 3 Altar of Zeus, 4 Altar of Hera, 5 Altar of the Mother of the Gods, 6 Oenomaus's pillar.

Fig. 4: The altis in geometric times (9th and 8th centuries BC). The figures refer to: 1 Olive tree, 2 Pelopium, 3 Altar of Zeus, 4 Altar of Hera, 5 Altar of the Mother of the Gods, 6 Oenomaus's pillar, 7 Altar of Hestia.

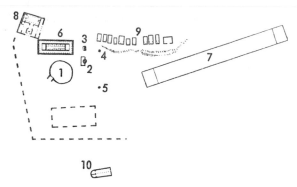

Fig. 5: The altis in archaic times (7th and 6th centuries BC). The figures refer to: 1 Pelopium, 2 Altar of Zeus, 3 Altar of Hera, 4 Altar of the Mother of the Gods, 5 Oenomaus's pillar, 6 Temple of Hera, 7 Stadium, 8 Prytaneum, 9 Treasuries, 10 Buleuterion.

Once a year the epheboi of the Peloponnese allowed themselves to be scourged at Pelops's grave until the blood flowed from their backs.[27] It is hardly possible that this ceremony was simply a test of manly courage; it seems far more likely that it represented a watered-down version of a human sacrifice once performed in ancient times.

Hero-worship was to the Greeks what the adoration of the saints was to the Christians. But the Greek hero differed from the Christian saint: he did not distinguish himself by great virtue nor an extraordinary love of God; his principal quality was his superhuman strength. According to Hellenic belief heroes were exceptional men with extraordinary powers, which they continued to exercise from the grave. Because the hero was powerful in life he remained powerful in death. Consequently the acts of veneration performed at the graves of dead heroes may conceivably have been prompted by a desire to partake of their strength and also to receive their protection.[28]

The Rule of the Olympian Gods

When Zeus took over the altis in Olympia great changes were wrought in the divine hierarchy. At Homer's bidding all the immortal gods of the Olympian household donned their shining armour and followed in the wake of the divine conqueror, appearing at the sanctuary on the Alpheus in the first bloom of their eternal youth; there they were met by Cronus and Rhea, the parents of Zeus, whom Hesiod had summoned from distant Crete. And so Olympia developed from a simple pre-Hellenic sanctuary of purely local interest into the illustrious abode of Olympian Zeus, a centre of pan-Hellenic significance.

When this god came to Olympia he brought Hellas with him. His shrine became a place of pilgrimage for the citizens of every Greek state. The rituals, the competitions and the art of Olympia were dedicated to him. Thus the religious tradition emerged from the darkness of prehistory into the clear light of the classical period, which encompassed a whole millennium (776 BC to AD 393). The sacred character of the sanctuary, its religious continuity and the hierarchy of the gods decided the constitution and the destiny of Olympia.

4. The Altis

The altis proper, 'in which one of the strangest and most beautiful periods of human culture was enacted',[29] was not large. The stadium and the hippodrome, the palaestra and the gymnasium, were situated outside the sacred grove, which consisted of a more or less rectangular area, flanked by the Hill of Cronus in the north and by walls in the south, east and west. We know from the excavations that it was 200 metres long and 175 metres wide.

In early times there were no temples and no statues of gods or victors in the sacred grove. Simple altars were erected among the trees and small votive offerings of clay or bronze were suspended from the branches of the wild olives and plane trees; these usually depicted horses, cattle, sheep and birds and were executed in a primitive, rustic style. The wealthy landowners dedicated tiny reproductions of their chariots and teams of horses, some with, some without a charioteer. There were also minute statuettes

19

which were no bigger than a man's finger and which appear to have been symbolic representations of the godhead.

Although the first official Olympiad took place in 776 BC, and although the temple of Hera, which is one of the oldest of all Greek temples, was erected in the seventh century BC, the altis did not acquire its incomparable reputation as a centre of the arts until the Eleans had wrested absolute control of the games from the Pisatans, who had organised them from 668 to 572 BC.

It was in 472 BC that the Olympic festival was extended to cover a full five-day period. By then the magnificence of the festival was matched by the splendour of the altis, which was subsequently even further enhanced by successive generations right down to Roman times. In the end the sacred grove was literally strewn with altars, temples, effigies of the gods and votive offerings. Following the destruction of the small pre-Dorian colony in Olympia it was not men who settled there but gods; apart from the priests who performed the 'opus dei' for the Hellenes nobody actually lived in Olympia; and even the priests did not live in the altis. First came the god and it was 'to the greater glory of this god' that the Greeks matched their skills in the games.

Chapter Two

The Cult of the Olympian Gods

The Olympian gods were the youngest and the most important of the deities in the altis. The liturgy performed by their devotees was unlike that observed in the older earth and fertility cults: the votaries were different, the rites were different and they were practised at a different time of day. In the Olympian cult there were daily and monthly sacrifices: Zeus was honoured every day, the lesser gods every month.

1. The Great Altar of Zeus

The religious centre of the altis was the great altar of Zeus, which stood close to the sacred spot where the god had hurled his thunderbolt. This altar was built in two sections: there was a base called the *prothysis* on which the victims were offered in sacrifice and a mound of ash on which the legs of the victims were burnt. According to Pausanias the upper part of the altar itself was made from the ashes of the victims sacrificed to Zeus. The circumference of the base, *i.e.*, the prothysis, was 125 feet and that at the top of the mound 32 feet; the overall height of the altar was 22 feet. Stone steps gave access to the base on two of its sides and from the base to the top of the mound there were a further two flights of steps cut into the ash. Virgins were allowed to ascend the steps to the prothysis, as were married women when they were not actually banned from Olympia; but only men were allowed to ascend the high altar.[1]

The Olympic foot measured 0.32 metres, so the circumference of the base would have been 39 metres and that at the top of the mound of ash 10 metres. Unfortunately we have no means of establishing the relative heights of the base and the mound; we simply know that the overall height was 7 metres. Pausanias

prefaces his description of the altar of Zeus with a reference to the altars at Pergamum and Samos. Excavations have shown that these had a rectangular base, from which it may be reasonably assumed that the same was true of the altar at Olympia.[2] In his account of the altar of Zeus, Pausanias goes on to say: 'And annually the seers observe the 19th day of the month Elaphius by carrying the ashes from the prytaneum and kneading them with...water from the river Alpheus and so construct their altar. No other water is ever used for this purpose and that is why the Alpheus is considered more friendly to Olympian Zeus than any other river.'[3] The *prytaneum*, which was the administrative centre for both the sanctuary and the games, contained the hearth of Hestia. Each year the ash from this hearth was removed to the altar of Olympian Zeus and, again according to Pausanias, the height of that altar was 'largely due to these contributions'.[4]

The archaeologists have found no trace of the altar of Zeus. Perhaps it was destroyed by the Christians in accordance with the decree promulgated by Emperor Theodosius II on November 13, AD 426.[5] But this widely held view has been opposed by Friedrich Adler who was present in Olympia throughout the entire course of the early excavations. He argues that, once it had fallen into disuse, a structure as flimsy as the altar of Zeus would quickly decay and that since the materials of which it was made were such useful commodities—the bones and ash for farming and the stones of the prothysis for building — it was almost inevitable that it should have been lost without trace. From this he concludes that Christian fanaticism would scarcely have been a major factor in the destruction of the altar.[6]

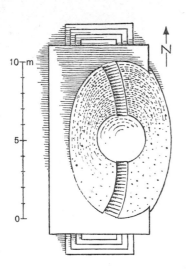

Fig. 6: Altar of Zeus in Pausanias's time (*c.* 170 AD).

2. The Daily Sacrifice

Although the priests sacrificed to Olympian Zeus on the great altar every day they did not always make burnt offerings to him; on many ordinary days they almost certainly made no more than a simple incense offering, burning frankincense and cakes kneaded with honey. On such occasions it was also customary to pour libations of wine. But when an animal was sacrificed it had to be burnt, strictly according to ritual, on a pyre of white poplar, the same kind of wood as that used in the annual sacrifice to the hero Pelops. We have already observed that, before making an animal sacrifice to Zeus, the priests had to offer up a preliminary sacrifice to Pelops.

The sacrificial victims attracted birds of prey, which hovered over the altars waiting to pounce on the offal. But the altar of Zeus in Olympia possessed a remarkable property which distinguished it from all other altars. Pausanias tells us that the kites never harmed the priests who sacrificed at Olympia and that on the rare occasions when a kite seized upon the entrails or the flesh of a sacrificial victim this was considered an ill omen for the officiating priest.[7] Pliny even maintains that birds of prey never stole anything from the altar in Olympia.[8]

There were also said to be no flies or midges near the altar of Zeus, even though it stood on low ground near the river. No doubt the smoke from the burnt offerings made them keep their distance. But it was not long before a mythical explanation was found for this phenomenon. According to Pausanias, when Hercules, the son of Alcmena, was sacrificing at Olympia there was a great plague of flies. But when he sacrificed to Zeus Apomyios ('the averter of flies') they were driven to the other side of the Alpheus.[9] Pliny also has a tale to tell of this plague of flies. In his version the Eleans sacrificed a bull at the great festival in honour of Zeus, whereupon the flies departed from the sanctuary in hordes.[10]

Hestia was a goddess of hearths and on her hearth in the prytaneum, which was also made of ashes, the sacred flame burnt night and day.[11] Before offering up a sacrifice to one of the gods it was customary for all devotees to pray to Hestia and also to one of the male hearth deities; this prayer to Hestia was normally accompanied by an offering if the ceremony was private but not if it was public.[12] From this it would follow that these were preliminary sacrifices and not sacrifices in their own right. Hestia, like all the other lesser deities in Olympia, received a full public sacrifice only once a month.

During the performance of the sacrificial rites in the prytaneum gnomic verses were spoken and hymns were sung in the Dorian dialect,[13] presumably to a flute accompaniment. This we know from

Pausanias. But he does not tell us the text of these verses and hymns, doubtless because he felt inhibited at the thought of revealing the secrets of the liturgy: 'But the words that they use in the prytaneum and the hymns which they sing I am not allowed to introduce into my account.'[14]

3. The Monthly Sacrifice

All in all there were seventy altars dedicated to the gods of Olympia, many of them to Zeus.[15]

Once a month the Eleans sacrificed at every one of these altars, following an established itinerary which began at the hearth of Hestia and finished at the altar of Pan. Pausanias has described this monthly ritual: 'They sacrifice in a...primitive fashion, for they burn frankincense on the altars and cakes kneaded with honey. And they decorate the altars with olive branches and pour out libations of wine. But they do not offer libations of wine to the Nymphs or the Mistresses or at the joint altar of all the gods.'[16]

When he speaks of the Mistresses, Pausanias is thinking of Demeter and Persephone, who, like the Nymphs, were pre-Olympian deities. The fact that they were not allowed libations of wine evidently goes back to a time when wine was unknown.[17] This taboo must have continued even after a goddess like Demeter had been received into the circle of the Olympian gods, and was evidently so powerful that it was able to assert itself at the communal sacrifice, which of course included both Olympian and pre-Olympian deities.

The heroes and the deities revered on the Hill of Cronus, namely Gē and Ilithyia and her child Sosipolis, were excluded from this monthly round. They were chthonic deities and as such very different from the gods of Olympus. They did not receive their sacrifices by the light of day but at the onset of night. Even Cronus, Zeus's father, was excluded from the monthly sacrifice, for he had been banished from the company of the Olympian gods. He received a sacrifice only once a year on the summit of the hill which bore his name.

It is striking to find that Dionysus was virtually disregarded in Olympia. Once a year a dance was staged in honour of Physcoa, his mortal mistress, but he himself, the god of wine and ecstacy, was obliged to share an altar with the Graces.[18] True, in the late days of the festival he received an altar of his own, but this was erected by private individuals[19] and was outside the altis.[20] Although by the time Pausanias visited Olympia the monthly ritual had been extended to include Dionysus, originally he had not belonged to the circle of the Olympian gods. On the contrary, there was open hostility between them, for the ivy, which was sacred to Dionysus, was not tolerated within the Olympic sanctuary.[21]

4. The Annual Sacrifice

Certain of the cults were practised only once a year and the cult of Cronus was one of these. Cronus occupied rather a special position in Olympia for he was not old enough to belong to the pre-Olympian gods and, since he had been dethroned by Zeus, could not be regarded as an Olympian deity either.

After castrating his father and usurping his throne Cronus had been threatened with the loss of his own throne if he bred any male children. He therefore devoured all the children of his marriage, both boys and girls. But when his wife Rhea was carrying Zeus she devised a scheme for saving the child's life. She bore it in secret and gave it to the Curetes, the benevolent earth spirits, who reared it in a cave on the island of Crete. When Cronus was told of the deception he set off in search of the child but failed to find it for, whenever the infant's cries threatened to reveal its hiding place, the Curetes performed a war dance with clashing shields and cymbals, thus drowning the sounds of the weeping child. And so Zeus grew up and eventually deposed his cruel father.

Although with the elaboration of the cult of Zeus the steep hill on the northern edge of the altis, which had not previously borne the name of any cult, was named after Cronus, this god remained a marginal figure in the Olympian pantheon. Pausanias tells us that the *basilae* sacrificed to Cronus on the summit of the hill at the vernal equinox in the month of Elaphius.[22] These basilae, who performed the annual sacrifice, were priests. But, although the word basilae means

23

'kings', it seems improbable that they really were priest-kings. It is far more likely that the members of this cult took their name from the god to whom they sacrificed for, unlike Zeus who was seldom referred to as 'basileus', Cronus was always accorded this title.[23]

There were many altars to Artemis in Olympia and she was also one of the deities to receive the monthly sacrifice. But once a year a special ceremony was held in her honour, which soon developed into a public festival. Strabo mentions it in his *Geography*. He also says that she had a grove situated at the mouth of the Alpheus, about eighty stades from Olympia, and that the whole district was full of sanctuaries dedicated to her.[24]

But as far as Zeus himself is concerned there are only a few fleeting references to an annual festival. One of these is to be found in the *Anecdotae Graecae*, where we are told that the smaller Olympics were staged each year.[25] And then the fact that Lucian refers to the great Olympics would seem to suggest that he was making a distinction between the Olympiads and some lesser festival.[26] But, although it is distinctly possible that there was a special annual sacrifice to Zeus, it is improbable that this festival was accompanied by sporting events, for then there would surely have been some record of them.

5. The Quadrennial Festival in Honour of Zeus

The fame enjoyed by Olympia both in antiquity and in modern times originated in the 'great Olympics', the five-day festivals of sport which were held every four years and which were inextricably bound up with the cult of Zeus. This relationship has been well described by Deubner: 'The Olympic games were sacred games, staged in a sacred place and at a sacred festival; they were a religious act in honour of the deity. Those who took part did so in order to serve the god and the prizes which they won came from the god. For when the wreath woven from the branch of sacred olive was placed on the victor's head it transmitted to him the life-giving properties with which that tree was charged. The Olympic games had their roots in religion.'[27]

There was also a splendid festival every four years in honour of Hera, at which the competitors were women. But this could not compare with the festival staged for her husband, Olympia Zeus.

6. The Oracle of Zeus

Olympian Zeus had taken the age-old oracle of the sacred cleft away from the earth mother Gē, the oldest goddess in Olympia, and transferred it to his own great altar.[28] The earliest Greek oracles were all earth oracles.[29] Gē had had another at Delphi, which she lost to Apollo when he began his reign on Mount Parnassus. Although far less important than the celebrated oracle of Delphi the Olympic oracle also enjoyed considerable fame from Pindar's time—the first half of the fifth century BC—down to the days of Strabo, a contemporary of Caesar Augustus.

Whereas in Delphi the god's answers were transmitted by a woman, the prophetess Pythia, in Olympia this service was performed by prophets from the families of the Iamidae and the Clytidae; the first of these families was probably of Pisatan, the second of Elean origin. Even in Cicero's day their powers of prophecy were still held in great respect[30] and the Clytidae were once described as men who spoke with the tongues of gods.[31] But they did not practise the ancient earth oracle of Gē and consequently were not given to the ecstatic form of soothsaying favoured at Delphi, which went back to pre-Hellenic times. As exponents of the new Olympian religion they restricted themselves to the interpretation of omens. They prophesied from the flames and smoke of the sacrificial pyres and interpreted the voice of the god when he spoke to them through his thunder; their prophecies were so accurate that Pindar was able to speak of Olympia as a mistress of truth:

> Hail, Olympia, mother of contests for the peerless crowns,
> Mistress of the shrine of Truth, where soothsayers make trial of the will of Zeus of the gleaming thunderbolt, seeking for a sign in the burnt-sacrifice,

Whether he hath aught to say concerning men whose hearts are hot to win high renown and solace for their toils and pains.[32]

They also predicted the future from the skins of the sacrificial victims by studying the incisions made by the knife.[33]

Since Delphi was so manifestly pre-eminent there was no question of rivalry between the two oracles. On the contrary, the priests actively cooperated with one another. Xenophon tells of the Spartan general, Agesipolis, who in 390 BC asked, first in Olympia and then in Delphi, whether he would be offending the gods if he were to subdue Argos before embarking on his campaign against Athens. Both oracles gave him permission to proceed.[34] A similar example of harmonious collaboration is cited by Plutarch. It seems that every nine years the Spartan magistrates, who enjoyed considerable powers and were even able to impose restraints on the kings of Sparta, waited for a moonless, starlit night and then proceeded to observe the heavens. If they sighted a shooting star they took it as a sign that the kings had offended the gods and suspended them from their office until such time as 'an oracle came from Delphi or Olympia' which authorised their reinstatement.[35]

7. The Officiants at the Sacrifices to the Olympian Gods

Pausanias tells us that the sacrifices were conducted by the *theekoleos*, aided by the seers, the libation-offerers, the flute player and the woodcutter.[36] It seems probable that the four seers, who were descendants of the ancient families of the Iamidae and the Clytidae, headed this religious hierarchy and that it was they who interpreted the oracle. But their duties did not end there; they also had to observe all the sacred days, a requirement involving highly complex computations, for the great quadrennial sacrifice to Zeus was a moveable feast, whose date they had to establish and proclaim in advance. In the spring of each year they carried the ashes from the hearth of Hestia to the great altar of Zeus, which had been placed under their special care. It also seems probable that these seers were the Apolline prophets who ensured that no unworthy persons approached the great altar of Zeus.

Literally theekoleos means 'one who tends the gods'. In fact these men were the priests, three in all, who took it in turns to preside over the sacrifices. A priest's period of office lasted for one month, during which time he lived at Olympia. These men all came from noble Elean families. The libation-offerers who took part in the monthly sacrifices also poured the annual libations for those heroes and their wives who were revered by the Eleans.[37] These libation-offerers were probably the cult lawyers; as such they would have acted as sponsors and ensured that all agreements concluded in Olympia were carried out. As the heralds of Elis they were also required to travel to every state in Greece to proclaim the sacred truce and announce the opening of the great festival of Zeus.[38] The flute player accompanied the sung liturgy at the sacrifices while *xyleus,* the woodcutter, procured the wood for the burnt offerings, which he sold to both municipalities and private individuals at a fixed price.[39] Finally there were the *exegetes* or guides, who took the pilgrims and visitors to Olympia on conducted tours and explained the sights of the sanctuary to them. Pausanias based many of his accounts on the evidence of these guides.

Together with the administrative personnel these officiants constituted the *collegium,* which held its sessions in the *theokoleon.*[40] There was also an Olympic Council, a permanent institution made up of members of the Elean nobility, which had its official residence in the *buleuterion* just outside the southern wall of the altis and which dealt with day to day administration.[41] The officiants who served the Olympian gods were all men. By contrast, the pre-Olympian deities had been served by priestesses. But then the older deities had all been goddesses and even where the goddess had been coupled with a god she had always been the dominant partner.

Chapter Three

Ritual Games in the Sanctuary

Zeus asserted his absolute supremacy over the ancient sanctuary of Olympia by eliminating all his male rivals: he destroyed Demeter's lover with a thunderbolt and he reduced Hera's partner to the status of a hero; Sosipolis, a mere child, was considered harmless and neither Ilithyia nor Gē had husbands. And so Zeus entered into the cult of Demeter and Hera. But he did not appear there in the role of prince consort, which was the position accorded to the male partner in the old fertility cult of the Magna Mater. On the contrary, he came as a conqueror with a conqueror's rights.

The liturgy used for the celebration of the birth, marriage and death of the god had been accompanied by ritual games, which had served a real and genuine purpose in the pre-Dorian religion. But with the erosion of this religion under the new regime of the Olympian gods the games gradually lost their original significance; for when Zeus succeeded his vanquished rivals and took over their consorts for himself—one as mistress, the other as wife—these age-old fertility games, which the goddesses brought with them into their new union by way of a dowry, were assimilated into the Olympian cult and underwent a profound transformation in the process. Thus the religious continuity in Olympia ensured the continuity of the games: after an initial phase of atrophy which was followed by a second phase of transformation and adaptation, the games previously associated with the ancient fertility rites were eventually re-established as part of the cult of the militant and immortal Zeus. They then acquired a degree of fame such as they had never known before.

1. The Foot-Race of the Sacred Marriage. Demeter and Iasius

The sacred marriage of the agrarian religion, the *hieros gamos,* was enacted at the festival of the sowing in order to fructify the womb of mother earth. After nature had bestowed its gifts on mankind it had to be made fertile again so that the new seed might germinate and grow to maturity. In the cult of Demeter the officiating priestess of the Magna Mater always represented the goddess at this ceremony, but in the cult of Hera this honour went to the winner of a special foot-race for girls. In both cults the agrarian god was represented by the winner of a chariot-race or foot-race for men.

Suitors' races are frequently mentioned in Greek legend and mythology. Odysseus, for example, won his bride in a race which Icarius staged for the suitors of his daughter Penelope.[1]

In the first thirteen Olympiads, which were held between 776 and 728 BC, the only contest was the foot-race for men. The competitors had to cover a distance of one stade—192.28 metres in Olympia— and consequently this event came to be known as the stade-race. Pausanias has recorded the legend purporting to relate the origin of this contest: It seems that after the Idaean Dactyli (the Curetes to whom Zeus had been entrusted as a child) had come from Crete to Elis, the oldest of them, Hercules, challenged his four brothers, Epimedes, Paeonaeus, Iasius and Idas, to a race. The winner of this race was to be crowned with a wreath cut from one of the wild olive trees which grew in such abundance in Olympia that the

Dactyli even used their branches to make a litter on which to sleep. Thus, according to legend, it was Idaean Hercules who inaugurated the Olympic games; he was also said to have given them their name and to have stipulated that they should be held every fifth year because he and his brothers were five in number.[2]

Since it is highly probable that the celebration of the pre-Dorian sacred marriage between Demeter and Iasius-Hercules 'on the litter of olive branches' was also observed in Olympia, the legend of the contest between the Dactyli may be regarded as a mythological account of an ancient, ritual suitors' race. The wild olive was sacred to Cretan Hercules and was inhabited by him. Consequently, when the victor in the foot-race was crowned with a wreath of wild olive, he assumed the properties of the god, became the representative of the god, and as such was allowed to enact the sacred marriage. His partner in this ceremony was the priestess of Demeter Chamyne. As the representative of the goddess she probably stood at the end of the track to mark the finish of the men's foot-race. Even after Zeus had killed Demeter's partner, Iasius, with a thunderbolt and taken the goddess for his mistress she was still accorded a special place in the stadium despite the fact that the ritual suitors' race no longer existed as such, having been completely assimilated into the cult of the victorious lord of the altis. The priestess of Demeter Chamyne was the only married woman allowed to watch the Olympic games, all others being banned from the stadium under pain of death. She sat enthroned on an altar of white marble opposite the judges' stand. The perpetuation of this privilege and the fact that the victors were still crowned with wreaths of wild olive furnishes clear evidence of the continuity between the old and the new games in Olympia.

2. The Chariot-Race of the Sacred Marriage. Pelops and Hippodamia

Although the representative of the goddess in the fertility cult of Hera-Hippodamia and Zeus-Pelops

was selected by staging a foot-race, a chariot-race was held to determine who was to represent the god, a practice in keeping with the way of life of the Pisatan nobility, who were the principal adherents of this cult. The old legend shows quite unmistakably that the first of these chariot-races, that in which Pelops won the hand of Hippodamia, was in fact a ritual suitors' race: 'Oenomaus had learnt from an oracle that he was to die at the hands of his son-in-law. Consequently, when any man came to court his daughter he insisted that he should first match his skill with him in a chariot-race, in which the loser must die. Oenomaus always gave his opponent a start but his pair of colts was so fast and his charioteer, Myrtilus, so skilful that he never failed to catch up with the suitor, whom he promptly transfixed with his lance. Twelve courageous men had already paid the price for their daring love when Pelops presented himself as a contender. At the start of each race Hippodamia always mounted the suitor's chariot at her father's request, who hoped in this way to distract the love-lorn charioteer from the business in hand. But when she came to mount Pelops's chariot she fell in love with him at first sight; his victory meant much to her. Pelops meanwhile, who had seen the heads of his predecessors nailed to the wall above the portal of the royal palace, had decided to resort to a stratagem: Myrtilus, the king's charioteer, was himself in love with Hippodamia but lacked the courage to enter the lists; Pelops promised to give

Fig. 7: Small bronze sculpture: chariot (reconstruction).

him Hippodamia for one night and so induced Myrtilus to remove the bronze pins from the wheels of the king's chariot and replace them with pins made of wax. As the race progressed the axle heated up, the wax melted and a wheel flew off the chariot, throwing Oenomaus to the ground. The victorious Pelops then killed his royal opponent and took both his throne and his daughter as his prize. When Myrtilus reminded the victor of his promise Pelops killed him as well by pitching him into the sea, thus disposing of an awkward witness to his deceit.'[3]

If we disregard the highly imaginative elaborations in this account, what remains is a story of a chariot-race in which a suitor wins a bride. Since Pelops was quite sure of Hippodamia from the outset, and took her with him in his chariot instead of winning her as a prize at the end of the contest, the above account, the so-called 'treachery version', must be a relatively late one. And in point of fact there is an alternative version of this same legend in which Pelops receives his bride as a reward for his labours. It seems probable therefore that this is the older of the two and that it has retained more of the religious substance of the myth. According to this second account Pelops was given, by Poseidon, a golden chariot drawn by four winged horses which struck fear into the heart of Oenomaus. But this did not deter the king from accepting the challenge, for he still placed great faith in the speed of his own horses. Poseidon then cast a spell on Oenomaus's chariot so that the wheels flew from their hubs and the rider was thrown to his death. After reaching the finish the victorious Pelops turned to see the royal palace, which had been struck by lightning, burning furiously; he raced to the scene and saved his bride from the holocaust. The only thing spared by the flames was a wooden pillar which then remained within the altis until late in its history.[4]

Although there is also a great deal of elaboration, in this version the nucleus of the myth remains, for Pelops wins his bride only at the end of the contest.

Pausanias gives a detailed description of Oenomaus's pillar, which he places between the great altar and the temple of Zeus. Apparently the timber was so old that the pillar was reinforced by iron clamps and protected by a roof which was supported by four further pillars. Pausanias then mentions a small bronze tablet bearing the following elegiac inscription:

> Of the splendid house, oh stranger, I am the
>   only vestige;
> Formerly a pillar in King Oenomaus's house,
> Now near Zeus I stand in iron clamps in honour.
> The destructive fire left me unscathed.[5]

But we know from the excavations that there was no palace within the altis. Consequently Oenomaus's pillar must have been a phallus, which was of course a customary and significant symbol in the old fertility cults. In the suitors' races a phallus was used to mark the finishing point and it was at the base of this phallus that the victors placed their votive offerings. This would certainly seem to be the implication of the following passage from Pausanias: 'Another curious thing happened...in my time. A senator of Rome won a prize at Olympia and wishing some record of his victory to survive in the form of a bronze statue...he dug for the foundations close to the pillar of Oenomaus and the diggers found fragments of arms and bridles and bits. These I myself saw dug up.'[6]

As a fertility god Pelops manifested himself not only in the seed corn but also in the ram, which was why a fillet of wool was bound round the head of the victor in the chariot-race. This stamped him as Pelops's representative; in him the god underwent his epiphany.

When Olympian Zeus succeeded Zeus-Pelops the chariot-race lost its original significance as a suitors' race and was simply held in honour of the victorious god. This of course was in the nature of things. But the process of integration did not stop there, for the legend of Pelops's chariot-race was subsequently represented in the eastern pediment of the great temple of Zeus built by Libon.

3. The Foot-Race for Girls

The festival of Hera, like the festival of Zeus, was celebrated every four years and was accompanied by

28

6.   Cult of Demeter. The goddess (left) is handing Triptolemus ears of corn and Persephone is crowning him.

7. A competitor in the race for young maidens at the festival of Hera in Olympia.

a foot-race for girls, which was organised by a group of sixteen of the most senior and most respected of the matrons of Elis, each of whom was assisted by a married woman. These games, which were called the Heraea, have been described by Pausanias: 'The contest is a race for maidens of various ages: in the first race are the youngest, and next those slightly older, and last of all the eldest. They all run with their hair down their back, a short tunic reaching just below their knees and their right shoulder bare to the breasts. They use...the regular race-course at Olympia but make it a sixth part of a stade shorter. And the victors receive crowns of olive and part of the heifer sacrificed to Hera...They trace this contest of the maidens back to ancient times, saying that Hippodamia, in gratitude to Hera for her marriage with Pelops, selected 16 matrons and in concert with them inaugurated these games to Hera.'[7]

The legendary account of this contest also states quite unequivocally that it had its origin in the marriage between Pelops and Hippodamia. But since they were both pre-Dorian fertility deities, who had only subsequently been reduced to the status of hero and heroine, this marriage, in which Pelops was personified by the winner of the chariot-race and Hippodamia by the winner of the foot-race, can only be regarded as a sacred marriage of the ancient fertility cult. Originally the prize given to the young girls who were victorious in the foot-race may conceivably have been a pomegranate, which was a symbol of fertility and was also sacred to Hera. Certainly, by eating of the flesh of the heifer sacrificed to Hera they became one with her, for Hera revealed herself to mankind in the form of a white heifer.

The simple litter made from the foliage of the wild olive which served Demeter for her nuptials was not grand enough for the former patron goddess of Mycenae: for her sacred marriage Hera-Hippodamia required a bed of state, which was subsequently preserved in the temple of Hera. Pausanias tells us that it was 'a bed of no great size adorned with much ivory... [which] they say was a plaything of Hippodamia.'[8] But this bed would not have been a child's toy. We must remember that the Hellenes thought of the heroes as giants and a giant's 'plaything' could well have been a normal sized bed. Moreover, since it was preserved in the temple of Hera it must have been connected with her cult and may therefore have served as a sacral couch at the celebration of the sacred marriage.

Pelops, Hippodamia's partner, was of course also regarded as a giant. This we know from Pausanias, who relates the legend of Pelops's shoulder blade. It seems that during the siege of Troy the soothsayers prophesied that the city would never fall until the Greeks had procured Hercules's bow and one of Pelops's bones. So they sent for Philoctetes, who had inherited the bow, and also despatched a ship to Pisa to bring back Pelops's shoulder-blade. But the ship was wrecked near Euboea on its return journey and the shoulder-blade was lost until 'Damarmenus, a fisherman of Eretria, cast his net into the sea and fished up this bone and marvelling at the size of it hid it in the sand.'[9] Eventually Damarmenus consulted the oracle at Delphi and was told to return the bone to the Eleans, which he did. In this way it was brought back to Olympia, although by the time Pausanias saw the sanctuary the bone was no longer there.

The fact that the competitors in the foot race for girls were divided up into three age groups would seem to indicate that the sowing took place three times in the course of each year. This is also suggested by the Iasius myth, according to which Iasius and Demeter lay together on a 'thrice-ploughed field'. Thus it would logically follow that the sacred marriage was also celebrated three times.

Once the new tribes from the north had taken over the sanctuary in Olympia the Heraea appear to have lost all their links with the ancient fertility cult and to have become more or less straightforward athletic events held in honour of Olympian Hera. Their original significance, like that of Hippodamia's bed in the temple of Hera, was no longer understood. And yet, at a deeper level, the continuity between the old Hera contests and the new ones survived, as is quite evident from the legendary account of their origin. On the other hand the fact that the victors in these foot-races for girls were crowned

29

with wreaths of wild olive would appear to be an innovation for it was only in the men's foot-race held in honour of Demeter that the olive wreath possessed any ritual significance.

4. Pelops's Funeral Games

The great festivals of the fertility cult were held to celebrate the birth, marriage and death of the vegetation god in the course of the vegetation year. The custom of organising funeral games upon the death of important persons is well vouched for among the Greeks. We need only recall the magnificent games which Achilles staged in honour of his friend Patroclus, at which the Greek heroes measured their skill in chariot-racing, boxing, wrestling, running, archery and in throwing the discus and javelin. Competitions such as these, in which the victors received valuable prizes, were called 'thematic *agones*' to distinguish them from the 'sacred *agones*',[10] in which the only prize was a wreath of wild olive, spruce, laurel celery or sometimes only an apple. For the sacred games possessed a religious character which went back to the pre-Olympian fertility cult. 'In historical times the great Pythian, Olympic,

Nemean and Isthmian festivals, at which the whole of Greece foregathered, were held in honour of the gods; but in ancient times it was generally recognised that these festivals had derived from the funeral games staged for the heroes...'[11]

Funeral games of this kind were held each year to mark the death of the agrarian god Pelops. According to ancient legend, when Pelops was a small boy he was slaughtered by his father Tantalus, who placed his limbs on the tables of the gods for them to eat. But the crime was detected by all save Demeter, who had grown melancholy following the abduction of her daughter Persephone and unthinkingly consumed part of the boy's left shoulder. The impious Tantalus was then condemned to eternal torment by the gods, who also restored the murdered boy to life, replacing his missing shoulder blade with one carved from ivory. The slaughter of Pelops, the destruction of Zagreus and the murder of Dionysus are myths which hint at ritual murders in the cult of the agrarian gods.

In myth, Pelops, the god who 'brings an abundance', symbolised the seed corn. After his marriage with the Magna Mater the seed had to die in the womb of the earth before it could be reborn. In the anthropomorphic view of the universe this phase of the vegetation year could only be expressed if Pelops was personified by a small boy who was then murdered in a ritual ceremony and devoured by the other members of the cult at a sacral meal. Subsequently, however, the murderers of the divine child had to submit to trial by ordeal, opposing one another with naked swords in mortal combat. Plutarch, who was himself a sacrificial priest at Delphi, confirms that such duels were fought in Olympia.[12] The blood sacrifice was supposed to appease the wrath of the god at his own violent death and so reconcile him to the living. It seems that the more arduous athletic events such as the wrestling, boxing and *pankration,* in which boxing and wrestling combined with pushing, strangling and twisting, were derived from these duels. The racing, discus and javelin events, the archery and chariot-racing on the other hand were not intended to appease the god but simply to delight him. The end object, however,

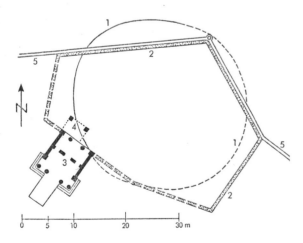

Fig. 8: Funeral mound of Pelops (Pelopium). The numbers refer to: 1 Pelopium I, 2 Pelopium II and III, 3 Gate III, 4 Gate II, 5 Water conduit.

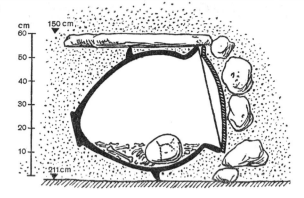

Fig. 9: Funeral urn (pithos grave) containing the bones of a child; found in Pelopium I (section).

remained the same, for these contests, from which all other events in light athletics have evolved, were held in order to persuade the god to return from the dead, to reappear in the form of a new shoot emerging from the dark womb of the earth into the light of day.

When Olympian Zeus usurped Pelops's position in Olympia the funeral games of the old fertility god underwent a complete transformation. Thenceforth they were held in honour of the new god, who exacted no blood sacrifices. And yet, even in the days of late antiquity, men were still aware that many of the contests staged at the festival of Zeus had originally been dedicated to the hero Pelops. This is clear from a comment made by Clement of Alexandria, one of the fathers of the church, who remarked that the funeral sacrifices once offered up to Pelops had been taken over by the Zeus of Phidias in the Olympic games.[13]

5. The Integration of the Fertility Games into the Cult of Olympian Zeus

It was not only Pelops's funeral games that were taken over by the Zeus of Phidias but also the chariot-race commemorating the hero's sacred marriage and the suitors' race held in honour of Demeter; the bridal race for girls Zeus ceded to his wife Hera.

The integration of these competitions into the Olympian cult was a lengthy process; within the completely different climate of the new religion they tended to retain their original character for some time to come. The Olympics opened in the year 776 BC with Demeter's suitors' race which, however, was presented in the form of a stade-race; it was won by Coroebus of Elis. From this simple stade-race the *diaulos*, or double stade, the *dolichos*, or long race, and the race in armour subsequently evolved. These were then supplemented in 708 BC by the funeral games for Pelops, i.e. by the wrestling and pentathlon (discus, long jump, javelin, stade-race and wrestling). In 668 BC and 648 BC respectively boxing and the pankration were also included. The fact that the stade-race was held twice, i.e. both as an individual event and also as part of the pentathlon, would indicate its dual origin in the suitors' race and the funeral games. Wrestling of course also featured as a double event, but this is best explained by the dual nature of the funeral games themselves. Then there was the ritual chariot-race of the sacred marriage, which was added in 680 BC and which subsequently gave rise to a variety of equestrian competitions. But the contests for boys, which were introduced in 632 BC, constituted a genuine innovation, for there cannot possibly have been any precedent for them in the old fertility cult.

The development of the Olympic games under the auspices of Zeus may be summarised as follows:

Olympiad	Year	Competition
1	776	stade-race
14	724	diaulos, or double stade
15	720	dolichos, or long race (competitors appeared naked for the first time)
18	708	pentathlon and wrestling
23	688	boxing
25	680	chariot-racing with teams of four
33	648	pankration and horse-race
37	632	foot-race and wrestling for boys
38	628	pentathlon for boys (immediately discontinued)
41	616	boxing for boys
65	520	race in armour

70	500	chariot-racing with mules *(apene)*
71	496	race for mares *(calpe)*
84	444	*apene* and *calpe* abandoned
93	408	chariot-racing with two-horse teams
96	396	competitions for heralds and trumpeters[14]
99	384	chariot-racing for colts with teams of four
128	268	chariot-racing for colts with two-horse teams
131	256	races for colts
145	200	pankration for boys[15]

In its final form the Olympic programme consisted of eighteen events. The most important was evidently the stade-race, for in contemporary references to the games the victor of the stade-race was frequently singled out for special mention. The following quotation from Pausanias is a case in point: 'Gelon the tyrant of Sicily was master of Syracuse when Hybrilides was archon at Athens in the second year of the 72nd Olympiad, in which Tisicrates of Croton won the race in the stadium.'[16]

The fame which Olympia acquired throughout the Hellenic world as a religious and athletic centre was due in the first instance to the new interpretation placed on these age-old games. It was one of the fruits of the new religion proclaimed by Homer, a doctrine compounded of joy instead of gloom, of good will towards men instead of bad will, a doctrine purged of murky sexuality. Homer told the Greeks that the Olympian gods were not monsters like the agrarian gods; although mightier than men, they were like men, for they had their virtues and their weaknesses; they loved to receive sacrifices but not human sacrifices, and, unlike the gods of vegetation who lived in the dark womb of earth and who grew old and died, they passed their days in the radiance of eternal youth on Mount Olympus.

Chapter Four

The Great Festival of Zeus

1. Hercules, the Mythical Founder of the Festival

Apart from the Dioscuri, Hercules was the only human being to be made immortal in the Olympian universe. As a man endowed with superhuman strength he was regarded as a hero, but as an immortal he belonged to the circle of the gods. Hercules accompanied the Greeks through every phase of their history. Even before the arrival of the early immigrants he was living in Crete as a Minoan god of vegetation, who inhabited the wild olive and was known to the Cretans as Iasius and to the Greeks as Hercules. The Achaeans then adopted him and he was reborn in Thebes in Boeotia as the son of Amphitryon and Alcmena. This Hercules was subservient to King Eurystheus of Mycenae, at whose command he performed his twelve great labours; he was a hero who served and suffered and overcame death. Subsequently Hercules was taken over by the late Greek immigrants, who claimed him as their mythical ancestor and justified their invasion of Mycenaean Greece on the grounds that, as the descendants of Hercules, they were merely returning to their homeland: this was the Dorian Hercules. In this version of the myth Amphitryon was replaced as the father by Olympian Zeus, who was said to have cohabited with Alcmena during her husband's absence by assuming his shape. This Dorian Hercules, the son of Zeus, was a martial hero, whose terrifying strength prevailed over all enemies and made them subject to the conquering tribes. Eventually, when he came to die on his funeral pyre on Mount Oeta, he was raised up to Mount Olympus and rendered immortal. Consequently, instead of being given a hero's grave in Olympia Hercules received sacrifices at the sacred altars.

Pindar sings the praises of the Dorian Hercules and names him as the original founder of the great festival of Zeus and of the Olympic games:

> Ye songs that lord it o'er the lyre,
> What God, what hero, and what man shall we
>   acclaim?
> Verily Pisa is the land of Zeus:
> And 'twas Herakles who stabilised the Olympian contest, as trophy of victorious war.[1]

According to Pindar, Hercules, the great hero of his home town of Thebes, actually created Olympia. Before him there was nothing:

> Now the ordinances of God have roused me to
>   sing of the peerless contest, of trials six in number;
> Which Herakles established by the ancient tomb
>   of Pelops...
> And having pegged the Altis all about, he cleared
>   it fair and free,
> And consecrated all the level plain around to solace
>   and festivity,
> Having honoured the stream of Alpheus in company with the twelve sovereign deities.
> And he called the hill by Kronos' name; for of
>   aforetime while Oinomaos ruled, it was nameless, drenched with many a snow-shower...
> And established the fifth-yearly festival with the
>   first holding of Olympian games and the winning of victories.
> Who was it then who won the fresh-woven crown
> By might of hand or swiftness of foot or chariot,
> Having set up in his heart the prayerful hope of
>   triumph in the contest and having in actual deed
>   achieved it?

The poet then gives the names of the victors in the stade-race, the wrestling, the boxing, the chariot-race, the javelin and throwing the stone.[2]

And so as far as Pindar was concerned Hercules did everything in Olympia, from determining the site of the altis to honouring the god of the Alpheus (a practice also observed by later visitors to the festival, who threw all manner of gifts into the water for the river god).[3] All that needs to be added to Pindar's list is the fact that Hercules fixed the length of the stadium by placing one foot in front of the other six hundred times,[4] that he organised the first contests and was himself victorious in the wrestling and the pankration.[5]

Thus Hercules appears as the mythical founder of the Olympic games, whose deeds were reflected in the achievements of the new immigrants, the Zeus-worshippers, when they raised Olympia to the status of a pan-Hellenic stadium.

2. Iphitus, the Historical Founder of the Festival

Although the early tribes with their mythical view of the world had accepted without question that the Olympic games and the festival of Zeus had been instituted by a divine being, with the passage of time men gradually came to grasp the nature of historical processes, thus ensuring that the part played by King Iphitus of Elis as the actual founder of the Olympics was preserved for future generations. The two principal facts handed down within this historical tradition were: the realisation that the new festival was a revival of older contests (which we have interpreted in the light of the ancient fertility games), and the recognition that the festival was supported by a religious community.

Pausanias comments on the restoration of the Olympic games: 'And as Greece was nearly ruined by civil wars and by the pestilence, Iphitus bethought him to ask of the god at Delphi a remission from these ills. And they say he was ordered by the Pythian priestess to join with the people of Elis in restoring the Olympic games.'[6] At the time of their revival, however, the Olympics did not comprise six events, as reported by Pindar in his mythical account, but only one, for Pausanias tells us that when 'the Olympic games were revived...prizes were first instituted for running [i.e. stade-race] and Coroebus of Elis was the victor'.[7] It was only gradually that the games were extended to cover a variety of contests. This we also know from Pausanias.[8] The extension took place in four phases, the last of which —the introduction of the contests for boys—had no historical precedent.[9] The religious community which celebrated the new festival of Zeus by staging these contests included the Eleans, the Pisatans and the Spartans.[10]

3. The 'Olive Beautiful For Its Crowns'

Coroebus of Elis, the winner of the stade-race at the first Olympiad, was not crowned with a wreath of wild olive; his prize was an apple. This we learn from Phlegon of Tralles, who tells us that nobody was crowned at the first five festivals. But when the time came round for the sixth Olympiad it seems that King Iphitus went to Delphi to enquire of the oracle whether they should crown the victors with a wreath. In his reply the god said:

> Iphitus, no longer give the apple tree's fruit as a prize to the victor,
> Crown him instead with a wreath from the wild and fertile olive
> Which is now enveloped in gossamer webs.

Upon returning to Olympia Iphitus found that one of the olive trees in the sacred grove was covered with cobwebs. He had it fenced in and thereafter the wreaths for the victors were woven from its branches. The Messenian Daïcles, who won the stade-race at the seventh Olympiad, was the first man to be crowned.[11] The ancients considered cobwebs to be a sign of rain and consequently this particular olive tree was thought to be especially fertile.

At the Pythian festival in Delphi it was customary to present the victor with an apple[12] and it would seem, therefore, that when the king of Elis reinstituted the Olympic games at the bidding of the

34

Delphic god he also adopted the type of prize favoured by Apollo. However, when Apollo subsequently advised him to crown the victors in Olympia with a wreath of wild olive the god was not introducing an innovation. It had long been the practice in Olympia to honour victors in this way, and Apollo was merely permitting Iphitus to revive an ancient tradition which had fallen into disuse. Victorious competitors from other Greek states also received a wreath of wild olive, as did the winners of the foot-race for girls. The object here was to demonstrate the unity and universality of the new religious conception underlying the Olympics and Heraea.

The wild olive, a tree of the genus *Elaeagnus,* differs from the cultivated olive. It is smaller, reddish brown in colour with fragrant yellow petals and its fruit is inedible.[13] The olive tree selected by Iphitus stood in the altis near the southern wall of the rear colonnade of the temple of Zeus. It was called the 'olive beautiful for its crowns' *(kotinos kallistephanos)*[14] because the wreaths for the victors were woven from its branches. In the *Mirabilia,* which has been ascribed to Aristotle, there is a description of this olive tree. According to this account, the tree differed from all olive trees for the leaves were pale green on the outside and not, as is normally the case, on the inside. Moreover, the branches—which were used for the wreaths—grew in a symmetrical pattern like the branches of the myrtle.[15]

This tree, which Iphitus had had fenced off, stood in the midst of a clump of wild olives; between them they formed a grove, which was called the *pantheon.*[16] The branches for the wreaths were cut from the sacred tree with a golden sickle by a young boy, both of whose parents had to be living. This we know from an ancient scholium on Pindar's Third Olympic Ode. It would seem that the boy cut just seventeen branches, one for each event.[17] (In 256 BC, when the race for colts was introduced, there were exactly seventeen events. But in 200 BC the first pankration was held for boys, which meant of course that the total number of events rose to eighteen.)

There are three traditional accounts concerning the origin of the olive trees in the altis. In the view of both Pausanias and Phlegon of Tralles the sacred olive tree was an indigenous product of the altis, where wild olive trees grew in great abundance, just as they do today in well-watered parts of Greece.[18] This is the Elean-Pisatan tradition. There are also a number of isolated references to what is probably an Athenian tradition, according to which Hercules first brought the olive tree to Olympia from the banks of the Ilissus in Attica.[19] This account quite evidently constitutes an attempt to claim greater antiquity for the Attic olive tree, which had been a gift of the goddess Athene, for we are told that the 'olive beautiful for its crowns' was a cutting of the Attic olive tree and as such a cultivated variety. Unfortunately there is scarcely any source material which could be said to bear this out. The third tradition, which is presented by Pindar,[20] the poet of Thebes, is mythical. According to this version, Theban Hercules brought the wild olive tree from the banks of the Danube in the land of the Hyperboreans and cultivated it in the valley of the Alpheus. He then ordained that the victors in the Olympic games, which he had founded, should be crowned with a wreath from this tree. But the wild olive cannot possibly have originated in the colder climate of the Danubian region. In fact, it cannot have been introduced into Greece at all since it was indigenous to that country and, according to Pausanias,[21] was even indigenous to the Alpheus valley; to this day the wild olive trees which grow there are amongst the biggest and most beautiful in Greece. But since historical causality was completely alien to mythical thought, the later immigrants, who regarded themselves as the descendants of the Dorian or Theban Hercules, found no difficulty in attributing the work of King Iphitus of Elis to their great ancestor. And where would one find a more willing propagator of this tradition than Pindar, who was so determined to exalt the hero of his own native city of Thebes?

But it was not only the 'olive beautiful for its crowns' that was held sacred. The other olive trees in the grove of the pantheon were also used in sacred rites. When the priests made their monthly round of the sixty-nine altars in the altis to offer up sacrifices and pour libations to the Olympian gods,

35

they also 'decorated the altars with olive branches'[22] which would have been cut from these trees. This was doubtless why the grove was called the pantheon, because the branches were dedicated to all the gods of Olympus.

Originally it was believed that those crowned with olive wreaths acquired divine status. Certainly this would appear to offer the only adequate explanation for the nation-wide fame enjoyed by the Olympic victors. But Olympia was not the only festival to reward its victors with a purely symbolic prize of vegetable origin. On the contrary, this was common to all pan-Hellenic festivals. In Lucian's work of the same name, Anacharsis, the Scythian philosopher, expressed his surprise at this practice, whereupon Solon explained to him that the prize itself was of little importance; what mattered was the personal fame acquired by the man who won the prize.[23]

Lucian then went on to say that the victors were 'placed on the same level as the gods'[24] and entered into communion with them. This bond was clearly demonstrated in the temple of Zeus in Olympia, for Phidias represented Zeus wearing a crown of wild olive. When the victors were honoured they wore the same mark of distinction as the god: a wreath woven from the evergreen branches of the wild olive tree.

4. The Sacred Truce

The festival of the old fertility cult was, of course, held annually, but there was always a special celebration every eighth year when—with the help of three intercalary months—the lunar year, by which the Greeks reckoned their calendar, coincided with the solar year. We have already seen that, when the contests associated with the fertility cult were adapted by the Zeus-worshippers to meet the requirements of their new liturgy, the whole character of the festival was changed. Eventually even the timetable of the agrarian celebrations was discarded and the festival was held every four years.

No doubt the adherents of the new religion wanted to celebrate the festival more frequently in any case. But the principal reason for this innovation was more likely their desire to remove the Olympian cult from the festive cycle of the old fertility ritual, even though this was bound to involve them in difficulties with their calendar, since there was no good astronomical reason for splitting the great lunar cycle. It may be assumed that the real significance of the festival of 776 BC was the decision to go over from an eight-year to a four-year Olympiad.

Until then Olympia had been a small sanctuary of purely regional interest. But due to the introduction of the festival of Zeus—and to its novel organisation—it became an important centre for the whole of the Peloponnese, whose inhabitants were predominantly Zeus-worshippers. In order to establish a supra-regional framework for his reforms, Iphitus had to come to terms with his neighbours and establish a sacred truce so that the pilgrims coming to Olympia could travel in safety. The initial treaty was concluded between Iphitus of Elis, Lycurgus of Sparta and Cleosthenes of Pisa and formed the basis of the religious community which then constantly grew until it embraced the whole of the Greek world.

No important measures were ever taken without the approval of the Delphic oracle. Consequently, when the three kings decided to revive the Olympic games in honour of all-powerful Zeus they first sent a delegation to ask the god whether he would advise them to proceed with their project. They were told that it could only be to their advantage to do so and that they should therefore proclaim a sacred truce to all the Greek cities who wished to take part.[25] The terms of the sacred truce were engraved on a bronze discus. Pausanias has commented on the 'quoit of Iphitus'.[26] It seems that the lettering of the treaty text was set out in concentric circles and not in straight lines across the face of the discus. This relic, the oldest and most sacred in the sanctuary, was kept in the temple of Hera.

When the time for the festival of Zeus drew near, heralds were sent out from Elis to every part of Greece to announce the sacred truce and the precise date of the forthcoming Olympiad. During the sacred truce nobody was allowed to take up arms, all legal disputes were suspended and no death penalties were carried out. The personal safety of all pilgrims was guaranteed, both on their journeys to and from Olympia and during the period of their stay. Initially the sacred truce lasted for only one month but it was later extended to two and then three months to cater for the needs of pilgrims from distant parts.

In the long term this kind of protection could only be extended to the Olympic sanctuary if it remained aloof from Greek internal affairs and its patron state of Elis remained permanently neutral. This is precisely what the Delphic priestess Pythia had told the Eleans to do:

> Leaders of Elis, who rule by the laws of your
> fathers,
> Safeguard your own land and do not have
> recourse to war.
> Instead be the leaders of Hellas in universal
> concord
> When every fifth year the festive season begins.[27]

Thanks to this religious neutrality the state of Elis enjoyed all the blessings of a lasting peace. This enviable state of affairs is described by Strabo. He explains how, after driving the Epei from their land and assuming the responsibility for the sanctuary at Olympia, the Eleans were able to obtain guarantees of nonaggression and even protection from the other Greek states. Foreign armies passing through their territory surrendered up their arms during the transit period and when the city of Elis came to be built no city walls were erected for none were needed. As a result of their neutrality the Eleans became economically powerful and also greatly increased their population, for the conditions obtaining there attracted large numbers of immigrants.[28]

But however advantageous this eternal peace may have appeared to be, after a while the absence of conflict and the lack of tension were bound to induce a certain degree of enervation. There was no incentive, no challenge, no great mission to be accomplished. The historian E. Norman Gardiner has described the consequences of this pacific life with considerable insight: 'Living in these easy circumstances the Eleans developed a distinctive character

of their own. They were farmers and countrymen living in scattered villages and farms. Their land provided them with all that they required. They multiplied and prospered, but they had little incentive to enterprise or adventure. Engrossed in their material comforts, they took no part in the restless activities of their more progressive countrymen. They cared little for politics and never took to city life. They seldom travelled, they founded no colonies, they had no inclination for the sea or for commerce, they won little distinction in literature or art, they took no part in the national struggles of Hellas. So they earned the reputation of being luxurious, addicted to the pleasures of the table, drunken and licentious, unwarlike and cowardly. But they often belied their reputation, and in the administration of Olympia at all events they showed no little ability and vigour.'[29]

The first disruption of this Phaeacian existence came when Elis intervened in the Peloponnesian War (431–404 BC), which was to lead to the decline of the Greek city states. The Olympic festival of 420 BC had to be staged under military protection for it was feared that Sparta, who had been excluded from the games, might launch an attack. This was the first rent in the Olympian cosmos.

5. The Pilgrimage to Olympia

Once the sacred truce was proclaimed, pilgrims and official delegations from every state in Greece flocked to Olympia. At the sanctuary the delegations often indulged in great displays of pomp; in 416 BC for example, the Athenians used vessels of gold for their sacrifices.[30] As the Olympic games developed from a regional to a pan-Hellenic festival, so the number of pilgrims increased until in the end people were setting out from the farthest corners of the Greek world and even of the Roman *orbis terrarum* to make their pilgrimage to Olympian Zeus. Livy, when writing about the Olympiad of 204 BC, commented on this aspect of the festival: 'The Olympic games, which are attended by a tremendous crowd of people from every part of Greece, were due to be held that summer.'[31] The stadium in Olympia was enlarged on various occasions and in its final form could accomodate 40,000 people.

In view of these great crowds the organisation of the festival was quite a major task. Roads and bridges had to be repaired, rivers dammed, springs purified and borders patrolled. Where necessary the sacred objects in the sanctuary were renovated, the altars and buildings were repainted, new votive offerings were manufactured and the vessels for the ritual sacrifices cleaned. An inventory had to be drawn up listing the precious articles in the treasuries while functional buildings (*e.g.*, stables for the race horses, many of which needed special care after their strenuous journey by land or sea) had to be repaired or replaced.[32]

Nobody has described the teaming life of the festival with greater insight than Ludwig Weniger, the celebrated Olympia scholar from Weimar:

'The Greek city states both at home and overseas sent delegates to the modest harbour at the mouth of the Alpheus. Like all great shrines Olympia was the terminus of many roads and footpaths which had been marked out over the course of time and were eventually thronged with pilgrims...

'In order to find suitable accomodation or camping sites it was advisable to arrive in Olympia in the first few days of the festival month. At that time the whole of the surrounding countryside was literally strewn with shelters. But even so, if the influx of visitors was particularly heavy, many were obliged to make shift for themselves. Sacrificial animals were driven to Olympia in great numbers. Oxen dragging their heels and herds of smaller animals moved slowly forwards, stopping to rest from time to time. Once they had reached their destination they were carefully inspected by experts and then prepared for the sacred ritual.

'The religious festival and the games had been accompanied since early times by a great fair. Bazaars were set up, which sold anything and everything, whilst the booths and eating places which ringed the altis made Olympia indistinguishable from the public festivals of all ages and all lands. East and West met in Olympia. The devotional requisites to be found in every shrine, votive offerings both large and small and made of bronze or clay, fillets, branches of palm, wreaths, incense and sacrificial vessels were offered for sale *en masse*. Goldsmiths displayed their precious wares and sculptors, stonemasons and brass founders held stocks of statues and plinths for victors and donators. There were booths selling food, sweetmeats, mementos, clothes, plaids and all the myriad wares which the traders with their knowledge of the market and of current fashions thought they might conceivably dispose of. Moneylenders set up their stalls and performing animals, circus artists and troops of travelling players were always to hand.

'Immediately after the prize-giving ceremony and the triumphal procession the masses broke camp and made off...'[33]

Part Two

The Games

Chapter Five

The Competitors

1. Eligibility for the Games

Neither foreigners nor slaves were allowed to take part in the Olympic games. Only men—and later boys—of pure Greek descent were eligible.

When King Alexander I of Macedonia, an ancestor of Alexander the Great and a contemporary of the Persian conqueror Darius, wanted to compete at Olympia he was asked to furnish proof of Greek descent, for the Greeks regarded the Macedonians as foreigners. After satisfying the judges that he was in fact an Argive he was allowed to take part and came equal first in his event.[1]

Initially this ban also applied to the Romans, but once Rome began to assert her power within the Greek world they were exempted.

We have already noted that the competitors had to be free citizens. This rule also applied to the boys, whose lineage was checked with great care. Philostratus tells us that, quite apart from ascertaining that the contestants for the boys' events were not overage, the judges also had to establish that they were members of a settled tribe, that they had a father and a family, and that they really were free-born and not simply the bastard sons of free-born fathers.[2] There were two principal reasons why the competitors had to be free-born citizens of Greek descent. In the first place, the Greeks despised foreigners and slaves; in the second, they wished to ensure that all the contestants approached the games in the same spirit. This has been well put by Ziehen, who points out that those who competed for the victor's crown in Olympia were free citizens of Greek communities who shared a common attitude to life. They were not men who practised sport for its own sake or for the sake of breaking a record. On the contrary, they used it as a means of pursuing the Greek ideal of physical perfection and military proficiency.[3]

It was felt that if the cream of Greek youth and manhood met in Olympia to compete with one another to this end, and if thousands of people from every part of Greece came to the festival to watch them, a sense of national unity and solidarity might well be engendered, which would bear fruit beyond the purely sporting sphere.[4]

Those who had committed murder or stolen from a temple or broken the sacred truce were also banned from the games. This last provision applied to both individuals and states, and in 420 BC, during the Peloponnesian War, Elis banned Sparta for having occupied the fortress of Phyrkos and the town of Lepreum within the period covered by the truce. The Spartans were also called upon to pay a fine of 200,000 drachmas, a considerable sum of money which would have bought more than 6,000 oxen in Athens.[5]

One Spartan, a man by the name of Lichas, defied the ban and entered his horses in the chariot-race by registering them as Boeotian. When his team won and the judges announced a Boeotian victory he stepped forward and placed a fillet on the charioteer's head to show that he, a Spartan, was the owner. Although he was an old man he was publicly scourged and driven from the hippodrome,[6] from which it would appear that the judges at Olympia not only imposed fines but also inflicted corporal punishment. On one occasion 'national disgrace' was also advanced as a reason for excluding a competitor from the games. Themistocles, the victor of Salamis (480 BC), raised this objection against Hiero, the tyrant of Syracuse. According to Plutarch he not only tried to have Hiero banned but also urged the assembled Greeks to storm his tent.[7] Presumably Themistocles's objection was prompted by the fact that Hiero had not taken part in the Greek war of liberation against the Persians. But this particular offence was not listed on the Olympic statutes and so Hiero's horses were allowed to compete. In the following Olympiad, in 476 BC, he gained a victory which was celebrated by Pindar.

Originally the judges had also been allowed to enter horses in the equestrian events. But this was subsequently forbidden in order to preclude all possible doubt as to their impartiality. Pausanias describes the events leading up to this decision. It seems that at the 102nd Olympiad Troilus, one of the judges, gained victories in both the two-horse chariot-race and the colts' four-horse race. As a result, the people of Elis passed a law banning the judges' horses from the track.[8]

There is an interesting passage in Herodotus on this question of impartiality. He tells us that Pharaoh Psammis was visited by a delegation from Elis. These envoys claimed that the administration of the Olympic games was so impartial that not even the Egyptians, who were the most intelligent people in the world, could devise a more equitable system. The king then sent for the wisest of his counsellors, who asked the Eleans to explain the rules governing the competition. This they did, whereupon the Egyptians, after consulting among themselves, asked whether the citizens of Elis were also entitled to take part in the contests. Upon being told that they were, the Egyptians declared that in that case the games could not possibly be equitable for, since the Eleans were also the judges, it was inevitable that they would discriminate in favour of their fellow citizens; if they really wanted to stage an impartial festival they would have to exclude the inhabitants of Elis.[9] This incident is said to have occured at the beginning of the sixth century BC.

Although women were forbidden to take any part in the festival several of them were nonetheless associated with the contests in the hippodrome. In the equestrian events it was not the charioteers or horse-

men who were proclaimed victors but the owners, and there was nothing to prevent a woman from owning horses. Cynisca, a daughter of King Archidamus of Sparta, was the first woman to enter a team at Olympia. Plutarch tells us that it was her brother Agesilaus who persuaded her to do so because he wished to impress on his fellow Greeks that victory in the equestrian events had nothing to do with ability but was simply a question of wealth.[10] And Cynisca's team won the chariot-race. But according to Pausanias Cynisca's one great ambition had been to win an Olympic prize; apparently she was the first woman ever to train horses. Subsequently, Pausanias tells us, many other women— chiefly Spartans—were victorious at the games but, of them all, Cynisca was the most famous.[11] She gained her victory between 390 and 380 BC. She also made a votive offering in Olympia and this, too, has been described by Pausanias: 'Near the statue of Troilus there is a basement of stone with a chariot and charioteer and also an effigy of Cynisca by Apelles.... There are also inscriptions to her.'[12] In the course of the excavations a fragment of limestone was unearthed on which a number of characters were engraved which had once formed part of one of these inscriptions. According to the ancient tradition the full text read:

> Sparta's kings were fathers and brothers of mine,
> But since with my chariot and storming horses
>   I, Cynisca,
> Have won the prize, I place my effigy here
> And proudly proclaim
> That of all Grecian women I first bore the
>   crown.[13]

Another votive gift of Cynisca's, a team of brass horses smaller than life-size, stood in the antechamber of the temple of Zeus.[14]

We do not know whether the competitors at the games simply registered in Olympia or whether they first underwent a selection process in their native cities. What is quite certain, however, is that they were required to complete a course of preliminary training in Elis, where their proficiency was also tested.[15]

42

The young Greek athletes trained very hard. Lucian's Anacharsis remarked on the fact to his friend Solon. He simply could not understand why the wrestlers and pankratiasts, who appeared to be on the best of terms and helped one another to prepare for their practice bouts, then proceeded to clash their heads together, throttle and throw each other and exchange the most fearsome blows.[16]

But if the general training in the Greek gymnasiums was hard, the more specialised training for the pan-Hellenic games was harder still. According to Antiphon, the price of victory at the Olympic, Pythian and other festivals was great hardship.[17] Of all the games, however, those at Olympia imposed the heaviest burden, for Lucian assures us that once a man had gained a victor's crown at Olympia none of the other stadia held any terrors for him.[18]

When they were in training the Olympic competitors lived extremely frugal lives; in the early days of the festival they even went without meat. Later, in the fifth century BC, this diet was changed by Dromeus of Stymphalus, a famous long-distance runner, who won twice at Olympia, twice at Delphi, three times at the Isthmus and five times at Nemea. Pausanias tells us that he was thought to have been the first man ever to have eaten meat while preparing for the games, 'for athletes in training before him used to eat only a particular kind of cheese'.[19]

During their period of preparation the Olympic competitors led a life that was far from enviable. Under the relentless supervision of the judges[20] they had to observe a strict diet, carry out set exercises and do exactly what their trainers told them. The Stoic philosopher Epictetus held up this harsh regime as an example to his followers, in order to impress on them that, before embarking on any undertaking, they should first consider what it involved.[21]

The athletes prepared for the games in the city of Elis. According to Philostratus they trained there for a period of one month,[22] according to Pausanias for a period of ten months. Certainly they had to swear on oath that they had 'carefully trained for the space of ten months'.[23] But since it is not clear from the wording of this oath whether the whole ten-month period had to be spent in Elis the most plausible explanation would seem to be that, while they were required to train for a total period of ten months, only one month, presumably the last, had to be spent in Elis. Incidentally, this must have been a relatively late innovation, for a ten-month training period could only have been prescribed for professional athletes, and, although these were a common feature of Roman life, at the early Olympics the competitors had all been amateurs. Even a thirty-day period of residence would have posed problems in the early days since the sacred truce, which was subsequently extended to three months, had originally covered only one month, and that had included the journey to and from the sanctuary. Later of course, when the *pax romana* had been established throughout the whole of the *orbis terrarum*, there was no longer any need for a sacred truce.

In early times the competitors presumably arrived in Olympia accompanied by their trainers (or, in the case of the boys, by their fathers and brothers) just a few days before the beginning of the games in order to practise on the actual course. Subsequently rules would have been made fixing the length of the training period to ensure that all competitors enjoyed equal facilities. The training could, of course, only have taken place in Elis from 472 BC onwards, since it was in that year that the city was founded.

But once the thirty-day rule had been established all competitors were required to present themselves in Elis in good time. Great importance was attached to punctuality and any late arrivals were automatically disqualified unless they were able to prove *force majeure*. Pausanias describes one such case involving an Egyptian boxer from Alexandria, by the name of Apollonius, who arrived late for the 218th Olympiad in AD 107. He pleaded that his ship had been delayed by adverse winds near the Cyclades. But Heraclides, another Alexandrian boxer, was able to disprove his story and alleged that Apollonius had actually broken his journey to win prize money at the Ionian games. Apollonius was then disqualified and Heraclides, the only boxer to arrive on time, won by a walk-over.[24]

Pausanias also describes the three gymnasiums[25] in Elis, in which the competitors prepared for their events: 'One of the notable things in Elis is an old gymnasium in which, before proceeding to Olympia, the athletes go through all the customary training. There are some lofty plane trees inside a wall growing all along the course and the whole enclosure is called the Colonnade...There is one course set apart for the races, which the local people call the sacred course, and another where they practise for the races and the pentathlon. In the gymnasium there is also a place called the plethrium [an arena 32 metres square] where the umpires pit the athletes one against the other...to test their capacities.'[26] It seems reasonable to assume that the qualifying heats were held on the sacred course. This would explain the derivation of the epithet for, like the finals, the heats were official, and consequently sacred, events.[27] The second gymnasium was really more of a palaestra, for Pausanias tells us that it was a smaller enclosure which was adjacent to the main gymnasium and was called the 'square' on account of its shape.[28] The third gymnasium, which was called the *maltho* after its soft floor, was reserved for the epheboi, who used it throughout the whole period of the festival.[29]

We are told nothing of the preliminary training for the chariot- and horse-races. But if this also took place in Elis then it seems probable that the market place served as a practice course, for in Pausanias's day the market place was called the hippodrome and was used by the local inhabitants to exercise their horses.[30]

The judges had their own official residence in Elis. This was the *hellanodicaeum* and was situated beside the market place beyond the tomb of Achilles. From there the *hellanodicae* (the judges) made their way to the gymnasium, where they began to test the runners in the early morning and the competitors for the pentathlon and the heavy events at noon.[31] The sophist Flavius Philostratus gave a discerning account of Elean training methods in the first half of the third century AD. Although he actually set out to explain why it was that the wrestlers in Olympia were the only class of athletes allowed to win by a walk-over, in doing so he also provided an interesting description of the kind of training undertaken by the other competitors at the festival. Certainly it would seem that the competitors in the light events had an easier time of it than their colleagues in the heavy events, for they practised in the morning before the full heat of the day. The dolichos men ran their eight or ten stades while the contestants in the sprint events practised either the stade-race or the diaulos or both. This, Philostratus considered, was comparatively easy. The heavy men, on the other hand, started their training at midday, when the heat was at its fiercest. Moreover, since it was midsummer, the ground was baked hard by the sun and the athletes were greatly troubled by choking dust.

Philostratus then went on to explain why it was that of the heavy events the wrestling was far and away the most strenuous. His observations are interesting for it seems that the boxers and pankratiasts not only could but actually did spare themselves during their training bouts. This the wrestlers were unable to do since by the very nature of their contest they had to come to grips with one another. In fact their training sessions were as hard as the actual competition. The Eleans recognised this and consequently were prepared to grant victory by a walk-over to a wrestler, which meant, of course, that they were really crowning him for his training.[32]

Before the contestants left their quarters in Elis for Olympia they were addressed by the judges. Although none of these speeches was ever recorded we know the general tenor of the judge's remarks on such occasions. Philostratus the Elder is our source, for in his history of Apollonius of Tyana there is a passage in which Apollonius reminds his companions, prior to their departure for Egypt, of the kind of exhortation made by the Eleans to the Olympic contestants before they set out for the stadium: 'If by your work you have rendered yourselves worthy to go to Olympia, if you have not been idle and ignoble, then go there with a good heart. But let those who have not trained in this fashion go where they will.'[33]

Accompanied either by their trainers or by their fathers and brothers the contestants were conducted

8. Bases of statues of Zeus (zanes) at the foot of the Hill of Cronus. The statues were paid for from the fines imposed on athletes who resorted to bribery.

9. Competitions for boys: two youths
fighting in the presence of a judge.

by the judges along the sacred road which led from Elis to Olympia. The journey almost certainly took two days for it covered some fifty-eight kilometres. On this route there was a fountain, in which the hellanodicae were required to perform a ritual cleansing ceremony before undertaking their office of judge. Pausanias comments on this rite: 'And the functions of...the umpires of Elis are never commenced until after the sacrifice of a pig and lustration with water. And the lustration takes place at the fountain Piera, which is situated in the plain between Olympia and Elis.'[34]

The month spent by the athletes in Elis was undoubtedly the last in the mandatory ten-month training period. Flavius Philostratus's reference to the hottest time of the year certainly bears this out, for the Olympic games were held in the summer. Moreover, special indoor training facilities were provided in Olympia in both the palaestra and the gymnasium so that the contestants could practise in winter and in the rainy season. It is difficult to see why the authorities should have gone to such expense if all ten months of training had to be carried out in Elis.

By stipulating that all contestants must spend a period of one month in their capital city the Eleans were presumably trying to demonstrate their monopoly over the Olympic games. It is conceivable that this regulation was introduced following the war of 365–363 BC, when the Arcadians conquered Pisa and joined with the Pisatans in staging the 104th Olympiad in 364 BC. But, although they lost the war, the Eleans won the peace, for the victors soon fell out. The result was that Pisa, and with it the control of the sanctuary and the Olympic festival, reverted to Elis.[35]

3. Training Facilities for the Contestants in Olympia

The mandatory month in Elis was preceded by a period of training in Olympia. In order to provide facilities for the athletes the palaestra and gymnasium were constructed to the west of the altis, where they formed a pendant to the stadium and the hippodrome in the east. These buildings almost certainly were a product of Hellenistic times, for it was then that the Greeks began to design their cities and sanctuaries along artistic lines; in the early days of the festival the athletes would have trained out of doors.

The principal feature of the palaestra, which was used to train young men in the arts of wrestling, boxing and the pankration, was a large square inner courtyard. The gymnasium on the other hand, which was used for training in light athletics, was built in the form of an elongated rectangle to accomodate long running tracks and provide sufficient space for throwing the javelin and discus. Contestants in the jumping events tended to practise in the palaestra because the soft ground suited their purposes. Subsequently the palaestra lost its separate identity and both buildings, which were contiguous, were referred to as the gymnasium.

In the fullness of time the Greek gymnasium was able to offer an all-round education; it became a centre, not only of sporting but also of intellectual life, where philosophers and rhetors sought to train the minds of their youthful charges. The younger boys received their instruction in the palaestra, and the older ones—those between 18 and 20—in the gymnasium proper.

Pausanias has furnished us with a contemporary account of the gymnasium and palaestra at Olympia,[36] while the modern excavations have revealed the lay-out of the entire installation.[37]

The Palaestra

Vitruvius, the celebrated architect who lived in the age of Augustus, gave precise specifications for the construction of Greek palaestrae: 'The palaestrae should be surrounded by quadrangular or oblong colonnades with a total circumference of two stades ...Three of these should be single structures but the fourth, the one facing south, should be double so as to prevent high winds from penetrating into the interior. Spacious rooms should be built contiguous to the single colonnades and provided with benches so that the philosophers and rhetors and those who take pleasure in intellectual conversation may do so

45

seated. The double colonnade should also be furnished with rooms but of a different kind: in the centre would be the *ephebeum* [the room for the epheboi], a very large rectangular hall with a length to width ratio of 3 to 2; in the right would be the *coryceum* [the boxers' training hall] and the *conisterium* [the room in which the wrestlers coat themselves with dust and sand]; the *conisterium* would give access to the cold bath, which the Greeks call the *lutron* and which would be situated at the end of the colonnade. To the left of the *ephebeum* would be the *eliothesium* [the storeroom for the ointments and salves] and then the *frigidarium* [a second cold bath], from which a corridor would lead to the heating installation at the end of the colonnade. Next to the *frigidarium* would be a vapour bath with a vaulted ceiling and a length to width ratio of 2 to 1; in one corner this would contain...a *laconicum* [a Spartan-type vapour bath] and in the opposite corner a hot water bath.'[38]

Fig. 10: Propylaeum of the palaestra (reconstruction).

The palaestra in Olympia, which was built towards the end of the third century BC, departed from these specifications, for the spacious bath, 1.38 metres deep, in the room in the north-eastern corner, which Vitruvius would have called a frigidarium, and the washroom in the north-western corner, *i.e.* Vitruvius's 'frigida lavatio' or 'lutron', were the only bathing facilities provided within the actual building. This was because a washroom and hip-bath, the oldest

installation of its kind in Greece, were already in existence when work was begun on the palaestra. Consequently the Olympic palaestra was smaller than the type designed by Vitruvius. It covered an area of 66.35 metres by 66.75 metres and was therefore almost a perfect square. The circumference of the colonnades was rather less than a stade, for the sides of the inner courtyard were only 41 metres long. But the southern colonnade in Olympia, which measured 38 metres in length, was in fact double and so conformed to Vitruvius's specification. A row of fifteen columns separated the outer from the inner colonnade and afforded protection against high winds. There were large and small study rooms in both the east and west wings. These all gave open access to their respective colonnades and, apart from two rooms, one in each wing, all were fitted out with benches. The rooms in the north wing corresponded exactly to Vitruvius's plan. The large central room was given over to the epheboi: it had a length to width ratio of 3 to 2, there were benches along all of its walls, it afforded open access to the colonnade and had a marble floor. (The floors in the other rooms were either of stamped clay or light soil.) There were also communicating doors between the ephebeum and the rooms on either side. Although it has not been possible to establish their separate identities, one of these rooms would have been the eliothesium, where the athletes first anointed themselves, and the other the conisterium, where they then threw dust and sand at one another to roughen their bodies. At the eastern end of the northern colonnade there was the cold bath and at the western end the washroom. The coryceum, it will be remembered, was the room in which the boxers trained; in the centre of this room hung a leather sack the size of a man which was filled with sand, fig seeds or corn and served as a punchbag. It is to be assumed that the coryceum was one of the two rooms without benches, the second of which may well have been used by the wrestlers. In both of these rooms the floor consisted of loose soil. The same was true of the southern colonnade which, because of its length, would have been particularly suitable for practising jumping.

The inner courtyard, whose surface consisted for the most part of the bare earth and which was open to the skies, was also used for practice by the boxers, wrestlers, jumpers and pankratiasts. Those who wished to watch the athletes training were of course able to do so from the colonnades.

In inclement weather the contestants remained either in the two rooms without benches or in the southern colonnade, which also had no seating accommodation. Even when the athletes were practising in these covered rooms spectators were able to watch them either from the northern colonnade or from the inner part of the southern colonnade. All in all the palaestra contained nineteen rooms.

In the northern part of the inner courtyard an unusual pavement of ceramic tiles, 24.20 metres long

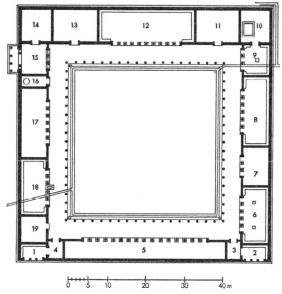

Fig. 11: Ground plan of the palaestra. The figures refer to: 1 South-western entrance, 2 South-eastern entrance, 3 Eastern interstice, 4 Western interstice, 5 Southern colonnade, 6 Auditorium, 7 Room without benches, 8 Auditorium, 9 Room with benches, 10 Corner room with wash basin, 11 Storeroom, 12 Epheboi's room, 13 Storeroom, 14 Washroom (cold water), 15 Entrance hall with propylaeum, 16 Room containing well, 17 Exercise hall, 18 Auditorium, 19 Storeroom (or steward's room?).

and 5.44 metres wide, was unearthed in the course of the excavations. An 80-centimetre strip of plain tiles runs lengthwise down the centre of this pavement, dividing it into two halves, both of which are laid out with fluted tiles. So far nobody has succeeded in establishing a fully authenticated explanation of this find. Julius Jüthner and Carl Diem are of the opinion that it was a practice track for the hop-step-and-a-jump.[39] No comparable installation has been discovered elsewhere.

The columns of the colonnades were Doric while those of the inner rooms were Ionian. The walls consisted of framework faced with tiles and were erected on a firm base of porous stone. A stately propylaeum, supported by four columns near the north corner of the west wing, formed the main entrance to the palaestra. There were two exits in the south which led to the outside baths while a small door in the rear wall of the ephebeum gave access to the gymnasium. During the recent excavations the columns of the palaestra were re-erected in order to give the modern visitor to Olympia a general impression of the lay-out of the building.

The Gymnasium

The gymnasium was built later than the palaestra. The southern part of the building has been excavated: work was first started on this project by the nineteenth-century expedition between 1875 and 1881 and has since been continued by modern archaeologists from 1936 onwards. As a result of this work the foundations of two colonnades have been unearthed, which join to form an almost perfect right angle. The southern colonnade, which was 120 metres long, was contiguous to the north wing of the palaestra but extended far beyond it towards the river Cladeus; the eastern colonnade ran 220 metres to the north to the foot of the Hill of Cronus. This means that the gymnasium was even larger than the stadium, which measured 212.75 metres from end to end. The western side of the gymnasium, which contained the accommodation for the athletes mentioned by Pausanias and which ran parallel to the eastern colonnade, was washed away by the Cladeus; part of the southern colonnade was also destroyed in this way. There is sufficient evidence to bear out the assumption of a northern colonnade running parallel to its southern counterpart. Thus the complete installation would appear to have been a rectangular building supported by Doric columns enclosing an inner courtyard large enough to accomodate running tracks and provide adequate space for throwing the discus and javelin. In the courtyard the Eleans erected a victory memorial, whose base is mentioned by Pausanias. All the colonnades opened on to the courtyard. The southern colonnade, which presumably had a bench running along the whole of its rear wall to allow the athletes to rest in the shade, was a single structure. But the eastern colonnade, which was over ten metres wide, was double: two rows of Doric columns, sixty-six in each, supported a wooden roof that was 220 metres long; the floor was strewn with soft sand and when the weather was bad the competitors were able to practise the stade-race in this colonnade on two separate running tracks, each of which was 192

metres long. There can be no doubt about the length of these tracks, for the starting and finishing lines at either end are still plainly visible.

But impressive though this installation was it was not impressive enough for the Eleans, who added a magnificent triple-arched propylaeum at the south-eastern corner, where the gymnasium abuts on to the palaestra just a few yards away from the northern entrance to the altis. Pausanias tells us that an athlete by the name of Paraballon, who had won the diaulos, 'excited the emulation of posterity by writing up the names of the victors at Olympia in the gymnasium...'[40] But if these names were engraved on stone, no trace has yet been found of them.

4. The Bathing Facilities for the Contestants

During the excavations carried out between 1939 and 1941 a number of baths were unearthed to the south and south-west of the palaestra. The oldest of these go back to the first half of the fifth century BC,

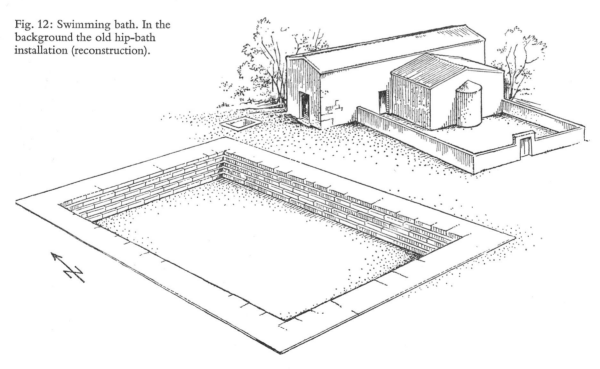

Fig. 12: Swimming bath. In the background the old hip-bath installation (reconstruction).

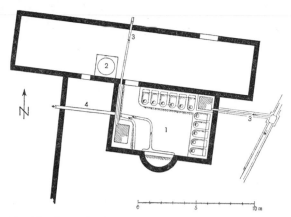

Fig. 13: Ground plan of the old hip-bath installation (reconstruction). The figures refer to: 1 Room containing hip-baths, 2 Well, 3 Water conduit, 4 Waste conduit.

while the most recent, the so-called Cladeus baths, were built about AD 100 by the Romans.[41] Kunze comments on these installations in his work on Olympia: 'The fact that these baths were situated so close to the palaestra would suggest that they were used by the athletes... We know of no other great Greek sanctuary where baths were in continuous use over a period of centuries.'[42] There were three separate bathing installations: a hip-bath, a swimming bath and a vapour bath. In the first half of the fifth century BC, before the palaestra had been built, a narrow, rectangular, covered building measuring twenty metres by four was erected and fitted with a fountain (Installation 1) to enable the athletes to sluice themselves down with cold water after their training sessions, which took place in the open air in those early days. Shortly afterwards this modest washroom received a back addition which contained hip-baths along two of its walls. A few decades later heating arrangements were installed so that the athletes might also take hot baths (Installation 2). Eventually these bathing facilities proved inadequate, and in early Hellenistic times a new room was added containing a large number of hip-baths (Installation 3). The old hip-bath installation then fell into disuse and the hip-baths themselves were filled in when a new stone floor was laid. After its conversion this room was

probably used for cold baths. But in the early part of the second century BC the whole installation was destroyed. We are able to fix the date with a fair degree of accuracy, for a large hoard of treasure, consisting of over one thousand silver coins, most of them minted by the Achaean League, was buried in the ruins and discovered in the course of excavation; none of these coins is more recent than 170 BC, which would suggest that the destruction of the installation took place at about that time. For the best part of seventy years the ruins just lay there until, in about 100 BC, a Roman-type bath heated by a hypocaust was installed (Installation 4). A bath of this kind was something quite new in Greece at that time.

Like the hot hip-baths the swimming bath to the south-west of the palaestra is of great archaeological significance. It was a large, rectangular, open-air pool which was probably built in the fifth century BC and, as far as is known, was the only open-air swimming bath in classical Greece. It was 24 metres long, about 16 metres wide and 1.60 metres deep. A row of five steps led down from the edge of the

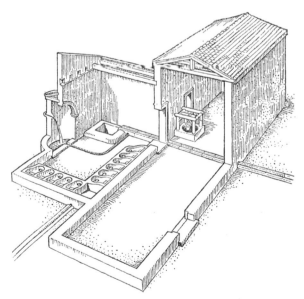

Fig. 14: Section of the old hip-bath installation (reconstruction).

49

pool to the bottom on all four sides. But once the hypocaust was installed the swimming bath also fell into disuse. The southern end was then built over in about AD 100 to make room for the Roman baths while the northern end was eventually washed away by the Cladeus.

The athletes in Olympia also had a vapour bath. This was built shortly after 450 BC and consisted of a circular bathroom together with an annexe in which, no doubt, the baths would have been warmed and the water heated. The vapour bath was also abandoned following the introduction of the hypocaust. Subsequently a simple altar was built in the *tholos*—the circular part of this installation—and dedicated to an unnamed hero.

The vapour bath, the swimming bath and the hip-baths were all installed in the fifth century BC, which shows that the Greeks in Olympia were aware of the importance of hygiene at a very early stage.

South of the altis, between the Leonidaeum and the buleuterion, Roman-type baths were built, which are usually referred to as the southern baths. These have only just been excavated and, since the report on the excavations has not yet been published, it is

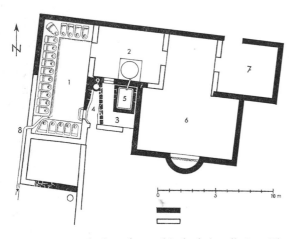

Fig. 15: Ground plan of new hip-bath installation. The figures refer to: 1 Room containing hip-baths, 2 Room containing well, 3 Service corridor, 4 Room with cauldrons for heating water, 5 Water tanks, 6 Cold bath(?), 7 Ante-room, 8 Waste conduit, 9 Chimney.

unfortunately not possible to give any details about the date and manner of their construction or about any later modifications.

In Roman times the baths were in greater demand than ever before. In order to cater for the growing needs of contestants and spectators alike the northern baths were then built at the foot of the Hill of Cronus. A number of mosaics have been discovered on this site in the course of the excavation work in Olympia but no full-scale investigation of this installation has been carried out.[43]

5. The Classification of the Contestants

Before leaving Elis for Olympia the contestants were classified by the hellanodicae according to age and the events in which they wished to compete. There were only two age groups: boys and men. The intermediate group of the *ageneioi, i.e.,* 'the beardless', was not recognised in Olympia. All those of twenty years of age and over were automatically placed in the men's class. Pausanias tells us that 'Archippus of Mitylene, who beat all comers at boxing, ... was crowned at the Olympian, Pythian, Nemean and Isthmian games when he was only twenty.'[44] We are told nothing of a minimum age for the boys and it seems likely that there was no fixed limit, for the judges had adequate opportunity of testing a young candidate's physique and general fitness before admitting him to the boys' events. Pausanias describes a case in point: it seems that Pherias the Aeginetan was not allowed to take part in the 78th Olympiad because he seemed so young.[45] At the other end of the scale there was the case of Nicasylus of Rhodes who, although only eighteen, was refused permission to compete in the boys' events because he was quite obviously too powerful for his opponents. Instead he was made to compete with the men, whom he promptly defeated.[46]

The hellanodicae were also called upon to classify the horses for the equestrian events. The chief point at issue here was whether the younger horses should be entered as colts or as fully grown horses. This, of course, was no easy task and the judges sought the help of experts and especially of ex-victors at Olympia.[47] At the oath-giving ceremony both the judges and their assistants were required to swear that they had arrived at their decisions fairly and had taken no bribes; they also had to give an undertaking that they would not divulge their reasons for accepting or refusing a given candidate.[48] And yet occasionally attempts were made to bribe or influence the judges. King Agesilaus of Sparta, for example, did all he possibly could to ensure that a certain Eualkes, who had fallen in love with a handsome Persian youth then residing at his court, was allowed 'for his sake' to compete in the boys' events, although he was far bigger than any of the other boys.[49]

The classification of the competitors according to contests and age also formed an important part of the judges' official duties. This too was done in Elis.[50] The judges arranged the groups of wrestlers in the gymnasium.[51]

6. The Draw

We might have expected to find that the draw to decide the composition of the heats and eliminating bouts would also have been made in Elis. But there is no evidence to suggest that this was the case, and according to Lucian the heavy athletes, i.e., the wrestlers, boxers and pankratiasts, were paired off in Olympia. It would therefore be reasonable to assume that this was standard practice for all events.

The stade-race was not run straight off. Instead the competitors were divided up into groups of four[52] and the winners of these heats then competed in the final; consequently the man who was crowned victor in the stade-race had to win twice.[53] In the course of the excavations the starting and finishing lines in the stadium were unearthed. They were found to consist of a double row of narrow limestone sills with holes for posts every few feet to separate the contestants. Since there was room for twenty starters it seems that some of the contests were for large groups of runners.

In the heavy events the weight of the contestants was not taken into consideration. According to Lucian, who watched the draw for the wrestlers and pankratiasts from a seat close to the judges, paired lots were thrown into a silver urn, each pair being marked with a different letter of the alphabet. Thus the urn contained one pair of Alphas, one pair of Betas, one pair of Gammas[54] and so on, the total number of paired lots corresponding to the total number of contests. After sacrificing to Zeus the competitors drew their lots and were paired off accordingly by the officials. In the event of there being an uneven number of competitors a single unpaired lot was thrown into the urn and the contestant who drew it received a bye; this was, of course, no mean advantage for it meant that the man concerned came fresh to the fight when his opponent was already tired.[55] A contestant who received a bye was called an *ephedros* and was not too highly thought of by Pausanias: 'I...know some who won the crown of wild olive from unexpected good fortune rather than their own exertions.'[56] Since such men had done nothing praiseworthy Pausanias refused to record their names or to describe their statues unless these possessed particular artistic merit.[57]

If only one competitor presented himself for a particular contest then, provided it was one of the heavy events, he won 'without dust', i.e., by a walk-over. To win in this way was not considered unworthy, for the heavy events were often dangerous and the contestants were by definition courageous men.[58]

A walk-over was also granted if one of the finalists arrived too late—for this involved instant disqualification—or if one of them withdrew from the contest.[59] In 460 BC Theagenes of Thasos, who had entered for both the boxing and the pankration, withdrew from the pankration after having overextended himself in the boxing. His opponent Euthymus, a native of Locri in southern Italy, was then declared the winner and Theagenes was fined.[60]

Occasionally there was a draw or a dead heat. The olive wreath was then dedicated to the god and consequently such contests were always referred to as 'sacred contests'.[61] It also seems probable that the wreath would have been offered to the god when there were no contenders for a particular contest.[62]

In the equestrian events both the traps and the starting positions were allocated by lot.[63]

7. Cheating at the Games

In the solemn oath which they gave before the festival began the competitors had to swear that they would 'not cheat at the Olympic games'.[64] But there were some who violated their oath. The transgressions took three principal forms: breaking the rules, bribing opponents and competing on behalf of a foreign nation. In point of fact there was nothing in the regulations to prevent a competitor from representing a foreign nation, but those who did so were felt to have cast a slur on their motherland, which then brought its own punishment.

Breaking the Rules

Although our records of the ancient Olympics are incomplete, it seems that throughout the thousand and more years during which they were held there were very few infringements of the rules. Undoubtedly the rules in force then were less stringent than those applied today, which would of course offer a ready explanation for this phenomenon. Here too our knowledge is far from perfect. But there is one thing which we can say with certainty, namely that the competitors were not allowed to carry the contest to the point of endangering their opponent's life. Naturally this only applied to the more violent events such as the boxing and the pankration. The boxers were allowed to wound one another on the head and the face with blows of their heavily thonged fists, while the pankratiasts could apply strangleholds and even break their opponents' fingers and toes. An unlucky blow or excessive pressure on a stranglehold could easily prove fatal and some men actually were killed in Olympia: in 564 BC the Arcadian Arrhichion of Phigalia, who had already won the pankration at two previous Olympiads, lost his life when competing for the third time in this event. His opponent was disqualified and the crown was awarded to the dead man.[65] As far as we know disqualification was the only punishment inflicted on this occasion. In 492 BC the boxer Cleomedes of Astypalaea killed his opponent Iccus of Epidaurus. According to Pausanias, when the judges disqualified Cleomedes he 'went out of his mind'.[66] Here, too, disqualification appears to have been the only punishment imposed, for Pausanias makes no mention of anything else. But we know of one case in which the judges were far more severe. A boxer by the name of Diognetus of Crete, who appears to have been a rough fighter, killed his opponent Hercules in the heat of the contest, for which he was not only disqualified but also expelled from Olympia.[67] This was an extremely harsh decision for, since victory at Olympia brought such great fame, expulsion brought absolute disgrace.[68]

But, even though our knowledge is admittedly imperfect, from the available evidence it would seem that the number of accidental or wilful deaths which occurred in the long history of Olympia was relatively small. This should not really surprise us if we consider that the games were dedicated to Zeus and the competitors were all required to swear a solemn oath that they would abide by the rules. During the early period of the festival at least, when the Olympian deities were still a very real force, this must have had considerable effect.

Bribing Opponents

It sometimes happened that a contestant at Olympia would try to bribe the opposition. This kind of conduct was considered to be particularly infamous. Themistius refers to the practice in his *De Humanitate,* where he describes it as odious and sordid.[69] There is no mention of bribery prior to the Peloponnesian War (431–404 BC), which sapped both the political and the moral fibre of the Greek cosmos. Whenever bribery was discovered fines were imposed, not only on the individuals directly concerned but also on their tribes and native towns. The money acquired in this way was used to build statues to Zeus. These were the *zanes,* seventeen in all, fourteen of which stood at the foot of the Hill of Cronus beneath the terrace of treasuries. There were two more at the entrance to the stadium, one on each side, and there was another in front of the echo colonnade. The bases of the statues bore inscriptions warning the contestants not to buy or sell victory in the games. The first six of these zanes were paid for by the fines imposed on the Thessalian boxer Eupolus and those of his adversaries who had accepted bribes from him.[70] This happened in the year 388 BC. The city of Athens was subsequently called upon to pay for six further statues. Pausanias tells us that, following Eupolus's conviction, the Athenian Callipus was accused of having bribed his opponents in the pentathlon at the 112th Olympiad in 332 BC. After Callipus and his fellow contestants had been fined by the Eleans the Athenians sent Hyperides to Elis to ask that the fine be rescinded. When this plea was dismissed the Athenians simply refused to pay. Not even their expulsion from the Olympic games could induce them to relent and it was only when the god in Delphi declared that he would furnish them with no more oracles until such time as they had paid the fine that they finally gave way.[71]

Even the Eleans themselves, who were the custodians of the sanctuary, accepted bribes, a fact which elicited the following remark from the virtuous Pausanias: 'It is a wonder in any case if a man has so little respect for the god of Olympia as to take or give a bribe in the contests; it is an even greater wonder that one of the Eleans themselves has fallen so low.'[72]

Pausanias's accounts of the corruption at Olympia have been supplemented by Dionysius of Halicarnassus. He tells us that contestants who had given or taken bribes sometimes received corporal punishment. It seems that they were scourged in full view of the spectators. This was of course particularly shameful, since public whippings were normally reserved for slaves.[73] But here too, if we consider that the Olympic games were celebrated from 776 BC to AD 393, we are forced to the conclusion that cases of bribery—even assuming that some escaped detection or were not preserved in written records—must have been relatively rare.

Representing a Foreign Nation

When registering at Olympia the contestants had to state their country of origin. This was important for, if they were victorious, their native land shared in their fame. It sometimes happened however that, for one reason or another, a competitor would lay claim to some other nationality. Consequently, if he won his event, it was the name of his adopted nation and not that of his native land which was proclaimed by the heralds. To offend against one's homeland in this way was a serious matter and those who did so were duly punished by their fellow countrymen. In 484 BC Astylus of Croton, who had won both the stade-race and the diaulos, had himself proclaimed victor as a native of Syracuse in order to curry favour with Gelon, the ruler of Syracuse. Pausanias tells us that the people of Croton then took their revenge on him by turning his house into a public prison and removing his statue from the temple of Hera.[74] His statue in Olympia, however, was left standing.

Another and far more onerous form of punishment in such cases was that of banishment. At the 99th Olympiad in 384 BC Sotades, a Cretan, won the dolichos, which was then duly announced as a Cretan victory. But at the following Olympiad he accepted a bribe from the Ephesians and registered in their name. For this he was banished from Crete.[75]

Although banishment posed a serious threat to all those who contemplated offending against their native land in this way, there was another side to this question. A man who had been banished from his homeland and was granted asylum and citizenship rights in another country was at liberty to register at Olympia under his new nationality. Pausanias tells us that Ergoteles the son of Philanor, who twice won the dolichos at the Olympic, Pythian, Isthmian and Nemean festivals as a citizen of Himera, was in fact a Cretan from Cnossus. It seems that, after having been banished from Crete due to the machinations of his enemies, he was granted rights of citizenship in Himera and was therefore proclaimed as a native of that Himera at the games.[76]

It was also possible for a man to have his banishment rescinded if he won a victory at Olympia. This was the case with Cimon, the father of the celebrated victor of Marathon, Miltiades, who was banished from Athens by the tyrant Pisistratus. Herodotus tells us that, after winning the chariot-race at Delphi with his team of four, he repeated the performance with the same team at Olympia, where he had Pisistratus proclaimed as victor. A reconciliation was then effected between the two men and Cimon was allowed to return to Athens.[77] Cimon won the four-horse chariot-race at three successive Olympiads, namely in 532, 528 and 524 BC.

A contestant who competed under an assumed nationality was only breaking the Olympic regulations if his native country was banned from the games at the time. This was the case with the Spartan Lichas who registered his chariot as a Theban entry in 420 BC when Sparta was excluded from the games. His team won its race but when he stepped forward to place a fillet on the charioteer's head he was recognised as a Spartan and scourged by order of the judges. It was on Lichas's account that Agis and the Lacedaemonians invaded Elis. After the war, although this race was still listed as a Theban victory in the official records, the Eleans were forced by the victorious Spartans to permit Lichas to erect his statue in the altis.[78]

8. The Judges

The judges were responsible for the administration of the Olympic games: they sent out heralds to issue formal invitations to all of the Greek states; they supervised the upkeep and renovation of the various buildings and arranged accomodation for foreign envoys and guests of honour; they decided the order of events and organised police supervision for the whole assembly; but their principal task was to test the athletes, sort them into pairs and groups and umpire the games.[79]

The number of judges officiating at Olympia fluctuated considerably. When King Iphitus of Elis introduced his great reforms and founded the games in honour of Zeus he was the sole judge. The purple cloak worn by his successors as an emblem of their high office was a legacy from this period of royal patronage. In the year 580 BC a second judge was appointed,[80] although strictly speaking they were not called judges in those days but *agonothetae, i.e.,* 'games organisers'. Over the course of time, as the Olympic games gradually developed into a pan-Hellenic festival, this expression was replaced by the term *hellanodicae (i.e.,* 'judges of the Greeks'), which was eventually adopted as the official title. As a matter of interest, the foremost member of the Spartan king's retinue was also called *hellanodicas.*[81]

Later, Pausanias tells us, nine judges were appointed, 'three for the horse-race, three to watch the pentathlon and three to preside over the remaining games...'[82] The number subsequently rose to ten, then twelve, only to return to ten again in 348 BC, after which it remained at that level until the days of imperial Rome.

Apollonius of Tyana criticised the system of electing the judges. He felt that to choose them by lot was imprudent, since there was then no guarantee that the best men would be chosen; he also objected to the rigid insistence on a fixed number, arguing that the number of judges selected should be determined by the number of just men available.[83]

Those chosen to act as judges were instructed by the 'guardians of the law' in all matters appertaining to the games. This instruction was given in Elis in the hellanodiceum, the judges' official residence.[84] We have already considered the judges' duties during the training period in Elis. In Olympia, where their word was law, they supervised all contests, ensured that the competitors abided by the rules and acted as adjudicators. They also handed each victor a branch of palm[85] as an initial mark of distinction—the olive wreaths were not presented until the end of the festival at the great prize-giving ceremony—and entered his name on the list of victors while the herald proclaimed it to the spectators.

The judges had very considerable powers. The principal offences which they were required to punish were failure to obey their orders, infringements of the rules and bribery. They could impose fines, disqualify competitors, banish them from Olympia and have them publicly scourged. They frequently

IV Vase painting of horseman.

resorted to corporal punishment, even for relatively trivial offences, for example when an athlete or a trainer failed to comply with their instructions.[86] They had a number of assistants to help them maintain discipline, including the *mastigophorae,* the whip-bearers, with their dreaded scourges.

Appeals against the judges' decisions could be made to the Olympic Council, whose members—all of them Eleans—appear to have been elected for life.[87] Pausanias has described such an appeal.

It seems that on one occasion the three judges who presided over the stade-race were unable to reach a unanimous decision. Two of them declared that Eupolemus of Elis was the winner while the third opted for the Ambraciote Leo. Leo then lodged an appeal with the Olympic Council in which he claimed that Eupolemus had bribed the two judges, who had found in his favour.[88] We do not know what the Council's decision was in this case. In fact, we do not even know whether it was possible to question the judges' decisions as such or whether bribery constituted the sole ground for appeal. But complaints of this kind would almost certainly have been few and far between, for the judges at Olympia were renowned for impartiality. It will be remembered that in order to safeguard this reputation it was decided in 372 BC that from then onwards the judges should no longer be allowed to enter their horses for the equestrian events. The fact that the Elean delegation, which visited Pharaoh Psammis[89] in the early sixth century BC, sought his advice as to how they might improve the organisation of the festival also shows how eager the Eleans were to retain their good name. Even after Greece had lost her independence and become part of the Roman empire the Olympic judges remained as impartial as ever. Apollonius of Tyana, who lived in the first century AD, praised the conscientious way in which they performed their duties.[90]

It was virtually impossible to bring influence to bear on the judges. Letters of recommendation, even those written by Romans or on behalf of Romans, were not opened until after the festival. There was only one law in Olympia, which was applied to both conquerors and conquered alike. Dion Chrysostom, who lived from about AD 40–120, praised the judges on this account. He also pointed out that, far from exposing themselves to any dangers by refusing to open the letters of recommendation presented to them on behalf of the athletes until the games were over, they actually gained in prestige, for this showed that they were worthy of their office. The Romans, he said, were not so unintelligent or inept as to forbid any display of independence or nobility of mind on the part of their subject peoples, for they had no desire to rule over slaves.[91]

There was only one occasion on which the hellanodicae bowed to *force majeure.* It was when Nero had the 211th Olympiad postponed from AD 65 to 67 so that he himself might take part in the Olympic games on his journey through Greece. Suetonius tells us that Nero competed at various festivals as a charioteer and that in Olympia he even appeared with a ten-horse team. But it seems that he was thrown from his chariot and, although he was helped to remount, was unable to complete the course. This, however, did not prevent him from being crowned. On leaving Olympia he granted the whole province of Achaea its freedom; he also bestowed considerable sums of money on the judges and made them citizens of Rome.[92]

After the tyrant's death in AD 68 this Olympiad was declared invalid and Nero's name was removed from the list of victors. The bribe which the emperor had paid to the judges was said to have amounted to 250,000 drachmas. At all events this was the sum which his successor Galba insisted should be repaid.[93] The freedom granted by Nero did not last long either, for the Emperor Vespasian, who reigned from AD 69 to 79, ordained that the Greeks should again pay taxes and be subject to a praetor, since they no longer knew the meaning of liberty.[94]

Chapter Six

The Spectators

1. The Ban on Married Women

Although strict rules were laid down for the competitors, anyone could come to the games as a spectator with the virtual exception of married women; even foreigners and slaves could attend and 'virgins were not refused admission'.[1] The one married woman who was allowed to watch was the priestess of Demeter Chamyne, who sat enthroned on an altar of marble, representing the goddess in whose honour the stade-race had first been inaugurated in early antiquity, when it had taken the form of a suitor's race. Consequently the office of priestess, which was conferred anew at each Olympiad, was much sought after and was once held by Regilla, the wife of Herodes Atticus, Olympia's great benefactor in Roman times.

The penalty for a married woman who transgressed against the strict Elean law was death. Pausanias has commented on this: 'On the way to Olympia from Scillus, before crossing the river Alpheus, the traveller comes to a high mountain with steep cliffs called Typaeum. There is an Elean law which provides that married women who come to the Olympic festival or even cross the Alpheus on days when they are forbidden to do so, are to be cast down from this mountain. But as far as is known no woman has yet been detected save Callipatira, known to some as Pherenice. Upon the death of her husband she dressed herself up as a trainer and brought her son to Olympia to compete in the games. When Pisidorus was victorious Callipatira leaped over the enclosure in which the trainers were confined and exposed herself in the process. Although she was then detected she was pardoned out of consideration

for her father, her brothers and her son, who had all been victorious in their events. Following this incident a law was passed requiring all trainers to appear naked at the games.'[2]

Callipatira was a daughter of the celebrated boxer, Diagorus of Rhodes,[3] the first of a famous line of heavy athletes, and it was her family's reputation that saved her life.

It has been argued that the story of Callipatira may well have been fabricated in order to justify[4] the unusual practice whereby the trainers and contestants at Olympia went naked and, although it is not possible to furnish proof of this view, it does appear distinctly plausible. But a more difficult problem is posed by the religious taboo, which was imposed on married women but not on virgins and young girls. It is to be assumed that this ban was tied up with the religious reform whereby the old fertility games of the sacred marriage were transformed into competitive games in honour of Olympian Zeus.

One of the results of this reform was that, in the strictly patriarchal climate of the new tribal system, the married woman was deprived of the religious pre-eminence which she had formerly enjoyed. As a mother it was the married woman who had symbolised fertility and not the young girl.[5]

Pausanias records only this one transgression of the ban on married women. But Dion Chrysostom, who lived a whole generation before him, maintains that even women of dubious character were admitted to the pan-Hellenic games,[6] although this observation, assuming that it is to be taken seriously and was also meant to apply to Olympia, must surely have referred to unmarried women.

2. The Pleasures and Hardships of a Visit to Olympia

A visit to Olympia was not unmitigated joy. The journey there in the height of summer was a strenuous undertaking and so too was the actual period of the visit, for the sanctuary had been conceived as a residence for gods and not for men. From the middle of the fourth century BC onwards the guests of honour were accomodated in the Leonidaeum, which had been specially built by Leonidas of Naxos for this purpose. Subsequently, in late antiquity, it became a residence for the Roman praetors in Greece. But the remaining guests slept either in tents or beneath the stars, an arrangement which was, however, rendered tolerable if not indeed refreshing by the mild summer nights in that part of Greece. The competitors of course had their own special accomodation in the western colonnade of the gymnasium.

The pilgrims bought their food from itinerant merchants for, in view of the great crowds which flocked to the festival, it was only natural that a sort of trade fair should have developed in Olympia. Cicero once observed that many of those who travelled to the games were not inspired by a desire for fame and a victor's crown but by the prospect of profitable business.[7]

But how were these enormous crowds, who only came once every four years, to be provided with adequate supplies of drinking water in the midsummer drought? This was doubtless the most difficult of the tasks facing the organisers. Drinking water was supplied by nine fountains from a number of subterranean channels. But supplies were never really adequate until Roman times, when Herodes Atticus built a special conduit, from his own private resources, which carried a large volume of water from the hills along subterranean channels several kilometres long and delivered it to a central well, which was subsequently fashioned into the beautiful fountain known as the exedra of Herodes Atticus. A magnificent marble bull, which was one of the ornaments on this fountain, has survived and is inscribed with the name and Olympic title of the wife of Herodes: Regilla, priestess of Demeter.

Lucian tells an interesting story in this connection about a contemporary of his, a man by the name of Peregrinus, who was always making speeches in order to attract attention. Eventually, when his oratory no longer drew the crowds, he announced that he intended to burn himself to death, which he actually did on a pyre not far from Olympia. But in one of the speeches which he gave in Olympia, Peregrinus inveighed against Herodes Atticus for supplying the crowds at the festival with abundant supplies of water. This was turning the Greeks into women, he said, arguing that it would be far better for them to suffer from thirst, even if it meant succumbing to the epidemics which ravaged the sanctuary during the festival period. In the course of this speech Peregrinus did not hesitate to drink from the self-same water to which he was taking such violent exception. In the end, when the crowd turned ugly and was about to stone him, our bold orator sought refuge in the altis at the statue of Zeus. This alone saved him.[8]

But it was not just a question of accomodation being difficult, of food and drink being hard to come by: life was altogether hectic at Olympia. A distant echo of the hardships endured by the spectators at the festival resounds in the words of the Stoic philosopher Epictetus: 'There are enough onerous and disagreeable things in life; don't they exist in Olympia too? Aren't you scorched there by the fierce heat? Aren't you crammed together there? Isn't bathing a problem there? Don't you get soaked to the skin? Aren't you troubled by the noise, the din and other nuisances? But it seems to me that you are well able to tolerate and gladly endure it all, when you think of the gripping spectacles [which Olympia affords].'[9] If we imagine this great surging mass of spectators, these vivacious and boisterous people from the Mediterranean world, pushing and jostling one another for the best places in the stadium, then it is not difficult to see why Epictetus should have chosen Olympia to illustrate his point. 'You expect me to live in such a fearful din? You talk about a din? Amongst so many people? What's so unpleasant about that? Imagine what it would be like in Olympia: the crush, the noise, everybody trying to do everything at once, everybody pressing and pushing and shoving...'[10]

The spectators in the stadium were not allowed to wear headdress of any kind, presumably because it would have impeded the view of those behind. But many of the Greeks were able to sit in the fierce summer sun for hours on end without apparent discomfort. This point is well brought out by Lucian in his *Anacharsis*. In a conversation with Solon, the Greek sage, Anacharsis, who was a Scythian, complained of the scorching heat in the stadium at Olympia and expressed his surprise that, unlike himself, Solon was not even perspiring and showed no sign of discomfort.[11]

Of course not all of the spectators would have been as hardened as Lucian's Solon. A visit to Olympia was a very taxing affair, so much so that, according to Aelian,[12] a citizen of Chios who was angry with one of his servants once threatened to take him with him to the Olympiad as a punishment.

But those who made the pilgrimage to Olympia gladly suffered all the inconveniences which this involved in order to witness the great athletic festival in the stadium. When the games were over they waited patiently for transport to take them home. Even Lucian was unable to set off immediately, there being no carriage available 'because too many were departing at the same time'.[13] Lucian's Solon explained to the young foreigner Anacharsis why it was that the Greeks considered athletics to be so important: 'If the Olympic games were being held at present, my dear Anacharsis, you would be able to see for yourself why we attach such great importance to athletic exercises. For it is impossible for anybody to describe in mere words the extraordinary...pleasure which these afford and which you yourself would enjoy if you were seated amongst the spectators feasting your eyes on the courage and steadfastness of the athletes, on the beauty and power of their bodies, their incredible dexterity and skill, their invincible strength, their boldness, ambition, patience and perseverance and insatiable passion for victory. You would never stop...applauding them.'[14]

But the games were not the only great experience for the visitor to Olympia. There was also the com-memorative service to Zeus, in which he was allowed to take part, and the impressive sight of the buildings and statues. The festival was both a pan-Hellenic occasion and a forum where famous men foregathered because they could be certain of finding a nation-wide audience. And so the pilgrim was caught up in a world of great events. For a brief period he lived in a state of extreme tension, deeply moved by the rich and colourful spectacle with which he was confronted, and then for the rest of his days he fed off the things which he had seen and heard in Olympia. After returning to his home district the traveller became the local authority on Olympic events and thus he helped to spread the fame of the sanctuary.

3. Olympia as a pan-Hellenic Centre

Lucian rightly observed that more people visited Olympia than any other national centre.[15] Ever since their inception the Olympics had gradually assumed the character of a pan-Hellenic festival, where contestants and spectators alike shared a common language and a common culture. The Peloponnesian War (431–404 BC) destroyed this unified cosmos. Small wonder then that, following this war, orators with pan-Hellenic views came to Olympia to urge the assembled Hellenes to carry the harmony of the festival period over into everyday political life so that they might once again oppose their common enemies, the Persians, from a position of strength and unity.

In his 'Olympic Oration' Lysias urged the Greeks to pay homage to Hercules, who had founded the Olympic games in order to forge a bond of unity between the Greek states, which were then torn by dissension and strife. It had been his hope that, if the Greeks came to this festival to see the contests in which men matched their strength and their wealth and to hear the dissertations of the philosophers, it would plant the seed of friendship in their hearts.[16]

And so the Olympic games continued to exercise a harmonious influence even after the Peloponnesian

War had swept through Hellas and the ensuing disturbances and pernicious peace settlements had further undermined the stability of the city states. In Olympia the Greeks forgot the things which divided them and concentrated on their common interests. In 380 BC, when he made his eloquent appeal for a reconciliation between the Spartans and the Athenians, Isocrates referred to the beneficial effect of the sacred truce and the pan-Hellenic assembly.[17]

But within this assembly the individual Greek states were nonetheless intent on claiming what they considered to be their due. According to this same Isocrates it would seem that in his day, apart from the host nation of Elis, Sparta enjoyed the greatest prestige at Olympia. But in 371 BC the Spartans lost the battle of Leuctra and with it their hegemony within the Greek world. One of the peace conditions laid down by the victorious Thebans was that the Messenians, who had been in thrall to Sparta for centuries, should be restored to liberty. In Isocrates's 'Panegyric', Archidamus, the son of King Agesilaus of Sparta, speaks the following words before the Spartan national assembly: 'We have good reason to feel ashamed of ourselves if we recall that at Olympia every one of us was envied and admired even more than the athletes who had been victorious in the games. But who of us would now dare to attend the festival if, instead of being honoured, we were despised, if, instead of being singled out for our courage, we were known to all for our cowardice?'[18] Archidamus then urged his countrymen not to cede Messenia.

4. Olympia as a Political Forum

The fact that Olympia was a pan-Hellenic centre made it a highly suitable place for honouring statesmen and leaders of merit. The homage paid to Themistocles at the first Olympic festival following the Persian Wars was particularly impressive because it was so completely spontaneous. Plutarch tells us that as soon as the great admiral, who had defeated the Persians at Salamis in 480 BC, appeared in the stadium the spectators forgot all about the games and spent the rest of that day applauding Themistocles and pointing him out to one another. The admiral himself is said to have been extremely moved and to have told his friends that he was now reaping the reward of his labours on behalf of Greece.[19]

Orators advocating pan-Hellenic policies, who naturally wished to reach a large audience, came to the assembly at Olympia because they knew they could command the attention of people from every part of Greece. This was why men like Lysias and Isocrates were tempted to enter the Olympic forum following the Peloponnesian War and the internal disorders which followed it. Olympia was admirably suited to their purposes for there they could build on the sacred truce in order to call the Greeks to unity and concord. But even during the war, when Greece had already been divided and ravaged for a full twenty years and both the Spartans and the Athenians were vying with one another for the favours of their erstwhile common enemy, the Persians, the celebrated sophist Georgius of Leontinoi delivered an oration in Olympia in which he implored the Greeks to call off their civil strife and unite against the Persians. We possess only two small fragments of this oration, which was given in 408 BC.[20]

In his 'Olympic Oration' in 388 BC Lysias described the dangerous situation facing the Greeks, who were then threatened by traitors within their own ranks—men who had been bought by the Persians—and also by direct naval action on the part of Dionysius, the tyrant of Syracuse. He begged the Greeks to set aside their differences and form a united front to meet their external enemies. Lysias's hatred was directed primarily against the 'tyrant Dionysius', a fellow-countryman of his, who, although a Greek himself, had subjugated the Greek colony in Italy on the river Eleporus, destroyed Rhegium, enslaved its inhabitants and made the whole of south-western Italy a sphere of Syracusan influence. Lysias so incited the visitors to the festival against the tyrant that there were demonstrations against Dionysius. Diodorus of Sicily gave an account of these events: 'Since the Olympic games were due to take place he [Dionysius] had sent several teams of four to the festival, which were very much faster than the other teams, and also a magnificent tent, whose fabric was interwoven with gold and which was fitted out with brightly coloured carpets. He had also commissioned the best readers to recite his poetry at the festival and so establish his fame in this sphere, for he was consumed by a burning passion to be hailed as a celebrated poet. His brother Thearides acted as his lieutenant. The beautiful tents and the splendid teams of horses caused a considerable stir and were admired by one and all. Then the readers began to recite Dionysius's poems. At first the trained voices of the readers drew the crowds and the fine artistry of these men was much admired. But the people soon realised just how paltry and worthless the poems were and they laughed and mocked at Dionysius for his stupidity and nerve; they then banded together and attacked and looted his tents.'[21] A large part of Lysias's oration has been preserved for us by Dionysius of Halicarnassus, who quoted it as an example of the declamatory style of oratory. Dionysius prefaced his quotation with a brief synopsis of the entire oration, from which we learn that Lysias urged the spectators at Olympia to topple the tyrant Dionysius from his throne and liberate Sicily and to open hostilities there and then by plundering the tyrant's tent.[22]

The Athenian orator Isocrates also pursued a political aim in his 'Panegyric', which was composed for the Olympic festival of 380 BC. Following the shameful peace concluded by Antalcidas in 387–6 BC, by which the Greek cities of Asia became tributary to the Persian monarch, this pan-Hellenic thinker and orator urged the Greeks to settle their disputes and unite against the Persians. He closed his long and artistic oration by inviting his audience to consider the affluence which the Greek territories might enjoy if, instead of wrangling amongst themselves, they fought together against the Persians, thus acquiring the wealth of Asia for Europe; and he exhorted those able to bring influence to bear to join forces in an attempt to effect a reconciliation between the Athenians and the Lacedaemonians.[23] It would seem that his speech, which was distributed in pamphlet form, may well have had some effect, for two years later Athens assumed the leadership of a newly formed naval league which was directed against Persia.

Plutarch tells us that Alexander the Great had little liking for athletics. Although he was always prepared to stage contests for tragedians, lyre and zither players, and even for wandering minstrels, and was by no means averse to hunting competitions and gladiatorial games, it would not have occurred to him to put up a prize for a boxing match or a pentathlon.[24] But Alexander recognised the great significance of Olympia, for in 324 BC, when he drafted his edict in favour of the Greek exiles, it was in Olympia that he had it promulgated. Diodorus explains that shortly before his death Alexander decided to help all the Greek exiles to return to their native cities; apparently he did this partly in order to enhance his personal prestige and partly to increase his following in the Greek cities and so safeguard himself against disturbances and possible defections. Consequently, when the time for the festival drew near, he sent Nicanor of Stagira to Greece with a copy of his edict, which was then read out by the herald at Olympia: 'King Alexander to the exiles from the cities of Greece. We were not responsible for your banishment but—with the sole exception of those who are under a curse—we are prepared to accept responsibility for your return to your native cities. Accordingly we have written to Antipater authorising him to use force in those cities which withhold their assent.' Diodorus reports that this announcement was greeted with tumultuous applause by the crowd, which included more than 20,000 exiles.[24a]

Alexander had long held both Olympia and its victors in high esteem. He made this perfectly clear after the battle of Issus in 333 BC when the Greek envoys to the king of Persia—one of whom was the Olympic victor Dionysodorus of Thebes—were among the prisoners taken by his troops for, 'although Dionysodorus was a Theban, he immediately released him because of his victory at the Olympic games'.[25] And towards the end of 324 BC, when the Greek states sent delegations to him at

10. Charioteer from Delphi.

Babylon, he received the Elean delegates first 'on account of their famous sanctuary'.[26]

As a focal point of pan-Hellenic life, Olympia was an ideal place for preserving documents and records of national importance.

In eternal memory of the crucial victory won by the combined Greek forces over the Persians at Plataea, the army command dedicated a statue to Zeus in Olympia and the names of the twenty-seven states which had fought in this war of liberation were engraved on its base.[27]

The text of the thirty-year peace signed between Athens and Sparta in 445 BC was engraved on a bronze tablet which was also placed in the altis.[28] In fact, the peace lasted for only fourteen years. Then came the Peloponnesian War. Ten years later peace was declared and ratified in a treaty which was to have remained in force for the next fifty years. In the event this peace turned out to be no more than a temporary armistice despite the most solemn oaths given by both parties. Thucydides tells us that the articles of the treaty had to be affirmed not only by the Athenians and the Spartans but also by their allies and that this affirmation was to have been repeated annually. It was also decreed that pillars should be erected at the sites of the Olympic, Pythian and Isthmian games, in the citadel in Athens and the amyclaeum in Lacedaemon and the text of the agreement engraved on them.[29]

Because of the prestige and power enjoyed by the parties to this treaty these documents were a matter of direct concern to the whole Greek nation. But in 420 BC, just one year after the conclusion of this peace, Athens entered into a hundred-year alliance against Sparta with Argos, Mantinea and Elis. (On this occasion the vow of perpetual neutrality enjoined on the Eleans as the custodians of the Olympic sanctuary was blatantly disregarded.) The text of this agreement was to be engraved on stone tablets, which were to be erected in Athens, Argos and Mantinea. 'And then', Thucydides tells us, 'a bronze column was also to be erected in the name of all four states at Olympia on the occasion of the forthcoming festival.'[30] In Pausanias's day this column stood in the temple of Zeus.

This particular record was of course by no means pan-Hellenic. Nor for that matter were the documents deposited both in the Capitol and in Olympia[31] to commemorate the anti-Macedonian treaty concluded in 212 BC in the course of the Second Punic War between Rome and the Aetolian League (which was enlarged in the following year by the accession of Sparta, Messenia, Elis and Pergamum), for at that time another group of Greek states was fighting for Hannibal's ally, Philip V of Macedonia.

Olympia's status as a pan-Hellenic centre was not restored until the whole of the Mediterranean had been pacified by Rome, when 'the Romans came to regard Olympia as a sort of capital for the whole of the Greek world'.[32]

The great festival in Olympia also provided an opportunity for holding political talks, especially in times of war when, because of the Eleans' neutrality and the protection afforded by the sacred truce, it was the one place where the belligerents could get together. In the early years of the Peloponnesian War, when Mytilene appealed to Sparta for help, the Spartans and their allies discussed this appeal during the festival of 428 BC.[33]

Olympia was again used as a venue for political discussions in the Second Punic War. In 208 BC the Romans sent Titus Manlius to Greece in order to report on the situation there and also to establish contact with the Siculi and the Tarentines who, after being driven from their territories by the Carthaginians, had made their way to Olympia.[34]

Olympia was also, of course, an excellent place for settling private transactions. Herodotus tells us that, after winning the victor's crown in the four-horse chariot-race, Clisthenes of Sicyon bade the herald announce that any citizen who considered himself worthy to become his son-in-law should present himself in Sicyon within sixty days, for he was prepared to offer his daughter Agariste to the bravest and noblest Greek he could find. At this, Herodotus says, every man who took pride in himself and in his native city set out for Sicyon, where Clisthenes prepared a running track and a prize-ring.[35] There the suitors matched their strength and their skill for a period of twelve months, at the end

61

11. Racing chariot and charioteer (votive offering).

of which time Megacles, an Athenian of the house of Alcmaeon, won the bride and became Clisthenes's son-in-law, while his rivals each received a silver talent as a consolation prize. This private contest took place in the middle of the sixth century BC.[36]

5. The Absence of Artistic Contests in Olympia

Artistic contests were an important part of the Pythian games in Delphi, the Isthmian games in Corinth and the Panathenaea in Athens. Apart from their temples and stadiums these sanctuaries also had theatres, so their festivals could really be said to promote the harmony of body, mind and soul.

Although Olympia with its gymnastic, athletic and equestrian festival would have been quite capable of fulfilling a similar role as a centre of the arts virtually all the evidence would seem to indicate that this was not the case. In his 'Olympic Oration' of 388 BC Lysias tells us that Hercules's object in founding the Olympic festival was to establish a 'contest of physical strength, a contest of wealth and an exhibition of the mind *(gnomes epideixis)*'.[37] But this is the only statement which might conceivably be construed as a reference to artistic contests and the evidence to the contrary is so unequivocal that we are bound to assume that there were no intellectual competitions as such in Olympia. Isocrates openly lamented the fact in his 'Panegyric' in 380 BC. Speaking as an intellectual he took the administrators of the Olympic games to task for placing too much emphasis on the physical attributes of the contestants. His censure was justified by events, for in the course of time the athletic contests lost their religious significance and eventually became an end in themselves. In this oration Isocrates made the telling point that, no matter how strong a wrestler was, other people were not likely to benefit from his strength, whereas the wisdom acquired by men who had patiently devoted themselves to their studies might well prove a source of comfort and help to their fellow men.[38]

A much later writer, Flavius Philostratus the Elder, who lived in the third century AD, also referred to the lack of intellectual and, more especially, artistic activities in Olympia: 'When the visitors arrive in Pytho [Delphi] they are met by the flautists, entertained with music and song, honoured with performances of comedies and tragedies; it is not until much later that naked combat comes to the fore. But Olympia dispenses with such things as inappropriate and worthless and, in accordance with the statutes framed by Hercules, immediately confronts the visitor with naked athletes.'[39]

It is true that Nero appeared at Olympia in the role of singer and actor. But he was the only one ever to do so. At the 211th Olympiad, which was postponed from AD 65 to 67 at his command, Nero won a triple crown: in the chariot-race with a team of ten, in which he fell from his chariot, in a contest for tragedians and in a competition for singers, presumably with zither accompaniment.

The excavations have shown that Olympia possessed neither an odeum nor a theatre. From this it is quite obvious that Lysias's 'exhibition of the mind' cannot have been a reference to artistic competitions. What he must have meant by this phrase was that Olympia was intended to provide a suitable forum for the presentation and discussion of literary, artistic and scientific ideas. There is, of course, abundant evidence that this was the case. Indeed, the Olympic festival offered scholars, poets and artists a unique opportunity of reaching a nation-wide public.

6. Cultural Life in Olympia

The prospect of appearing in Olympia before an audience which was numbered in tens of thousands must have been a very enticing one for the Greek intellectuals. There they could acquire the personal renown which was the elixir of life to the peoples of antiquity. We know from Lucian that Herodotus of Halicarnassus, the historian of the Persian Wars, sought and found fame in Olympia: 'As he was travelling from his native land of Caria to Greece he wondered how he could make himself and his works famous as quickly and with as little trouble

62

as possible. For he thought it a wearisome business to travel from place to place, reading his works first to the Athenians, then to the Corinthians, now to the Argives, now to the Spartans; he also considered that this would waste a great deal of time... And so he was intent on finding some place where he could reach large numbers of people from all parts of the Greek world at one and the same time. When therefore the time for the great Olympics drew near it seemed to Herodotus that here was the favourable opportunity he had been longing for. He waited until the festival was at its height and the best people had flocked to Olympia from every corner of Hellas and then proceeded—not as a spectator but as a contestant—to the rear portico [of the temple of Zeus], where he read his history and so charmed all present that they praised his works most highly, saying that they were comparable to the Muses themselves, who were also nine in number.

'Soon Herodotus was far more famous than the Olympic victors. Everybody knew his name. Some had heard it in Olympia, others had learnt it from those who had returned from the festival. Wherever he appeared people pointed to him and said: "That man is Herodotus who recounted the Persian Wars in the Ionic tongue and glorified our victories." The success which he achieved by reading his works at this one assembly brought him recognition throughout the whole of Greece.'[40]

It is significant that this account should have come from Lucian, for he himself visited Olympia on five separate occasions, the last being in AD 165. No doubt he was following Herodotus's example and seeking fame and recognition for himself at the festival.

The philosophers and sophists also liked to go to Olympia, some—such as Gorgias, Lysias and Isocrates—in order to pursue political aims, others in order to display their knowledge and powers of rhetoric. We know, for example, that Prodicus of Ceos, Anaximenes of Chios, Polus of Agrigentum and the native sophist, Hippias of Elis, all quickly made their mark in Olympia.[41] Hippias, who has furnished us with a list of Olympic victors, once boasted at the festival of his many accomplishments, which

Socrates subsequently enumerated for him in a distinctly ironical vein: 'You said that once, when you came to Olympia, every article you had on you had been the work of your own hands: first there was the ring you were wearing (you began with that) for you knew how to engrave rings, and then there was your seal, which you yourself had made, and also a scraping-knife and an oil flask, which you had manufactured. And you told how you had fashioned the sandals which you were wearing and had woven your cloak and robe. And then, as proof of your great dexterity, you recounted the most amazing thing of all, namely that the sash on your cloak was the same as the sashes worn by wealthy Persians and that you yourself had plaited it. And then you explained that you had brought poetic works with you—epics, tragedies, dithyrambs and prose writings on a wide variety of subjects. You had come, you said, as an outstanding master of the arts which I have just mentioned and also of rhythm and harmony and autography and many other things besides if my memory serves me correctly. And of course I had forgotten your mnemonics, an art in which you considered yourself pre-eminent.'[42]

The itinerant preacher and miracle worker Apollonius of Tyana, a contemporary of the early Roman emperors, also came to Olympia to preach. Philostratus tells us that in his sermons Apollonius dealt with matters of common concern; he spoke of wisdom, courage, temperance, in fact of all the virtues. He addressed his audience from the threshold of the temple and astounded them not only by the range of his thought but also by his powers of rhetoric.[43]

Lucian tells us that the painter Aetion exhibited one of his works at Olympia, in which he had portrayed the nuptials of Alexander and Roxana. This painting was received with great acclaim and Proxenides, who was one of the judges at that particular Olympiad, was so delighted with Aetion's art that he gave him his daughter in marriage.[44] Although this is the only substantiated case of an artist exhibiting his work at Olympia this may well have been standard practice since the festival also provided painters and sculptors with an ideal public. There is even some evidence that scientists availed themselves of the Olympic forum in order to publicise the findings of their enquiries for we know that the astronomer Oenomides exhibited a bronze tablet inscribed with his calculations.[45]

Poets and philosophers may actually have competed with one another at the festival but, although it has been assumed by some authorities that the victors in such contests would have been crowned, there is no firm proof that this was the case.[46] The only reference to a crown for intellectuals occurs in Philostratus's history of Apollonius of Tyana. Apollonius was said to have visited the king of India and to have conducted a conversation with him to the following effect:

'What has brought you here?' the king asked.
'These gods and wise men', Apollonius replied.
'Tell me stranger, am I mentioned in Greece?'
'As much as the Greeks are mentioned here.'
'I do not consider anything which the Greeks do worthy of mention', the king said.
'I will tell them so', Apollonius replied, 'and they will crown you in Olympia.'[47]

The irony underlying these words is so obvious that it is difficult to see how they could be regarded as furnishing satisfactory evidence that a crown was awarded in Olympia for intellectual achievements.

7. Famous Men in Olympia

It seems surprising to us today that so many philosophers should have journeyed to Olympia. Thales of Miletus, the first of the Greek philosophers, even died there. Diogenes Laertius tells us that he succumbed to the effects of the intense heat, due partly to lack of water and partly to his advanced age.[48] Cheilon—the early Greek seer who is said to have been the author of the maxim: 'Know thyself'—also died there. It seems that when his son was victorious in the boxing contest he was so overcome with emotion that he dropped dead on the spot.[49] The Ionian philosopher Anaxagoras demonstrated his powers of prophecy in Olympia. According to

Philostratus he appeared in the stadium during the games, *i.e.* at a time of year when rain was virtually unheard of, wearing a sheepskin because he knew that it was going to rain.[50] Empedocles of Agrigentum—the seer, prophet and miracle worker who leaped into the crater of Mount Aetna—travelled to Olympia, where he sacrificed an effigy of a bull made of dough[51] mixed with incense and precious herbs.[52] Plato and Aristotle also visited the sanctuary on the banks of the Alpheus; Plato describes his visit in his letters[53] and we know from Plutarch that Aristotle saw the 'quoit of Iphitus' in the temple of Hera.[54] Demosthenes, the most celebrated of all ancient orators, came to Olympia at the head of an Athenian delegation.[55] Pindar, who celebrated many of the Olympic victors in his Odes, stayed there, and his contemporary Bacchylides, who also praised the athletes in epic verse, probably did so; the latter's uncle Simonides certainly did. He composed epigrams to the Olympic victors which were subsequently engraved on their statues. Archilochus, a poet of the seventh century BC who sang the praises of Hercules, the mythical founder of the festival, and was the first man ever to compose verse in honour of the Olympic victors, presumably visited the sanctuary.

But our list of famous men in Olympia is still far from complete. Lycurgus, the legendary Spartan legislator, was one of the first to go there. It was in Olympia that he was instructed by a voice from heaven to allow his people to take part in the games; this then led to the conclusion of the sacred truce with Iphitus and Cleosthenes.[56] And there were many others: Pythagoras, Socrates, Diogenes, Aeschylus, Thucydides[57] and Dion Chrysostom, the 'golden mouth', whose penetrating intuition saw deep into the soul of Phidias, thus enabling us to share in the vision which was the source of the Olympian Zeus, the most important work by the greatest of all Greek sculptors.[58] And there must also have been many great thinkers who made their pilgrimage to Zeus in his Olympic sanctuary without our knowledge.

Some of those who attended the festival were undoubtedly motivated by a false sense of their own importance and a morbid desire for recognition.

One such was the painter Zeuxis, a man of considerable wealth who appeared at Olympia wearing a cloak on which his name was embroidered in letters of gold.[59]

There were also celebrated rulers who sought to enhance their fame by gaining victories in the games, although the most celebrated of them all, Alexander the Great, did not take part. His father Philip had even had special coins minted to commemorate the victories won by his horses at Olympia. But, although Alexander was a good runner, when asked if he would like to run at the Olympic games he replied: 'Certainly, provided my adversaries are kings.'[60]

Chapter Seven

The Sequence of Events

1. The Reconstruction of the Sequence of Events

There were two principal aspects to the festival in honour of Olympian Zeus. On the one hand there were the religious rites, such as the solemn processions and sacrifices, and on the other hand there were the games, although strictly speaking, since these were held *ad majorem dei gloriam,* they too formed an integral part of the cult. The ancient Olympiads lasted for more than one thousand years. Initially the festival had been a simple affair, consisting of a sacrificial service to Zeus and the stade-race, for which a single day had sufficed. But with the diversification of the games and the growth of Olympia's importance as a pan-Hellenic centre the festival began to take up more and more time until eventually a fundamental reappraisal of the whole proceedings became necessary. Consequently, in 472 BC, following the Greek victory over the Persians, reforms were introduced which fixed both the duration of the festival and the sequence of events. These reforms were still in force in AD 174 during the reign of Marcus Aurelius, when Pausanias was revising his journals on Elis.[1]

Although it is difficult to state the overall sequence of events with absolute certainty, the information gleaned from a wide variety of sources has enabled us to establish a number of individual sequences. Thus we know that in the five days covered by the festival the boys' contests preceded the men's, the pentathlon and the equestrian events took place on the same day (first the horse-races and then the pentathlon) and that these both preceded the great sacrifice to Zeus; we also know that the various foot-races were held on a single day and that the normal sequence was dolichos, stade-race and diaulos; the heavy events—wrestling, boxing and pankration—took up a further day, while the race in armour was either the last of the foot-races or, as in Delphi, the final event of the whole athletic festival.[2]

It should be borne in mind, however, that the judges were at liberty to change the sequence of any single group of events. This they did in 212 BC when, at the request of one of the contestants, they reversed the normal order of the boxing and pankration.[3]

But, although it is not possible to establish the overall sequence of events from the source material, we can perhaps reconstruct a more or less satisfactory sequence by tracing the ritual development of the games. The sacrifice to Zeus and the stade-race, which were the original basis of the festival, must of course form the point of departure for any such enquiry. Initially both of these took place on the day following the full moon in the eighth month of the Elean year and, for both religious and traditional reasons, they would have remained the focal point of the festival, even when it was extended in later times. According to the legendary account of the chariot-race between Pelops and Oenomaus the two contenders first made their sacrifice and then engaged in their contest;[4] so too did Hercules in Pindar's ode.[5] Philostratus on the other hand tells us that the victor in the stade-race at Olympia was privileged to light the pyre on the sacrificial altar, which would mean of course that the race preceded the sacrifice. In this version the competitors lined up for the start of the race at a distance of one stade from the altar, where a priest with a burning torch in his hand waited to proclaim the victor, who then

VI Scenes from the pentathlon.

took the torch and lit the pyre.[6] This, however, is the only account in which this sequence is observed and consequently we may safely disregard it. In Delphi the altar pyre was not lit after the stade-race but at the end of the solemn procession.[7] It seems probable that the same procedure would have been adopted in Olympia.

Whereas the stade-race, which went back to the suitors' race in honour of Demeter, and the various other foot-races, which had been derived from it, were associated with the festival of Zeus from its inception, the other athletic events staged in Olympia, all of which were derived from Pelops's funeral games, were absorbed into the new cult at a later stage. When this happened, the festival was extended to cover two days, the first of these being given over to the more recent innovations, which were concluded at nightfall with obsequies in honour of Pelops in the altis. This was of course the eve of the first full moon of the eighth lunar month and, since the Greek day was calculated from sunset to sunrise, it was also the beginning of the day on which the Greeks made their great quadrennial sacrifice to Zeus. Thus the first full moon of the eighth lunar month linked the nocturnal rites of the cult of Pelops with the diurnal sacrifice to Zeus.

When the equestrian events—which had been derived from the suitors' race of the cult of the divine marriage—were incorporated into the cult of Zeus they were also held on the day devoted to the hero. Because the actual funeral games, i.e., the pentathlon, the wrestling and the other heavy athletic events, were more closely connected with the cult of Pelops they came at the end of the day's events immediately before the obsequies.

It is to be assumed that with the diversification of the contests and the constant growth in the number of contestants it would eventually have proved impossible to accomodate all the events within the specified two-day period, and that the wrestling, the boxing and the pankration, which took up a great deal of time and were also extremely popular with the spectators, would have been removed from the programme as it then stood and an extra day set aside for them. But this extra day cannot have come before the other two, for then part of the funeral games would have preceded the chariot-race of the sacred marriage and, given the natural conservatism of religious organisations, such a sequence of events would have been quite impossible.

Although the passage in Pausanias dealing with the reorganisation of the Olympic programme at the 77th Olympiad is corrupt, the view advanced above would appear to be more or less in accord with it. He tells us that the order of the games in his day was for the sacrifice to come after the pentathlon and the horse-races 'according to the programme established in the 77th Olympiad, for before this horses and men contended on the same day. And at that time the pankratiasts did not appear till night for they could not compete sooner, so much time having been taken up by the horse-races and pentathlon. But for the future they took care that neither the pentathlon nor the horse-races should stand in the way of the pankration.'[8] Since Pausanias makes no reference to the stade-race it would appear that it was not affected by the reorganisation. On the other hand it would seem that the sacrifice to Zeus took place after the equestrian events and the pentathlon but before the wrestling, boxing and pankration. A further inference which might perhaps be drawn from this quotation is that the pentathlon was held before the equestrian events on the day preceding the sacrifice to Zeus, i.e., on 'Pelops's festival', for Pausanias mentions them in that order. But this would be at variance with the clear statement made by Xenophon in respect of the Olympiad of 364 BC when the Arcadians and the Eleans fought a battle in the altis: 'They had already finished the horse-race and also the foot-race in the pentathlon.'[9]

In the light of this evidence we are now able to advance the following hypothetical sequence for the first three days of the festival:

First day:
Equestrian events, pentathlon, obsequies for Pelops.
Second day:
Sacrifice to Zeus, foot-races.
Third day:
Heavy events—wrestling, boxing, pankration.

When the competitions for boys were included in the programme they were treated as a separate class of event altogether and staged before the men's contests. This of course extended the festival by yet another day.

Finally we have to consider the question of the prize-giving ceremony. Originally, when the festival had lasted only a single day and had consisted simply of the sacrifice to Zeus and the foot-races, this ceremony would probably have been held on the evening of the same day. The extension of the festival to two days, so as to include the games and obsequies in honour of Pelops, would have made no difference to this arrangement since this additional day preceded the day of the sacrifice. But when the festival was extended by a third day in order to cater for the growing needs of the contestants in the heavy events this did make a difference, for this third day came after the day of the sacrifice. Naturally the prize-giving ceremony had to be deferred. In 472 BC, by which time the games covered a full five days, the Eleans placed the prize-giving ceremony on the final day of the festival.

This reconstruction of the sequence of events at the five-day festival takes account of all the available evidence and would therefore appear to be soundly based. The principal virtue of this hypothesis is the fact that it places the great sacrifice to Zeus and the foot-races which accompanied it firmly in the centre of the festival, *i.e.*, on the third day of the Olympiad, for since this was the day following the full moon, and consequently the mid-point of the lunar month, it was of course the most significant in religious terms. It was in fact the fourteenth day of the 'sacred month'.[10]

2. The First Day

The Inauguration of the Festival and the Oath-taking Ceremony

The solemn inauguration of the festival was performed in the altis and was attended by the whole of the Olympic community. There are no extant accounts of the proceedings but it would be natural to assume that they were initiated by purification rights. As in Eleusis, so too in Olympia those excluded from the games on the grounds of blood-guilt or sacrilege would no doubt have been solemnly called upon to quit the altis. The law banning married women from the sanctuary would also have been proclaimed. With this the purification of the festival community would presumably have been completed. The judges of course had already undergone their purification at the fountain of Piera on their journey from Elis.

The oath-taking ceremony was then performed in the buleuterion in front of the statue of Zeus. Pausanias tells us that this statue, which was called 'Zeus God of Oaths', was most awe-inspiring. It seems that the athletes, their fathers and brothers and also their trainers were required to swear over the entrails of a boar that they would not cheat at the Olympic games. The athletes were then called upon to give a further oath to the effect that they had carefully prepared for the games over a period of ten months. The judges, who had to assess the eligibility of the boys and the colts for their respective events, were also required to give a solemn oath that they would deliver their verdicts honestly and would refuse all bribes.[11] But this statement of Pausanias's would appear to contain contradictions. The oath relating to the ten-month training period, which Pausanias says was given in Olympia, must in fact have been given in Elis since a competitor's eligibility for the games depended on it.[12] Moreover, if the contestants had already been classified in Elis on the basis of age and ability, then the judges would already have delivered their verdicts in respect of the boys and the colts. Consequently, these two particular oaths can only have been a formal reaffirmation of the solemn undertakings already given in Elis.

The Contest for Heralds and Trumpeters

From 396 BC onwards the games were opened by a contest for heralds and trumpeters.[13] This probably followed immediately after the ritual inauguration

12. Small bronze figure of horseman.

and was held to decide which trumpeter was to give the signal for the start of the various events and which herald was to proclaim the judges' verdicts. Originally the Eleans would no doubt have simply provided heralds and trumpeters from their own ranks. Subsequently, however, there was a general demand for a contest in which all states might participate. According to Pausanias, the competition was held near the entrance to the stadium, the contestants standing on an unconsecrated altar.[14]

The trumpeter's principal task in the equestrian events was to give the signal for the beginning of the final lap or the finishing sprint and then to accompany it with lively and encouraging blasts on his instrument. Pausanias refers to this trumpet call in the following account of an Olympic horse-race which was won by a riderless horse: 'The mare of the Corinthian Phidolas was called... Aura and, although its rider was thrown at the beginning of the race, it ran straight on and turned at the pillar and, when it heard the sound of the trumpet, ran on all the faster and beat all the other horses...'[15]

The most famous trumpeter of all was undoubtedly Herodorus of Megara who won the prize in ten successive Olympiads (328–292 BC). According to some accounts he actually won the contest eleven times in all, according to others seven times. He was said to have been so strong that he could blow two trumpets at once.

The Contests for Boys

The opening ceremonies and the competitions for heralds and trumpeters occupied the morning of the first day, which means that the afternoon would have been left for the boys' contests. Initially these consisted of the running, the wrestling and the boxing events, but at the Olympiad of 628 BC a pentathlon for boys was also introduced. This, however, was immediately discontinued. According to Pausanias the Eleans abandoned it because the victor was a Spartan,[16] but the truth of the matter may well have been that this particular event proved too strenuous for the boys and over-taxed their strength. The pentathlon was, of course, also extremely time-consuming and may conceivably have overrun the schedule fixed for the boys' events.

Although it was generally recognised that physical training formed a necessary part of adolescent education these contests did not meet with unqualified approval. Aristotle pointed out that, while nobody doubted the need for physical exercise, it was important that this should be graded to suit the requirements of the individual concerned. Youths, he said, should practice light exercises and should neither overeat nor overtax their strength. The dangers of such over-indulgence were only too obvious, for of all the boy victors at Olympia no more than two or three had gone on to gain victories as men.[17]

Philostratus also dealt with this question. In his *Gymnasticus* he took a number of trainers severely to task for feeding and training their young charges as if they were fully grown men, thus making them muscle-bound and lethargic instead of encouraging their natural vivacity and speed of movement.[18]

Polymnestor, a goatherd from Miletus, acquired great fame in the stade-race for boys; it was said of him that he could quite literally run like a hare.[19] At the 126th Olympiad in 276 BC Cratinus of Aegira in Achaea was so outstanding in the boys' wrestling that both he and his trainer were allowed to erect their statues in the altis.[20] From this it is evident that Greek wrestling called for a special expertise, which was imparted by the trainers; physical force was not the only requirement. The Spartans, however, who prided themselves on their brute strength evidently thought differently for in a boastful epigram penned by a Spartan youth we are told: 'The other wrestlers are stylists. I win by my strength, as is only right and fitting for a Spartan youth.'[21] Since the Spartans despised wrestling as an art they did not employ trainers.[22]

In the boxing it was considered particularly meritorious if a contestant won his event without taking a blow. Hippomachus of Elis achieved this feat in the boys' competition; Pausanias tells us that he overcame three opponents without receiving a single blow or wound.[23]

3a. Four-horse chariot.
3b. Horseman.

The best of the boy pankratiasts was almost certainly Artemidorus of Tralles who began his career by being defeated in Olympia but subsequently achieved great things at Smyrna. There, we are told, he not only defeated his former adversaries from the Olympic festival[24] but also took on both the 'unbearded' and the men and defeated them too.[25] At the 212th Olympiad in AD 69 Artemidorus won the men's pankration at Olympia.

We also learn from Pausanias that horse-races for boys were held at Olympia for he refers to the statues of 'Tymon and his son Aesypus, a lad on horseback [who] won the prize on his race horse'.[26] He also mentions two other statues of boys on horseback at Olympia on a later page.[27] But we have no detailed knowledge of these equestrian events for boys. We do not know whether they were a regular feature of the games or occurred only on isolated occasions; nor do we know whether they formed an integral part of the contests for boys or were merely an adjunct to the equestrian events for the men. It is also conceivable that these young lads mentioned by Pausanias may simply have inherited a horse which then gained a victory at Olympia in their name.

3. The Second Day

The Equestrian Events

The men's contests began on the second day of the festival, which opened with the equestrian events.[28] These took up the whole of the morning. In the early days of the festival they consisted of chariot-races with teams of four. At first the draught animals were fully grown horses but subsequently colts were also used and for a while even mules. Then in 480 BC chariot-races with two-horse teams were introduced, which were also restricted to fully grown horses at first but were subsequently extended to include colts. Most of the animals in the horse-races were stallions, although mares and perhaps even geldings would have been used to some extent, while a special race for colts was introduced at a later stage.[29]

We do not know whether the chariot-races or the horse-races featured first on the programme of equestrian events, although the chariot-races certainly preceded the horse-races in the development of the games, the former being introduced in 680 and the latter in 648 BC. All forms of horse-racing were the prerogative of the rich, who hired charioteers and riders to race for them. They themselves did not normally take an active part. But if their horses won at Olympia then they, as the owners, were proclaimed victors and received the crown of olive while their charioteer or rider was adorned with a fillet of wool.[30]

Racing chariots were low-slung and were mounted on an axle without springs which was fitted with two small wheels, the majority of which had four spokes. The car itself was open to the rear but had a knee-high framework on its other three sides. In the four-horse team the middle pair was harnessed to the yoke, which was then attached to the pole, while the other pair acted as trace-horses. The charioteer carried a whip or a goad. Larger wheels would undoubtedly have produced higher speeds but the smaller type of wheel made for greater safety, which was an important factor on rough ground.[31]

The ancient style of horse-racing was very different from our own, for the Greeks had neither saddles nor stirrups. The modern bridle was also unknown to them; they used a snaffle, a plain, slender, jointed bit without a curb, which passed through the horse's mouth. The Greek rider controlled his steed by the use of knee pressure, reins and whip. Although spurs had been invented they were rarely used.[32]

Riding without saddle and stirrups must have been quiet a strenuous undertaking, which would suggest that the races were not very long. Unfortunately no trace has been found of the race track in Olympia and so we cannot be absolutely certain of its exact length. But Pausanias does tell us that at Nemea the length of the horse-race was 'twice the double course',[33] i.e., twice as long as the diaulos or the equivalent of four stades. The Olympic stade was of course 600 feet or, to be more precise, 192.28 metres. Assuming that the horse-race at Olympia was also run over four stades this would mean that the Olympic course measured 769.12 metres. If we now recall the race held at Olympia in which Phidolas's mare, after throwing its rider, 'ran straight on and turned at the pillar and...beat all the other horses'[34] it would seem that the course in the Olympic hippodrome consisted of a single circuit measuring four stades or 769.12 metres. From this it would follow that a single length of the race track at Olympia measured two stades or 384.56 metres.

The chariot-races at Olympia were considerably longer. In the events for teams of four, the fully grown horses had to cover the course twelve times and the colts eight times; thus these races were run over distances of 9229.44 metres and 6152.96 metres respectively. In the later contests for two-horse teams the fully grown horses had to cover eight circuits, i.e., 6152.96 metres, and the colts three circuits, i.e., 2307.36 metres.[35]

In the ancient seraglio of Constantinople a metrological manuscript was discovered which contained a description of the hippodrome at Olympia. With the information obtained from this manuscript it has proved possible to reconstruct the original race course with a fair degree of certainty.[36]

The equestrian events were open to all comers. In Delphi the chariot entered by Archaesilaus of Cyrene won out of a field of forty.[37] With so many competitors heats would have been essential. Often, in order to create an impression, a single owner would enter a number of chariots in the one event. Alcibiades for example boasted that he had seven chariots running at the Olympiad of 416 BC.[38] Despite the great numbers involved, however, it was entirely feasible for the equestrian events to be completed by noon, when a break was made on account of the heat, for the races began very early in the morning.

But what were these chariot-races like? Sophocles has provided us with a graphic account in the speech in which the Tutor informs Electra of her brother Orestes's supposed death in the chariot-race at Delphi:

'The day for the chariot-races came, and the contest was to start at sunrise. Orestes was there, with many another competitor: an Achaean, a Spartan, two drivers of teams from Libya, and Orestes with his Thessalian horses—that makes five—an Aetolian with chestnut colts, six, a Magnesian, seven—an Aenian with a white team, and one from the sacred walls of Athens, eight, nine—and a Boeotian ten.

'The appointed stewards cast the lots for position and ranged the chariots on the starting-line; then, at the sound of the bronze trumpet, off they started, all shouting to their horses and twitching the reins in their hands. The clatter of the rattling chariots filled the whole arena, and the dust flew up as they sped along in a dense mass, each driver goading his team unmercifully in his efforts to draw clear of the rival axles and panting steeds, whose steaming breath and sweat drenched every bending back and flying wheel together.

'To begin with all went well with every chariot. Then the Aenian's tough colts took the bit in their teeth and on the turn from the sixth to the seventh lap, ran head-on into the African. This accident led to other upsets and collisions, till the field of Crisa was a sea of wrecked and capsized chariots. The Athenian driver had seen what was coming and was clever enough to draw aside and bide his time while the oncoming wave crashed into inextricable confusion. Orestes was driving last, purposely holding his team back and pinning his faith to the final spurt; and now, seeing only one rival left in, with an exultant shout to his swift horses he drove hard ahead and the two teams raced neck and neck, now one now the other gaining a lead.

'At each turn of the lap, Orestes reined in his inner trace-horse and gave the outer its head, so skilfully that his hub just cleared the post by a hair's breadth every time; and so the poor fellow had safely rounded every lap but one without mishap to himself or his chariot. But at the last he misjudged the turn, slackened his left rein before the horse was safely round the bend, and so fouled the post. The hub was smashed across, and he was hurled over the rail entangled in the several reins, and as he fell his horses ran wild across the course.

'When the people saw his fall from the chariot, there was a cry of sympathy for the poor lad—the hero of such magnificent exploits and now the victim

71

of such a terrible misfortune. They saw him now pinned to the ground, now rolled head over heels, till at last the other drivers got his runaway horses under control and extricated the poor mangled body, so bruised and bloody that not one of his friends could have recognized him; and shortly some men of Phocis will be bringing you a little urn of bronze that contains, alas, the dust of one of the greatest of men, so that you may lay him to rest in his native soil.'[39]

The Pentathlon

On the afternoon of the second day the pentathlon was staged, the sequence of events being discus, jumping, javelin, running and wrestling.[40] Since running and wrestling were also contests in their own right, only the discus, javelin and jumping were regarded as 'disciplines specific to the pentathlon'.[41] The order of events had been well thought out, for

Fig. 16: Bowl painting illustrating the pentathlon. Above: discus thrower (left-handed?), javelin thrower, a pair of wrestlers; Centre: discus thrower wearing boxer's cap and javelin thrower; Below: judge with pegs to mark jumps, jumper with jumping weights and javelin thrower.

72

the first four tested the athletes' arms and legs in an alternating sequence while the last tested the whole body. The pentathlon was composed of both light and heavy events. Philostratus laid down the canon for it in his *Gymnasticus,* where he defined the stade-race, the dolichos, the race in armour and the diaulos as light events; the pankration, wrestling and boxing as heavy events, and the pentathlon as a combination of both. In this combination the heavy events were the wrestling and the discus.[42]

Aristotle considered the contestants in the pentathlon to be the most attractive athletes since they were both fleet of foot and strongly built. To succeed in the pentathlon therefore a man had to be an all-rounder and this called for a particular kind of physique, which has also been described for us by Philostratus, who was the great authority on athletics in ancient times. In his view the ideal type was a tall, slim, well-built man of medium weight, whose muscles were well-developed but not over-developed; his legs needed to be long rather than well-proportioned and his back supple and flexible, for this facilitated the back-swing in both the javelin and the discus and was a distinct advantage in the jump; he also needed long hands and slender fingers, for this would afford him a stronger purchase on the discus and enable him to handle the throwing thong of the javelin without straining.[43]

Throwing the Discus

The discus was a Greek invention. Presumably the round smooth stones which were to be found on the banks of their rivers and seashores gave the Greeks the idea of manufacturing bronze discs in various sizes suitable for throwing. Most Greek discuses were 1.4 centimetres thick, 21 centimeters in diameter and weighed 2 kilogrammes. But there were exceptions to this general rule and the weight of the discuses discovered to date actually ranges from 1.353 kilogrammes to 4.758 kilogrammes.[44] The three discuses used in Olympia were stored in the treasury of the Sicyonians.[45] Assuming that all three were of equal size and weight we might reasonably infer

14.   Preparing for the pentathlon.

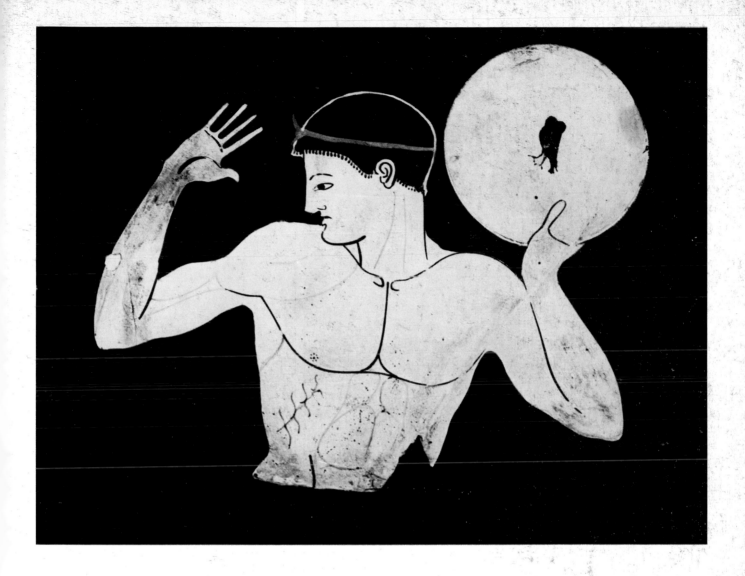

15. The first event in the pentathlon:
throwing the discus. Discobolus of Myron.

16. Discus thrower.

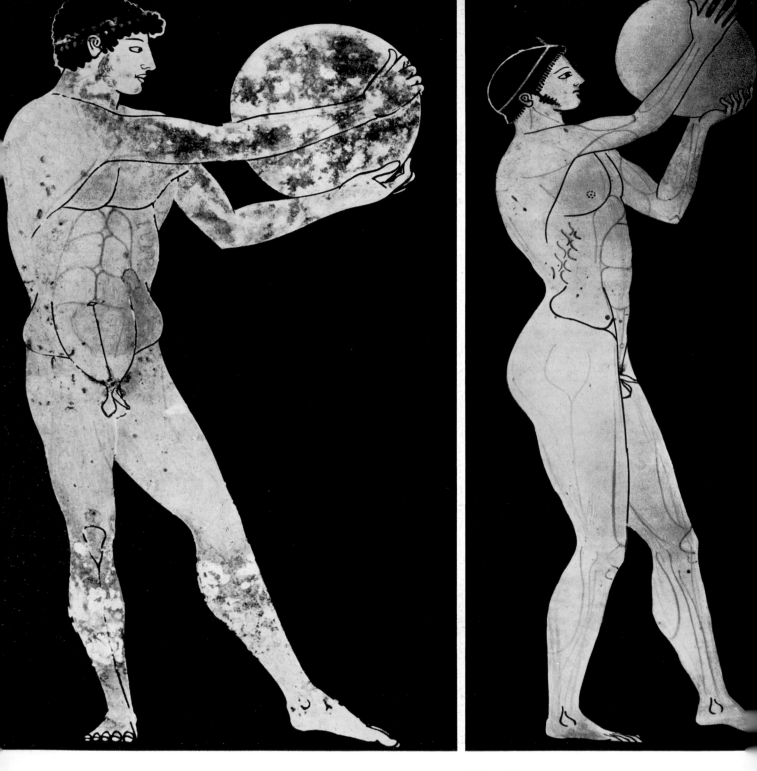

17a/b. Discus throwers.

18. Competitor in the pentathlon throwing the discus:
he is represented here as victor in the discus, javelin and
wrestling events.

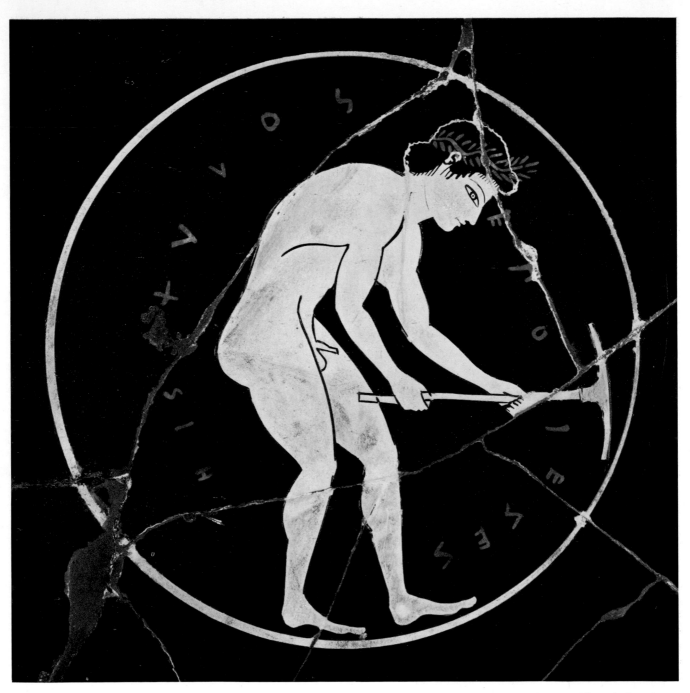

19. The second event in the pentathlon: the long jump.
The landing pit was first broken up with picks and then
levelled.

20. Competitor in the pentathlon holding jumping weights. He is represented here as victor in the jumping, running and javelin events.

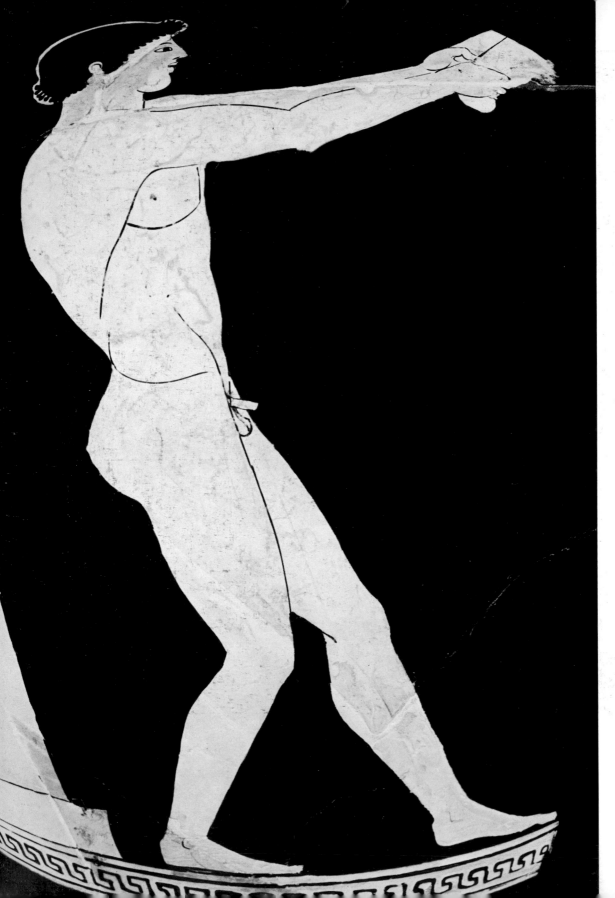

21. The first stage of the
preliminary swing, carried
out with jumping weights

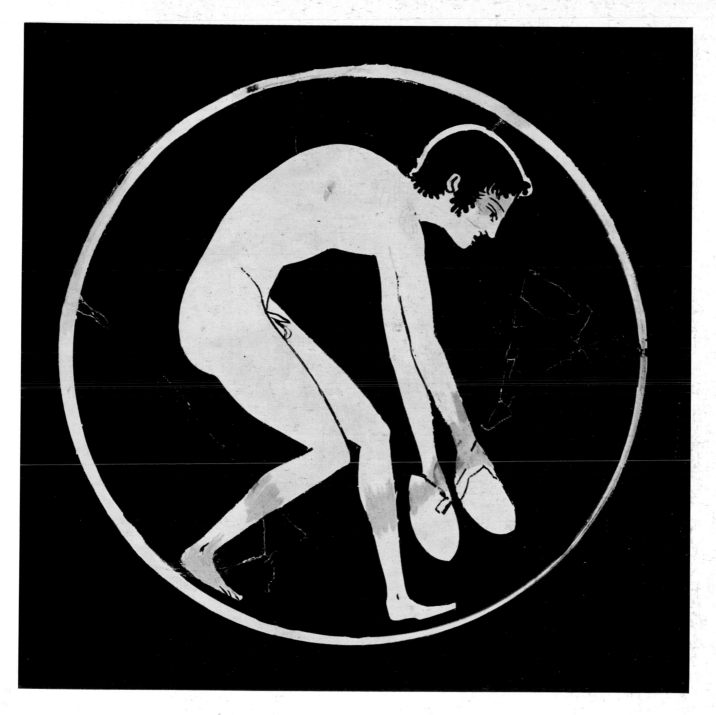

22. Jumper about to take off.

23.   Two jumpers and judge.

24.   Amphora painting depicting a jumper, flute player and discus thrower.

25. Stone jumping weight belonging to Acmatidas (seen from both sides). The inscription reads: 'Acmatidas the Lacedaemonian made this votive offering for his victory. He won the pentathlon without dust' (*i.e.*, by a walk-over).

either that the contestants were divided up into groups of three or that three different heats were held at one and the same time.[46] But this second alternative seems improbable since it would have made it difficult for the spectators to follow the course of events. A third possibility—and one which appears distinctly plausible—is that each of the contestants threw all three discuses one after the other, his best throw being marked by a peg. In this way no time would have been lost and the spectators would have known exactly how the competitors stood at any point of the contest.

The method of throwing the discus and the place from which it was thrown (the *balbis*) are described by Philostratus in a passage in which he refers to the death of Hyacinthus, who was accidentally killed by Apollo with a discus. According to Philostratus's account, the balbis consisted of a raised mound which sloped away to the front. The thrower stood with his right foot stemmed against the mound while his left foot rested on the sloping surface. He then bent his head backwards until he could see the right hand side of his body and threw the discus as if he were lifting an object from the ground, putting the whole force of his body into the movement.[47] (Some modern authorities, incidentally, do not consider that the discus was always thrown from a raised platform.) Philostratus's description of the actual throw is virtually identical with the stance portrayed by Myron in his 'Discobolus'.[48] His account is also very similar to one given by Lucian. Judging by these accounts, which were evidently based on drawings, it would seem that the Greek discus thrower executed a standing throw. But this need not have been the case, for we must remember that the artists of the sixth and fifth centuries BC lacked the technical knowledge which would have enabled them to portray the turn in perspective.[49] The discus thrower presented himself 'at the balbis carrying a discus either on his shoulder or in his left hand. After taking up his initial position he transferred the discus to his right hand and went into his throw, using the same technique as his modern counterpart.'[50]

The greatest of the Olympic discus throwers was undoubtedly Phlegyas. He would often amuse him-

self by throwing a discus across the Alpheus at its widest point and never once did his discus fall into the river.[51] Now even in the summer, when the water level is low, the Alpheus is some fifty or sixty metres across, and since we have no reason to suppose that the river has widened its course since Phlegyas's

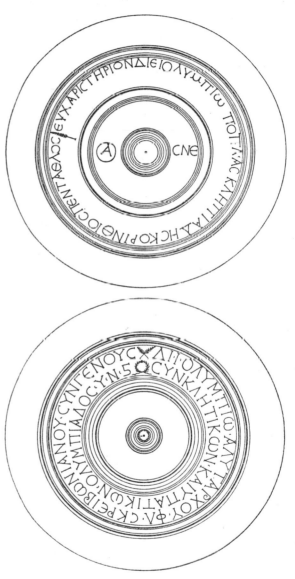

Fig. 17: Discus given as votive offering by Poplius Asclepiades (seen from both sides).

73

time this achievement of his appears quite incredible. The only plausible explanation would be that he used a lighter discus.[52] The best performance in the actual games at Olympia was probably put up by Phayllus, credited with a throw of ninety-five feet (30.44 metres) by the author of an ancient epigram.[53]

The victors in the pentathlon often dedicated their discus or a replica of it to the deity. The discus of the Corinthian Poplius Asclepiades, which was dedicated to Zeus at the 225th Olympiad in AD 241, has been discovered in Olympia in the course of the excavations. But the weight of this votive discus is of course no guide to the weight of the discuses used in the actual competition. Consequently, the question of weight remains undecided.[54] In early times, before the emergence of the discus as an artifact, the athletes would probably have thrown, or putted, heavy stones. The excavators have also discovered an enormous oval stone at Olympia which weighs 143.5 kilogrammes and bears an inscription dating from a very early period. Two different interpretations have been placed on this inscription. The first of these reads: 'Throwing with one hand from above his head Bybon beat Ophoias' and the second: 'Bybon, ...the son of Pholus, threw me over his head with one hand.'[55] The second reading is probably the correct one for it seems virtually impossible that men should actually have competed with one another in throwing a stone that weighs the best part of three hundredweights. It is far more likely that an athlete by the name of Bybon used this stone to demonstrate his strength and subsequently dedicated it to the gods.

Fig. 18: Inscription on Bybon's stone.

The only kind of jump practised in Olympia was the long jump, although whether this was a standing jump or whether the competitors used a run-up is not entirely clear. A form of pole vaulting, in which the competitors used a lance as pole and vaulted over a horse, was also in vogue in Greece at that time but it was never introduced in Olympia. The use of springboards in the long jump was quite unknown to the ancients but they did employ a *bater,* a sort of sill or threshold which afforded additional purchase for the take-off. This sill marked the beginning of the *skamma, i.e.,* the landing pit, which was simply a piece of ground fifty feet long that had been broken up with picks and subsequently raked over to form a level surface of soft earth.[56]

The jumping events in the Olympic pentathlon were accompanied by the flute player. It seems that this custom was first established in honour of Apollo who, according to ancient legend, defeated Hermes in the stade-race and Ares in the boxing. Pausanias tells us that 'the Pythian flute playing was introduced in the leaping contest in the pentathlon because the flute was sacred to Apollo and also because Apollo was on several occasions the victor at Olympia'.[57]

The jumpers used jumping weights or *halteres* which were roughly semi-circular in shape and so constructed that the fingers could pass through them.[58] These dumbbells were made of lead, iron or stone. From the finds made in the course of the excavations it would seem that their length varied from 12 to 19 centimeters, and their weight from 1.48 to 4.629 kilogrammes.[59] Clearly, the lighter weights would have been used by the boys and the heavier ones by the men. There was also another type of dumbbell which, instead of being pierced, was provided with grooves. This type was simply gripped in the hand, the grooves affording a better purchase for the fingers.

These jumping weights served two main purposes: they helped the jumper to keep his balance and also to make a good clean landing in the pit. Whereas at the moment of take-off the competitor swung his

VII Runners, discus thrower and judge.

arms forwards with considerable force in order to gain greater momentum, at the moment of landing he swung them backwards with equal force in order to prevent himself from toppling over. For the jumper had to make a clean landing; if he slithered or fell the jump was not counted.[60] We know this from Philostratus, who tells us that if the imprint of the jumper's feet was imperfect his jump was not measured.[61]

The jumping weights would of course also have been designed with a view to improving performances. In fact, we know that this was the case for, in a comparison which he made between running and jumping, Aristotle pointed out that a runner will run faster if he uses his arms and a jumper will jump further if he uses his jumping weights.[62]

Recently experiments were carried out in which a number of modern athletes executed both the standing and the running jump using dumbbells weighing 2.5 kilogrammes. In the running jump the weights proved a hindrance, reducing normal performances by more than a metre. In the standing jump, however, performances were improved by fifteen to twenty centimetres. The best standing jump achieved measured 2.84 metres. In this connection Ebert has observed that a standing jump of three metres must be regarded as a very good performance.[63]

We know of two quite extraordinary performances in the long jump in ancient times. At the 29th Olympiad in 664 BC Chionis of Sparta jumped 52 feet while in Delphi Phayllus of Croton jumped 55 feet. Since the Olympic foot measured 0.32047 metres and the Delphic foot 0.296 metres Chionis actually jumped further than Phayllus (16.66 metres as opposed to 16.28 metres).[64] But neither of these performances appears at all credible if we regard them as single jumps. Consequently, unless the texts in which these figures were quoted are corrupt, we can only assume that the long jump in the pentathlon actually consisted of a sequence of jumps. Themistius seems to imply as much in his commentary on Aristotle's *De Physica,* where he argues that only those phenomena may be said to be continuous which 'omit nothing either from the time or from the activity through which they move'. The jumpers in the pentathlon, he suggests, do not move continuously because they 'omit part of the space through which they move'. Now if the jumpers 'omit part of the space through which they move' this could mean that they do not cover the whole distance in one leap because they come into contact with the ground in the course of that leap.[65] From this it would then follow that the jump in the pentathlon was a noncontinuous multiple jump, in other words a sequence of jumps.

But what are we to make of all this? The view advanced by Julius Jüthner and Carl Diem that the amazing performances of Chionis of Sparta and Phayllus of Croton were not set up in the long jump at all but in the hop-step-and-a-jump is scarcely tenable today. At first sight Ebert's hypothesis appears far more attractive. He argues that the jumping event in the pentathlon consisted of a sequence of standing jumps. In order to explain the fifty-foot-long pit and the tremendous distances put up by our two famous contestants he is of course obliged to assume a sequence of five jumps. Five jumps of three metres each would be about fifty feet. So far so good. But when Ebert tries to substantiate his theory of the quintuple jump by suggesting that the figure five also played a part in the other events in the pentathlon[66] his argument is far less convincing. In the discus and the javelin each competitor had three throws, in the wrestling victory went to the contestant who succeeded in throwing his opponent three times, and to become overall winner of the pentathlon a man had to win three separate events. Consequently Ebert's hypothesis of the quintuple jump receives no support from the procedures adopted in the other events.

Throwing the Javelin

The Greek competition javelin was about six feet long. It was both shorter and lighter than the military javelin, although it had the same metal point. Before making his throw the contestant fitted an *amentum,* or throwing loop, to the shaft just behind the point of balance, in which he placed the index

75

and perhaps also the middle finger of his right hand while the actual shaft rested on his thumb. The effect of the throwing loop was to increase the carry and perhaps also to impart a rotary movement to the javelin, which would have stabilised its flight and controlled its direction.

The old controversy as to whether the contestants in the javelin event at Olympia had to aim at a target or simply throw for distance, or both, is not at all easy to resolve, for none of the sources provides any firm evidence to go by. We might perhaps feel inclined to assume that, since the contestants had already demonstrated their ability to throw for distance in the discus, the judges would have been more likely to have tested their accuracy with the javelin. A wooden post, a suspended shield or a circle painted on the ground could have served as a target. The javelin was thrown from a horizontal position above the right shoulder with the left leg serving as fulcrum.[67]

We have already mentioned the balbis or raised platform in connection with the discus. This was also used in the javelin event. If a contestant moved out of the balbis in the execution of his throw the throw was discounted.

Although we have no proof that the competitors at Olympia were each allowed three throws we may reasonably assume that this was the case. On the island of Cos it was customary to give the victor in this event three javelins as a prize; this we know from an ancient inscription. There are also ancient Greek monuments on which athletes are represented holding three javelins in their hands.[68] It

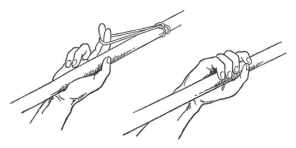

Fig. 19: Amentum (loop attachment) and methods of gripping the javelin.

is not, unfortunately, possible to give any precise information about the actual performances in this event since there are no reliable records.

The Foot-Race

Although we do not know the precise length of the foot-race in the pentathlon the widely held belief that it was a stade-race, in which the competitors covered a single length of the stadium, is almost certainly justified.[69] The stade-race was the most convenient distance for a sprint event and for this reason alone it was likely to have been adopted for the pentathlon.

Wrestling

Wrestling was the last contest in the pentathlon; it was also the most difficult and the most exacting. The rules were the same as for the independent wrestling event although the type of wrestling was very different. The pentathlon wrestlers were basically light-athletics men, which meant that they depended far more on the correct application of strength and on general expertise than on brute force. The fact that wrestling remained a highly intricate and attractive sport, which could justly be called an art, was largely due to its inclusion in the pentathlon. 'All the enthusiastic and laudatory assessments of wrestling...which are to be found in virtually every account of Greek sport were really inspired by the wrestling contests in the pentathlon.'[70] As in the individual contest, so too in the pentathlon only upright wrestling was allowed. In order to win, a contestant had to throw his opponent three times.

Victory in the Pentathlon

Numerous hypotheses have been advanced purporting to explain the requirements for victory in the pentathlon. But only one thing is certain, namely that the victor had to win three of the five events.

This is evident from a passage in Pausanias according to which Tisamenus, an Elean of the family of the Iamidae, was told by an oracle that he would win five notable victories; he interpreted this statement as a reference to the Olympic pentathlon, for which he then entered (probably in 492 BC). But, Pausanias tells us, although he won the prize in two of the five events, beating Hieronymus of Andros in the foot-race and the jump, he was defeated by him in the wrestling and so failed to gain the victory.[71] From this it would follow that Tisamenus's successful opponent won the discus, the javelin and the wrestling. Whether it also follows from Pausanias's account that, in order to win the pentathlon, one of the successful contestant's three victories had to be in the wrestling is still a subject of controversy. It can of course be argued either way, for with the score at two-all the wrestling was bound to decide the issue in any case. The fact that wrestling was also staged as a competition in its own right would tend to militate against the theory that it enjoyed a special position within the pentathlon; on the other hand, if everything did depend on it, this would certainly have ensured that the spectators' interest did not flag, for the wrestling was always the last of the five events.

But all this is speculation. The only thing we can be sure of is that the successful contestant had to win three individual victories. In this respect Pausanias is borne out by Plutarch in his *Quaestiones Convivales*[72] and also by Photius, who states quite unequivocally that it was by no means necessary for the competitors in the pentathlon to win all five events since three were enough to ensure overall victory.[73]

But what of the many questions which still remain unanswered? Joachim Ebert has tried to deal with these in his recent study, in which he takes account of all the available source material. Acting on the basis that three individual victories ensured outright victory he arrived at the following conclusions:

1. As soon as one of the contestants had won three events he was declared winner overall and the pentathlon was then broken off. This would mean of course that the foot-race and the wrestling were both subject to cancellation.

2. If one of the contestants was beaten by the same opponent in three different events he had to retire since he had no further chance of winning. This contingency could of course only arise after the completion of the first three contests.

3. If no contestant succeeded in defeating all of his opponents in three specific events the overall victory was conferred on aggregate, the victor then being the contestant who had defeated each of his opponents in any three of the five events. Victory on aggregate could of course only be conferred upon completion of the fourth or fifth contest.

4. Finally, Ebert argues that, since the whole object of the pentathlon was to establish the winner, once this had been done the climax would have been reached and consequently the cancellation of the rest of the programme would not have detracted from the excitement of the crowd.[74]

The Funeral Rites for Pelops

The second day of the festival closed with the obsequies for Pelops, which were held at nightfall. The chariot-races, which were originally dedicated to the hero as a ritual representation of his own suitor's race, had been staged in the early morning. After the noonday heat had passed the pentathlon was put on and, although this combination of events had not existed as such in the early pre-Olympian phase of the festival, the individual contests of which it was composed had all formed part of the original funeral games held in honour of Pelops. And then, in the evening, this memorable day was concluded by the obsequies at the grave of the great hero.

But these funeral rites were not only the culmination of the day's events, they were also the central point of the eighth lunar month, the 'sacred month' in which the festival was held; and to mark the occasion the full moon appeared above the altis.

At Pelops's funeral mound within the altis a black ram was slaughtered—all animals sacrificed to the dead were black—and its blood was poured into a hole in the grave for the hero to drink. The flesh of the animal—with the exception of its neck—was burnt to ashes on a pyre of white poplar. No sacrificial meal was eaten, since the hero, unlike the immortal gods, was separated from the living by the impenetrable barrier of death and so could not have taken part in such festivities. Instead he took sustenance by inhaling the smoke from the burnt offering. Presumably libations would have been poured for Pelops and solemn dirges chanted in his honour, for this was customary among hero-worshippers on such occasions.[75] We learn from Pindar that the *enagismos* of heroes was staged for Pelops at the Olympic games:

> And now as he lieth in rest by the ford of Alpheus,
> He hath fellowship in the fair blood-offerings,
> His tomb being in near neighbourhood by the
>   altar of the High God, whereunto men from
>   all lands come:
> And the glory of the Olympian contest in the
>   running-courses of Pelops
> Sendeth a gleam throughout the world:
> 'Tis there that swiftness of foot is tried in strife,
> And the highest pitch of strength, bold to brook
>   all toil.
> But the man who conquereth there
> Hath the sweet calm of repose...[76]

Private Victory Celebrations

Only the wealthy could afford to compete in the equestrian contests and it is understandable that those who were successful, and so acquired the life-long fame enjoyed by the Olympic victor, should have wished to share their happiness with their fellows. Thus in 416 BC Alcibiades celebrated his overwhelming victory, in which three of his seven chariots took first, second and third place,[77] by entertaining the whole of the festival community. In doing so he was accorded generous help by his country's allies. Plutarch tells us that the Ephesians presented him with a magnificent tent, the people of Chios provided fodder for his horses and large numbers of sacrificial animals, while the Lesbians contributed great quantities of wine and other necessary commodities for his banquets.[78] Similar grand banquets in celebration

78

of equestrian victories were given by Anaxilas and his son Leophron, the tyrants of Rhegium, and also by Empedocles of Akragas.[79]

4. The Third Day

The Great Sacrifice to Zeus

Early in the morning of the third day, following the obsequies to Pelops of the preceding evening, the main sacrifice was made. This consisted of the official offering of a hecatomb to Olympian Zeus by the Eleans and it was the central point of the whole festival. A large solemn procession, which included the delegations from the other Greek states, approached the great altar of Zeus, presumably from the prytaneum. There the hundred bulls were slaughtered in front of the prothysis and their legs carried to the top of the altar, where they were burnt in honour of Zeus and in order that he might draw sustenance from the smoke. This hecatomb was a gift from the people of Elis to the great Olympian god, a token of gratitude and an expression of praise. The delegations from the other Greek states also offered sacrifices, as did many private citizens,[80] who presumably used the many lesser altars dedicated to Zeus within the sacred grove.

All of these ceremonies had to be concluded by midday, for the time prescribed for ritual observances to the Olympian gods was the morning.

The Foot-Races

The foot-races were held in the afternoon. We know the order of events from Pausanias: dolichos, staderace, diaulos.[81] It is surprising to find that the stade-race, the most venerable of all the Olympic contests, was not run first. The dolichos was of course the longest of these events and also the least spectacular. This, presumably, was the reason why it was used to open the programme for it gave the spectators time to settle down.[82] In the stade-race the competitors had to run a single length of the stadium, a distance

VIII Boxers preparing for the fight.

of 192.28 metres. In the diaulos, which was the middle-distance event at the ancient Olympics, they ran twice the length of the stadium, once in each direction, which means that they covered 384.56 metres. In the long-distance event, *i.e.*, the dolichos, they had to run twenty-four lengths of the stadium, a total distance of 4614.72 metres.[83] Pausanias tells of one outstanding performance in the foot-races. It seems that at one Olympiad a runner by the name of Polites won all three events, a remarkable feat considering that they were held on the same afternoon.[84] We know nothing of the times set by the Greek athletes, but then they never tried to establish records. Their only object was to win.

We have already mentioned that the starting and finishing lines were designed to accommodate twenty runners. But in both the stade-race and the diaulos the competitors were first divided by lot into groups of four. These groups then ran in preliminary heats, the winner of each heat going on to compete in the final.[85] It would seem that only the one set of heats was run.

Before getting to their marks the runners warmed up with a few final exercises. Statius describes how they practised running on the spot, then dropped on to their haunches, beat their chests and set off on short sharp sprints, which they suddenly broke off.[86] They then went quickly to their places where they stood panting and waiting impatiently for the trumpet to sound.[87] Since there was a contest for heralds and trumpeters at Olympia it is to be assumed that the trumpeter gave the signal for the start of the foot-races there. At other festivals the runners were often started either by word of mouth or by dropping a rope and sometimes even a barrier.[88]

If a contestant jumped the start it appears that he was scourged by the *alytes*, *i.e.* the policeman. Certainly this would seem to be the implication of the passage in which Plutarch reproduces the conversation attributed to the Spartan admiral Eurybiades and the Athenian Themistocles at the battle of Salamis. Themistocles wanted to engage the enemy in the Bay of Salamis but encountered fierce opposition from the Spartan, who preferred to launch an attack at the isthmus. As admiral commanding the Greek fleet Eurybiades eventually threatened to strike Themistocles. But first he warned him not to be impetuous, recalling that those contestants at athletic contests who jumped the start received a beating. Themistocles's reaction to this threat is justly celebrated: 'Strike me, but hear me.'[89]

From this we see just how determined the ancients were that the contests should be conducted in a spirit of chivalry and, although in relating this incident Plutarch does not refer to Olympia by name, it seems highly probable that this practice was in force there as well.

Carl Diem has described the start of the Greek foot-race: 'From ancient times the runners stood on a stone sill which ran diagonally across the track and was fitted with two parallel grooves, usually fifteen centimetres apart. By pressing his feet against the concave surfaces at the rear of the groove and gripping the front rims with his toes while at the same time slightly extending and raising his arms he was able to attain the maximum angle of inclination. And so the runner stood poised for the start like a coiled spring.'[90]

In the sprint events the athletes made extensive use of their arms, swinging them vigorously backwards and forwards and raising their hands head-high in order to increase their speed. This is in line with Aristotle's observation that 'a runner will run faster if he uses his arms'.[91] The long-distance men on the other hand usually held their arms high and in front of their bodies like boxers and only began to flail about with them during the final sprint.[92] Philostratus draws this distinction in his *Gymnasticus*, where he also points to the difference in the physical requirements between the sprint and the long-distance men. The latter, he says, should have slender legs, like the competitors in the stade-race, and they should be much stronger in the neck and shoulders, since they need to hold their arms in front of them throughout almost the entire course of their event.[93] But this was not the only style practised by the Greek long-distance runners. They also used the modern technique of running with bent arms swinging freely at their sides. This is quite evident from the illustrations on the Panathenaic

79

amphorae which have been preserved.[94] In fact, most of our knowledge of the foot-races has been derived either from the illustrations or from artifacts.

As for the finish of the foot-races, this was judged by the naked eye. The hellanodicae had no recourse to technical aids of any kind.[95]

The title of *triastes, i.e.* triple victor, was conferred on men such as Polites, who won all three foot-races at the same Olympiad, and was a mark of special distinction.[96] (It is also an indication that the race in armour was not regarded as one of the foot-races and consequently was not staged with them. It seems more likely that it was held on the following day together with the heavy events.)

Pausanias tells us that the most remarkable victories in the foot-race were gained by Leonidas of Rhodes, for over four Olympiads, *i.e.* a period of twelve years, he was 'twelve times conqueror through his swiftness of foot'.[97]

Ladas appears to have been the fastest runner. Solinus said of him that after he had run over the sand, where all the other athletes left a deep imprint, there was no sign to show that he had passed.[98]

There were two long-distance runners who not only surpassed themselves but who could even be said to have surpassed Pheidippides, the original Marathon runner. One of these was Ageus of Argos, who won the dolichos at the 113th Olympiad and then ran the one hundred kilometres to his home, where he announced his victory on the same day.[99] Incredible though Ageus's achievement may seem it was eclipsed by that of his fellow countryman Drymos, who carried news of his Olympic victory to Epidaurus, one hundred and thirty kilometres from Olympia as the crow flies, and which he also reached within the day. Both runners had to cross the mountains of Arcadia. Drymos's achievement is vouched for by an inscription found in Epidaurus.[100]

The Ritual Banquet

Although there are no written records to go by we may safely assume that the third day of the festival closed with a ritual banquet in the prytaneum at which the guests ate the flesh of the sacrificial victims.

The god was present in spirit at this meal and sat at table with his people, for the Hellenes envisaged the gods in human form and so sought their company at ritual meals.

5. The Fourth Day

The heavy events were held on the fourth day of the festival. These consisted of the wrestling, boxing and pankration, which were presumably followed by the race in armour. Although Philostratus classifies this race as a light event everything about it would suggest that it was really one of the heavy events: the Greeks called it the hoplite race, *i.e.* the race for heavily armed men, for the contestants were encumbered with shields, helmets and greaves. In fact the race in armour fitted into the programme for the fourth day of the festival extremely well.

The Wrestling

From contemporary accounts and illustrations we know that the Greek wrestlers massaged their bodies with oil to keep the skin soft and prevent it from cracking in the sun and then splattered one another with sand to ensure a better grip.

Ancient Greek wrestling was less brutal than either the boxing or the pankration. The most recent enquiry into this sport was carried out by Werner Rudolph who summarised his findings under the following five headings:

1. Holds on any part of the body were allowed, although the Greek wrestlers appear to have concentrated more on the upper part of the body.
2. Leg-holds and tripping were both allowed, the latter being more prevalent.
3. Three clean throws ensured victory.
4. The decision as to what constituted a clean throw was taken by the judges.
5. Contestants were not allowed to deliver painful blows, to throttle their opponents or twist their limbs in order to force them into submission.[101]

And yet there were instances of brutality in the

IX *(above)*. Competitors in the foot-race.
(below). Competitors in the race in armour.

wrestling event at the Olympic games. Leontiscus of Sicily was quite prepared to break his opponents' fingers if he were unable to throw them. By using such tactics he won twice at Olympia and the Eleans did not withhold the victor's crown from him.[102] Another Olympic wrestler, Cleitostratus of Rhodes, won by applying strangle-holds and then suddenly throwing his opponents.[103] These may, however, have been isolated incidents which were recorded because they were so unusual or there may even have been some confusion with the pankration, in which the competitors were entitled to use strangle-holds and to break one another's limbs.[104]

Certainly ground wrestling, in which the contest was continued until one of the two combatants ceded victory, would appear to have been restricted to the pankration.[105] In standing wrestling it was not possible for contestants to cede victory in this way, since the outcome of the contest was determined by the judges. For this reason the Spartans did not take part in the pankration. Seneca reports that for a Spartan to acknowlege defeat was considered too humilating and consequently the Spartan rulers forbade their citizens to participate in either the pankration or the boxing. They did not object to the other events, for in their view a runner who lost the race was not necessarily inferior to the winner in the will to win. Similarly, although a wrestler who was thrown three times did not take the palm, neither did he yield it. What mattered to the Spartans was that their people should not risk the reputation which they had acquired for indomitable courage. Consequently they held aloof from those contests in which the loser was required to acknowledge defeat.[106] The Spartans gained forty-five victories at Olympia. Of these none were in the pankration and only one was in the boxing (at the 57th Olympiad in 552 BC).

It was considered particularly meritorious for a wrestler to defeat his opponent in three straight bouts. The maximum number of bouts was of course five.

After the contest the wrestlers scraped the oil and sand from their skin with a strigil. Lysippus of Sicyon portrayed a wrestler using this instrument and a Roman copy of the work is in the Vatican Museum.

The athletes carried their strigil together with a flask of oil and a sponge suspended from an armlet.

The most celebrated of all ancient wrestlers was Milo of Croton. After winning as a boy wrestler at Olympia he went on to take the men's crown at five different Olympiads, starting with the 62nd in 532 BC. He also gained victories at the other pan-Hellenic festivals. According to Julius Africanus he won six times at Delphi, ten times at the Isthmus and nine times in Nemea.[107] Pausanias mentions only his Olympic and Pythian victories. He also informs us that at his seventh appearance at Olympia Milo was defeated by a younger opponent, who skilfully frustrated his efforts to get to grips and so tired him out.[108] This, however, is at variance with the account given by Simonides, who refers to Milo's seven victories.[109] Milo was so strong that he carried his own statue, which had been made by his fellow countryman Dameos, into the altis and erected it there unaided.[110]

The Boxing

'Of all the Olympic contests the one which is most alien to us today is the boxing; no matter how hard we try we are still unable to conceive how a highly cultivated people with such discriminating aesthetic tastes could derive pleasure from this barbaric spectacle, in which two men beat one another about the head with their heavily mailed fists... until one of them acknowledged defeat or was reduced to such straits that he was unable to continue the fight. For not only under the Romans but under the Greeks as well this form of contest was no longer a sport; it was a deadly serious business. ...More than one Olympic competitor lost his life in the stadium.'[111] This critique, made in 1882 by Adolf Boetticher, one of the early Olympia scholars, is valid today. Like their colleagues in the wrestling and the pankration, the boxers were determined to win at all costs. This should not really surprise us if we consider that their event was derived from the ritual funeral games, which in their original form had actually been 'duels to the death'.[112]

81

The boxers at Olympia were not classified according to weight any more than the wrestlers were. There was no boxing ring, the bouts being fought on an open piece of ground inside the stadium.[113] The target area was the head and face. Holding was forbidden but it would seem that the contestants were allowed to parry blows with the flat of their hand. The fight went on until one of the two combatants was no longer able to defend himself or acknowledged defeat. This he did either by raising his index finger or extending two fingers towards his opponent. It is quite possible that there were official intervals; certainly there were unofficial ones when the boxers momentarily broke off the engagement and went down on one knee to rest.[114] But the fight had to be carried to a conclusion. If this took too long the judges produced a 'climax' by ordering the combatants to exchange blows without trying to defend themselves until one of them yielded.[115]

The ancient Greek boxer bound his hands with long leather thongs, leaving his fingers free. According to Philostratus these thongs were originally made of soft leather which was subsequently replaced by a much harder variety. It seems that the thong was bound around the upper part of the four fingers, allowing sufficient freedom of movement for the hand to be clenched, and was held tight by a cord fastened to the forearm. In later times, Philostratus tells us, a special thong was made from tanned ox-hide. This was fitted with a ring of between three and five strips of hard, thick leather with sharp, projecting edges which encompassed the knuckles.[116] Small wonder that Greek boxing was such a painful procedure: many of the contestants left the stadium with broken teeth, swollen ears and squashed noses; many sustained serious injuries to their eyes, ears and even their skulls. One such was Androleus, who said in an epigram which he wrote on himself:

Now Pisa has one of Androleus' ears and Plataea
One of his eyes; in Pytho they thought I was
dead.[117]

Given this brutal form of fighting, cases of accidental death were of course inevitable. Although manslaughter was forbidden it did not carry a heavy

penalty save in terms of personal honour. The judges awarded the victor's crown to the dead man and banned his opponent from the stadium. But no other action was taken against him. The most violent case of manslaughter is reported by Pausanias. He tells us that at the Nemean games two boxers, Damoxenus and Creugas, agreed to exchange blow for blow in order to bring their contest to an end before nightfall. Creugas had first strike and delivered a blow to Damoxenus's head which the latter survived. Creugas then removed his guard and as he did so Damoxenus struck him 'under the ribs with his fingers straight out, and such was the hardness of his nails and the violence of the blow that his hand pierced his side, seized his bowels and dragged and tore them out'.[118] Damoxenus was then driven from the stadium, the dead Creugas was awarded the victor's crown and a statue was erected to him in Argos; this still stood in the temple of Lycian Apollo in Pausanias' day.

(There were also the two cases of accidental death referred to earlier.[119] But if we consider that the boxing contests at Olympia were staged for more than a thousand years the incidence of fatal accidents would seem to be extremely low.)

There were some ancient Greek boxers who were so skilfull that they were able to defeat their opponents without giving or taking a single blow. Melancomas of Caria, who was the friend of Emperor Titus, was one of these. His guard was so effective that his opponents were never able to penetrate it and were eventually obliged to cede victory from sheer exhaustion. In his funeral oration on Melancomas, Dion Chrysostom explained the latter's attitude to boxing. It seems that Melancomas regarded his art as a test of endurance. In his view a boxer who tried to force victory by mixing it with his opponent was simply demonstrating his lack of stamina. Moreover, if a boxer acknowledged defeat because he had sustained a wound he was really succumbing to the wound. But if he gave up the struggle unmarked his defeat was absolute, for then his whole body would have been forced into submission and not just the one part which had been wounded.[120]

26. The third event in the pentathlon: throwing the javelin.
Javelin thrower and judge.

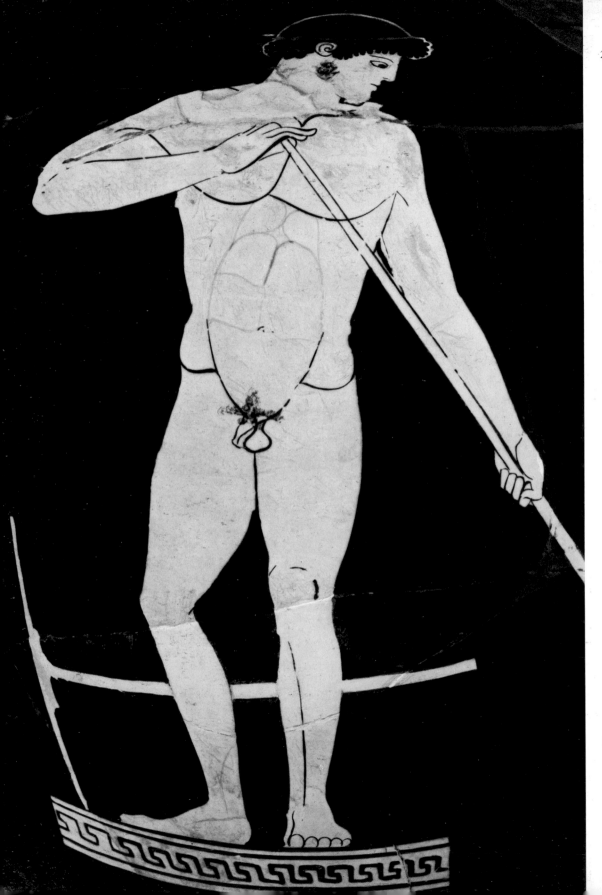

27. Javelin thrower.

28. Javelin thrower.

29. Pentathlon:
javelin throwers,
discus thrower
and judge.

30. Foot-race in
the pentathlon.
Runner with jud[ge]
discus thrower.

31. Stade-race. Group of runners.

32. Runners, boxers and judges.

33. The fifth event in the pentathlon: wrestling.

34. Two wrestlers.

35.   Palaestra scene: pair of wrestlers practising, runner in
start position and javelin thrower. Relief on base of statue.

36.   Statue of seated boxer in bronze by Apollonius of Athens.

37. Boxers.

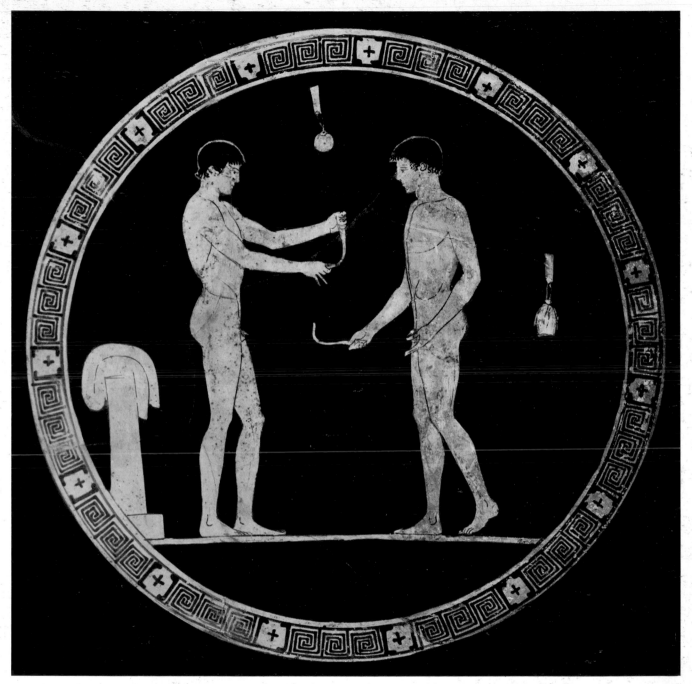

38. Heavy athletes cleaning themselves with the strigil
(skin-scraper).

39. Armed runner (hoplite) with helmet, shield and greaves.

40a/b. Armed runners.

The Prize-giving Ceremony.

41a.   A judge handing a victor his fillet
of wool (taenia).

41b.   A victor with the symbols of victory:
olive crown, palm branches and fillet of wool.

This was the greatest achievement to which a boxer might aspire. The next greatest was to win without receiving a blow, a feat accomplished by Hippomachus of Elis in the boys' boxing at Olympia, who defeated three opponents 'and received no blows or hurt'.[121]

But victory did not depend on ability alone. The support of the crowd was also an important factor and could easily influence the outcome. This is quite evident from the account given by Polybius of the contest between Cleitomachus of Thebes and Aristonicus of Egypt. It seems that King Ptolemy IV of Egypt was determined to humble the celebrated Cleitomachus and had Aristonicus especially trained in order that he might defeat him. The crowd at Olympia, delighted to find that somebody had the courage to face the invincible Cleitomachus, sided with the underdog and, when they discovered that he was well able to hold his own, cheered him on all the more. Eventually Cleitomachus interrupted the contest to address the crowd and chide them for backing a foreigner instead of their Greek compatriot. His appeal caused such a revulsion of feeling that, according to Polybius, Aristonicus was vanquished not so much by Cleitomachus as by the crowd.[122]

The most famous of all Olympic boxers was Diagorus of Rhodes, who won the contest at the 79th Olympiad in 364 BC and is celebrated in Pindar's Seventh Olympic Ode. He was the first of a long line of boxers and pankratiasts, whose statues stood side by side in the altis, for his sons and nephews were also successful in many a contest. At the 83rd Olympiad two of his sons won prizes on the same day. They then lifted their aged father on to their shoulders and carried him around the stadium. As they did so they were approached by a Spartan who congratulated the old man in the following words: 'Die, Diagoras, for you will not ascend into heaven.' Cicero, who recorded this statement for us, added his own interpretation. He explained that victory at Olympia was important to the Greeks, perhaps too important, and that consequently what the Spartan had meant to imply was that, since both Diagoras and his two sons had all been victorious in the games,

the old man would do well to quit this life, in which he was subject to the whims of fate, at such a propitious moment.[123]

The Pankration

In the pankration wrestling and boxing were combined to form a new type of contest. The pankratiast did not wear thongs like the boxer but he did oil and sand his body.

Franz Mezö has described this contest: 'In the pankration the competitors fought with every part of their body, with their hands, feet, elbows, their knees, their necks and their heads; in Sparta they even used their feet. The pankratiasts were allowed to gouge one another's eyes out ... they were also allowed to trip their opponents, lay hold of their feet, nose and ears, dislocate their fingers and arms and apply strangle-holds. If one man succeeded in throwing the other he was entitled to sit on him and beat him about the head, face and ears; he could also kick him and even trample on him. It goes without saying that the contestants in this brutal contest sometimes received the most fearful wounds and that not infrequently men were killed'.[124] The pankration for the Spartan epheboi was probably the most brutal of all. Pausanias tells us that the contestants quite literally fought tooth and nail and bit and tore one another's eyes out.[125]

If one of the two contestants wished to submit he either raised his hand or tapped his adversary on the shoulder. In 564 BC Arrhichion of Phigalia, who had already won the pankration at two previous Olympiads, was killed in the final contest. According to Pausanias his opponent obtained a combined leg and strangle-hold on him and, although Arrhichion succeeded in breaking one of his adversary's toes, the strangle-hold proved fatal. As usual the dead man was proclaimed victor, but we are not told whether the surviving pankratiast was punished.[126] Commenting on this incident Philostratus observed that, although Arrhichion had already achieved great things by winning two Olympic crowns on merit, his final achievement—which had cost him his life—was greater still.[127]

83

Because it was the hardest of the Olympic events the pankration was held in high esteem and was extremely popular with the spectators. It was, as Philostratus observed, 'the fairest of all Olympia'.[128] This explains the disappointment felt by spectators and judges alike when the famous heavy athlete Theagenes of Thasos, who had entered for both the boxing and the pankration at the 75th Olympiad, withdrew from the pankration after over-extending himself in the boxing. For this he was fined.[129] So too was Sarapion of Alexandria, who ran away the day before the pankration was due to be held at the 201st Olympiad because he was afraid of his opponents.[130]

The athletes who entered for the pankration needed great strength of will; they were not allowed to show fear. The trainers were important here for they had to engender self-reliance. Philostratus tells us that he once heard Mandragones of Magnesia say that the powers of endurance which he had demonstrated in the pankration as a young man were due entirely to his trainer. His father had died and his mother had assumed her husband's responsibilities as head of the family. Mandragones's trainer had then written her the following laconic letter: 'If you are told that your son is dead, you may believe it, but if you are told that he has been defeated, you should not believe it.' The effect of this letter, Mandragones said, was to make him summon up all his courage lest his mother should be disappointed and his trainer branded as a liar.[131]

Those contestants who won both the wrestling and the pankration at the same Olympiad were especially renounced. The list of double victories begins with the mythical hero Hercules and, to the best of our knowledge, contained just seven names in all.[132] But the victor in the pankration alone still enjoyed great fame, which was less if he won with the help of a bye and least of all if he won by a walk-over.

The most celebrated of the Olympic pankratiasts were Theagenes of Thasos and Polydamas of Scotussa. They both erected their statues in the altis and both became legendary figures, the heroes of many stories.[133]

84

The hoplite race, or race in armour, was the final event of the festival.[134] Like the competitors in the other contests the hoplites were naked apart from their helmets, greaves and shields. Subsequently the greaves and then the helmets were discarded.[135] In order to ensure that the contestants all carried the same weight special bronze shields were manufactured which were identical in all respects and twenty-five of these were stored in the temple of Zeus.[136] This would suggest that the organisers anticipated a relatively large field for this particular contest. Carrying the circular shield on their arms the hoplites had to cover the length of the stadium in both directions, a total distance of nearly four hundred metres.[137]

There are two traditions purporting to explain the origin of the race in armour. One of these is Elean and is referred to by Philostratus. According to this version the Eleans once fought a war with the Dymaei which was so bitter that it was even allowed to encroach on the sacred truce. It appears that during the actual festival the Eleans won a conclusive victory, whereupon one of their soldiers ran into the stadium dressed in full armour to bear the glad tidings to the Elean officials.[138] This, it is claimed, was the origin of the hoplite race. But this explanation is too cut and dried to be entirely credible. Moreover, it presupposes a breach of the sacred truce, which also seems unlikely. According to the other tradition, which is described by Pausanias, the race in armour was first introduced in 520 BC at the 65th Olympiad as a military exercise.[139] This is far more plausible, for the contest was staged at other festivals as well, which would suggest that it was a general development and may well have been prompted by military requirements.

Heliodorus describes a race in armour at the Pythian games in Delphi in his *Aethiopica,* a Greek romance which dates from the third century AD. Theagenes won this race, his lover, the priestess Chariclea, standing at the finishing line holding a burning torch in her left hand and a branch of palm in her right.[140]

X   Two pairs of wrestlers.

6. The Fifth Day

On the fifth day the Olympic festival was brought to a conclusion with the prize-giving ceremony, a service of thanksgiving and a banquet.

The Prize-giving Ceremony

In the morning the victors, judges and the members of the various delegations probably proceeded in solemn procession, watched by the whole Olympic community, to the temple of Zeus, where the victors were crowned with their wreaths of wild olive. Each had already been proclaimed victor immediately after winning his event and this proclamation, which was made by the herald at the judge's bidding, was a necessary part of the prize-giving procedure. Maximus of Tyre tells us that neither at the Pythian nor the Olympic games could a contestant claim victory until his name had been proclaimed by the herald.[141] After the proclamation the athletes received a palm branch as a temporary symbol of victory and in the procession to the temple of Zeus, where they were to receive the coveted olive wreath, they carried this palm branch in their right hands.

We know from Pausanias that it was common practice to hand palm branches to the victors at athletic meetings. After enumerating the prizes conferred at the four pan-Hellenic festivals—the olive wreath at Olympia, the laurel wreath at Delphi (from 582 BC onwards the victors at Delphi received a laurel wreath in addition to the traditional apple), a spruce wreath at the Isthmus and a wreath of wild celery at Nemea—he goes on to say: 'Most games have a crown of palm as the prize and everywhere the palm is put into the right hand of the victor.' This custom went back to Theseus who is supposed to have instituted games to Apollo at Delos and crowned the victors with palm.[142] On Delos stood the sacred palm tree to which Letho had clung while giving birth to Apollo and his sister Artemis. Thus we see that the practice of giving a palm branch as a prize also had its origin in ancient ritual. This practice appears to have been adopted

in Olympia at the time of Alexander the Great. Among other writers[143] of late antiquity Horace has testified to its existence there.[144]

According to Gellius, who based his observations on statements by Aristotle and Plutarch, the palm branch was chosen as a symbol of victory because it was so resilient. If pressure was applied to it in an attempt to flatten it, instead of buckling, it resisted the pressure. Consequently—and here Gellius quotes Plutarch—the palm was chosen as a symbol of victory because this tree does not give way under pressure.[145]

But there was another symbolic prize which was even older than the palm branch: the *taenia* or fillet of wool.[146] In historical times fillets were bound round the heads of the victorious charioteers and riders.[147] (The owners were the official victors and they received the olive wreath.) It would seem that this custom, which in the early stages of the festival was observed only in the hippodrome, later made its way into the stadium as well. It could well be that in the course of time all victors were adorned with the taenia.

At some point on the way to or from the temple of Zeus, or perhaps even from the gallery of the temple itself, the spectators threw leaves and flowers over the victors,[148] a custom which is said to be even older than that of crowning them with wreaths.[149] Originally this *phyllobolia* ('throwing of leaves') no doubt possessed some religious significance for it is clearly derived from the vegetation cults, in which the games themselves had their origin.

And so, with a palm branch in their right hands and a fillet of wool on their heads, the victors made their way to the temple of Zeus. There the branches, which had been cut from the 'olive beautiful for its crowns' by a young boy with a golden sickle, lay in readiness. In the early days of the festival they were laid out on an iron tripod, which was still kept in the antechamber of the temple of Zeus[150] in Pausanias's day; later they were placed on a table of ivory and gold which had been made by Colotes and was kept in the temple of Hera.[151] The Olympic victors received their crowns in the presence of Olympian Zeus, who also wore a wreath of wild olive to commemorate his victory over Cronus. This ceremony constituted an act of communion between man and god, in which the victor's achievement was solemnly offered up to Zeus and graciously accepted by him.

Rodenwaldt has commented on the prize-giving ceremony: 'One of the Elean judges, who wore a purple cloak, placed the wreath on the victor's head, which already bore a fillet of wool. The wreath was always made from a single branch. The reason for this was an extremely ancient one and implied magical associations, for this wreath linked the victor with the god, and at the moment when it was placed on his head—which was one of the great moments of his life—he felt not only the pride and joy of victory but also the sense of pious awe induced by a divine sacrament. Certainly this was the case for as long as the sacred games retained their religious character.'[152]

The day of the prize-giving ceremony was the sixteenth of the festival month. This is vouched for by an ancient scholium on Pindar.[153] We also possess documentary evidence which shows that the victors were crowned in a joint ceremony at the end of the games.[154] It must be pointed out, however, that there are a number of isolated accounts which would seem to indicate that each victor received his olive wreath immediately following his event.[155] Since it is virtually impossible to reconcile these two different sets of evidence we can only assume that over the ages changes were made in the various ceremonials which accompanied the games.

Service of Thanksgiving and Banquet

Although there is no positive evidence we must assume that the contests staged in honour of Olympian Zeus closed with a service of thanksgiving. It is not difficult to imagine the scene as the crowned victors, the judges, the leaders of the national delegations and the spectators all stood around the great altar of Zeus and watched the smoke from the burnt offering ascending to heaven. Afterwards a banquet was held in the prytaneum, at which the flesh of the sacrificial animals was eaten.[156] The festivities reached their peak as night descended on the altis and the moon rose up above the hills. There was great eating and drinking and the songs of the victors and their companions rang out over the Alpheus valley. Pindar has caught this festive spirit quite admirably in his Tenth Olympic Ode:

> And the whole fellowship of warriors blazéd
>   forth into a mighty shout.
> The lovely light of the sweet-faced moon
>   kindled the evening sky;
> And with the delightful feastings the holy place
>   was full of song, tuned to the fashion of the
>   victor's hymn of praise.[157]

Chapter Eight

The Stadium and Hippodrome

1. The Stadium

The athletic events were held in the stadium and the equestrian events in the hippodrome. According to ancient legend Dorian Hercules determined the length of the Olympic stadium by placing one foot in front of the other six hundred times, this gave a total distance from start to finish of 192.28 metres, making the stadium at Olympia the longest in Greece. Of course the early Hellene with his mythological view of the world did not think of it in rational terms. To him the Olympic stadium was simply very big and consequently only a giant such as Hercules could have paced it out.[1] There is an alternative version of the Hercules legend in which the hero is supposed to have fixed the length of the stadium in accordance with the distance which he was able to cover with a single breath. Isidore of Seville, the sixth-century Spanish encyclopaedist, derives the name 'stadium' from this method of measuring. Hercules called this distance a stadium, he says, because upon completing it he was obliged to stop for breath.[2] This etymological derivation (from Latin *sta-re,* Greek *hi-ste-mi* = to stand) is not all that far-fetched, even if modern etymologists have opted for an alternative solution.[3] The word stadium (or stade) subsequently acquired three distinct meanings. Firstly it was a distance of 600 feet (*i.e.* a stade); secondly it was a race run over that distance (a stade-race); and thirdly it was a running track 600 feet in length (a stadium). In the foot-race for girls the stade was reduced by one-sixth to give a distance of 500 Olympic feet or 160.23 metres.[4]

As early as the eighteenth century the German archaeologist Johann Joachim Winckelmann planned to excavate the stadium. But of course Winckelmann had never seen the site and so had no idea of the problems involved. Ever since the fourth century BC the stadium had been surrounded on all four sides by earth embankments. However, during the Middle Ages, when the Alpheus changed its course, it was covered by something like 75,000 cubic metres of sand and clay. By the eighteenth century there was not even a 'shallow depression left in the terrain to show where the original site had been'.[5]

The first team of archaeologists, led by Ernst Curtius, worked in Olympia from 1875 to 1881 and was unable to move these enormous quantities of earth. The team had to content itself with fixing the positions of the starting and finishing lines by digging a number of carefully planned trenches. But in 1936, the year in which the modern Olympic games were held in Berlin, a new German team set out for Olympia under the leadership of Armin von Gerkan—who was soon succeeded by Emil Kunze—in order to clear the whole terrain. Work was interrupted during the war but this objective has been achieved. The members of the expedition first carried out a series of excavations on the four embankments, salvaging as they went. The results exceeded all expectations: 'The inventory of the excavation lists over 4,000 bronze objects alone. Then there are all the terracotta and marble figures, not to mention the iron work, the inscriptions, the enormous quantities of ceramics and clay lamps which have filled a whole warehouse and the innumerable coins dating from earliest times right up to the Byzantine era.'[6] The whole of the northern embankment of the stadium, which was also the foot of the Hill of Cronus, was excavated. A complete network of exploratory trenches was dug running parallel to the axis of the stadium. At this stage the expedition was equipped with twenty-five tipper trucks which had been placed at its disposal by Krupps of Essen. Later, when mechanical excavators were provided, it was possible to proceed with the removal of the alluvium, which covered the stadium to a height of five metres and which naturally contained no objects of value. Later this earth was used to build new embankments similar in respect of height and lay-out to those which had existed in the late classical period, *i.e.* from about 350 BC onwards. This replica of the ancient Olympic stadium was duly inaugurated on June 22, 1961 with a display of gymnastics by Greek and German teams.

As a result of this excavation work, which involved the removal of some one hundred thousand cubic metres of earth, it was discovered that five different stadia were built in Olympia in the course of its history.[7] For the period prior to the construction of the first stadium in *c.* 550 BC we can only speculate as to the site chosen for the games. On the other hand we know that originally they were ritual games, from which it would logically follow that the very first contests must have been held in the altis itself. The sacred olive tree, from which the branches for the victors' wreaths were cut, stood within the sanctuary and for as long as the foot-race remained integral to the ancient fertility cult and represented a ritual suitors' race, the sacred olive tree would have marked the finishing line. When King Iphitus removed the foot-race from its original context and staged it in honour of Olympian Zeus he may conceivably have chosen a different finishing point—the altar of Zeus perhaps—and have established a fixed length for the race. At all events we may assume that the oldest running course in Olympia lay in the heart of the sacred grove, where the temple of Zeus was later built in the fifth century BC.

The funeral mound of Pelops was also situated within the altis and the funeral games staged by the ancient Pisatans were centred on this mound. Consequently, since the foot-race was one of the events in these games, we may reasonably infer that the mound served the Pisatans as a finishing point. Subsequently, when Pelops's funeral games were absorbed into the new Olympian cult, it seems likely that this foot-race would have been moved to the new course, which we assume must have ended at the altar of Zeus, and that the other athletic contests staged in honour of Pelops would have been transferred with it. Once the games had all been concentrated on this new course there was good reason for building a special stadium.[8]

The Archaic Stadium (I)

Olympia's growing importance as a pan-Hellenic centre attracted more and more pilgrims. They pitched camp near the sacred grove, especially to the east of the altis at the base of the Hill of Cronus. Although this area was subsequently incorporated into the stadium the archaeologists discovered clear signs of human habitation there dating from *c.* 600 BC onwards. These included pottery fragments, pieces of bronze and lead, and also traces of fires. Even in the days of the archaic stadium numerous wells were sunk: simple circular shafts measuring between 0.70 and 1.10 metres in diameter. There were forty-three of them at the base of the Hill of Cronus alone. One of these wells (No. 34), which penetrated the rock to a depth of 12.60 metres, yielded valuable finds. All in all there were over one hundred and fifty wells in the vicinity of the stadium, which would suggest that large numbers of people camped at Olympia, all of whom were attending the festival.[9] To make it easier for the crowd to watch the contests a low earth embankment was built on the south side of the stadium in the middle of the sixth century BC. No embankment was needed at that time on the north side, for the base of the Hill of Cronus, on which the spectators had already pitched their tents, provided them with a natural stand. Later, when this part of the hill was incorporated into the stadium, they lost their favourite camping site.

This then was the archaic stadium, 'a very modest installation (I), of which just enough has been preserved to enable us to identify it with certainty'.[10]

From the archaeological evidence it is clear that votive offerings, most of them weapons or armour, were placed on the artificial embankment as symbols of victory *(tropaea)*. But votive offerings were always associated with the altis, which would indicate that the stadium must have formed an integral part of the sacred grove. A very high percentage of the articles discovered on the embankment were shields and helmets. We know that these were hung up on posts for, although there was no trace of holes at this level, the next layer of earth (which was added to the embankment when the second or early classical stadium was built) revealed clear traces of post-holes, which were spaced out at irregular intervals along its entire length. Iron cauldrons standing on tripods or conical bases and with ornamental heads of lions and griffins on their rims were placed between the arms and armour. These were also symbols of victory and thanksgiving. Although there were no traces of post-holes in the natural embankment formed by the Hill of Cronus on the northern side of the stadium, it would seem that this, too, was decked out with such emblems, for the weapons and armour found there were undoubtedly votive offerings.[11]

These weapons and pieces of armour, most of which were taken as booty in wars fought in the sixth century BC, were arranged in complete sets, which the Greeks called *panoplia,* and which consisted of shields, helmets, coats of mail, greaves, arrows and lances. The heads and sockets of the weapons, which were made of either iron or bronze, have survived and one of them bore a votive inscription. Inscriptions of this kind on weapons dedicated to the gods usually referred to the battle in which the particular weapon was taken and were often extremely terse. 'Danklaioi Rheginon' is a case in point. Literally this reads 'Zanclians from Rhegium', which means that the Zanclians (or Messinans) were dedicating part of the booty captured in Rhegium. Amongst those who made votive offerings were victors from Argos, Sicyonia, Tanagra, Athens, Tarentum, Syracuse and Messina.[12] But in setting up his tropaeum the victor was not only giv-

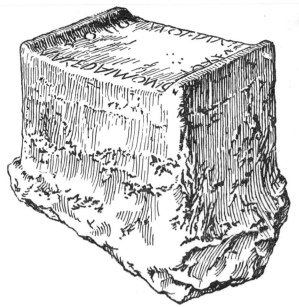

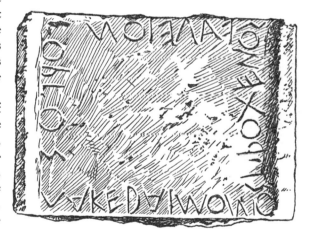

Fig. 20: Marble seat from the archaic stadium (I).

ing thanks to the god, he was also proclaiming his own fame and providing other competitors with an example and an incentive. The fact that war trophies were used for this purpose would suggest a close association between military combat and sporting contests in the mind of the early Greek.[13]

No trace at all was found of the actual course in the archaic stadium. But the fact that it ran towards the altis and was not separated from it by any kind of barrier is a sure sign that the athletic contests and the cult were still closely related. The games held in this early stadium, which was a very simple affair, were those celebrated by Pindar and Bacchylides. Virtually all of the spectators at these games sat on the ground on the two embankments for no special seating was provided for them. One man who did have a special seat was a Spartan by the name of Gorgos, who acted as consul for the Eleans in his native land. We know this from an inscription on a marble seat which was discovered in the early Roman layer of the southern embankment. (The inscription dates the seat to the period of the archaic stadium.) But this is all we know about Gorgos. How he came to acquire his seat of honour remains a mystery.[14]

The Early Classical Stadium (II)

We have seen how the Olympic programme was gradually extended in order to accomodate the increasing number of contests and contestants until in 472 BC the festival lasted a full five days. Because of this expansion the archaic stadium was eventually no longer adequate for the games. Consequently just before the middle of the fifth century, probably immediately after the completion of the temple of Zeus in 456 BC,[15] 'the first monumental stadium (II)' was built, 'whose lay-out we are able to reconstruct with a fair degree of certainty'.[16] This new, early classical stadium was laid out at a much lower level than its predecessor. As a result a considerable quantity of earth was removed from the actual course, which was then used to raise the southern embankment to a height of three metres. In the process the posts which stood on the old embankment were uprooted and the trophies which hung from them thrown on the ground beside the tripods, where they were duly buried. This development was readily identifiable because the finds made in the embankment at this level were all buried in a layer of green clay which could only have come from the stadium. The front face of the southern embankment

sloped gently down to the stadium while the whole of the rear elevation was supported by a tiered retaining wall. This impressive structure was built of blocks of conglomerate stone and was four metres high. It 'provided the southern side of the stadium with an architectonic barrier'.[17] When the architects who designed stadium III increased the height of the southern embankment still further they did away with this retaining wall. The rear face of the embankment then fell away in a steep slope, although it too was supported—in the west at least—by a much lower wall.[18]

In the eastern part of the natural embankment formed by the Hill of Cronus on the northern side of the stadium there was a gap caused by a sudden dip in the terrain. Consequently the principal task in this section of stadium II consisted of filling up this gap with surplus earth. Although the amount of work involved was less than that required on the southern embankment it was by no means inconsiderable. Here too the excavations revealed a layer of green clay, which must have come from a lower stratum, i.e. the stadium. But despite the great quantities of earth which were shifted to fill this gap the northern embankment remained an irregular structure. Nor was there any 'axial similarity'[19] between the two embankments, for the one in the north was both wider and higher than its counterpart in the south.

The distance from the top of the northern embankment to the edge of stadium II was about seventy-five metres at its widest. The corresponding distance in the south was thirty-five metres.[20] This difference in size between the two major embankments was a permanent feature of the Olympic stadium. When the natural embankment was plugged the votive offerings which had been set out on it were collected and sunk in the numerous disused wells in the vicinity. Well No. 34, mentioned above, yielded a breastplate, a shield and a Persian bronze helmet bearing the inscription: 'taken from the Medes by the Athenians [and offered] in honour of Zeus'. This helmet, which is in a wonderful state of preservation, was presumably a trophy captured at the battle of Marathon.[21]

90

XII Head of the boxer Satyrus.

Although no trophies were set up on the embankments of this second stadium the close association with the field of battle remained. The new stadium was probably shifted further to the east but it was still open-ended, which meant that it was not cut off from the altis by any artificial barrier. In fact its western end still lay well within the precinct of the sacred grove.

The actual track lay about 9.30 metres south of the track in the third stadium. With a width of 25 metres it was also a little narrower but it was of course 600 feet long. Each side of the track, which was raised about half a metre above the foot of the two embankments, was rimmed with stones.[22] This obviated the need for special stone gulleys since the rim trapped any rainwater or snow which fell on the slopes.[23] The water which collected in this way was then conducted along a conduit which ran under the embankment in the south-west corner of the stadium and discharged its contents into the Alpheus valley. When the third stadium was laid out this conduit was extended and bends were introduced. As a result it was often blocked up and was soon abandoned.[24]

The finishing line in the second stadium lay in the altis seventy-five metres west of the stone sills which marked the finish in the third stadium. The exact position of this finishing line was determined by deep excavations beneath the echo colonnade, which revealed that the stone sills had extended right up to the barriers on either side of the stadium. The track had continued nineteen metres past the finishing line to provide an over-run terminating in a stone verge.[25] The stone sills of the finishing line had been removed when stadium III was laid out, but the archaeologists were able to establish their original position because the trenches which had been dug to hold them were still identifiable. The eastern end of stadium II could not, however, be located. The stone rim at the western side of the track did not continue beyond the starting line.[26] The southern embankment also broke off at this point leaving no trace of either a retaining wall or a slope, one of which must have existed.[27]

There were no special seating arrangements for the spectators in stadium II either. Presumably the altar of Zeus was in line with the running track, and the newly-erected temple of Zeus, the base of which was one metre higher than the top of the embankment, towered up before the contestants.[28] At that time the stadium and the sacred grove were all one —this was the great discovery made by the new archaeological expedition. 'As far as the critical and historical exegesis of the athletic contests is concerned it is difficult to overestimate the significance of the fact that, until the middle of the fourth century BC, the finish of the stade-race took place in full view of the great altar and temple.'[29]

But the construction of a proper stadium, rimmed with stone verges and flanked by spectator embankments, was also a very important advance and pointed the way for future developments. 'For the first time ever the accommodation for the spectators and the running track were joined together into a unified whole.'[30]

The Late Classical Stadium (III)

In the middle of the fourth century BC, *i.e.* about one hundred years after it was built, the early classical stadium was replaced by a new and much more spacious installation. Although the significance of the games as a factor in the ethical and political life of the nation had actually diminished, their popular appeal had been greatly enhanced due to the emergence and gradual development of professional athletics. As a result spectator accommodation at Olympia had to be increased by nearly fifty per cent.[31] But the late classical stadium was not just a bigger and better version of its predecessor. The whole site was shifted so that the bottom of the western embankment of stadium III lay some eighty-two metres east of the western end of the running track in stadium II. The site was also moved northwards by between 7.5 and 9.5 metres. The re-alignment naturally entailed radical changes.

The southern embankment was extended inwards, raised by a further metre and made somewhat steeper. The earth used for this purpose was not taken from the surface of the stadium but brought in from outside. Some of it must have come from the sacred grove for it contained large numbers of fragments from votive offerings. These offerings could not have been trophies set up on the embankments of the early classical stadium and then buried, for in that case they would surely have remained in the same excellent state of preservation as those which had come from the archaic stadium. All that was found at this level were fragments, which were scattered over fairly wide areas. Most of them came from iron tripods, shields and jumping weights. But they also included a few valuable finds, among them a terracotta figure of Zeus and Ganymede, which is 1.10 metres high and has been dated to the period following the Persian wars.[32] There was also a head of Athene, an important work also in terracotta and extremely well preserved. This originally formed part of a group but insufficient fragments were recovered for it to be reconstructed.[33] Strangely, however, those fragments which were recovered were found in both the early and late classical layers of the embankments. This would suggest that the lower layer was disturbed in the course of the construction work on stadium III, a not unlikely contingency considering the enormous quantities of earth which had to be shifted.

Finally a Corinthian helmet was unearthed. This was very badly damaged but its inscription was quite legible and is of considerable interest: 'Miltiades dedicated [it] to Zeus'. The striking thing about this inscription is the name. It is unqualified. There is no mention of the man's father or of his native town; nor is there any reference to an enemy or a battlefield. Clearly the donator was a person conscious of his own worth, for by omitting personal details he was assuming equality with the Greek city states and placing his offering on a level with theirs. This, together with the date attributed to the helmet, would suggest that he was in fact the great Miltiades, son of Cimon, who defeated the Persians at Marathon in 490 BC. It seems reasonable to assume that this votive offering was made to Olympian Zeus in thanksgiving for the victory, although there is no actual proof that this was the case.[34] Since no enemy is named in the inscription it appears unlikely that the helmet was taken as booty. It was probably Miltiades's own helmet, worn in battle and subsequently dedicated to the god.[35]

When the stadium was moved to the east the northern embankment at the foot of the Hill of Cronus was extended until it abutted on to a sandstone hill, which then marked its eastern limit. At the same time the front of the embankment was cut away to allow the stadium to expand northwards. Consequently—since no new earth was added to the northern embankment at this stage—no new finds were made which would have enabled us to date this development.[36] By this time of course the embankment was steeper than it had been before although both its depth and its gradient fluctuated as much as ever. Towards the section where the gap had once been the width increased and the gradient decreased. The failure to effect any improvement in these conditions would suggest that this embankment was no longer quite as important as it had once been. Although the southern embankment had been made much wider—between forty-three and forty-four metres from top to bottom—it was still narrower than any part of the northern embankment despite the fact that this had been cut back nearly fifteen metres. The gradient in the south, where overall height had been increased to five metres, was now one in nine, while in the north, where maximum height was eight metres, it averaged one in six. Thus the differences which had existed between the two embankments in stadium II were preserved in stadium III.[37]

Additional spectator accommodation was also provided in the east and west. Previously of course the stadium had been open-ended. Now, for the first time, it was enclosed, thus assuming its definitive shape. In the west a new earth embankment had to be built, but in the east the rise in the terrain provided a natural embankment. It would seem, however, that this was shunned by the spectators for nothing was found on this site, whereas the northern embankment yielded a hoard of bronze coins dating from the second century BC.

The course in the new stadium was thirty centimetres higher than its predecessor, presumably to improve drainage. The surface consisted of a layer of sand thinly strewn on a thicker layer of greenish clay which had been well levelled. The edge of the course was rimmed on all four sides by a sill consisting of porous stone blocks inclined at obtuse angles. These marked the outer limits of the course and separated it from the embankments. There was a channel eighty-five centimetres in from this sill. This was also made of blocks of porous stone, which were fluted and laid end to end. During the festival this channel conducted drinking water around the stadium to a number of fountains, which were more or less equidistant from one another. At all other times the channel was used for drainage. When the old waste conduit in the south-west corner of the stadium had to be abandoned a new one was built at the eastern end of the stadium. But this also seems to have been inefficient for, when the early Roman stadium (IV) was built, the track had to be raised once again. The fact that the stadium eventually fell into decay was due in no small measure to the inadequacy of the drainage system.

A sill, or balbis, consisting of a row of limestone blocks was set in the ground at either end of the stadium and served both as a starting and as a finishing line. These sills, which were fitted with grooves, were first discovered by the nineteenth-century expedition. Their overall width was 48.5 centimetres while the width of the grooves was 4.5 centimetres. The blocks afforded the runners a better start. The leading edge of each groove was perpendicular, to afford purchase for the toes, while the rear edge was angled and slightly concave to receive the balls of the feet. The distance between the inner edges of these two rows of grooves ranged between 12.5 and 13.5 centimetres. Holes were bored in the sills at intervals of approximately 1.28 metres (four Olympic feet). Posts were then placed in these holes to separate the various starting positions. There were twenty-one holes in the sill at the eastern end, which means of course that it could accommodate twenty runners. The sill at the western end was divided into equal halves, each of which had ten starting positions.[38] The exact distance between the centres of these two sills was 192.28 centimetres (and not 192.27

centimetres as stated by the nineteenth-century archaeologists).[39] Behind each of the two sills there was an over-run. The distance between the eastern and western water channels was 212.54 metres and between the bases of the two embankments 215 metres. The running track widened a little towards the centre so that the stadium assumed a slightly oval shape. It was not a true oval, however, for the bulge was more pronounced in the south than in the north and the widest point was not in the centre but about Hirteen metres west of centre.[40] At this point the distance between the two embankments was 34.33 metres whereas the corresponding distance at the western end of the stadium was 30.74 metres and at the eastern end 31.87 metres. The eastern sill was fifty-two centimetres longer than that in the west. It also lay fifty centimetres further south, although it may quite conceivably have shifted by this amount due to the effects of water or a boggy subsoil.[41] Since the northern and southern embankments followed the line of the stadium, the two sections opposite the bulge offered the best view of the games.[42] In the course of the modern excavations the cathedra or judges' stand was discovered. It was about sixty metres short of the finishing line. In their report on the excavations the archaeologists suggested that it was placed as this particular point because the runners displayed their smoothest, most perfect style just before the final spurt.[43] While the spectators in stadium II sat on the bare earth, the judges could follow any contest in which they themselves were not involved seated on wooden chairs—between ten and twelve in all—set out in a single row on this raised platform. Subsequently the cathedra was extended and fitted with several rows of stone seats for one hundred and ten people. In the late Roman stadium (V) the cathedra sat five hundred people.[44] Those judges who were adjudicating the track events of course stood at the finishing line.

Since the judges' stand was nearer the western sill this must have been the finishing line for the track events, which would have been in keeping with ancient tradition, since the altis lay in the west. This means that the stade-race, in which the runners covered only one length of the track, started in the east

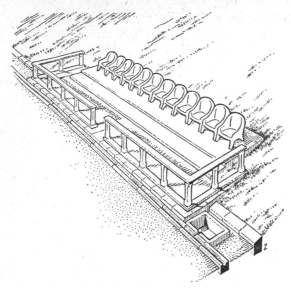

Fig. 21: Judges' stand in the late classical stadium.

while the diaulos and the race in armour, which were run over two lengths, and the dolichos, which was run over twenty-four, started in the west. This would explain why both sills were fitted with a double row of grooves. The over-run in stadium III, *i.e.* from the sill to the water channel, (10.8 metres) was much shorter than that in stadium II (18.5 metres)[45] and the extension at the other end of the track was very nearly as great.

When the western embankment was installed the architects had to build an entrance leading into the stadium from the north-eastern corner of the altis. At first this entrance, which was reserved for the judges and contestants,[46] was uncovered but in either the third or second century BC, *i.e.* in Hellenistic times, it was vaulted[47] and the vault covered with earth to enlarge the embankment. From then onwards this entrance passed through a tunnel 32 metres long, 3.70 metres wide and 4.45 metres high.

The tunnel entrance on the altis side was concealed by a gateway made of blocks of conglomerate stone and fitted with twin trellised gates. A single course of this covered entrance has been re-erected, using the original stones, which were cut to

shape and held in position by a keystone to form a mortarless arch.

We have mentioned that the late classical stadium has been reconstructed in its original form. But, significant though this achievement is, its implications are even more important. We now know that when the stadium was shifted to the east the course on which the contests were held was removed from the sacred grove, and the ancient bond, which had united the athletic competitions with the religious cult, was severed. In the early classical stadium the contestants still ran into the temenos towards the altar of Zeus, which was its central feature. But now the altis was cut off by the western embankment and the rear of the newly erected echo colonnade which rose up behind it. There were two reasons for this trend, which had first set in towards the end of the fifth century BC. In the first place the Greeks had a new concept of architectural design in which the emphasis was placed on bold, regular outlines. Consequently they revealed a general preference for enclosed spaces and it was partly for this reason that they erected the echo colonade at the eastern end of the altis. But there was another and more important reason, namely 'the growing secularisation of the games, which eventually led to the complete isolation of the stadium from the sacred grove'.[48]

The First Roman Stadium (IV)

The late classical stadium remained unchanged for more than three hundred years. During that time, when Rome was embroiled in a civil war whose repercussions made themselves felt throughout the whole of Greece, Olympia entered into a temporary decline. But when peace was restored and Greece began to revive under the protection of the *pax romana* the Olympic festival emerged from the relative obscurity to which it had been reduced and acquired a new ecumenical role. Caesar Augustus was well disposed towards Olympia. The chariot-racing, which had been abandoned in 72 BC, was revived during his reign and his stepson Tiberius won this event with a team of four in 4 BC. After this the

42. Zeus and Ganymede.

chariot-racing was once again dropped from the programme but was permanently reinstated in AD 17 at the first Olympiad following Tiberius's accession to the imperial throne. Tiberius's nephew Germanicus, who enjoyed immense popularity throughout the whole of the Roman world, appeared in Olympia in person, where he also won the chariot-race with a team of four.[49]

This revival of interest in the Olympic games was accompanied by further work on the stadium, which was carried out towards the end of the last century BC and resulted in the installation of stadium IV. The whole southern embankment was reshaped and raised by a further 0.75 metres. The major part of the material used for this purpose was taken from the sacred grove and consisted of building rubble. There was no need to raise the northern embankment for it was already steep enough but a certain amount of renovation was carried out. Apart from the guests of honour, for whom stone seats were provided, the spectators still sat on the ground in stadium IV.

The Second Roman Stadium (V)

In the second century AD, when Hellas and its classical culture were experiencing a renaissance, which reached its peak under the philhellenic Emperor Hadrian, AD 117–138, Olympia achieved world-wide importance for the last time. During this period interest in the festival was probably keener and more widespread than ever, for it was in the second century AD that the majority of contemporary accounts were written and many of their authors were natives of Asia Minor. They include Dion of Prusa, Phlegon of Tralles, Lucian of Samosata in Comagena and, above all, Pausanias of Lydia, who was probably a citizen of Magnesia, the town at the foot of Mount Sipylus, and who has provided us with a very lucid description of the Olympic sanctuary. It was in the middle of this philhellenic century that the stadium was renovated for the last time.

The course was raised by twenty centimetres, presumably to improve the drainage, and both the

Fig. 22: Reassembled altar of Demeter from the second (Roman) stadium.

channels and the sills at the foot of the embankment, which had been buried by falling earth, were abandoned. The southern embankment was made still higher by means of earth and rubble taken from the altis. At certain points, chiefly in the vicinity of the judges' stand, low ramparts made of pebbles and lumps of rock were built into this embankment. The workmanship was so bad and the mortar used so weak that they 'could only have been intended as bases for wooden benches'.[50]

In the north the width of the embankment was cut to between ten and fifteen metres to provide for deep trenches running the whole length of the stadium. These were meant to catch the rainwater, which flowed down from the Hill of Cronus, and to prevent it from flooding the track. Five rows of benches, each at least thirty-two metres long, were erected one behind the other on this drastically pruned terrace. The stone pillars which supported the wooden planks have been preserved. In the middle of the second century AD the altar of Demeter Chamyne was then built behind the last of these rows of benches. This altar, which was made of hard limestone and not marble (lithos leukos) as reported by Pausanias, was 1.064 metres high, 1.574 metres long and 1.03 metres wide. The priestess of Demeter was enthroned upon it.

We have mentioned earlier that Regilla, the wife of Herodes Atticus, once held this office.[51] This was

95

43.   Head of Ganymede (compare plate 42).

in AD 155 and it seems probable that this particular altar was erected in her honour. However, it can hardly have been the first of its kind for it seems quite impossible that an altar to Demeter should have been erected in the second century AD without a precedent. We are obliged to assume therefore that it was a replacement for an older, less imposing and less durable altar, which would explain why it aroused no comment and why no trace of it has been found. The new altar was itself dismantled in late antiquity—perhaps even later—on account of its metal brackets and lead fittings. All that was found on the original site was one of the foundation stones. The rest of the altar had been scattered about the terrain.[52]

By the time Pausanias visited Olympia in AD 174 work on the fifth and final version of the stadium had been completed.[53] This stadium then remained in use for two and a half centuries until the festival was abolished. During that time a great deal of necessary maintenance work was not carried out. Although the surface of the track was twice raised and further trenches were cut on the side of the Hill of Cronus to trap the rainwater, these undertakings smacked more 'of a long drawn out but hopeless struggle against the inevitable processes of decay... than of new and vital life'.[54]

It is generally accepted that the last Olympiad took place in AD 393 and that the games were then abolished by Theodosius I (AD 375–395). But a coin has been found in the top soil of one of the embankments showing the head of Honorius, emperor of the western empire from AD 395 to 423. This find would appear to bear out the tradition that the Olympic games were abandoned during the reign of Theodosius II, who ruled the eastern empire from AD 408–450.[55]

After the abolition of the festival at Olympia nature took command. The rainwater from the Hill of Cronus poured on to the track. Subsequently the Alpheus changed its course, inundated the whole of the stadium and swept away the top of the southern embankment. The whole expanse eventually was hidden beneath a uniform layer of mud; not even a shallow depression remained to mark the site of the great stadium where 40,000 people had once watched the Olympic games.

2. The Hippodrome

Its Separation from the Altis

The hippodrome lay to the east of the altis and was used for the equestrian events, the oldest of which was the chariot-race. Originally this had been a suitors' race staged in honour of Pelops and therefore presumably ran over a course finishing at Oenomaus's pillar.[56] Whether the chariot-race was run over the same course during the early period of the Olympian festival or whether a more appropriate finish was chosen, e.g. the altar of Zeus or the 'olive beautiful for its crowns', is unknown. There is only one thing which we know for certain, namely that the finish was surrounded by olive trees which—according to Pindar—had been planted by Theban Hercules:

> Then he halted and gazed with wonder on the trees,
> And sweet desire possessed him to plant shoots of
>   them around the twelve-times-circled goal of his
>   horsecourse.[57]

Until the temple of Zeus was built—between 468 and 456 BC—there was nothing to prevent the charioteers and riders from reaching their ritual goal in the altis. But once this great building had been erected the end of the race track had to be moved further east. It was then—at approximately the same time as the early classical stadium—that the first hippodrome was laid out. Unfortunately, when the course of the Alpheus was diverted northwards in the Middle Ages, the whole site was washed away. Consequently there is no archaeological evidence upon which to reconstruct the ancient hippodrome or identify any later modifications or extensions. Thus, though it is generally thought that the hippodrome was subsequently moved further east, we cannot be entirely sure. We do, however, have the evidence of contemporary writers, which enables us to form a reasonably clear idea of the installation.

It would seem that the original race course ran from west to east between the stadium and the Alpheus and that it was parallel to the running track. In the middle of the fourth century BC the hippodrome, like the stadium, was separated from the altis and shifted further east. The horse- and chariot-races then lost their ritual association with the ancient fertility games. Agnaptus probably built his colonnade as a pendant to the echo colonnade, which separated the stadium from the altis. The southern colonnade was presumably erected in conjunction with the colonnade of Agnaptus, for they stood roughly at right angles to one another and so formed two sides of a spacious square which probably served the riders and charioteers as a paddock. The colonnade of Agnaptus almost certainly extended from the southern embankment to a point in line with the finishing post, i.e. over the whole of the southern half of the hippodrome, and would therefore have been at least one hundred and twelve metres long.

In an attempt to preserve the ritual association between the equestrian events and the sacred grove fourteen altars were built, five of them in front of the colonnade of Agnaptus and the other nine at the starting line on the edge of the race track. These altars were incorporated into the religious services performed in the altis. After the priests had made their monthly round of the seventy altars in the sacred grove they proceeded to the hippodrome and honoured the gods and goddesses worshipped there, i.e. the Fates and a number of equestrian deities.[58]

The Reconstruction of the Hippodrome

In attempting to reconstruct the Olympic hippodrome we must remember that the only events held there were flat-races and chariot-races. Consequently the actual race track probably consisted of an elongated stretch of ground divided down the middle to form two separate straights, with a post at the far end (i.e. the eastern end) to mark the turn, and another in the west to mark the finish. In the chariot-races, which were run over longer distances, the finishing post also served as a second turning point.

In Greek this post was called a *nyssa* and in Latin a *meta* while the barrier which separated the two straights was a *spina*. This may have consisted of a low wall, a wooden fence, a hedge or simply ropes.[59] The hippodrome must have continued for some distance beyond the two metae to allow adequate space for the turn. In making their turn the competitors of course described an arc, which means that the two ends of the track were roughly semicircular and the whole of the hippodrome elliptical. We must assume the existence of a perimeter track and either artificial or natural embankments for the spectators. Pausanias says the hippodrome was flanked by an earth embankment in the south and by rising ground in the north.[60] There is no means of telling how the embankment was separated from the track but it would be logical to assume that there was a strong barrier of some kind to prevent shying horses from breaking out. This barrier was presumably fitted with gates to facilitate the removal of wrecked chariots and injured horses, riders and charioteers. Pausanias refers to a gate at the *taraxippus* ('the terror of horses').[61]

There are a number of written accounts which enable us to determine the various measurements in the hippodrome. It is mentioned in chapter seven that the horse-race, which consisted of a single circuit, was run over a distance of four stades.[62] Consequently a single length of the race track, i.e. the length of the spina, would equal two stades or 384.56 metres. The race track constructed for Emperor Hadrian in Rome was of equal length.[63]

Other measurements have been furnished by a manuscript found in the ancient seraglio of Constantinople. Its validity has been questioned by many authorities and flatly rejected by others, who claim that the text is corrupt and the figures meaningless.[64] Up to now it has been generally assumed that the length of the race track was twice its width. This means of course—since the length was two stades—that the width had been fixed at one stade. But if, instead of one stade, we assume a width of one and one-sixth stades, or 700 Olympic feet, then the figures quoted in the manuscript are seen to be remarkably accurate. The text reads as follows: 'At the Olympic games there is a hippodrome which has eight stades [1538.24 metres]. One side [*i.e.* the length] measures three stades and one plethron [1900 feet = 608.887 metres]. The width at the start is one stade and four plethra [1000 feet = 320.47 metres]. At the funeral mound, which is called taraxippus...' There is a gap in the text at this point. '[Horses of] all ages run six stades. In the two-horse chariot-races the foals cover three circuits, the fully grown horses eight. In the four-horse chariot-races the foals run eight circuits, the fully grown horses twelve.'[65]

If we assume a width of one and one-sixth stades (*i.e.* 700 Olympic feet or 224.327 metres), then the width of a single track would be half this amount, *i.e.* 112.63 metres. So, too, would the radius of the turning circles at the two ends of the hippodrome, since these would necessarily equal the width of a single track. If we now add the length of the spina to the combined length of these two radii we obtain an overall length for the hippodrome of 608.887 metres, which is the precise figure given in the manuscript. Thus there are three measurements which may be regarded as authentic: the length of the spina, the overall length of the hippodrome including the turning circles and the width of the two tracks.

When we read in the manuscript that the hippodrome 'has' eight stades this could quite conceivably be a measure of circumference. But eight stades would correspond to 1538.24 metres whereas according to the figures which we have just established the circumference of the actual hippodrome would work out at 1473.862 metres (*i.e.* twice the length of the spina plus twice the circumference of one of the turning circles). Might we perhaps be justified in assuming that the hippodrome proper was surrounded by a perimeter track for the use of the spectators and that the figure given in the manuscript included this track? If so, the track would have to be 10.246 metres wide.[66]

But there is a further problem posed by the manuscript. We are told that horses of all ages ran six stades, which would appear to contradict the clear statement by Pausanias that the horse-races were run over a distance of four stades. Could it be that the author of the manuscript was quoting an average distance? A single circuit of the track measured four stades only at its shortest point, *i.e.* on the inside lane which ran along the sides of the spina. A complete circuit of the outside lane would have been eight stades. Even if the competitors were allowed to change lanes, those who drew the outside positions still had further to run than their opponents. It is perhaps conceivable therefore that the figure of six stades mentioned in the manuscript was an attempt to establish an average distance for the horse-race.

Finally, there is the question of the width of the hippodrome at the start, which according to the manuscript was 1000 Olympic feet, or 320.47 metres. We of course have assumed a width of 700 feet or 224.327 metres. This figure of 1000 feet could still make sense but only if it included a spectators' stand a full 300 feet or 96.141 metres wide. The starting line would have been the ideal place for a spectators' stand. From such a vantage point the guests of honour could have watched the horses and chariots getting into position, they would have seen the start and the finish of every event, and also have seen the charioteers rounding Hippodamia's pillar. This hypothetical spectators' stand would have stood opposite the judges' stand, which was of course in line with the finish. It would not be surprising therefore if the embankments were especially deep at this particular point.

Pausanias says that the judges' stand in the stadium was near' ... the ground appointed for the horse races'.[67] From this it would follow that the hippodrome was situated immediately to the south of the stadium. In fact, all the judges had to do in order to pass from one to the other was to climb over the embankment.

Special Features of the Hippodrome

Although Pausanias says nothing about the size of the actual track he mentions many of its special features, *e.g.* the starting gate, the taraxippus and the pillar which marked the finish.

44. Gorgon mask in wheel-vane.

45.   The end of Caeneus (bronze fitting on chest).

He describes the starting gate in some detail, comparing it to the prow of a ship with its narrow leading edge pointing towards the course and its rear edge flanking the colonnade of Agnaptus.[68] There were starting traps set out along the other two sides of this triangular installation. The riders and charioteers drew their positions by lot and then entered the corresponding traps, the fronts of which were barred by ropes. At the apex of the triangle there was a bronze dolphin and towards the centre an altar of unfired brick on which a bronze eagle stood. When the clerk of the course released the mechanism built into this altar the dolphin fell to the ground and the eagle rose up in the air to signal the start to the spectators. At the same time the ropes in front of the horses or charioteers nearest to the base were lowered. As they drew level with the next position the ropes there were also lowered and so on until the whole field was strung out in a straight line at the apex, which was the actual starting position. This gate was devised by Cleoetas of Athens and later modified by Aristides. This apart, we know nothing about either of these men.

The object of the device was to ensure a clear start. The traps were presumably staggered and, since the two sides of the gates were over four hundred feet long and the base took up the whole width of the southern track (one hundred and twelve metres), probably as many as ten four-horse teams, twenty two-horse teams and forty race horses could be accommodated on either side. The traps presumably were simple affairs without roofs and with low sides, for this would have enabled the spectators to watch the start of the race from the very beginning. Once the chariots or horses were drawn up in line at the dolphin a signal—perhaps a blast on a trumpet—would start the actual race.

The dolphin was sacred to Apollo, the eagle to Zeus, and the fact that these two creatures were represented in the hippodrome is an indication of the close links which existed between these equestrian events and the Olympian cult. The finishing post also had ritual associations, for on it Hippodamia was represented binding a fillet about the head of Pelops.[69]

Pausanias also says that one side of the hippodrome was longer than the other.[70] This must in fact have been the case for the apex of the triangular starting gate abutted on to the western turning circle at a point midway across the southern track and would thus have been three hundred feet west of the finishing line. Thus the starting straight was 96.141 metres longer than the finishing straight.

Pausanias goes on to speak of the taraxippus, the circular altar situated at the edge of the southern embankment which was said to terrify the horses without any apparent reason.[71] Many mythological explanations were adduced for this phenomenon and these are enumerated by Pausanias, including one in which Pelops was supposed to have erected the altar as a cenotaph to Myrtilus and called it taraxippus because it was Myrtilus who had frightened Oenomaus's horses.[72] Pausanias tells us that there was a taraxippus at the Isthmus and also at Nemea but that neither of these was as terrifying as that at Olympia.[73]

Boetticher has advanced a plausible explanation. He points out that the equestrian events began at sunrise, which means that as the horses ran along the southern track of the hippodrome they had the sun in their eyes.[74] Consequently it could well be that, as they drew level with the taraxippus—which stood just short of the turn—and proceeded to execute this intricate manoeuvre, both charioteers and horses were so dazzled by the rising sun that they were unable to see the turning post clearly. The turn was difficult to negotiate in any case and placed heavy demands on the charioteer's skill for he had to round the post as closely as possible but without allowing the hub of his wheel to brush against it. In the *Iliad* Nestor explains to his son Antilochus how to guide the horses round the turning post at the funeral games held in honour of Patroclus: 'As you drive round it you must hug it close, and you in your light chariot must lean just a little to the left yourself. Call on your off-side horse, touch him with the whip and give him rein; but make the near horse hug the post so close that anyone might think you were scraping it with the nave of your wheel. And yet you must be careful not to touch the stone,

99

or you may wreck your horse and smash up your car...'[75]

Pausanias concludes his description of the hippodrome with a reference to a temple of Demeter Chamyne which, he says, stood on 'a hill of no great size'[76] that was used in lieu of an embankment in the north. This observation fits in exactly with our reconstruction of the hippodrome. On the northern side of this site no embankment would have been needed for there is a gentle rise in the terrain which would have served the purpose. Although no trace of the temple of Demeter has been found as yet it must have stood on this rising ground.

In the north-western corner of the hippodrome stood the *octagon*. This building, erected in Roman times, has now been excavated. Originally it was dedicated to the Roman emperors, the octagon being a symbol of perfection. It was made of two interlocking squares, one of which represented the four elements, the other the four seasons, and since it symbolised nature its eight corners were aligned with the eight principal points of the compass. Perhaps this octagon, which was erected at Olympia in honour of the emperors, served as an imperial lodge, for it gave the best possible view of the start, the turn and the finish.

Chapter Nine

The Fame of the Victor

1. Fame as a Reward for Victory

The fame of the Olympic victor was nation-wide and in ancient times nothing was as highly valued as fame. It lifted a man out of the anonymity of the daily round. This we know from Pindar, who sang the praises of so many Greek athletes:

> But if a man winneth the grace of renown in
>   the athletes' strife or in the battlefield,
> Then words of praise, the flower of speech
>   of citizens and strangers, he receiveth as his
>   highest gain.[1]

Those who acquired personal fame received a further lease of life for they lived on in the memory of posterity. This was the reward which the Olympic victor expected. Writing on this aspect of the games Dion Chrysostom of Prusa stated that the competitors placed posthumous fame above life itself. The whole object was to ensure that their names lived on when they themselves were dead.[2]

From this it is clear that in their quest for fame the contestants at Olympia were really seeking immortality and that the simple wreath of wild olive was their guarantee. The adherents of the pre-Christian cult of Olympian Zeus were offered no reward in heaven in return for a virtuous life. When they died they went down to their joyless existence among the shades. Their only hope of immortality therefore was to perform some great deed which would live on in the minds of men. The deed was not important in itself. What mattered was that it should be celebrated by the world. This is confirmed by Pindar:

> And when a man, Agesidamos, having done
>   fair deeds with no poet to sing of them, hath
>   come to the hall of Death,
> All his high hopes are barren,
> And with all his toil he hath won but a scanty
>   measure of delight.[3]

But, however much a man might long for fame, he could never hope to acquire it without the help of the gods. Human endeavour was ultimately dependent on the mysterious workings of grace. Alone man could achieve nothing. Consequently, since every great deed was inspired by the god, any fame which it acquired was really due to the god; for, as Pindar tells, us,

> The great mind of God piloteth the course of
>   the guardian spirit of the men he loves.[3a]

The poet attributes the victory gained by Hippocleas in the boys' diaulos at Delphi to the deity alone:

> Tis by impulse divine, oh Apollo, that man's
>   achievement from its beginning to its close
>   waxeth sweet.[3b]

And so we see that victory at the games was a gift from the gods. There was no appeal against their decision and consequently no point in resenting it.

Later of course, during the period of Greek enlightenment, this simple and absolute faith in the power of the gods to determine the outcome of human events was undermined and men tended more and more to claim personal credit for their own deeds. This development also made itself felt in Olympia for, although the prescribed rituals were still performed there, they gradually lost their original import. However, the desire for personal fame survived all changes. If anything it became more pronounced over the years. The names of the victors at each Olympiad were entered on a roll of honour and the Olympiad itself was named after the winner of the stade-race. All those crowned at Olympia were entitled to erect their statue in the altis. Kings were allowed to have special coins made to commemorate their victories; Gelon of Syracuse and Philip II of Macedonia actually did so. But the most splendid monument the Olympic victor could hope for was to have his praises sung in great poetry, for the poet's words were the one really enduring thing in his transient world.

2. Songs of Praise

In classical times men were aware of the gulf which separated them from the gods. The gods were immortal, all-powerful and eternally young; men, on the other hand, were frail, grew old and died. And yet men were related to the gods.

A man whose achievements were celebrated in a song of praise was raised above his fellows and acquired something of the aura which surrounded the deities. Fame in itself was also mortal for, although it might survive the individual, it would scarcely survive his family or race. Consequently, if a man was to achieve immortality, if he was to live on in the reflected glory of the Olympian deities, his deeds had to be celebrated by the poet in a song of praise. It has of course always been part of the poet's task to praise noble deeds and thus to preserve them from oblivion. Pindar leaves us in no doubt about this:

> There is a saying among men, not to hide
> beneath a bushel the light of a noble
> deed accomplished:
> Right meet for it is a wondrous song with
> the proud words of ancient story.[4]

Pindar sang the praises of many Olympic victors in his odes: Hiero of Syracuse following his victory

in the horse-race; Theron of Akragas after his victory in the four-horse chariot-race; Psaumis of Camarina and Hagesias of Syracuse after their victories in the mule-race; Diagoras of Rhodes after his victory in the boxing; Alcimedon of Aegina after his victory in the wrestling; Epharmostos of Opus after his victory in the boys' wrestling; Agesidamos of western Locris after his victory in the boys' boxing; Ergoteles of Himera after his victory in the dolichos; Xenophon of Corinth after his victory in the stade-race and the pentathlon; Asopichos of Orchomenus after his victory in the foot-race. In his poetry they still live on.

3. Folk Tales and Legends

But only very few Olympic victors found a poet to sing their praises and those who did so all lived during the early period of the festival when its ritual character was still sufficiently marked for a victory in the games to be experienced by the spectators as a deeply moving religious act. The names of other victors have survived because of the legends which grew up around them. This applied above all to the heavy athletes, whose great strength appealed to the popular imagination and made them ideal subjects for the ancient storytellers.

Stories about Wrestlers

The most celebrated of the ancient wrestlers was Milo of Croton. This town in southern Italy had already produced many great athletes before Milo appeared on the scene, probably more than any other in the Greek world. Strabo has commented on both the town and the man: 'Croton's fame was further increased by the great numbers of Pythagoreans and also by Milo, the greatest of all athletes and a student of Pythagoras, who had been living in the town for some time. They say that once, when one of the pillars in Pythagoras's dining room began to tremble, Milo supported it and so saved the lives of all present; afterwards he succeeded in escaping himself.'[5]

46. Bronze tripod.

47. Horse from a team of four (bronze).

48a/b. Ponies (bronze).

49, 50. *(overleaf)*
Bronze head of griffin.

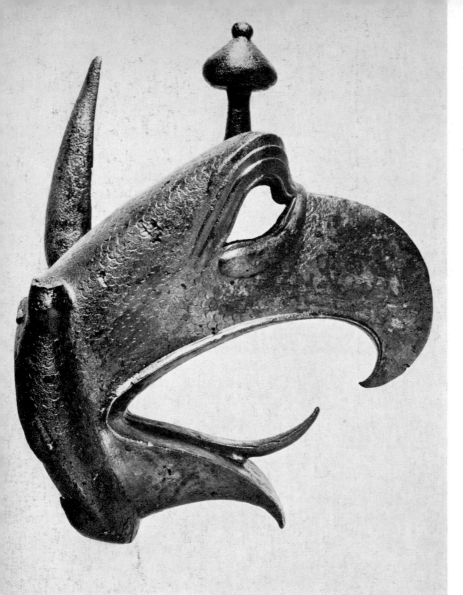

51a. Bronze head of griffin;
ornament on cauldron.

51b. Bronze head of battering-ram.

52a. Helmet of Miltiades. Of Corinthian origin and bearing the inscription: 'Miltiades dedicated [it] to Zeus.'

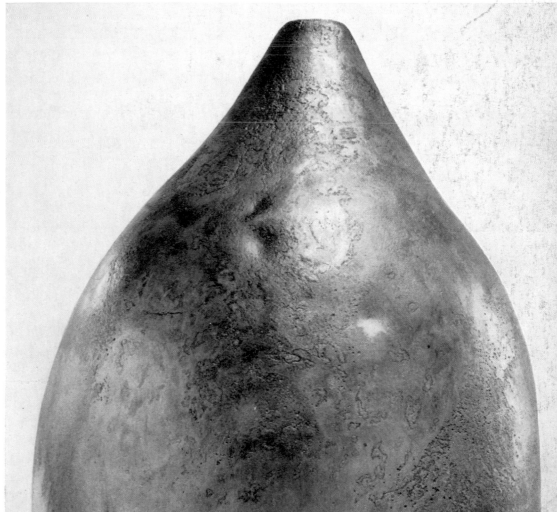

52b. Oriental helmet taken from the Persians and bearing the inscription: 'Taken as booty from the Medes by the Athenians [and dedicated] to Zeus.'

53. Starting line at
eastern end of the
stadium. The groove
provided footholes
for the runners to ge
purchase. Posts were
placed in the holes to
mark the various
starting positions.

Probably more tales and legends were told about this great wrestler than about any other Olympic victor. Pausanias, who saw Milo's votive statue in the altis, recounts some quite incredible anecdotes about his feats of strength. Milo, it seems, carried his own statue into the altis. And then there was the occasion when he gripped a pomegranate in his hand and defied anybody to take it from him. Many tried but none succeeded and when Milo opened his hand the fruit was unblemished. He also amused himself by tying a piece of string around his head as if it were a fillet and then snapping it by expanding the veins in his forehead.[6] He once lifted a live bull on his shoulders and carried it around the stadium at Olympia to the huge delight of the crowd. He then slaughtered the animal and ate every bit of it within the day. (There were many such tales about his enormous appetite and also his thirst.)

Eventually Milo, whose fame had even reached the ears of King Darius in Persia,[7] met his death by presuming too much upon his strength. Strabo relates that Milo was walking in the country near Croton when he chanced upon a withered tree, into which wedges had been driven in an attempt to split the trunk. Thinking to finish the work he placed both his hands and his feet in the cleft and tried to tear the trunk apart. But the wedges slipped out and the trunk sprang back, imprisoning him and leaving him an easy prey for the wild beasts.[8] According to Pausanias these wild beasts were wolves, which roamed the countryside around Croton in great numbers.[9] The French sculptor, Pierre Puget (1622–1694), carved a marble statue of the death of Milo, which is now in the Louvre.

Stories about Boxers and Pankratiasts

Glaucus of Carystus, the Olympic boxer, was also a legendary figure. Originally he had been a farmer and it was due to this circumstance that his boxing talent was discovered. One day the ploughshare came away from his plough and his father discovered Glaucus hammering it back with his bare fist. Impressed by his son's great strength the old man decided there and then that at the next Olympiad he would take him to Olympia to compete in the boxing. This he did and Glaucus fought his way through to the final. But he was inexperienced and so took a great deal of punishment in the preliminary bouts. Consequently, when he came to face his last opponent, he was so badly wounded that everybody thought he would have to give up. But his father called out to him: 'My boy, remember the ploughshare',[10] whereupon Glaucus hit his opponent so hard that the contest was ended there and then.

Pausanias tells an interesting story about Cleomedes of Astypalaea, the boxer who went out of his mind when he was refused the Olympic crown after having killed his opponent. Following this incident Cleomedes returned to his native city, where he soon became an outcast. It seems that one day, when he was in the schoolroom, he tore out the main pillar of the building, bringing the roof down on the heads of some sixty boys. His fellow citizens then began to stone him and he sought refuge in the temple of Athene, where he is said to have hidden in a chest. After vainly trying to raise the lid of this chest his pursuers eventually broke in the sides only to find that it was empty. They immediately sent emissaries to Delphi to seek an explanation. The emissaries were told by the Pythian priestess:

The last of the heroes is Cleomedes of
  Astypalaea:
Honour him with sacrifices, for he is no
  longer a mortal.

From that day onwards the people of Astypalaea honoured Cleomedes as a hero.[11]

Theagenes, son of Timosthenes, a Thasian boxer and pankratiast, was also declared immortal by his fellow citizens, who claimed that he was the son of Hercules. Theagenes's achievements were truly legendary: at the age of nine, on his way home from school he picked up a bronze statue of a god in the market place at Thasos and carried it off because he had taken a liking to it. He won 1,400 crowns at various Greek festivals. After his death a former opponent made a practice of scourging his statue every night until eventually it took its revenge by toppling over and crushing him to death. The dead man's sons then had the statue indicted for murder and when they won their case the Thasians ordered the statue cast into the sea. But from that moment on their land became barren. They sought advice in Delphi and were told to bring back to Thasos all those who had been exiled. This they duly did, but the dearth continued. They sent again to Delphi, where they were told that they had forgotten their 'great Theagenes'. But how were they to recover his statue from the sea? Eventually fate intervened. The crew of a fishing boat caught the statue in a net and brought it to shore. It was returned to its original site and from then onwards sacrifices were made at its base and Theagenes was worshipped as a god.[12]

Many other pankratiasts were celebrated in legendary accounts. Polydamas of Scotussa was said to have killed a lion with his bare hands and to have stopped a chariot dead in its tracks by seizing hold of it with one hand as it flashed past him. Like Milo, he also died by presuming too much upon his strength. He was in a mountain cave one day with several companions when the roof began to fall in. His companions fled but Polydamus stood his ground and tried to support the roof, as if refusing to accept that the mountain was stronger than he, and so died.[13] Timanthes of Cleonae is said to have committed suicide when he found that his strength had temporarily deserted him.[14]

4. The Votive Statue in the Altis as a Symbol of Fame

Each Olympic victor was entitled to erect a statue in the altis and to have his name and a brief statement of his victory engraved on its base, thus ensuring that a record of his achievement was preserved. The statues of boy victors at Olympia were erected by their parents or relatives. The girl victors in the foot-races staged in honour of Hera were allowed to dedicate a portrait of themselves to the goddess.

These portraits, and this very ancient tradition, may well have been the inspiration for the statues.[15]

But it was not only the Olympic victors who were allowed to erect their effigies in the altis. Special statutes were introduced by the Eleans so that men of outstanding merit in any sphere might be honoured in this way. Thus the Samians erected a statue to Lysander, the Spartan general who won the Peloponnesian War, for having liberated them from the Athenians.[16] The Achaeans did the same for Pantarches, a native of Elis who negotiated a peace between his country and their own and arranged an exchange of prisoners.[17] The Aetolians honoured Cylon, who freed the Eleans from the despotism of Aristotimus by killing the tyrant at the altar of Zeus where he had sought sanctuary.[18] A statue was also erected in the sacred grove to Aristotle, who had taken a keen interest in the history of the festival.[19] Finally there were the group statues which were erected by the various tribes to commemorate their great deeds and in which their tutelary heroes were often represented.[20]

It seems that the choice of material for these votive statues was left to the victors. Most were in bronze, some in marble or stone, and a few of the earlier specimens were carved in wood. 'The first athletes who had effigies at Olympia were Praxidamas the Aeginetan, who won the prize for boxing in the 59th Olympiad, and the Opuntian Rhexibius, who won the prize in the pankration in the 61st Olympiad... Their effigies are made of wood, Rhexibius's of fig wood and the Aeginetan's of cypress.'[21] The size of the statues, however, was subject to strict supervision by the judges. Lucian tells us that they were vetted even more closely than the contestants, and that if any were found to be larger than life they were toppled over.[22] For a man to erect a statue larger than himself was presumably regarded as a mark of hubris. Superhuman proportions were reserved for the gods.

The victors were also forbidden to erect statues which reproduced their own features for, since victory was a gift from the gods, the votive offerings had to be presented in an ideal form. An exception was made in the case of triple victors, who were allowed to erect realistic statues. No doubt it was felt that, if a man won three times, the grace of the gods could not have been the only factor at work. Commenting on this custom, Pliny the Elder pointed out that it was only men whose deeds were so outstanding that they deserved to be immortalised whose features were carved in stone. Such realistic statues were called *iconica*.[23]

In the idealised portrait the victor respectfully subordinated himself to the god who had granted him victory. He was a committed man and by this commitment to a goal which lay outside of himself, by this involvement in other-directed activity, he both elevated himself and found himself; for man attained to the highest level of humanity only when the god appeared in him. A small bronze statuette representing a runner and dating from the first decade of the fifth century BC, *i.e.* from the period immediately preceding the Persian wars, has been preserved and bears the inscription: 'I belong to Zeus'. The runner stands poised for the start, his body leaning forwards, his hands outstretched, his right leg braced, his left leg bent and the heel slightly raised. This runner, his achievement and his victory all belonged to the god.[24]

The realistic statues, which were erected by the triple victors, were probably inspired by Hellenistic attitudes. The respect and reverence which had prompted the god-fearing victors of earlier times to dedicate an ideal portrait to the god who ruled their lives was supplanted by personal ambition, which could only be satisfied by a votive statue bearing the features of the individual victor. In this period of the festival the athletes were no longer inspired by the deity but by the sense of their own power. Their votive offerings were really dedicated to themselves and consequently had to bear their likeness. 'I belong to myself' would therefore have been an apt inscription.

Apart from the victors in the equestrian events—who were the owners and not the charioteers or riders—the Olympic victors were portrayed in the nude, for that was how they competed. Moreover, even the realistic statues were idealised; the Greek artists strove always to represent the human form at its most beautiful. Consequently all these statues of athletes, like the anthropomorphic statues of the gods, had the added effect upon the contestants of a constant spur to emulation. Lucian observed in this connection that the athletes took care to ensure that their bodies were in perfect condition lest they should bring shame on themselves when they undressed before so many people and so proved unworthy of victory.[25]

Many of the statues indicated the type of contest in which the athlete concerned had been victorious. Pentathletes were depicted holding jumping weights, discuses or javelins; hoplite runners were shown wearing helmets and greaves and carrying a shield; victors in the equestrian events were portrayed with their horses or chariots. Often the statues were arranged in groups according to nationality, contemporaneity or athletic category.

Not every Olympic victor had his statue erected in the altis.[26] Many lacked the means, and, although there were some Greek cities who were prepared to cover the cost,[27] this was by no means universally the case. Lack of means would also explain why some of the statues lacked artistic merit. Pausanias mentions only the better work—of the Greek sculptors he names Myron, Polyclitus and Lysippus—and those which commemorated athletes of outstanding ability.[28] He nonetheless lists one hundred and ninety-two statues in the sacred grove.

But Pausanias does more than present a list of victors. He also tells us their story whenever he can. Eubotas of Cyrene is a case in point. When this young athlete came to Olympia he brought his statue with him, for he had been told by the oracle in Libya that he would win his event. The oracle did not lie and Eubotas was able to erect his statue on the very day on which he was proclaimed victor.[29] This incident occurred in 408 BC.

Of the hundreds of votive statues which must have been set up virtually all that has been recovered are a few odd bases and a number of fragments, the most important of which is the head of the boxer Satyrus by the sculptor Silanion. Were it not for Pausanias's accounts we would know very little indeed about this open-air hall of fame in the altis.

5. The Victor's Fame in His Native Land

In view of the fact that the Olympic victor was acclaimed by the whole of the Greek world it should not surprise us to find that a special welcome was prepared for him in his native land, which shared in his fame.

But first the victor had to inform his fellow countrymen of his success. We have already seen that Ageus of Argos and Drymos of Epidaurus ran all the way home—one hundred kilometres in Ageus's case and one hundred and thirty kilometres in the case of Drymos—to announce their victory in the dolichos.[30] Taurosthenes of Aegina, who won the wrestling at the 84th Olympiad, also reported his victory in a novel fashion. Aelian tells us that immediately prior to his departure for Olympia Taurosthenes removed a pigeon from a nest of baby birds and took it with him. After his victory he tied a red ribbon round the pigeon's leg and released it, knowing that it would make straight for its nest. The bird arrived in Aegina the same day after a flight of one hundred and seventy kilometres. When Taurosthenes's father saw the red ribbon he knew that his son had been successful.[31]

The Olympic victor came home to a magnificent reception, entering his native city in a state carriage drawn by a team of four.[32] In 420 BC the people of Akragas in Sicily arranged a particularly splendid reception for Exaenetus following his second victory in the stade-race.[33] When he entered the city in state he was escorted by three hundred of its leading citizens, each of whom rode in a chariot drawn by a pair of white horses.[34]

According to Suetonius it was customary to breach the city wall so that the victor could enter by his own private gate. This author tells us that when Nero returned from Greece and entered Naples in state a breach was made in the city wall 'as was customary for victors in the sacred games'.[35] Nero subsequently entered Antium, Alba and Rome in the same way. It seems likely that this custom derived from the early period of the festival when the victor assumed the identity of the god and consequently would have been entitled to a private entrance. In later times it was doubtless reinterpreted and may well have been regarded as an indication that a city which produced such valiant sons had no need of city walls.[36]

The reception ceremony was of course continued within the city. Mezö suggests that the procession proceeded first to the main square and then to the temple of the city's tutelary god, where the victor offered up a sacrifice and dedicated his wreath to the deity. This ritual would then have been followed by a great banquet with a choir singing a song of victory composed especially for the occasion. Later songs were sung for the victor outside his house.[37]

Nero's reception in Rome was the most splendid ever accorded to an Olympic victor. Dio Cassius says that after entering the city through a breach in the wall he proceeded via the circus and forum to the Capitol and thence to the palace; the whole city was decked with garlands of flowers and the streets were sprinkled with fragrant wine while the populace, including the senators, lined the streets to acclaim the great victor.[38] This account is confirmed by Suetonius, who also mentions the large number of sacrifical animals slaughtered in Nero's honour and the songbirds released by the crowd when he passed by.[39]

The victors also received very considerable material benefits. Vitruvius states this quite specifically: 'Throughout the whole of their life they enjoy great privileges from their native land.'[40] Athenaeus tells us that the names of Olympic victors were entered on their country's roll of fame and that they themselves were invited to all great banquets and given a place of honour in the theatre.[41] This would appear to have been general practice. Over and above this, however, the victors also received special tokens of distinction, which varied from country to country. In Sparta they enjoyed the highest privilege to which a 'peer' might aspire for they were allowed to fight beside the king in battle.[42] In Athens the Olympic victors were given free meals in the prytaneum.[43] Socrates referred to this practice in the *Apology* and suggested that the privilege should really have been extended to him instead: 'What then is suitable to a poor man, a benefactor, and who has need of leisure in order to give his good advice? There is nothing

54. Remains of arched gateway leading into the stadium from the altis, *i.e.,* from the west.

55.   Four-horse chariot rounding the turning post
(nyssa) in the hippodrome.

56.   The poet Pindar (*c.* 518 — *c.* 438 BC) who composed
many odes in praise of victorious athletes.

so suitable, O Athenians, as that such a man should be maintained in the prytaneum, and this much more than if one of you had been victorious at the Olympic games in a horse-race or in the two- or four-horsed chariot-race: for such a one makes you appear to be happy, but I, to be so: and he does not need support, but I do.'[44]

This was not all that the Athenian victors received. Solon, the sovereign legislator of Athens, decreed that money prizes should be given to all Athenian victors at the Isthmus and at Olympia—one hundred drachmas for the Isthmus and five hundred for Olympia.[45] If we consider that in Solon's timocracy one drachma was equal in value to a sheep or a bushel of corn[46] for purposes of property assesment and that an annual income of five hundred drachmas placed a man in the top income group, we see how valuable the prize for the Olympic victor was. Plato could conceive of only one group of people who would receive even greater blessings, namely the 'guardians' in his republic. 'And their life will be blessed as the life of Olympic victors and yet more blessed.'[47] But the rewards offered by other Greek cities were even higher than those enjoyed by the Athenians. Dion Chrysostom tells us that some cities gave their victors as much as five talents.[48] The value of the Attic talent was fixed by Solon at six thousand drachmas, the equivalent of 26.2 kilogrammes of silver. A reward of five talents was the equivalent of eight thousand dollars.[49]

6. Great Men in Search of Olympic Fame

It was Cicero who said that victory at Olympia meant more to the Greeks than the most splendid triumphal procession meant to the Romans.[50] Small wonder then if important public figures and even kings and princes were eager to take part in the Olympic games, although it must be said that their interest was more in the hippodrome than the stadium. This is not altogether surprising if we consider that horse- and chariot-racing were decidedly the prerogative of the rich, for they were extremely costly. By and large, of course, it would be true to

say that, prior to the advent of the professional athlete, the contestants in all the Olympic events were relatively wealthy, for the poor could afford neither the loss of income nor the expense which competition entailed. Consequently, although the stade-race was the most important of the Olympic contests in terms of ritual associations, from the point of view of the competitors it was one of the least important. They not unnaturally assessed the contests in the light of their own social position, which meant that, as far as they were concerned, the equestrian events took pride of place. The heavy events came next while the light events, which included the stade-race, were last. The wealthier and more powerful the contestants were, the more they tended to regard the games as a means of raising their own prestige and consequently the prestige of their state. The most conspicuous example was that of Alcibiades, who entered seven chariots in the same race in 416 BC and took the first three places.[51] Isocrates says that his object was to belittle the achievements of previous victors and to ensure that nobody should surpass him in the future.[52] King Philip II of Macedonia took part in the games on a number of occasions. His victory of 356 BC was a famous one, for it formed part of the auspices under which his son Alexander the Great was born. Plutarch reports that immediately after he had conquered Potidaea Philip received three dispatches, each of which brought good news. The first informed him that Parmenio had defeated the Illyrians, the second that his horse had won at the Olympic games and the third that his wife had borne him a son. The proud father, Plutarch tells us, was prouder still when the seers advised him that a son born under such auspices would be invincible.[53] Subsequently Philip won the chariot-race at a number of Olympiads. He then had special coins minted to commemorate his victories[54] and erected the Philippaeum, the circular Ionic temple which graced the altis.

In fact, there were many royal contenders from the city states of Greece and subsequently, following the temporary eclipse of the festival, many Roman aristocrats competed. We have already seen that Tiberius and Germanicus competed in the chariot-race and that the Emperor Nero—a famous if unworthy contestant—appeared in person both as singer and charioteer.

7. Famous Horses at Olympia

In the equestrian events the owners of the horses were proclaimed victors and in view of the importance attached to Olympic fame it is not difficult to understand why these owners felt both attached and indebted to their horses, although occasionally such feelings took rather an extreme form. Cimon (the father of the great Miltiades) who won the four-horse chariot-race at three successive Olympiads (532, 528 and 524 BC), had his horses buried in the family tomb and then had bronze statues erected to perpetuate their memory.[55]

The names of a few of the winning horses have been preserved for us. For example, there was Aura, the riderless mare whose victory was recorded by Pausanias and whose owner Phidolas was permitted by the Eleans to erect a statue of the horse. Phidolas's sons also won several races with a stallion by the name of Lycus. A statue was also erected to this horse which bore the inscription:

> Once in the Isthmian games, twice at Olympia,
>   did Lycus the swift courser
> Win the race and honour for the sons of
>   Phidolas.[56]

The horses of Cynisca—the first woman ever to win a victor's crown at Olympia—were also commemorated in a bronze statue which actually stood within the temple of Zeus.[57] The statues of race horses, most of which were in bronze, were all ideal representations. The statues of chariots on the other hand were usually 'realistic and of various sizes'.[58] Unfortunately none of the statues of these Olympic horses have been preserved. Modern archaeologists have found only a small bronze horse from a team of four. This was unearthed by the nineteenth-century expedition in the eastern part of the southern colonnade.[59]

Part Three

The Art

Chapter Ten

The Buildings in the Sanctuary

Art—at least in the golden age of Olympia—was exclusively in the service of religion. The temples, effigies and the altars of the Olympian gods, and the votive statues dedicated to them by the victors, were all direct expressions of religious feeling. The architects, the sculptors, the painters, the poets and rhetors, the dancers at the ritual ceremonies and the flute players at the sacred games all vied with one another in their devotion to the deity. In the early period of the festival there was no uncommitted art: both art and life revolved around the same religious centre. At Olympia the ancient Greeks gave expression to this divine quintessence of their universe in the altis, the sacred grove, which was cut off from the outside world by stone walls. This was where the deities lived, where Hera, Zeus and the mother of the gods had their temples.

1. The Temple of Hera

The History of the Temple

Up to the end of the geometric age the Greeks had worshipped their gods in tiny Mycenaean chapels or at altars in sacred groves. These early cults had no temples and in many cases no statues. But then, in the early sixth century BC,[1] a sanctuary was built to Hera in Olympia on the foundations of two older temples. It was at the foot of the south-western spur of the Hill of Cronus beneath the gaeum, a spot which had always been held sacred. Pausanias says that according to an Elean legend the first temple had been built by the people of Scillus in Triphylia about eight years after Oxylus had conquered Elis.[2]

Considerable quantities of earth had to be shifted in the process.[3] The style was supposed to have been Doric with pillars on all four sides, but we now know this was not the case: the oldest Heraeum did not have a peristyle, although it did have internal pillars and pilasters.[4] Nor was it built during Oxylus's reign, i.e., at the time of the Dorian migration: a bronze statuette of a helmeted warrior has been found 1.49 metres below the floor of the opisthodomos (the rear chamber) of the third temple of Hera which clearly belongs to the middle of the geometric age and has been dated to c. 750 BC.[5] Since this find was made beneath the level of the first Heraeum the temple must have been built after 750 BC. Jantzen suggests the middle of the seventh century BC as the probable date of erection.[6] The first temple was a wooden structure which was later destroyed by fire.

The second Heraeum was intended to have a peristyle but 'it appears that it [the Heraeum] was never completed. There are no stylobates and no sign at all of any superstructure. Before the temple was finished it was decided to raise it by a further 0.80 metre.'[7] Thus the second Heraeum would appear to have been little more than a blueprint and the Doric building which was eventually erected at the beginning of the sixth century BC was in fact the third Heraeum. It is one of the oldest extant Greek temples.

King Iphitus's object in introducing his great reforms in 776 BC was to propagate the cult of Olympian Zeus and ensure that homage was paid to the northern god. Thus the Olympian religion which, Pausanias says,[8] was first brought to Elis by the northern conquerors (i.e., the Eleans) in the twelfth century BC was finally established there in an enduring form four centuries later. But the cult of Hera, the former Magna Mater and tutelary goddess of Mycenae, was not integrated into the new Olympian cult and the foot-races for girls which were held in her honour were kept separate from the Olympic games. Initially Hera was worshipped primarily by the older tribes, *i.e.*, the Epei, Pisatans and other Achaean peoples, who had been conquered by the Eleans. It seems reasonable to assume therefore that the temple of Hera within the sacred grove was erected on their initiative. It can hardly have been an accident that all three of these Hera projects were undertaken during the 'Pisatan restoration', *i.e.*, between 668 and 572 BC, when the older tribes regained control of Olympia.[9]

We have already seen that Pausanias ascribes the building of the temple of Hera to the people of Scillus, a town in Triphylia. Only small bands of Eleans had advanced into Triphylia and consequently the displaced Achaeans had sought refuge in this territory. While the Eleans honoured Zeus in the sacred grove in accordance with northern tradition—which at that time still felt no need for statues of any kind—Hera, the ancient goddess of the Mediterranean world, received a temple containing a ritual effigy. This would also suggest that the temple was the work of the older tribes, for they had once belonged

to the Minoan-Mycenaean civilisation and temples and religious statues formed part of their cultural heritage. The goddess was represented seated on a throne while a bearded and helmeted Zeus stood at her side.[10] Hera as queen and Zeus as her prince consort. This surely is the correct interpretation of this statue, which is so reminiscent of the pre-Dorian cult of the Magna Mater and her lover. According to Dörpfeld the Doric architecture of the temple was a development of Mycenaean techniques[11] which may very well have survived among these conquered descendants of this ancient civilisation.

Description of the Temple

The foundations of the last of the three temples of Hera, the oldest of all the temples at Olympia, have been preserved. Unlike Heraeum I, which consisted of a simple elongated cella with an antechamber at its eastern end and two pillars between the antae, Heraeum III was already entirely classical in character. It had a Doric peristyle and was divided into three separate sections: pronaos, cella and opisthodomos. The upper part of the cella was made of unbaked brick and the lower part of stone blocks; its floor was paved. 'Tongue-walls', *i.e.*, partitions, projected from the sides of the cella every two metres, thus

Fig. 23: Temple of Hera (section).

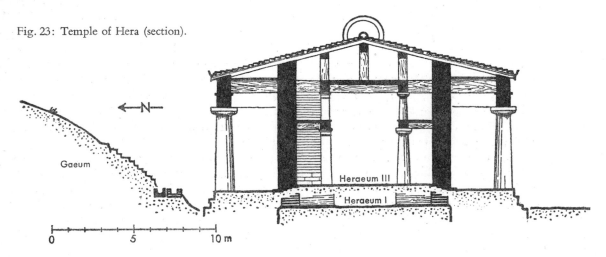

Gaeum

Heraeum III

Heraeum I

0   5   10 m

58.   Re-erected pillars at the south–eastern corner of the temple of Hera.

59a.   Capital of pillar from temple of Zeus.

59b.   Pillars from the temple of Zeus toppled by the earthquake and still lying where they fell.

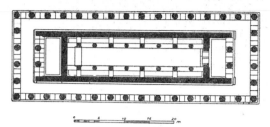

Fig. 24: Temple of Hera (ground plan).

forming niches on both sides. (It was in one of these niches that the nineteenth-century expedition found the Hermes of Praxiteles.) Subsequently the partitions were replaced by pillars. At the end of the cella, just in front of the rear wall, there was a rectangular stone dais. It was forty centimetres high and four metres across, which means that it covered the whole width of the nave. The inner temple, *i.e.*, pronaos, cella and opisthodomos, was surrounded on all four sides by colonnades. There were six pillars on each of the two narrow sides and sixteen on each of the two longer sides (counting the corner pillars twice.) The overall measurements of the foundations were 18.75 by 50 metres. This gives a width to length ratio of 3 to 8, which corresponds to the ratio between the pillars (6 to 16 = 3 to 8). The overall measurements of the inner area of the temple (pronaos, cella and opisthodomos) were 11.51 by 40.62 metres, a ratio of 1 to 4. The height of the pillars was 5.22 metres, which was half the internal width of the cella. And so here too a definite ratio was established, *i.e.*, 1 to 2.[11a]

Originally all the pillars had been of wood but, as these decayed, they were gradually replaced in stone. Because they were erected at different times these stone pillars differed considerably. Different kinds of stone were used, the fluting was different, the capitals were different, even the width was different. At first sight it appears strange that the Greeks did not replace all the wooden pillars at the same time. But presumably reverence inhibited them from interfering more than was necessary with this very ancient temple.

When the Heraeum was excavated in 1877 not one of its forty-four pillars was intact. Most had been reduced to stumps and some had disappeared altogether. Naturally none of the capitals was in position. Some had been destroyed, the rest lay on the ground. The two pillars which are to be seen on the site of the Heraeum today were re-erected in 1905.[12] The older of these has only sixteen flutes; it is surmounted by a broad circular capital which took the weight of the architrave. The pillars are ill-proportioned. The capitals are too massive and the pillars themselves too wide in relation to their height. Unlike those at the Parthenon, which describe an almost imperceptible curve, these pillars, which widen towards the base, are quite straight. As a result they appear clumsy and squat. No trace of the original rafters or roof timbers has been found. The roof was covered with alternating rows of concave and convex clay tiles. This 'male and female' system of tiling, known as the 'laconic system' in ancient times, is still used in the Mediterranean area. Both ends of the ridge-piece of the span-roof sported an enormous acroterium consisting of a terracotta disc from which one quarter had been removed to allow it to straddle the ridge. These discs, which were decorated with geometric shapes painted black, white, yellow and red, gave the roof a picturesque appearance.

Although one of the original wooden pillars of the temple was still standing when Pausanias visited Olympia the building was no longer used exclusively as a shrine: by then it also served as a treasury and was filled with works of art. (The aisles, which contained the original niches, were of course particularly suitable as repositories for votive offerings and may well have been designed with this purpose in view.) Pausanias lists the votive offerings: the cella contained gold, ivory, bronze and marble statues of various gods including the Hermes of Praxiteles, while in the antechamber and the colonnades the statues quite literally stood shoulder to shoulder. Their bases, many of which bore the names of Elean gentlewomen (presumably priestesses of Hera), were discovered by the members of the nineteenth-century expedition, who also found four statues of women with drapery and the head of an older woman with frizzed hair. On the pillars of the southern and eastern colonnades indentations have been

113

discovered which may have been caused by inscriptions. Dörpfeld has suggested that these were in fact the inscriptions made by the young girls who won the foot-race in the Heraea[13] and who were entitled to dedicate their portraits to Hera.[14] The most precious article in the temple was the cedar wood chest placed there as a votive offering by Cypselus, the tyrant of Corinth in the seventh century BC. Pausanias describes this chest in minute detail.[15] Three other objects of great religious significance were kept in the temple of Hera: Hippodamia's nuptial bed, the bronze 'quoit of Iphitus', on which the terms of the sacred truce were inscribed, and a table of ivory and gold, on which the wreaths for the victors were laid out.[16]

Thanks to Pausanias's accounts and the evidence discovered by modern archaeologists we are now able to form an impression of the temple of Hera. Kirsten and Kraiker have given a brief description of the shrine in their recent book on classical Greece: 'Although it is not possible to establish the exact height of the building it probably stood about 15 ells or 7.80 metres high. But in view of its elongated structure it must have appeared much lower than it actually was and will have made a very different impression than that created by the Doric stone temples of a later date.'[17]

2. The Temple of Zeus

The Erection of the Temple

Although there were several layers of ash and many votive offerings[18] in the earth beneath the site of the great temple there was no sign of earlier foundations. We must assume therefore that there was only one temple of Zeus.

The architect was the Elean, Libon, and the construction of the temple took about ten years. The year of completion was 456 BC. This we know because, following the battle of Tanagra, the Spartans dedicated a golden shield to Olympian Zeus which was hung from the eastern pediment of the temple. The battle of Tanagra took place in 457 BC.[19]

But there is some confusion concerning the events leading up to the erection of the temple. Pausanias says that 'the temple and statue of Zeus were built out of the spoils of Pisa, which the people of Elis razed to the ground'.[20] Then, in a later chapter, he goes on to say that war broke out between the Pisatans and the Eleans when 'Pyrrhus the son of Pantaleon succeeded his brother Damophon on the throne'.[21] Now Damophon was king of Pisa at the time of the 48th Olympiad in 580 BC,[22] which means that, if Pausanias was referring to this particular war, the Eleans allowed over a century to elapse before commissioning the temple.

But was Pausanias referring to this war when he spoke of the Elean booty? It seems more than likely that the minority groups in the districts of Pisa and Triphylia would have rebelled against the Eleans when they proceeded to establish their city state and to destroy the identity of all the lesser tribes by their process of synoecism, which was probably inaugurated in 472 BC. At all events we know that the Eleans had to fight the 'Minyae', i.e., the descendants of the older tribes, shortly after the Persian wars.

Herodotus tells us that the various towns in the neighbourhood of Elis, including Lepreum, Phrixae, Pyrgus and Epium, were destroyed by the Eleans 'in our days'.[23] It would not be unreasonable to assume therefore that this was the war to which Pausanias was referring. If so, then work on the temple of Zeus would have started soon after the war ended, i.e. around about 468 BC.[24]

In both of these engagements the Eleans defeated the pre-Dorian tribes, including the people of Scillus who had built the temple of Hera in the altis during the 'Pisatan restoration'. Pausanias makes a specific reference to the destruction of their town.[25] Following this Elean victory over the Pisatans and their allies the conception of the Magna Mater with Zeus as prince consort began to wane. The Elean Zeus-worshippers gave tangible expression to their victory by building a temple to their northern god, the great father and lord of the universe, which surpassed the temple of Hera in size, beauty and splendour. Phidias represented almighty Zeus seated on his great throne

XIII Temple of Hera.

as the sole ruler of heaven and earth. And so Dorian Zeus finally won his long and arduous battle with the Mycenaean goddess.

Description of the Temple

Pausanias has described the temple of Zeus and its statues in considerable detail[26] and consequently we are able to form a fairly accurate picture of the building as it was in his day. Libon had built it in the Doric style using stone hewn from local quarries. This temple, which had a peristyle, was the largest in the altis. The height from the ground to the top of the pediment was 68 feet, the width 95 feet and the length 230 feet.[27] The roof was not covered with ordinary terracotta tiles but with slabs of Pentelic marble cut especially to shape.

A gilded nike hovered above the apex of the pediment while gilded tripods at its two outer corners symbolised the fruits of victory. Below the goddess hung the golden shield which the Spartans and their allies had dedicated to Zeus after the victory at Tanagra; the head of the Medusa was painted on this shield to protect the temple from evildoers. The architrave, which rested on the lofty pillars, supported a frieze which ran round the whole building. Twenty-one gilded shields were attached to the panels of this frieze.[28] The Roman general Mummius had sent them to Olympia as a votive offering after the suppression of the last Greek insurrection, in which he destroyed Corinth and dispersed its inhabitants. Zeus himself was the central figure of the facade. He stood in the middle of the pediment with the nike and the golden shield immediately above his head and with Oenomaus on his left and Pelops on his right; these two ancient rivals were portrayed with their chariots and retinues as if waiting to enter the lists.

After climbing the steps to the temple and passing through the outer colonnade the visitor entered the spacious gallery which encircled the naos, the inner sanctuary. The entrance to the antechamber was flanked by two pillars and fitted with three bronze gates. The wall of the antechamber was covered with

Fig. 25: East front of the temple of Zeus.

metopes depicting six of the labours of Hercules, symbols of endless tribulation and a reminder to the athletes that, like their great ancestor, they were expected to strive and suffer hardship in order to acquire immortal fame. Just to the right of the bronze gates, immediately in front of the pillar, was a statue of King Iphitus being crowned by a woman for having established the sacred truce. Inside the antechamber, to the right of the entrance, stood the bronze horses dedicated by Cynisca. This room also contained the bronze tripod on which the Eleans once placed the wreaths at the prize-giving ceremony. The twenty-five bronze shields which were used for the race in armour probably hung on the walls.

The shields dedicated by Mummius were not the only evidence of Roman rule. There were also four wreaths, which were a votive offering made by Nero, and two statuettes, one of the Emperor Hadrian, the other—which was paid for by a Greek national contribution—of the Emperor Trajan.

From the antechamber the visitor entered the sanctum sanctorum, the cella. Two rows of pillars ran the length of the cella, dividing it into three parts and focusing attention on the far end of the room where Phidias's towering Zeus, fashioned in gold and ivory, was enthroned. As the ruler of heaven and earth the great god held a golden sceptre

115

surmounted by an eagle in his left hand and as the source of victory a golden nike in his right hand. As a victor himself he also wore a wreath of wild olive on his head.

The cella had two levels, for the pillars on either side of the nave also supported a gallery, which afforded a closer view of Zeus. From this gallery a spiral staircase led to the roof. At ground level access to the base of the statue was cut off by a series of barriers, the first of which was painted blue while the rest were decorated with paintings. An Assyrian woven curtain in various shades of Phoenician purple, supported by ropes descending from the ceiling, served as a backcloth. This had been a votive offering from King Antiochus.[29] The floor immediately in front of the base was of black flagstones bordered by a rim of white Parian marble[30] to prevent the oil used for cleaning the statue from running into the nave. In front of the barriers a bronze water jug marked the spot where lightning had struck after Phidias had asked Zeus to vouchsafe him some sign that he was pleased with his work.

The cella did not afford access to the opisthodomus, or rear chamber, and so, to reach the back of the temple, the visitor had to walk round on the outside. On the rear elevation of the pediment was a representation of the furious battle between the Centaurs and the Lapithae at the nuptials of Pirithous. Entry to the opisthodomus was through the western colonnade. This was always open, for it had no doors. The Eleans probably kept the steles on which the texts of their treaties were inscribed in this chamber. Here too the entrance was flanked by pillars and the whole of the upper wall was given over to metopes depicting the other six labours of Hercules. It was because he had founded the Olympic games to please his father Zeus that Hercules's deeds were recorded in the temple.

The Archaeological Survey

The foundations for the new temple[31] did not lie on the solid gravel of the diluvial layer. They were only one metre deep and rested on alluvium. To

116

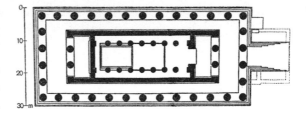

Fig. 26: Temple of Zeus (ground plan).

compensate for the instability of the subsoil seven layers of massive Poros blocks were laid on top of the foundations and covered over with earth. These blocks, which rose three metres above the general level of the surrounding terrain, served as a support for the base of the temple, which consisted of three tiered platforms, each fifty centimetres high. The length of the top platform, i.e., the stylobate, was 64.12 metres and its width 27.68 metres. But these platforms were not solid stone. Although the load-bearing surfaces, i.e., the supports for the walls and the rows of pillars, consisted of individual courses of stone-work, the rest was simply an earth filling. The proportions between the various components of the superstructure (naos and peristyle) were precise, as is typical of Doric architecture. The unit of measure was the ell or 521 millimetres. The 78 pillars of the superstructure, 'which were 10.42 metres in height, supported the 4.17-metre-high entablature with its frieze of metopes and triglyphs. ...The combined area of the cella, pronaos and opisthodomos was 16.40 × 46.85 metres, which would suggest a basic width to length ratio of 1:3 (30 × 90 ells of 521 millimetres each). The distance between the pillars of the peristyle [i.e. the inter-columniation] was the same as the distance between the pillars in the antechamber (10 ells or 5.21 metres) and will have been derived from it... The width of the side colonnades (5 ells or 2.605 metres) and of the rear and front colonnades (20 ells or 10.42 metres) was also derived from this basic measure, as was the height of the pillars (20 ells or 10.42 metres). Thus the elevation was determined by the ground plan. The same was true of the temple of Hera, although there the system was applied in a different way.'[32]

Although the longitudinal colonnades of the temple of Zeus were longer than those in the temple of Hera they had fewer pillars—thirteen instead of sixteen— and these were twice as high. The overall height of the temple of Zeus has been fixed at twenty metres as compared with 7.80 metres for the temple of Hera. As a result the temple of Zeus was much simpler and better proportioned. There were twenty flutes on each of its pillars. The lower diameter of the side pillars was 2.21 metres and that of the end pillars 2.25 metres, which means that they all had a height to width ratio of approximately 5 to 1. They were strong but well balanced.

There was no marble near Olympia so Libon used the local conglomerate stone and covered it with a thin coat of stucco to give it the appearance of marble. Parts of the stucco were painted, e.g., the fillets beneath the echinus of the white capitals, which were painted red. The architrave was extremely colourful: the triglyphs were painted dark blue and the metopes sported the golden shields donated by Mummius. The panels alternated blue and gold, rimmed above and below by red fillets. They were surmounted by the great projecting marble gutter, whose pale-blue ground was offset by gilded meanders and foliage.[33]

Since the high steps of the base were ill-suited to ceremonial needs a wide ramp was built to facilitate access to the antechamber at the eastern end of the temple. Originally this ramp, which was faced with marble in Roman times, had been decorated with a mosaic representing a boy riding on a triton and surrounded by fishes and seabirds.

The nave was divided into four sections. The first extended from the entrance to the second row of pillars, where a gated barrier ran across the entire width of the nave. The gate was fitted with a lock. The floor of this section was made of white limestone blocks. Originally these had run the whole length of the nave but Phidias subsequently faced the area between the barrier and the base of the throne with black Eleusinian marble in order to reduce the glare set up by the reflection from his gold and ivory statue. This part of the floor was surrounded by a rim of white Pentelic marble. The base of the statue, which was made of slabs of blue-black limestone, occupied the third section of the nave, an area measuring 6.65 metres by 9.93 metres. The fourth and final section consisted of a passage behind the base of the statue by which the priests and visitors passed from one aisle to the other. This was also fitted with a barrier, which then extended along both sides of the nave, linking the last six pairs of pillars and joining the barrier at the front. Thus the whole of the statue area was enclosed. A few of the limestone slabs from the base of the statue have survived; but that is all that remains of one of the seven wonders of the world.

The ceiling of the cella was a timber structure. The roof was covered with tiles cut from Parian marble, some of which were later replaced by tiles of Pentelic marble. The roof was fitted with a gutter which carried the rain water to gargoyles and so to the ground. The gargoyles were marble and shaped like lions' heads. There were one hundred and two of them; thirty-nine have been preserved. They damaged very easily and, because the marble was so heavy, also had a tendency to snap off. Consequently many had to be replaced and the replacements were not nearly as impressive as the originals.

Plutarch relates a story according to which the tyrant Philanthropus once set fire to the temple in order to avenge himself on Zeus for failing to answer his prayers. Subsequently, when he was returning to Elis with his retinue of three hundred men, he and his whole company were supposed to have been struck down by lightning.[34] But this story of a fire seems dubious for no other author has recorded it. On the other hand, a tale such as this might well have been deliberately spread by the Eleans in order to frighten off malefactors and to preserve the sanctuary from sacrilege.[35]

This magnificent temple survived for about a thousand years before it was destroyed. The great statue of Zeus was carried off to Constantinople, where it perished in a fire, while the temple itself was first damaged by flames and then completely demolished by an earthquake in the sixth century AD, after which its ruins were slowly covered by deposits of earth.

3. The Temple of the Mother of the Gods

Previous History

Once the northern immigrants had arrived in the Peloponnese and begun to establish the cult of the great Indo-European god Zeus in Olympia, once Homer and Hesiod had proclaimed the Hellenic version of this cult and anthropomorphised the insubstantial nature god, he acquired both a family and a retinue. The ancient mythical world of Cretan Zeus stood ready to hand. The victorious Eleans, who were determined that their god should receive all the honours to which he was entitled in their newly-conquered territory, imported his relatives from nearby Crete.[36] Zeus's father Cronus was given an altar on the hill which then bore his name.[37] Rhea, the mother of the gods, who was also known as Meter, received her altar at the foot of the same hill. The Curetes had their altar and there was even an Idaean grotto on the lower face of the hill.

Curtius and his team unearthed a small, narrow sanctuary behind the exedra on the western side of the treasury of the Sicyonians which had been built into the side of the hill. This sanctuary, which was rather like a chapel and was made of limestone, consisted of a cella measuring 2.74 by 2.84 metres and a narrow antechamber.[38] Dörpfeld then carried out further excavations on this site and identified the tiny sanctuary as the Idaean grotto mentioned by Pindar.[39] When the various treasuries were combined into a single terrace, part of which was then elevated, the lower part of the grotto, which has been preserved, was buried under a bank of earth.[40] This happened at the beginning of the fourth century BC.

In the first half of the same century a temple was erected to the mother of the gods in the altis. This would suggest that by this time there may have been some connection between the Idaean grotto and the cult of Rhea and that the temple was built in order to compensate for the destruction of the grotto. Sacrifices were offered at the altar of Rhea in the altis from the early geometric period onwards. This has been demonstrated by the archaeological excavations, for primitive animal statues and the kind of cymbals associated with her cult were found in the immediate vicinity of the altar. These votive offerings lay very deep in the earth, which revealed strong traces of ash.[41] It was at the side of this altar that the fourth-century temple was built to the mother of the gods.

The Late Classical Temple of Meter

The new sanctuary was erected on the eastern side of the altar of Rhea. The site appears to have been completely fresh for none of the ancient authors refers to an earlier temple on this particular spot and no evidence of previous building works was discovered in the course of the excavations. In actual fact the temple should really have been built on the western side of the altar, for in Greek shrines the altar always stood in front of the entrance to the temple, which invariably pointed to the east. But in this particular case the architects had no choice, for the land to the west of the altar of Rhea was already occupied by the altar of Hera; consequently the entrance to the temple must have pointed to the west. Unfortunately the archaeological evidence is too insubstantial to prove the point beyond doubt.

The temple of Rhea—or temple of Meter as it is usually called—was built from blocks of Poros stone in the Doric fashion. It had a peristyle with six pillars at each end and eleven on each side. It was a very small building, a fact which would also suggest that it was designed as a replacement for the minute Idaean grotto. Its stylobate was 20.67 metres long and 10.62 metres wide, an area only one-ninth the size of that covered by the temple of Zeus. Its other proportions were of course correspondingly small: the distance from the top of the stylobate to the apex of the pediment was only a little over 7.50 metres while the slender late classical pillars which supported the architrave measured about 4.75 metres overall. The pediments at the front and rear had the customary height to width ratio of 1 to 8. Each end of the temple had two pillars between the antae and a frieze of triglyphs and metopes, the latter made of Poros stone.[42] Like the other buildings at Olympia the *metroum* or temple of Meter

XIV   The stadium.
60.   Model of Olympia.

was painted in bright colours, the dark blue triglyphs and guttae contrasting with the red moulding beneath the cornice.[43] One figure from the pediment —a marble torso of Dionysus—has survived.

The Cult of the Roman Emperors in the Temple of Meter

In Roman times the temple of the great mother of the gods underwent a complete transformation. The metopes were removed and all the external surfaces received a coat of roughcast plaster.[44] The effigy of Meter was removed from the sanctuary and has completely disappeared. It was replaced by statues of various Roman emperors. The first was of Caesar Augustus; Claudius, Titus, Domitian and their wives were later represented. The temple of Meter thus became an imperial temple.[45]

Of these marble statues that of Caesar Augustus was three-and-a-half times life size and represented

Fig. 27: Temple of the mother of the gods (Metroum) with figure of Divus Augustus (reconstruction).

Augustus as Zeus with a thunderbolt in his right hand. It seems to have been intended as a counterpart to the Zeus of Phidias. Not only was Augustus a god but the highest god of all. Imperial Zeus presumably stood opposite the entrance while the other emperors and their consorts lined the side walls.[46]

The aura of mysticism which surrounded the Roman emperors owed its inception to the *pax romana*, which Augustus had established. The emperor appeared in the eyes of mankind as a saviour. This is apparent from an inscription which was discovered on the architrave of the pillars in the peristyle: 'The Eleans to the son of god, the noble Caesar, the saviour of the Hellenes and of the whole of the inhabited world.'[47] This can only have referred to Augustus. There was a definite link between the new imperial cult and the ancient cult of Rhea or Meter: salvation which had once come from the mother of the gods was now dispensed by divine Caesar. Eventually the new world order was depicted with all of Meter's attributes.[48] Since the beginning of the Hellenistic age religious syncretism had been gaining ground; various deities who had once been entirely separate were linked and in some cases even identified. In the course of this development Rhea, as the mother of the gods, was identified with the Phrygian Magna Mater Cybele, who was also known as the 'Berecynthian mother'. Virgil compares the Roman empire with Cybele for the Cumaean Sibyl says to Aeneas:

His are the auguries, my son, whereby great Rome
Shall rule to the ends of the earth, shall aspire to the highest achievement,
Shall ring the seven hills with a wall to make one city,
Blessed in her breed of men; as Cybele, wearing her turretted
Crown, is charioted round the Phrygian cities, proud of
Her brood of gods, embracing a hundred of her children's children—
Heaven-dwellers all, all tenants of the realm above.[49]

119

XV Zeus and Ganymede.

Associations of this kind no doubt hastened the transformation of the temple of the mother of the gods into a temple of the Roman emperors.

4. The Treasuries

The treasuries were storerooms for objects of value and objects which could not be exposed to the elements. Most of these were votive offerings but the sacrificial vessels and utensils used by the delegations from the other Greek states at the ritual ceremonies were also included. In all, twelve treasuries were erected in Olympia, the earliest *c.* 600 BC. The foundations of all twelve were unearthed in the course of the modern excavations. Pausanias mentions only ten of these treasuries because by his time two of them had already been demolished to make way for a new road leading from the altis to the Hill of Cronus, the old road having been built over when the exedra was erected.

Ten of the twelve treasuries have been identified. They were the treasuries of Sicyon, Syracuse, Epidamnus, Byzantium, Sybaris, Cyrene, Selinus, Metapontum, Megara and Gela. Although these towns were scattered throughout the whole of the Greek world they were all Dorian. But this is not really

surprising since Olympia was the principal sanctuary of the Dorian motherland. By erecting their treasuries there the Dorian colonies overseas were probably trying to gain recognition and acquire prestige at home. But Dorian does not necessarily mean Spartan, for not one of the Dorian colonial towns represented at Olympia was a Spartan satellite. Sparta founded only one colony and that was Tarentum in southern Italy. It then took no further part in the Greek colonisation programme.

The treasuries, which were themselves votive offerings, were rather like miniature temples. They stood side by side on a tiered terrace of Poros stones three metres above the level of the altis at the foot of the Hill of Cronus. A retaining wall strengthened with buttresses ran along the rear of the terrace. This wall also formed the northern limit of the altis, which means that the treasuries lay within the sacred grove, where they enjoyed the protection of the gods.[50] All the treasuries, with the single exception of the treasury of Gela at the eastern end of the terrace, were based on the megaron and consisted of a single rectangular room, with generally two columns in front, engaging the side walls towards the front of the building, thus providing a tiny antechamber. They all had a span roof and a pediment above the entrance. Some pediments

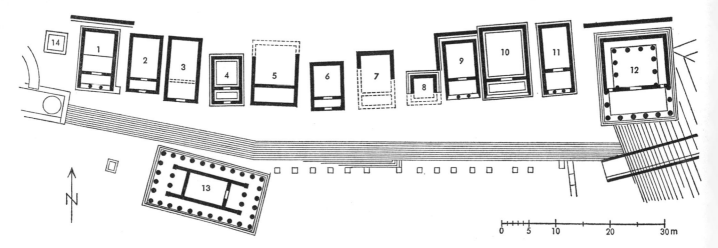

Fig. 28: Treasuries of Sicyon 1, Syracuse 4, Epidamnus 5, Byzantium 6, Sybaris 7, Cyrene 8, Selinus 9, Metapontum 10, Megara 11, Gela 12, Metroum 13, Idaean grotto 14. (The ownership of treasuries 2 and 3 is not known.)

were decorated with sculptures. The fact that the treasuries stood side by side and faced the altis suggests that they were planned as a unit.[51]

The treasury of the Sicyonians, which lay at the western end of the terrace, was erected as early as the sixth century BC. It was a Doric building of sandstone blocks especially imported from Sicyon and measured 12.46 by 9.30 metres. Among other things it contained the three discuses used in the pentathlon, the sword of Pelops with its golden hilt and an ivory cornucopia which had been dedicated by Miltiades, the victor of Marathon. The Syracusans also imported their own building material— white Syracusan limestone. To the east of their treasury stood the treasury of the Megarians, on the pediment of which the battle between the gods and the giants was depicted in high relief. Remnants of these rough-hewn sandstone figures were discovered by the modern archaeologists. They still bore traces of paint, from which it would seem that the figures themselves were painted blue and the weapons red.[52] At the eastern end of the terrace stood the treasury of the Gelani. This was also built in the sixth century BC. Originally it had pointed east and had been rather more elaborate than the later treasuries. Subsequently, however, when the terrace was laid out, this building was converted so that its entrance faced south, which brought it into line with the other treasuries. It was also provided with an antechamber.[53]

Money was also deposited in Olympia and presumably was kept in the treasuries where it enjoyed the protection of the gods. Olympia thus became a financial centre. This enhanced its reputation and also gave it a position of power. Sparta's allies in the Peloponnesian War reckoned with financial aid from the Elean authorities. Thucydides tells us that when the war broke out in 431 BC the Corinthians suggested to their allies that they should buy up the services of all the professional sailors by offering them higher wages than the Athenians were paying, thus weakening the Athenian navy by depriving it of manpower. To finance this scheme they proposed to draw on deposits held at Delphi and Olympia.[54]

But fear of the gods was not always an effective deterrent. There were occasions when avaricious rulers were prepared to defy them. Plutarch says that Sulla[55] took treasure from Epidaurus, Olympia and Delphi in order to finance his wars. It should be added, however, that he later indemnified all three sanctuaries by giving them one half of the territory of the Thebans, whom he wished to punish for their repeated defections.[56] As a result of such inroads the treasuries were sadly depleted by the time Pausanias saw them in AD 174. Then, in the third century AD, when the altis was reduced in size, they were demolished and the stones and rubble used to build a new wall to protect the sanctuary against the assaults of the Heruli. Consequently only the foundations were discovered by the archaeologists.

5. The Philippaeum

The Philippaeum was a circular building with a peristyle which was a votive offering from Philip II of Macedonia.[57] It was the most graceful building in the altis. The triple-tiered marble base rested on a foundation consisting of two circular stone walls with an overall diameter of 15.24 metres. The peristyle of eighteen Ionic pillars of Poros stone and covered with a yellowish stucco supported a conical roof with marble tiles and marble lions' heads and with a brass poppy-head which served as a central clamp. The ceiling of the inner chamber was made of wood while the ceiling of the peristyle consisted of trapezoid coffers of Poros stone.

The entire interior was given over to the cella, the circular wall of which was of conglomerate stone faced with tiles on the outside and sectioned off by nine engaged pillars on the inside. Opposite the entrance stood a semicircular base on which statues of the Macedonian royal family were displayed. There was a passage about 1.5 metres wide behind this base to enable visitors to view the statues in the round. The room was lit by two windows, one on either side of the door.

Pausanias says that the Philippaeum was built by Philip of Macedonia after he had defeated the Greeks at Chaeronea. The statues of the members of the Macedonian dynasty which were in the cella were sculpted by Leochares in ivory and gold.[58] Leochares, who was the most famous Attic artist of his day, probably designed the building as well. Philip II of Macedonia died in 336 BC, just two years after his victory at Chaeronea. It seems probable therefore that his son Alexander the Great completed the temple. If so, it would certainly have been finished before his Asian campaign, which began in 334 BC.

This circular temple tells us a great deal about the development of the Olympian cult. It seems highly probable that the altis was extended westwards to make room for the building, for there is a bend in the wall between the Philippaeum and the prytaneum for which there would appear to be no alternative explanation. Certainly this monument can only have been a votive offering and would quite naturally have been placed within the altis. There is also the highly significant fact that the statues of Philip and his family were made of gold and ivory, materials which in classical Greece were normally reserved for statues of the gods, *e.g.*, the Zeus of Phidias. Consequently the nature of the materials used for these statues served to distinguish the Macedonian royal family from the lesser mortals whose effigies stood in the sacred grove. Originally these had been carved in wood, a material which subsequently gave way to marble and bronze. The object of choosing gold and ivory was not simply to display the great wealth of the Macedonian monarchs but was also to show how like the gods they were. Certainly these statues were far too precious to be left in the open and some sort of shelter was undoubtedly called for. But a simple building—something along the lines of the treasuries—would have served perfectly well. Philip surely chose to build a circular temple with cella and peristyle in order to demonstrate the similarity —although not the identity— of the Macedonian kings and the Olympian gods.

The fact that the temple was a circular building is also significant for this form had its origin in the ancient funeral cults. The beehive tombs of Mycenae and the heroes' funeral mounds with their circles of obtusely angled stones were early examples of tholos construction. We have seen that, initially, Pelops's grave in the altis was a circular installation.

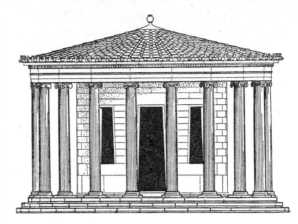

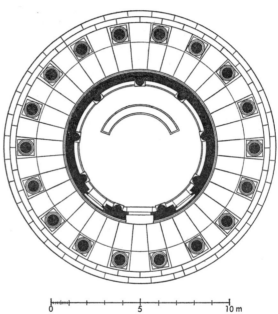

Fig. 29: Philippaeum (reconstruction).

Fig. 30: Philippaeum (ground plan).

So too was Hippodamia's, which still existed in its original form when the Philippaeum was built. In view of this association it is tempting to speculate that this tholos temple may also have been envisaged as a cenotaph.

There is, moreover, a direct link between the size of the Philippaeum and the size of the two funeral mounds in the altis. We know from archaeological

122

XVI The Philippaeum.

evidence that the diameter of Pelopium I[59] was one plethron and Pausanias says that Hippodamia's grave (which has not yet been located) was of equal size.[60] If we take the Olympic foot (0.32047 metres) as our basic unit of measure the diameter of the mound works out at 100 Olympic feet or 32.047 metres, which means that it was almost exactly twice the diameter of the Philippaeum (15.24 metres). From this it would not necessarily follow, however, that the Philippaeum was used for hero-worship. Indeed, this seems improbable since the entrance, which should have faced west if the tholos had been intended as a heroum in the normal sense of the word, actually faced south.[61] On the other hand it could quite conceivably have been envisaged as a heroum of a very special kind, one in which living heroes were to be honoured. The sun rose in the east and set in the west. Consequently the east was sacred to the Olympian gods and the west to the dead heroes. But when the sun reached its zenith it stood due south of the altis and it could be that in placing the entrance to the Philippaeum in the south, i.e., mid-way between east and west, Alexander was trying to create a symbol of the human condition.

It would seem therefore that the Philippaeum gave expression to a number of religious attitudes, which had once been quite distinct but had gradually coalesced due to Hellenistic syncretism. This building was a monument to an Olympic victor—for Philip had won the chariot-race on various occasions—and by the same token it was a votive offering to the gods on the part of an individual and his nation; it was a cenotaph for the Macedonian royal family and it was also a heroum, but a heroum for living heroes; at the same time—because of the choice of gold and ivory for the statues—it was a temple of 'god-like' kings; and finally it was a treasury of a particular kind, which it had not been possible to accommodate on the terrace and for which a special site had to be found within the altis.

But was the Philippaeum also meant to commemorate the Macedonian victory over the Greeks at Chaeronea in 338 BC? Was it intended to serve as a constant reminder to the Hellenes of their lost liberty? Pausanias's account could be interpreted in this way. But if this were the case it is difficult to see why Philip II should have helped the Eleans by financing the conversion of the echo colonnade or why he should have visited Olympia—it seems almost certain that he did—following the general peace concluded in Corinth in 338 BC. And finally it must be remembered that the aristocracy of Elis had been supporting him from 364 BC onwards.[62] In the light of these considerations we are forced to the conclusion that, far from being a monument to the arrogance of a conquering nation, the Philippaeum was intended as an act of homage to the spirit of Greece and a token of conciliation.

6. The Remaining Buildings in the Altis

The Pre-Dorian Apsidal Houses

The horseshoe foundation walls of the six houses excavated by Dörpfeld at the foot of the Hill of Cronus go back to the period between 2000 and 1200 BC (middle and late Bronze Age). These houses had been built on a solid base which was one metre thick and consisted of boulders mixed with alluvium and a certain amount of conglomerate stone. The upper walls were made of clay reinforced with brushwood and cane. In one of the houses the apse was cut off from the principal room by a partition wall; all the entrances faced the Hill of Cronus. The largest of the apsidal buildings (II) was about eleven metres by four metres and its walls were a half metre thick. Three children's graves were discovered in the vicinity. The urns were of the kind commonly found in the middle and late Bronze Age and they prove that the houses were lived in. Presumably this settlement, which may well have been called Pisa, was destroyed in the course of the Dorian migration.

Pelops's Funeral Mound

The Pelopium in the north-western section of the altis is still visible today. The older installation

(Pelopium I) consisted of a mound which may or may not have been artificially raised. It was enclosed by a circle of stones which were inclined to each other at obtuse angles and had a diameter of between thirty-one and thirty-four metres. The circle was probably inspired by similar Mycenaean installations, although it would almost certainly have been post-Mycenaean since it was built on top of the foundation walls of one of the apsidal houses (V). In house No. VI, which stood in the immediate vicinity of the circle of stones, a fragment of Mycenaean pottery has been found which dates this particular house to the thirteenth or twelfth century BC. It seems therefore that Pelopium I must have been built towards the end of the second millennium BC.[63] The archaeological evidence indicates that the mound was a cenotaph, although an urn containing the bones of a child was discovered at a spot lying between the centre of the circle of stones and apsidal house No. V.

Subsequently—probably in the sixth century BC—the Pelopium was rebuilt. The circular enclosure was abandoned and a new wall of Poros stone built in the form of an irregular hectagon. Its propylaeum (entrance gate) was in the west, this being standard practice for such installations. In the fifth century BC the propylaeum was enlarged and in Roman times it was given a new coat of roughcast.

The Prytaneum

The prytaneum, which was named after the prytanes or magistrates who administered the festival, stood at the foot of the Hill of Cronus near the temple of Hera. It was probably built in the sixth century BC. The original site was square with sides of 100 Olympic feet or 32.80 metres. But the subsequent conversion, which was carried out in Roman times, was so extensive that little trace has been left of the original installation. In the prytaneum the sacred fire burned night and day on the altar of Hestia, the goddess of hearths. All processions started in the prytaneum for the pyres on all the other altars in the sacred grove were always lit with the fire

from the hearth of Hestia. Her altar, of which not even fragments have been found, stood in a square room which measured 6.5 metres by 6.5 metres. This room was the inner sanctuary of the whole building and consequently it was left unchanged when the conversions were carried out. Deep excavations beneath the colonnade to the west of the altar have revealed the foundations of a navicular installation composed of large boulders. Although it has not been possible to date this installation with any degree of accuracy it almost certainly was built in the geometric period, probably in the ninth or eighth century BC.[64] Perhaps the original altar of Hestia stood on this site.

The victors in the games and important visitors to the festival were feasted in the prytaneum at the expense of the host state. This was a high honour, which called for a special reception room. The spacious colonnade on the northern side of the building doubtless served as a banquet hall and the kitchens, sculleries etc. presumably occupied the smaller rooms at its western end. The ordinary dining room was situated immediately to the south of the kitchen area. In this western section of the prytaneum archaeologists discovered tables and cooking utensils and fragments of earthenware preserving jars.

The Echo Colonnade

Shortly after 350 BC, when the stadium was removed from the altis and cut off from it by the new western embankment, a colonnade 96.5 metres long and 12.5 metres wide was built along the eastern edge of the sacred grove. This new building, which opened on to the altis, also underlined the segregation of games and cult. Pausanias says that it was first called the 'painted colonnade' on account of the pictures which were painted on its walls but that it was also commonly referred to as the echo colonnade because it echoed the sound of a man's voice seven times and more.[65] This echo must have been particularly impressive when the heralds and trumpeters competed with one another at the beginning of the festival, for their contest was held near the

61. Head of Hera (early archaic).

62a. Gargoyle depicting head of lion (temple of Zeus).

62b. Bull of Regilla, marble sculpture from the exedra (or nymphaeum) of Herodes Atticus.

entrance to the stadium, *i.e.*, in front of the northern end of the colonnade.[66]

With forty-four Doric pillars the echo colonnade provided the sacred grove with an impressive eastern boundary, one which was in keeping with contemporary taste, for the Greeks of that period revealed a marked preference for wide, open spaces flanked by colonnades. The deep roof, supported in the centre by a second row of pillars, offered the spectators a place of refuge from the fierce rays of the sun. The marble floor would suggest that no expense was spared on this building. Numerous votive statues were erected in front of it and some of their bases have been recovered.[67] Of the colonnade itself only the foundations and a few isolated members have been preserved.

Immediately behind the colonnade there was a court, which was much narrower but of equal length. The rear wall of this court marked the eastern extremity of the altis and also served as a retaining wall for the western embankment of the stadium. It was probably used as a storeroom for athletic equipment.

Various technical and artistic details of the echo colonnade would suggest that it was built at the same time as the Philippaeum. Wiesner assumes that Philip himself donated the building following the battle of Chaeronea; by embellishing the altis in both the east and the west he hoped to effect a reconciliation with the Greeks.[68] Extensive renovations were carried out in the echo colonnade under Emperor Hadrian.

The South-Eastern Colonnade

In the first half of the fourth century BC a rectangular building was erected immediately south of the site subsequently occupied by the echo colonnade. The main body of this building, which had colonnades on three of its sides, contained two square rooms which were separated from one another. The western colonnade, which faced the altis, measured 36.42 by 14.56 metres and had a single row of nineteen Doric pillars. The northern and southern colonnades each had eight pillars. Whether there were further rooms in the eastern wing of the building is still uncertain. Opinions differ as to whether this building was an administration block for the judges, a covered stand *(proedria)* for guests of honour[69] or perhaps a sanctuary of Hestia.[70] We shall probably never know for certain. Under the Romans this building was demolished and a large villa built on its foundations, presumably to provide accommodation for Nero on the occasion of his visit. After Nero's death the western doors of the villa were bricked up, which effectively eliminated it from the sacred grove.[71]

The Exedra of Herodes Atticus

At the height of its popularity under the Roman emperors Olympia received one last great monument. This was the fountain built by Herodes Atticus, a rich Athenian, who also erected splendid buildings in Athens and Delphi, thus acquiring both contemporary and posthumous fame. Following the recent excavations German archaeologists have renamed the fountain the *nymphaeum* of Herodes Atticus after the nymphs who inhabited the woods, fields, rivers and springs of ancient Greece. In the English-speaking world, however, it is commonly referred to as the *exedra*, a term first used by Friedrich Adler because of the apparent similarity between this installation and the classical exedra, *i.e.* a semicircular bench, which was usually covered by a hemispherical dome. Adler's assumption that the fountain was also fitted with such a dome has since been proved false.[72]

The provision of drinking water for the spectators had always posed problems[73] and these were rendered even more critical when the Romans built their baths, which made heavy demands on existing supplies. And so Herodes Atticus decided to conduct water into Olympia from a tributary of the Alpheus. This new conduit started near the village of Miraka, then passed through the Hill of Cronus and so into the altis. All in all it extended over some three kilometres. At the point where the tunnel emerged into the altis stood the exedra. Basically, this consisted of an upper semicircular basin, which

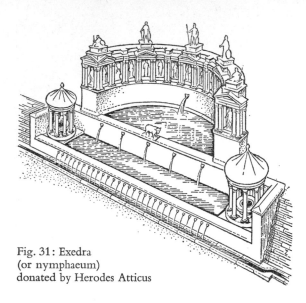

Fig. 31: Exedra
(or nymphaeum)
donated by Herodes Atticus

stood the statues of three emperors: Hadrian, Antoninus Pius and Marcus Aurelius. Herodes and his wife Regilla, the donators of the fountain, each had their statue in a special niche situated at either end of the semicircular wall and facing the front, a position which testified to their importance but did not exalt them above the emperors. Seventeen of these statues have been attested either by archaeological finds or by inscriptions, but unfortunately it has not been possible to determine the respective positions of the statues in the niches. These works appear to have been without artistic merit.

A marble bull, which is now in the museum in Olympia, stood on the wall between the two basins. It faced east and bore the inscription: 'Regilla, priestess of Demeter, the water and the installation to Zeus.' In her capacity as priestess Regilla had of course been allowed to watch the games despite the fact that she was a married woman. It seems probable that Herodes Atticus donated this expensive fountain and dedicated it to Zeus out of gratitude for the high honour accorded to his wife.

received the water as it flowed from the tunnel and conducted it through five marble lions' heads into a lower rectangular basin, from which it issued through eighty-three gargoyles into a runnel. It was then carried to a number of channels leading to various parts of the altis and stadium. The area of the rectangular basin was 21.90 by 3.76 metres and the length of the leading edge of the semicircular basin 16.62 metres.

But the exedra—which stood at the western end of the terrace of treasuries—was not a purely functional installation; it was also a monumental building, which stood sixteen metres high and whose facade covered thirty-two metres. It was made of brickwork faced with marble and its lower basin was flanked on either side by a tiny circular temple complete with peristyle and containing a miniature fountain. The rear semicircular section of the upper basin was attached to a tall and very powerful socle. This was surmounted by a decorative wall, which followed the curve of the basin and was fitted with pilasters to form individual niches. There were thirteen in all, some with, some without a pediment. The statues in the gabled niches were of members of the imperial family, those in the plain niches of members of Herodes's family. On top of the wall

The Walls and Gates of the Altis

The altis was cut off from the outside world. It formed a *temenos,* or sacred precinct. Everything connected with the cult—the temples, altars, treasuries and votive offerings, the 'olive beautiful for its crowns' and the pillar of Oenomaus—stood within this grove, which was two hundred metres long and one hundred and seventy-five metres wide.

Originally the altis was probably enclosed by a fence or a hedge. (Legend has it that the enclosure was made by Hercules.) But in the middle of the fourth century a low wall of Poros stones was built, presumably with gaps to serve as entrances. We have already noted that the eastern boundary of the altis, *i.e.,* the wall bordering the stadium, was formed by the rear wall of the porch behind the echo colonnade. In the north the boundary was probably marked by the retaining wall which supported the terrace of treasuries at the foot of the Hill of Cronus. It is possible, however, that the hill also formed part of the sacred grove for there appears to have been no wall between the exedra and the prytaneum.[74]

During Nero's reign, i.e., between AD 54 and 68, the altis was extended by two metres in the west and twenty in the south. Four entrance gates were made in the two new walls which were then built and a triumphal arch was erected especially for the emperor. After the emperor's death the arch was demolished.

The festival procession moved from the hearth of Hestia in the prytaneum along the outside of the western wall of the altis, which it entered by the south-western gate. It then proceeded to the great altar of Zeus after skirting the southern and eastern walls of his temple.

7. The Buildings Outside the Altis

Without exception all secular buildings and installations stood outside the altis. This is why the removal of the stadium and hippodrome from the sacred grove was such a revolutionary step, for it signalled the secularisation of the ancient ritual games: the gods had their abode within the temenos, from which all secular institutions were banished. These included the theokoleon, i.e., the priests' residence, the Leonidaeum or Greek guesthouse, the Roman guesthouses and the buleuterion or council house.

The Theokoleon

The three Olympic priests, who were all members of noble Elean families, were required to offer up the sacrifices in the altis. To this end they each lived in Olympia for one month at a time. Eventually —probably in the middle of the fourth century BC— they were given a special residence of their own, namely the theokoleon. This was a square building consisting of eight rooms grouped round an inner courtyard containing a draw-well. The building was twice extended and in its final form was nineteen by nineteen metres. The Greeks added three rooms to the east wing, and this was later completely

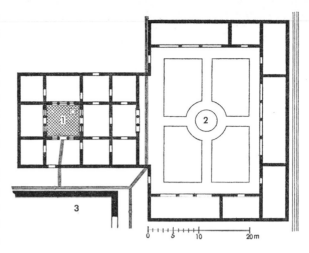

Fig. 32: Ground plan of the theokoleon after it had been extended by the Greeks. The figures refer to: 1 The courtyard, 2 The gardens and 3 The outer wall of Phidias's workshop.

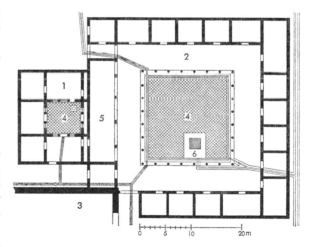

Fig. 33: Ground plan of the theokoleon after it had been converted by the Romans. The figures refer to: 1 The old Greek building, 2 The new buildings added by the Romans, 3 The outer wall of Phidias's workshop, 4 Courtyards, 5 A hall and 6 An altar.

127

remodelled by the Romans, who added a courtyard lined with rooms in the form of a peristyle.

The Leonidaeum

Between 330 and 320 BC Leonidas of Naxos built a large guesthouse at his own expense, which was named after him. This building, the Leonidaeum, covered eighty by seventy-four metres and was constructed around an inner courtyard, which was laid out with gardens and fountains. It was almost a perfect square and it had both an inner and an outer peristyle. Apart from one large hall in the centre of the west wing the entire building was given over to small rooms suitable for guest accomodation. The base of the Leonidaeum was made of conglomerate stone while the walls were probably framework and brick. The main entrance was in the east.

Although this building was modernised during Hadrian's reign, *i.e.*, between AD 117 and 138, the basic structure remained unaltered. It is possible that these renovations were carried out prior to a visit by Hadrian himself. Certainly the Leonidaeum was used by important visitors to Olympia, including the Roman praetors.[75]

The Roman Guesthouses

Modern archaeologists have excavated two large residences immediately south of the Cladeus baths, which were built in the first and second centuries AD. Both of these houses could accomodate large numbers of guests and both had a central courtyard with gardens and a peristyle. The draw-wells in these courtyards were surrounded by mosaic pavements.

The Buleuterion or Council House

The buleuterion consisted of two elongated apsidal houses which were separated from one another by a square courtyard. The overall length of the southern building was 30.79 metres, that of the northern building 30.53 metres. Both were approximately fourteen metres wide. The sides of the courtyard measured 14.24 metres. The terracotta tiles on the southern building date it to *c.* 600 BC; its northern counterpart was built a little later. The apsidal form of these houses, which was pre-Hellenic, suggests that, like the temple of Hera, they were built by the pre- and early Hellenic tribes when they regained control of the Olympic sanctuary from their Elean overlords during the 'Pisatan restoration' (668–572 BC). In fact, this appears to be the only feasible explanation, for it is hardly likely that the Eleans would have chosen to build in a style which was so intimately associated with their Pisatan rivals. In the buleuterion the Olympic council, which was the body ultimately responsible for the administration of the games, held its meetings and heard any appeals lodged by the competitors against the judges' decisions.

Each of the apsidal buildings had its entrance in the east. The architrave was supported by three pillars set out at regular intervals across the entrance while the ridge-piece and roof timbers rested on a row of pillars running down the centre of the building. Above the apex the roof sloped away. This hemispherical end section, *i.e.*, the actual apse, was partitioned off from the main chamber and divided into two separate rooms by a wall which formed an extension to the central pillars. Access to these rooms, which probably housed the Olympic archives, was by separate doors which led off from the main chamber.

Pausanias says that the statue of Zeus Horkios, the god of oaths, was kept in the buleuterion. It is to be assumed that this statue stood in the square inner courtyard and that it was there that the athletes foregathered—accompanied by their fathers, brothers and trainers—to swear over the entrails of a boar that they would not cheat at the Olympic games. In ancient Greece all oaths to the gods had to be given in the open, from which it would follow that the courtyard must also have been an open structure. The pedestal which was discovered in the centre of this part of the site presumably formed the base for the statue of Zeus Horkios. An Ionic colonnade was erected across the face of this three-part installation

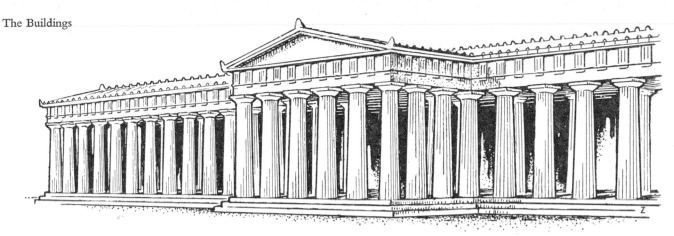

Fig. 34: Southern colonnade (reconstruction).

in Hellenistic times (probably in the fourth century BC when the south-eastern, southern and echo colonnades were built).[76] Under the emperors a further courtyard was laid out in front of this colonnade; this was enclosed by Doric pillars.

The Southern Colonnade

In the fourth century BC a monumental double colonnade eighty metres long and eleven metres deep was erected south of the buleuterion overlooking the Alpheus. The rear, which was in line with the altis, was closed. The outer row of pillars was Doric and the inner row Corinthian. In the centre of the colonnade was a portico seven metres deep and fourteen metres wide with a pediment above its six main pillars. This portico relieved the uniformity of the colonnade and gave the whole installation a pleasing appearance. In its shade the visitor to Olympia could promenade or stand and watch the teaming life of the encampment in the valley of the Alpheus. Foreign delegations, processions and important visitors were probably welcomed here, for the road from Elis to Olympia ended in front of the southern colonnade.

Chapter Eleven

The Statues in the Sacred Grove

1. Lost Groups

For the peoples of Greece the sacred grove was a hall of fame in which not only Olympic victors but also important public figures and events were commemorated. Many of the statues were erected singly; others, particularly those inspired by tragic or glorious events in the life of the Greek city states, were in groups. Pausanias is our authority in respect of these groups, which have unfortunately been lost without trace. He relates one touching incident involving thirty-five boys, members of a choir, who had been lost at sea with their choirmaster and flautist when returning to Messina from Rhegium, where they had taken part in a national festival. The Messinans were so affected by this tragedy that they sent statues of all thirty-five boys, and of the two men, to Olympia.[1] Another group of boys' statues was dedicated by the people of Akragas in Sicily but in happier circumstances. This bronze group, in which the boys were depicted with their right arms outstretched as if in prayer, was a votive gift to Zeus for the victory granted to the people of Akragas over the Libyans and Phoenicians of Motye. The group was erected on the wall of the altis.[2]

The subject matter of these group compositions was not restricted to historical events. Myth and legend were depicted as well. There was one group representing the Greek heroes drawing lots to see who should face Hector at Troy[3] and another depicting Hercules fighting a mounted Amazon for her girdle.[4] There were even groups in which the gods appeared. Micythus of Rhegium dedicated a whole series of statues representing various gods. He

did so 'in fulfilment of a vow for the recovery of his son who was wasting away in a consumption'.[5]

2. Lost Statues of Gods

Within the precincts of the sacred grove magnificent dwellings were built for the gods, in which their presence was invoked by ritual statues. The first was the temple of Hera, then the temple of Zeus and finally the temple of Meter. But even in the grounds of the altis, in the shade of the wild olives and plane trees, statues were dedicated to the gods; wherever the pilgrim turned he was sure to encounter deity. With very few exceptions these statues were erected either in honour of Zeus or of his son Hercules, the great hero who had prepared the ground for him.

Pausanias has four chapters describing the statues of Zeus[6] in the altis, which, he tells us, he enumerates in full.[7] He mentions twenty-four in all. All were in bronze and some were of considerable historical importance. One of these votive statues commemorated the great battle of Plataea, in which a combined Greek army defeated the Persians under Mardonius.[8] Another statue—which stood twenty-seven feet high—was dedicated by the Eleans themselves to celebrate the recovery of the Olympic sanctuary from the Arcadians, who had taken it by force.[9] The Arcadians and their allies controlled the sanctuary from 365–363 BC. The 104th Olympiad, which took place in 364 BC and was organised by the Pisatans with Arcadian backing, was subsequently declared an 'Anolympiad' by the Eleans. Their votive

63.   Head of Athene in terracotta (late archaic).

64a. Nike of Paeonius.
Standing figure of the
winged goddess of victory
dedicated to Zeus by the
Messenians after their
victory over the Spartans.

64b. Nike of Paeonius
(reconstruction).

65. Nike of Paeonius
(detail).

offering of course was not in any way connected with the war. It was intended as a token of gratitude for the reconciliation with their enemies and the restoration of the sanctuary to Elis. Hence the inscription on its base: 'From the Eleans for concord'.[10]

But Hellenic discord was also commemorated in the altis. The Spartans, for example, erected a twelve-foot statue to Zeus out of gratitude for their victory over the Helots of Messenia in the third Messenian war (464–456 BC).[11] In point of fact no statues should ever have been raised in this sanctuary to celebrate the victory of one Greek state over another.[11a] Monuments which reminded men of wars between Hellenic states were contrary to the whole concept of pan-Hellenism. But they were built, for each victory was a gift of Zeus, a sign of his great power and an expression of his will, which the victor was required to accept with reverence and his vanquished foe to endure as a divine dispensation. For as long as the Greeks were seized by a sense of religious awe such monuments were not likely to engender the sort of bitterness which they were bound to provoke in a secularised society. They also served to remind the Hellenes of the vicissitudes of fortune, for this Spartan statue to Olympian Zeus was soon joined in the sacred grove by the jubilant nike erected by the Messenians after they had gained their liberty early in the Peloponnesian War.

For later generations things were not quite the same. The Hellene of the second century BC, when he saw the statue of Zeus erected by the Roman general Mummius from the spoils taken from the Greeks,[12] would have been reminded of the utter defeat of the Achaean League; of the fearful sack of Corinth; of the cargoes of works of art shipped to Rome; of the forcible incorporation of the conquered states into the province of Macedonia, and of the absolute supremacy which Rome established over the whole Greek world in 145 BC. This monument to final victory was presumably erected in 146 BC when Mummius was pro-consul in Greece. Thus Rome entered the altis in Olympia as a victor.[13] This same Mummius donated the twenty-one gilded shields which were hung in the metopes of the temple of Zeus. A second statue of Zeus, which bore no inscription, was also attributed to him.[14] Lucius Mummius, a plebeian who received the surname of Achaecus after his military victories, then put up two equestrian statues of himself. Later, under either Augustus or Nero, he was again depicted on horseback—this time in the company of the ten legates responsible for the administration of Achaea—in a group composition which stood on a base ten metres long opposite the temple of Zeus.[15] Clearly the object of Mummius's votive offerings had been to impress on the Greeks that Zeus approved of the Roman victory and to persuade them to submit. This they had done, for the equestrian group was dedicated by the Eleans themselves in honour of the brutal conqueror who had destroyed Greek liberty. The full extent of their self-abasement was revealed by the inscription: 'For his proficiency and for the benevolence which he has shown to the people of Elis and the other Greeks'.[16]

If we add to the twenty-four statues of Zeus listed by Pausanias the seventeen zanes[17] which were paid for out of the money obtained from fines and placed beneath the terrace of treasuries we have a grand total of forty-one statues in all. Like all the other large bronze works which were displayed in the open these were eventually stolen, either for sale as works of art or for scrap. But a number of small bronze statuettes, including some of Zeus, have been preserved.[18] The limestone, marble and clay statues were also liable to be stolen, although clearly the bronze pieces ran a greater risk. Fortunately the figures on the pediments and metopes of the temple of Zeus escaped destruction.

3. Extant Statues of Gods

The Early Archaic Hera

Pausanias refers to a statue in the temple of Hera which depicted the goddess seated on a throne with a bearded and helmeted Zeus standing at her side. 'The workmanship', he says, 'is very simple.'[19] Undoubtedly this group was a representation of the Magna Mater and her lover. The base of the statue,

131

66. The Hermes of Praxiteles (compare plate 67).

which has been preserved, is made of conglomerate stone. Now the archaeologists have discovered, at a spot situated between the temple of Hera and the palaestra, an archaic female head dating from the beginning of the sixth century, which is also made of conglomerate stone. Earlier scholars believed it came from the statue of Hera described by Pausanias but recently this view has been challenged on the grounds that the head was not executed in the round and must therefore be a fragment from a high relief, perhaps part of the pediment on the temple of Hera.[20] This argument does not necessarily invalidate the older view, for the throne on which the Magna Mater was seated certainly had a support for the back and consequently the figure itself might well have been carved in high relief with the back of the throne serving as the ground. The other objection raised to this theory is that, according to Pausanias, the votive statue was made of gold and ivory and the head of conglomerate stone found in the altis must therefore have come from some other work. But was Pausanias referring to the statue of Hera when he made this remark? After describing this statue he went on to mention fifteen others before stating: 'What I have enumerated are in ivory and gold.'[20a] Whether the statue of Hera was meant to be included in this list seems questionable, for, if it really was made from ivory and gold, it is strange that Pausanias described it as 'haplus', a word which originally implied that an object 'consisted of the one material' and which by extension came to mean 'simple' or 'plain'. Neither the original nor the extended meaning of this word would suggest the use of ivory and gold. Conglomerate stone on the other hand would certainly be a 'simple' material. And then of course we do not know whether the pediments on the temple of Hera were decorated with statues or not.

From the evidence of this head it is quite clear that the cult of Hera in Olympia was of long standing. Quite apart from the fact that the style is undoubtedly archaic, there is also a remnant of a decorative device on the head immediately beneath the high crown which must originally have been a sprig of blossom.[21] (The suggestion that it formed part of a veil is untenable.) This decoration places Hera fairly and squarely in the sphere of the vegetation and fertility cults, to which the pre-Dorian tribes still paid allegiance after the Eleans under King Iphitus had severed the bonds between the cult of Zeus and these ancient rites.

The Late Archaic Athene

A few widely scattered fragments of painted terracotta have been found which once formed part of a group in which Athene[22] was depicted assisting her protégé Hercules in a duel. His protagonist was probably either the three-legged Geryones or Cycnus, son of Ares. There was certainly at least one other person in this group but unfortunately the number of fragments recovered is insufficient for a definitive interpretation. The group was placed on a socle with Athene standing on the left behind Hercules, whose opponent stood facing him on the right of the group; Hercules had seized the crest of his adversary's helmet with his left hand. Another helmeted warrior—perhaps Ares the god of war—also faced Hercules. This statue was made in Corinth c. 490 BC and then sent to Olympia as a votive offering. The figures were three-quarters life-size and the socle was 1.25 to 1.50 metres long. Firing a group such as this in one piece was a considerable technical achievement. And yet it was allowed to stand in the altis for only a few decades. By 450 BC it had been broken up and buried in the southern embankment of the early classical stadium, where the head of the goddess was discovered in 1940. This head of Athene is one of the most precious finds made in the stadium and, although it has been damaged in a few places, by and large it is fairly well preserved. The goddess wore the light Attic helmet which fitted close to the skull and protected the nape of the neck, leaving the face uncovered. A high slender crest surmounted the helmet, describing a wide arc above the head, to which it was attached by an iron bolt. The rim of the headpiece is missing but just above where it would have come a diadem of flowers adorns the goddess's head, which is inclined slightly to the left. Athene's left arm is bent and the forearm inserted in the loops of a circular shield about sixty centimetres in diameter. On her breast the goddess wore the protective aegis with the Medusa's head.

This terracotta figure was covered with a thin layer of lime to provide a key for the paint. The crest of the helmet, the diadem, the aegis, the Medusa's head and the shield were all painted. The shield was actually painted on both sides, which would indicate that the figure was executed in the round. The dark red of the shield, which has since turned purple, and the pale tint of the arm must have created a lively and artistic colour composition. But only very few pieces of Athene's equipment have been found and the colouring of the statue is best judged by the head, which is comparatively unblemished. The face and the rims of the ears were a chalky white and the curls, the lips and perhaps the inner part of the iris were painted red, while the pupils, the rims of the lids and the eyebrows, the ears, the helmet and the great mass of hair which protruded from beneath it were all painted black. This colour combination produced an extremely natural effect and gave a 'sense of direct physical contact'. The set, rather austere features of this late archaic goddess are already informed by a specifically spiritual quality.

Zeus and Ganymede

The most valuable find made by the modern archaeologists is a 1.10-metre-high terracotta group of Zeus and Ganymede. The fragments from which this group was reassembled were discovered when the stadium embankment was excavated.[23]

According to ancient legend Ganymede was a beautiful Trojan youth with whom Zeus fell in love and who was brought to Mount Olympus by an eagle to become the god's cup-bearer. In this group, however, Zeus is seen abducting the boy himself. With a pilgrim's staff in his left hand and the boy held firmly under his right arm the god strides quickly along, so quickly that his cloak appears to be slipping from his left shoulder. In the mysterious smile which hovers about his face triumph mingles with joy. The youth is perfectly content. As Zeus steps out with a powerful, buoyant step, Ganymede's naked body nestles against the god's hip and thigh. In his left hand the youth holds a cockerel, a present from his divine lover.

These two figures are welded together into a perfect organic whole. Perhaps the most delightful thing about the group is the way in which Zeus's movement is transferred to Ganymede, so that, although intrinsically passive, the youth nonetheless participates in the rhythm of the walking god. The group is also greatly enhanced by the fact that the colours have not faded: the bare skin is a pale yellow, Zeus's coat and hairband are a reddish brown, his hair, beard, eyes, eyebrows and eyelashes are all blue-black. When the head of Ganymede was discovered in 1942 the artist's view of the relationship between youth and manhood was revealed: 'The inner tensions within the group reach their incomparable climax in the contrast between the man's head, which radiates an aura of divine fulfilment, and the gentle face of the youth, which is like a bud about to blossom forth.'[24] This figure of Zeus was created c. 470 BC, just before the Zeus statues on the eastern pediment.[25] In neither of these groups had the god separated out from the world of mythological thought. This step was taken by Phidias; it was he who first conceived and created Zeus as the father of all things and guiding spirit of the universe.

The Zeus-Ganymede group was not a votive offering. It stood on the apex of the pediment of a building which has not yet been identified. Although we cannot say with absolute certainty that this acroterium was made for a competition it seems likely that it was, for the temple authorities often invited sculptors to compete with one another.[26] Paeonius, the Thracian sculptor who carved the winged victory which the Messenians dedicated to Zeus, won such a competition. An inscription on the base of his statue recalls his success.[27]

Paeonius's Nike or Winged Victory

All victories were a gift from Zeus. By association, therefore, Zeus himself was represented in this statue

133

of the winged victory. Phidias had already placed a nike in the great god's right hand before Paeonius created his work, which was dug out of the rubble in the altis in 1875. The statue was dedicated by the Messenians after they and their Athenian allies had broken the power of their Spartan overlords during the Peloponnesian War, which was to shatter the whole of the Greek cosmos. But when the Messenians donated their statue following the peace of Nicias in 421 BC—or possibly following their victory on the island of Sphacteria in 425 BC—the disintegration of Hellenic culture had not yet become apparent to those concerned. For the moment the Messenians were jubilant. Ever since 740 BC these Doricised Achaeans had been in thrall to the Dorian Spartans and now, after more than three hundred years of serfdom, they had regained their freedom. In their shortlived joy they created this effigy of the jubilant goddess who had swooped down from Mount Olympus to bring them victory.

And from the top of the tapering triangular pillar, which was some thirty metres east of the temple of Zeus and about nine metres high, Paeonius's winged victory also appeared to be swooping down to the ground below. This impression of movement was strengthened still further by the eagle which was attached to the pillar beneath her feet and itself appeared to be in full flight. Both the nike and the eagle symbolised the supreme power of the deity.

The impression created by the statue was also enhanced by strong colours: 'The black curls were set off by a golden fillet; the close-fitting drapery was red; the rhythm of the statue was greatly strengthened by the interplay of the bare limbs, which were the colour of marble, and those covered by the red drapery. This variegated figure stood out in high relief from the uniform ground of the billowing cloak.'[28] Paeonius was the first to solve the problem of flight in sculpture and he did so superbly.

The Hermes of Praxiteles

The Hermes of Praxiteles is a late classical work dating from the fourth century BC. The statue was

found in the temple of Hera on May 8, 1877 at the precise spot where Pausanias had seen it. The right arm and foot were missing and both legs had been broken off below the knee. Subsequently the foot was found and in all other respects the statue is in an excellent state of preservation. Ernst Curtius, the leader of the nineteenth-century expedition, regarded the Hermes as the 'crowning glory of the finds made in Olympia'.[29]

Praxiteles created the god in the image of man and accorded him those attributes which man finds most desirable and which in him are usually so shortlived: beauty, symmetry, youth and strength. But he expressed these properties in their highest form so that here too the superhuman and transcendental quality of the godhead was still present. In his statue the divine quintessence, by which man is elevated and inspired, is vested in the figure of Hermes, the messenger of the Olympian gods. On Hermes's left arm, which he has supported on the trunk of a tree and covered with his cloak, sits the infant Dionysus, whom the god had been ordered to carry to the nymphs of Nysa after Zeus had killed his mortal mother Semele by appearing before her as the god of lightning. Praxiteles represents Hermes resting on his journey. In his right hand (which is missing) Hermes originally held a bunch of grapes, dangling them just out of the infant's reach, toying with him as he tried to seize them. But the god is not really watching the child; he is lost in thought and appears almost unconcerned. This god lacks the severity and commanding majesty of the gods portrayed in earlier statues. The power is there but it has not been brought into action. This is the 'deus ludens', the god at play. For in the eyes of toiling humanity the life led by the gods was all play—a happy, carefree existence free from want and exempt from death. Man, who was driven by the fates, was a mere plaything in their hands. The gods toyed with him just as Hermes toyed with the infant Dionysus and whether he achieved fulfilment or succumbed to despair was no more important to them than whether a child was given a grape or denied it. And yet Praxiteles's Hermes was not entirely carefree. A slight shadow hovers around the eyes, the gaze

67. The Hermes of
Praxiteles.

68a. Eastern pediment of the temple of Zeus depicting the chariot-race between Pelops and Oenomaus.

68b. Central group from the western pediment of the temple of Zeus: Apollo and the Lapithae fighting the Centaurs.

69. 'Seer' from the eastern pediment of the temple of Zeus.

is introverted and there is a suggestion of sadness in the way he looks at the world without really seeing it, as if he knew deep within himself that in the final analysis the Olympian gods were inadequate. It is this sadness, this pain, which stamps the Hermes as a late classical work.

The discovery of this statue was important, not only for the history of the ancient cult but for the history of Greek art as well. The white marble revealed clear traces of colour: the sandals had once been red, the hair partly red and partly gilded, and the drapery had also been painted, although it is no longer possible to determine the original colour. Moreover, it seems the god had been attired with articles of bronze, *e.g.,* herald's staff, hairband and sandal buckles, which would have provided a further source of colour. The idea that Greek marble statues were unpainted had to be revised following the discovery of this work.

4. The Statues on the Temple of Zeus

The Artists

The great temple built by Libon was intended as a dwelling for Olympian Zeus. And so, before the god received his votive statue in the innermost sanctuary, his dwelling was decorated as splendidly as possible. Twenty-one brightly coloured statues of Parian marble were erected on each of the two pediments. These statues, which were one-and-a-half times life-size, have all been recovered, although many of them are defective and some are little more than fragments. The central point of each pediment was, of course, the section immediately beneath the apex, and the action in the friezes had to be arranged accordingly. Consequently the artist placed the god in the centre and the human beings on either side of him.

Pausanias attributes the frieze on the eastern pediment to Paeonius and that on the western pediment to Alcamenes, whom he describes as a contemporary of Phidias. But for chronological reasons alone

neither Paeonius nor Alcamenes could possibly have created these friezes. There are also stylistic objections in the case of Paeonius and above all there is the fact that in the inscription on the base of the Messenian nike he refers only to the acroterium as his work and makes no mention of the figures on the frieze.[30]

Modern scholars tend to assign both the friezes to the same artist: 'And so if we try to establish the authorship of the friezes by comparing the individual statues in purely formal terms all we find is a mass of contradictory evidence. But from this we would conclude that the artist concerned had mastered all the essential techniques practised in his day. ...The great master of Olympia stood quite alone. No artist either before or since is directly comparable.'[31]

It is widely held that the Hercules metopes on the outer walls of the pronaos and opisthodomos were created by another artist, whose name is also unknown. 'The artist who carved the metopes was a man with a sensitive and engaging temperament. ...His work is far removed both from the deadly serious scene depicted on the eastern pediment and from the ferocious battle enacted on the western pediment.'[32]

The figures from the pediments are now in the museum at Olympia. Together with the sculptures from the Parthenon they represent Greek plastic art at its greatest. But they are not as carefully executed as the Parthenon marbles and their proportions are often distorted, sometimes obviously so.[33] Originally of course, when the sculptures were still in position on the pediments, they could only be viewed from a distance. Consequently it was the overall impression which mattered and where necessary the individual figures were adapted accordingly. Unfortunately the descriptions of the pediments given by Pausanias, our only early authority, are partly faulty. This is clear from the heights of the various figures and from their relationship to one another. (The sequence adopted in the museum, where the sculptures are set out along the two principal walls of the building, has not gone unchallenged and a number of alternative sequences have been suggested.)

135

70. King Oenomaus.

The Frieze on the Eastern Pediment

The frieze on the eastern pediment depicts the scene immediately prior to the chariot-race between Pelops and Oenomaus. Pausanias describes this frieze as follows: 'And on the gable in bas-relief is the chariot race between Pelops and Oenomaus. . . . And in the middle of the gable is a statue of Zeus, and on the right hand of Zeus is Oenomaus with a helmet on his head, and beside him his wife Sterope, one of the daughters of Atlas. And Myrtilus, who was the charioteer of Oenomaus, is seated in front of the four horses. And next to him are two men whose names are not recorded, but they are doubtless Oenomaus's grooms. . . . And at the end of the gable is a personification of the river Cladeus, next to the Alpheus the most revered of all the rivers of Elis. And on the left of the statue of Zeus are Pelops and Hippodamia and the charioteer of Pelops and the horses and two men who are apparently Pelops's grooms. And where the gable tapers, there the Alpheus is personified.'[34]

The identity and arrangement of the figures has been long and hotly disputed. But by now there is a fairly wide consensus of opinion[35] in this respect and Pausanias's account has been corrected and reformulated. When he speaks of the 'left' and the 'right' of the frieze Pausanias is presumably referring to the viewer's left and right for then the two corner figures, 'Alpheus' and 'Cladeus', occupy the positions nearest to the rivers which they represent.[36]

In the centre of the pediment, towering above all the other figures, stands Zeus the protector of oaths with a thunderbolt in his left hand. On Zeus's left, i.e. on the northern side towards 'Cladeus', are King Oenomaus and his wife Sterope, on Zeus's right, i.e. on the southern side towards 'Alpheus', are Pelops and Hippodamia. Next comes Pelops's chariot and team of four with a groom kneeling in front of the team and a charioteer squatting behind the chariot and presumably holding the traces. Pelops's chariot is ready for the race. Oenomaus's is not, for he is to give his opponent a start. The figure squatting in front of his team is Queen Sterope's handmaiden and not the charioteer Myrtilus as stated by Pausanias. The semi-recumbent figure behind Oenomaus's chariot is neither a charioteer nor a groom but a seer, who stares anxiously into the distance because he senses Oenomaus's doom. Then, last of all, comes Myrtilus. On Pelops's side of the frieze the order of the seer and the charioteer is reversed. The two seers were probably meant to depict the progenitors of the families of the Iamidae and the Clytidae, who provided the priests for the Olympic sanctuary.

The artist has portrayed the scene immediately prior to the chariot-race. The figures are motionless. They stand or sit calmly in their places and watch as a sacrifice is offered up to the god. Pelops has a contemplative look; he has assumed a reverent attitude with his head slightly bowed. Hippodamia, the bride whom he hopes to win in the race, has also lowered her head and is supporting her chin in her left hand; she looks solemnly but calmly in front of her. On the other side of the god stands Oenomaus, self-assured and confident of victory, his head held high, his right hand planted imperiously on his hip, his left hand gripping the shaft of his

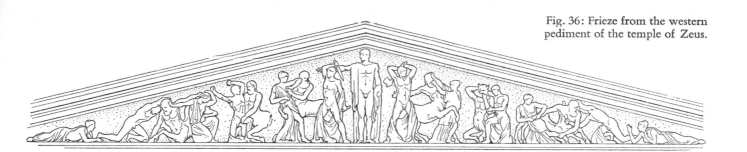

Fig. 36: Frieze from the western pediment of the temple of Zeus.

javelin, a picture of arrogant pride. His wife Sterope reveals a similar attitude of mind. Her self-satisfied demeanour is that of a proud and vain woman; she looks on with complete unconcern as if it were a foregone conclusion that the king, her husband, would win the race. This attitude was incomprehensible to the Greeks for it disregarded the absolute power of the god; they called it hubris. Only the seer seated behind Oenomaus's chariot is aware of the impending disaster. Although his features are perfectly controlled there is a look of horror in his eyes.

The frieze depicts the calm before the storm. In this solemn group the omnipotence of the god, who exalts the reverent and destroys the proud, holds invisible sway. Pelops will win the race because he reveres the god and so enjoys his protection. The 'treachery version', according to which Pelops bribed Myrtilus to wreck Oenomaus's chariot, could not possibly have been incorporated into this work, for here reverence defeats hubris, the fear of the god vanquishes human arrogance. Over and above this of course the frieze has a specifically Olympic significance in so far as it places the chariot race of the prehistoric heroes—i.e. the mythical contest between Pelops and Oenomaus from which the equestrian events were derived—under the aegis of Zeus, the lord of the altis. And since the chariot-race symbolised all other contests as well, the frieze actually placed the Olympic festival under his protection.

The two heroes and their followers are watching a preliminary sacrifice, and preliminary sacrifices were an integral part of the Olympic games. Zeus is represented as the protector of oaths, and oaths were sworn by all nations and individuals participating in the games. Two seers, Iamus and Clytius, are incorporated into the group, for Zeus also had an oracle in Olympia. And finally there are 'Alpheus' and 'Cladeus' who—like the rivers they personify—lie on either side of the course and so set the scene for the contest. Thus the symbolism of the frieze in the eastern pediment embraces every aspect of the sanctuary of Zeus in Olympia.

The Frieze on the Western Pediment

On the western pediment a Thessalian legend was depicted: the battle of the Centaurs and the Lapithae. Centaurus, the son of Ixion, mated with the mares of Magnesia, who then produced creatures which were half man and half horse. These were the Centaurs, the ferocious and dangerous neighbours of the Lapithae, who inhabited Thessaly in ancient times. When Pirithous, the king of the Lapithae, married Deidamia he invited King Theseus of Athens, with whom he had a friendly alliance, to attend his nuptials. He also extended invitations to the Centaur Eurytion, to whom he was related, and a number of his companions. During the celebrations the Centaurs suddenly ran amok; they seized the bride, the young girls and boys and tried to ravish them. This is the scene represented in the frieze on the western pediment. But the artist adds to the legend for he brings Apollo onto the field of battle. The god appears in regal splendour and commands the Lapithae to avenge the outrage perpetrated by the Centaurs.

137

As we look at this frieze, Pirithous, the bride-groom, is shown on the god's right hand side, drawing his sword to attack Eurytion, a bearded, hideous monster who has seized the struggling bride Deidamia with his left hand and is pawing at her breast with his right. On the god's other side Theseus has raised his axe and is about to strike the head of another Centaur who has seized a Lapithae girl. To the right of this pair a strongly built Lapithae youth is grappling successfully with his opponent; in a similar duel being enacted on the opposite side of the frieze it is the Centaur who is getting the upper hand. In the third and final group on either side, which extends almost to the edge of the frieze, a wrestling youth is depicted dragging a Centaur away from his victim and towards the corner of the pediment, where the handmaidens—two in each case—have sought refuge.[37]

This frieze is in complete contrast to its companion piece on the eastern pediment. The first composition is static, the second dynamic. The battle is a scene of unparalleled ferocity: in it the Centaurs are depicted with their faces distorted by lust, Theseus and the Lapithae appear as extremely noble but extremely powerful figures while the women retain an air of quiet dignity, uttering no sound despite their desperate situation. But it is the god Apollo, the central figure of the frieze, who portrays this combination of nobility and strength in its highest form. His slightly protruding lips express indignation, his rigid stance indicates a mental attitude which will brook no contradiction and his face is a study in majesty. With arm outstretched, pointing to the rapacious monster to his right as if commanding Pirithous to kill it and free Deidamia, he gives symbolic force to the whole scene: the cosmos imposes order on chaos, the law of the gods prevails over the violence of uncontrolled nature. By association the scene also depicts the victory of the 'civilised' Greeks over the 'barbarous' Persians, for the memory of the defeat imposed on Xerxes's armies was still fresh when this frieze was carved. In the noble figure of Apollo the artist created an ideal image, which his fellow Greeks recognised and accepted as exemplary and binding.

138

In this frieze, too, certain aspects of the symbolism were specifically Olympic: the breach of the peace caused by the Centaurs at Pirithous's nuptials was reminiscent of breaches of the sacred truce; the expulsion of the Centaurs from the wedding feast for their riotous behaviour was an indication that similar behaviour on the part of barbarians was not to be tolerated at the Olympic games, and that the festival should therefore remain an all-Greek occasion; finally there is the obvious implication that, unlike the Centaurs who attacked women and boys, the contestants at Olympia must compete with their equals and must abide by the rules laid down by the judges. In this western frieze the artist proceeded by negation. He depicted the kind of contest which must be banned from Olympia. But he also issued a warning, namely that those who behaved like the Centaurs and broke the sacred truce or cheated at the games would feel the god's wrath.

The Olympic Apollo

The preceding interpretation of the scene on the western frieze is based largely on Pausanias's description. But there is one major difference, for Pausanias makes no reference to Apollo. In his account Pirithous is the majestic figure in the centre while the swordsman who is about to deliver Deidamia from the grip of the Centaur is Caeneus: 'The carvings on the [rear] gable...are...by Alcamenes... On this gable is a representation of the fight between the Lapithae and the Centaurs at the marriage of Pirithous. Pirithous is in the centre and on one side of him is Eurytion trying to carry off Pirithous's wife and Caeneus coming to the rescue, and on the other side Theseus laying about among the Centaurs with his battle-axe: and one Centaur is carrying off a maiden, another a blooming boy.'[38] Thus far the factual description. But Pausanias then goes on to say: 'Alcamenes has engraved this story, I imagine, because he learned from Homer[39] that Pirithous was the son of Zeus and knew that Theseus was fourth in descent from Pelops.'[40] This account has been rejected by most Olympia scholars. But

71. Head of the Olympian Apollo.

74. Lapith maiden in the grip of a Centaur (western pediment of the temple of Zeus).

75. Hercules bringing Athene the Stymphalides (Stymphalides metope from the temple of Zeus).

76. Hercules carrying the vault of heaven (detail of the
Atlas metope from the temple of Zeus).

77. Hercules carrying the vault of heaven for Atlas, who
gives him the golden apples of the Hesperides (Atlas
metope from the temple of Zeus).

Pausanias is our only contemporary authority and his testimony should not be discarded without very weighty reasons. What then are the pros and cons of the matter?[41]

As a son of Zeus Pirithous was a hero, *i.e.* a man endowed with superhuman qualities, but a man for all that and consequently mortal. Hero-worship was still widely disseminated for it better satisfied the religious longings of the ordinary Greek than the formal ritual of the Olympian cult, which had been adopted as the national religion. Like the Christian saints the heroes were intermediaries between man and god. Consequently it would not have been incongruous if a hero had been depicted as the central figure on this pediment, especially if the hero in question were a son of Zeus. The pediment above the entrance to a Greek temple always pointed towards the east, *i.e.* towards the rising sun, which was sacred to the Olympian gods since they were gods of light. The statue of Zeus erected in the altis by the Greeks after the battle of Plataea also faced the rising sun,[42] as did Zeus Horkios, to whom the athletes swore the Olympic oath and who punished all perjurers.[43] But the west was the land of the setting sun. Consequently it was sacred to the dead, be they heroes or ordinary men. The entrance to the funeral mounds of the Greek heroes was always in the west. Moreover, all funeral rites and ceremonies were performed in the evening because of the obvious association between the setting sun and the ebbing away of life. The record of Hercules's labours presented on the metopes in the temple of Zeus begins on the outer wall of the opisthodomos in the west and finishes on the corresponding wall of the pronaos in the east. Why not the other way round? Surely because Hercules, who was born a mortal man, earned immortality by his great labours and was thus allowed to progress from the western to the eastern end of the temple, *i.e.* from the mortal to the immortal sphere. By this interpretation the western pediment of the temple of Zeus would seem the ideal place for a great statue of a hero. Moreover, if the central figure on this frieze really was Pirithous, the god in the east would have been thematically juxtaposed with the hero in the west. Almighty Zeus was able to see into the very depths of the human heart; he knew whether a man was fundamentally reverent or fundamentally arrogant. Thus the subject matter of the eastern frieze was human nature itself, man's *being* as seen by the omniscient god, which is why the composition was static. In the western frieze on the other hand men were shown in action: these men, the Lapithae, represented the power of good and their opponents, the Centaurs, the power of evil. In ancient times of course the heroes had fought mighty opponents and destroyed fearful monsters in order to create a national home for the Greeks, and Pirithous and Theseus had both contributed to the emergence of this ordered cosmos. But the world which the heroes had created was still threatened by the destructive power of chaos. Hence this ornamental group in which the Greeks were reminded of the outrage committed by the Centaurs at Pirithous's nuptials and of the need to defend their culture against the incursions of the barbarian hordes.

But this battle of the Centaurs also symbolised the struggle which went on in men's hearts between order and disorder, between the sense of harmony inspired in them by the god and the chaotic eruptions of their own instinctual urges. The implication of the frieze is clear: if a man fights the good fight he will acquire nobility of soul, which will stamp him in the same mould as the heroes who defeated the Centaurs. And so a definite thematic link is established between these two seemingly so different friezes. In both, man is exhorted to emulate the superhuman forces of good and to eschew evil.

A further probable link between the two groups is provided by the figure of the bride. Pelops is to marry Hippodamia, Pirithous has just married Deidamia. But in the older versions of the story of Pirithous's nuptials his bride is also called Hippodamia[44] and, since Hippodamia was revered as a heroine in Olympia, this similarity of name may well have prompted the artist to chose the Thessalian legend as the subject of his second frieze. Finally it is argued that Pausanias could not possibly have mistaken the identity of a god and that, for this reason alone, his account must be correct.[45]

139

78. Hercules cleaning the Augean stables with Athene at his side (Augean metope from the temple of Zeus).

These are the arguments in favour of the central figure being Pirithous. Yet the majority of archaeologists have always regarded this figure as Apollo. The principal reason is undoubtedly the overall impression created by the sculpture. The look of majesty and clarity on the face is so marked, and the gesture of the right hand so imperious, that one automatically thinks of a god. But is there any objective evidence to support this view?

In the first place there is a significant parallel with the temple of Apollo in Delphi. In the old temple in Delphi, which was erected towards the end of the sixth century BC, Apollo was represented with a team of four on the eastern pediment while Zeus appeared on the western pediment, also with a team of four. (When the new temple was built in the the fourth century BC, Zeus was replaced by Dionysus and the Thyades.[46]) Now the temple of Zeus in Olympia was built in the first half of the fifth century BC and in view of the close and harmonious relations which existed between Olympia and Delphi it is not unreasonable to argue that the figure of Apollo would have been placed in the centre of the western pediment to repay the courtesy extended by the Pythians when they honoured Zeus in their temple.

But Apollo was also important in his own right at Olympia. The Delphic oracles were recognised there and one of the two summer months in which the great festival of Zeus was celebrated was named after Apollo (the other being named after Hera in her capacity as a virgin). Apollo also possessed three altars of his own in Olympia and shared a fourth with Hermes. At one of these altars the god was honoured as Apollo Pythius, *i.e.* as Delphian Apollo, and at the other as Apollo Termius, *i.e.* as law-loving Apollo.[47] This second epithet must have been associated with the sacred truce and consequently it should not surprise us to find Apollo represented as the protector of the sacred truce[48] in this frieze depicting the battle between the Centaurs and the Lapithae, especially since he was the divine ancestor of the Lapithae.[49]

The same battle is depicted on the frieze of the temple of Apollo Epicurius (the preserver) at Bas-sae in Arcadia. There Apollo, the lord of the temple, is shown hurrying up with his sister Artemis in her chariot, which is drawn by a team of stags, to protect his people.[50] There too he 'punishes the wild creatures for their hubris and defends his followers against them'.[51]

Apollo was also the divine father of the Olympian seer Iamus,[52] the progenitor of one of the two families of priests in Olympia, who may well have advocated his inclusion in the Olympic frieze.[53] And we must consider the great difference in size between the central figure and the remaining figures in the group. It would be quite uncharacteristic for the hero Pirithous to measure 3.10 metres and his fellow hero Theseus only 2.60 metres. A discrepancy of this order would, however, be perfectly acceptable between a god and a hero.[54]

In the final analysis, 'even if we disregard his kinship with the Lapithae, Apollo is...a far more likely choice as the central figure than Pirithous, who would hardly have just stood there striking a splendid attitude while his companion dealt with the drunken Centaur who was attempting to ravish his young bride'.[55] The frieze also makes better sense in symbolic terms if we cast Apollo as the central character. We then have a situation in which man is exhorted to emulate the victorious heroes by striving to act with conviction in everything he does and to observe the laws and customs of the land in order that he may enjoy the protection of Apollo, who defends the law and punishes every violation of the peace.

The Hercules Metopes

The entablatures above the pillars flanking the entrances to the opisthodomos and pronaos in the temple of Zeus each had six metopes, on which the labours of Hercules were depicted. The first six were at the rear of the temple, the last six at the front. Pausanias lists them all with the single exception of the Cerberus metope.[56] His account—plus the evidence of the archaeologists, who discovered the metopes lying on the ground in the order in which they had fallen when the temple was destroyed—enables us to reconstruct the following sequence:

1. Hercules killing the Nemean lion with his club.
2. Hercules and Iolaus killing the Lernaean hydra.
3. Hercules presenting the dead stymphalides to Athene.
4. Hercules capturing the Cretan bull.
5. Hercules capturing the Arcadian hind.
6. Hercules seizing the girdle of Hippolyta, the queen of the Amazons.
7. Hercules bringing the boar of Erymanthus to Eurystheus.
8. Hercules capturing one of the man-eating mares of the Thracian Diomedes.
9. Hercules killing the giant Geryones.
10. Hercules supporting the vault of heaven for Atlas and receiving the golden apples of the Hesperides from him.
11. Hercules carrying Cerberus from Hades to the upper world.
12. Hercules cleaning the Augean stables.

The cleaning of the Augean stables was probably chosen as the subject of the final metope because of its associations with Elis and Olympia.

Fragments of some reliefs were excavated by the French expedition which visited the Peloponnese as early as 1829 and were sent to the Louvre. The German archaeologists subsequently recovered fragments of all the remaining metopes and also further fragments belonging to the French finds. Four of the metopes—the stymphalides (3), the Cretan bull (4), the golden apples of the Hesperides (10) and the Augean stables (12)—have been sufficiently well reconstructed to enable us to follow the main course of the action. As far as the other eight are concerned the fragments are so scant and in many cases so badly damaged that adequate reconstruction has proved impossible.

These metopes were an integral part of the entablature, which interlocked with the triglyphs in a tongue-and-groove structure. Consequently they must have been placed in position when the temple was built, which means that the reliefs were executed by 456 BC at the latest. They are all 1.60 metres high and so the figures are nearly life size. Originally the metopes were painted and from the traces of paint found on the fragments it would seem that blue and red were the dominant colours—either red figures on a blue ground or blue figures on a red ground. Thus the reddish-brown Cretan bull appeared on a blue panel and the blue hydra on a red panel. In the metope in which Hercules kills the Nemean lion the hero's hair, lips and eyes were all painted red. In fact paint was used to create his hair in every one of the metopes, the only sculptural indication given being a slight ridge at the hair line. Meanwhile of course the paint has worn away, which is why Hercules looks almost bald in the reconstructed reliefs.[57] The realisation that these marble statues were once painted was one of the most important facts to emerge from the nineteenth-century excavations.

The Stymphalides Metope

The stymphalides, the man-eating birds which Hercules slaughtered at Eurystheus's command, are missing from this metope. But presumably Hercules held them in his right hand, which he extends towards the goddess as he stands looking at her, an expression of deep reverence on his features. Athene, portrayed as a graceful and dignified young woman dressed in a full length gown, is seated on a rock. Prior to the hero's arrival she had evidently been looking in the other direction for we see her turning towards him, her gaze fixed on his right hand, i.e. on the stymphalides. The fact that the hero is standing and the goddess seated places the two figures in a firm hierarchical relationship. Athene is undoubtedly the patron goddess and Hercules her protégé. But the gap which divides them is bridged by the goddess's movement towards the hero and by the complete openness of his attitude towards her. Thus, while remaining within their respective stations, they nonetheless establish a condition of absolute unity and concord. Even without her aegis, i.e. the scalloped goatskin which she wears above her gown, there could be no doubt about Athene's divinity: the infinite grace of her gesture and the splendour of her look proclaim her origin quite unequivocally.

One half of this metope—the part on which the goddess is portrayed—is in the Louvre; the other half is in Olympia.

The Atlas Metope

When Hercules was told to bring back the golden apples of the Hesperides he applied to the giant Atlas for help, since he was the only person able to procure them for him. But Atlas was supporting the vault of heaven at the 'pillars of Hercules' in the far west (*i.e.* the straits of Gibraltar) and so, while he set off in search of the golden apples, Hercules carried the heavens for him. The artist depicts the scene as Atlas reappears with the apples, three in each hand, on the right of the metope. Hercules faces him in the centre, bearing his great burden while Athene stands behind him to give moral support. Although the vault of heaven is not represented in the relief it is cleverly implied by association with the architectonic structure surmounting the panel Hercules stands with his forearms and the palms of his hands raised above his head and running parallel to and just below the upper edge of the metope. A folded cushion is wedged into the space between his shoulders and the backs of his forearms to ease the pressure. But by filling this space the cushion also creates an impression of solidity with the result that the hero's body bears a striking resemblance to an architectural pillar surmounted by a capital. Immediately above the metope, *i.e.* immediately above the 'Hercules capital', came the cornice which—together with the triglyphs—supported the roof of the colonnade. It must therefore have appeared to the viewer as if Hercules were supporting the roof and consequently that the roof had become the vault of heaven.[58]

But, although Hercules stands completely motionless in the centre of the panel, he is not isolated. His relationship to Atlas is indicated by the apples which the giant brings him and on which his gaze is fixed, while his relationship to Athene is expressed

in their common task. The artist also avoids the danger of rigidity by placing his three figures at different angles to the viewer. Thus Hercules appears in profile, Atlas is turned slightly to the front, while Athene stands with her body square to the observer but with her head in line with Hercules's. Hers is a significant posture, for by facing the viewer she seems to imply that she belongs to all mankind, while by turning her head towards Hercules she also seems to imply that, at this particular moment in the hero's life, when he is being tested to the limit, he is her principal object of concern. The contrast between Athene and Hercules is another significant feature. While he strains every muscle her body is quite relaxed. Nor is she actually supporting the vault of heaven, for her hand is lower than his. Evidently her power is so great that all she needs to do to help mortals is to make a gesture.

These three upright figures are welded into a structural whole by the line of their arms and hands. Atlas's forearms are parallel with Hercules's and his forearms are in line with Athene's raised and open hand. This is where the movement starts, this is where it finishes: the goddess's helping hand is the true centre of this deeply religious relief.

The Atlas metope is in Olympia.

The Augean Metope

Augeas was a legendary king of Elis who took Hercules into his service. This was the link between Hercules and Elean tradition which prompted the artist to choose the cleansing of the Augean stables as the subject of his twelfth and final metope. Pausanias tells the story of Augeas and Hercules: 'The oxen and goats of this Augeas were so numerous that most of the country could not be cultivated for their dung. Hercules therefore, whether for a part of Elis or for some other reward, was persuaded by him to clear the country of this dung. And he effected this by turning the river Menius on to it. But, because the work had been effected by ingenuity rather than toil, Augeas refused to give Hercules his reward.'[59] There are various versions of this legend, most

142

79. Head of Athene
on the Augean metope
(detail from plate 78).

of which restrict the scene of the action to the Augean stables. The river also varies. Frequently it is the Peneus or Alpheus which Hercules diverts. The creator of the Olympic metope is even more severe in his treatment of the theme for he depicts Hercules as a farmhand shifting dung with a broom.

Despite the humiliating nature of his task Athene still helps her protégé. Between them the two figures fill the whole metope. Athene stands erect while Hercules adopts a stance which runs diagonally across the panel as he leans forward into his work. His right leg, which is advanced and bent at the knee, takes the weight of his body, while his left leg is thrust out behind him, the toes seeking a foothold from which to apply pressure. The diagonal line of this rigid back leg is continued first by the body, which is turned almost square to the viewer, and then by the head, which is inclined forwards and so appears in profile. The hero grasps the top of his broom with both hands, exerting a downward pressure along the handle of the broom, which also runs diagonally across the panel but at right angles to the line of the body. These two diagonals, which describe the two lines of force, converge half way up the metope to the left of centre. The artist makes no attempt to portray the outcome of this effort in terms of work. That was not his object. He brings the forces into play, directs them to a common centre and leaves the rest to the viewer's imagination. In this way attention is focused on Hercules, this immensely powerful figure, who is shown at the moment of maximum endeavour. As in the Atlas metope Athene stands with her body square to the viewer but with her head turned in line with the hero's. Even in this stable she remains a noble figure. She stands immediately behind her protégé dressed in a full length pleated gown and with all the accoutrements of a goddess of war: the two rivet holes in the temple indicate where her bronze helmet—now missing—was once attached to her head, which is still surmounted by its curved crest; she supports her shield on the floor at her side, gripping it at the top with her left hand, while her right arm, which once held a lance, extends into the stable, running parallel with Hercules's forearms. Her right hand is

positioned between the two lines of force delineated by the hero's left leg and his broom and forms both the structural and the thematic centre of the metope.

Judging by the general style of the relief it seems probable that the goddess's lance ran parallel to the hero's broom: Athene would have pointed it at the huge mound of dung to exhort Hercules to greater efforts. Thus the spatial corollation between the broom and the lance would have established a spiritual corollation between the hero and the goddess, between the human and the superhuman spheres.

This metope now stands in the museum at Olympia. Apart from Hercules's torso it is almost complete. This large fragment was actually found by the French expedition in 1829 but has since been lost.[60]

The Bull Metope

The metope in which Hercules captures the Cretan bull is a particularly fine piece. Poseidon gave a magnificent bull to King Minos of Crete in order that he might sacrifice it to him. But the king was unable to part with this superb beast and so he slaughtered a bull from his own herd and offered it up to Poseidon instead. The god was not deceived and in order to punish Minos he made his own bull run amok. In its blind rage the animal wreaked fearful devastation on the island. Eurystheus then commanded Hercules to capture the bull, to tame it and bring it to Mycenae. The hero succeeded in catching and binding the beast, whereupon it became quite docile and swam from Crete to the Peloponnese, carrying Hercules on its back.

On this metope the artist portrays the moment of capture. The bull rears on its hind legs as Hercules tugs with his left hand on the loop which he has already passed round its front hooves, leaning backwards as he does so in order to take the beast's weight when it falls; he has also raised his right hand and is about to bring it down on the animal's head in order to stun it. Thus the basic composition of this relief consists of two contrasting diagonals. Hercules's body extends from the bottom right to the

143

80. Hercules capturing the wild bull of Crete
(bull metope from the temple of Zeus).

top left of the metope, the bull's body from the bottom left to the top right. But these centrifugal movements are balanced by the centripetal action of the two heads, which are both turned inwards against the line of the bodies. The goddess Athene is not portrayed on this metope. Presumably the artist felt that the hero's natural powers were adequate to the task in hand. The style is also unusual. Instead of placing the figures next to one another as in the other metopes in this series, the artist places them one on top of the other, carving the bull in low and Hercules in high relief. The result is a work of tremendous and concentrated power.

Hercules's torso and head and the rear part of the bull's torso are in the Louvre in Paris. The head of the bull and the lower section of stone with the marks of the bull's hind legs, which were found by the German excavators, are now in Olympia.

God and Man

In these metopes Hercules appears as an uncomplicated but very dignified man who demonstrates not only his strength but also his self-control, and who, although not over-demonstrative, is by no means devoid of feeling. His actions and his attitudes are always attuned to the task in hand. There is no hint of boastfulness in him for he knows that there are only very few tasks which he can accomplish alone. He constantly needs divine assistance and this is furnished by Athene. Whenever she is needed she is at his side, a fine and noble figure, outwardly composed and even reserved, but inwardly both animated and engaged. Her gentle restraint stands in marked contrast to the great exertions of her protégé.

The artist did not indulge in unnecessary detail. He strove to create a great structure capable of expressing the great idea prevalent in his day, namely that, however powerful a man might be, he could achieve nothing without the help of the gods. And so in his reliefs we encounter the goddess who loves mankind and the man who loves the godhead.

A few decades after the renaissance of Greek culture under Emperor Hadrian, Lucian suggested that perfect beauty lay in the union of an excellent mind with a shapely body.[61] He then went on to define the components of mental excellence as gentleness, philanthropy, high-mindedness, modesty and a trained intellect.[62] It is significant to note that neither devoutness of soul nor reverence for the gods figures in this second century inventory of human virtues.

The transition from the religious conception of man obtaining in the classical age to the *humanitas* advocated in neo-classical times was brought about by the greatest of all revolutions: the secularisation of the world. Homer's legacy was soon frittered away. But in these metopes the world of man was still guided by divine power and love. Man had not yet been cast out into the void; he still lived in the presence of the invisible god, to whom he cried out and who answered his cry.

For the early Greek the god and the 'good' could only appear in a shapely body and a shapely body could only house a noble soul. The whole object of the early Olympic athletes was to dedicate their bodies to the god in the contest.

Chapter Twelve

The Zeus of Phidias

1. One of the Seven Wonders of the World

When the pilgrim passed through the bronze gateway and entered the cella in the temple of Zeus he entered the dwelling of the god. This was his abode, the house where his statue was kept and where he himself was actually present. Pausanias describes the statue of Zeus: 'The image of the god is in gold and ivory, seated on a throne. And a crown is on his head imitating the foliage of the olive tree. In his right hand he holds a victory in ivory and gold …and in his left hand a sceptre adorned with all manner of precious metal, and the bird seated on the sceptre is an eagle. The robe and sandals of the god are also of gold: and on his robe are imitations of animals and also of lilies. And the throne is richly adorned with gold and precious stones and with ebony and ivory. Upon it there are painted figures and wrought images'.[1]

This votive statue was of gigantic proportions. Its base occupied the whole width of the nave and one third of its length, an area of 6.50 by 10 metres, while the figure itself reached very nearly to the ceiling of the temple, which was over 13 metres high. The back of the throne, which was freestanding, blotted out virtually the whole of the rear wall of the cella. Although the temple of Zeus was the largest temple in the Peloponnese this statue was so colossal as to be out of all proportion if considered as a purely realistic work. Strabo draws attention to this; he points out that, if the god had stood up he would have lifted the roof off the temple.[2]

There were two floors to the cella. By mounting a spiral staircase the visitor gained access to the gallery, from which he was able to view the head of this pan-Hellenic Zeus from close up. The engraver who cut the die for the Elean coins on which the great god was represented no doubt made his sketches of the head from this gallery. Several of these coins, which were issued in AD 133 under the philhellenic Emperor Hadrian, have been preserved so that we actually possess miniatures of the lost masterpiece.[3]

This chryselephantine statue was the work of the Athenian sculptor Phidias, the son of Charmides. It was 'the most beautiful and most sacred effigy in the whole world', having been produced 'at enormous expense and with an artistry that was quite consummate'.[4] Phidias's work made such an impact and was so utterly inscrutable that it passed for one of the seven wonders of the world[5] and attracted pilgrims from the entire ancient world. The stoic philosopher, Epictetus, bears this out in one of his discourses: 'You all go to Olympia', he tells his

Fig. 37: Elean copper coins from Hadrian's time (AD 133) representing the Zeus of Phidias.

listeners, 'to see the famous work by Phidias and each one of you would think it a tragedy to die without having seen it.'[6]

It seems that after Phidias's statue had been lauded by his fellow men the sculptor also claimed to have received the approbation of Olympian Zeus. Pausanias reports the legend, according to which the god was supposed to have testified to the art of Phidias. 'For they say when the statue was finished, Phidias prayed him to signify if the work was to his mind, and immediately Zeus struck with lightning that part of the pavement, where in our day stands a brazen urn with a lid.'[7]

2. The Technical Achievement

The task which faced Phidias when he started work in Olympia after completing the chryselephantine statue of Athene for the Parthenon in 438 BC was a daunting one. A large section of the floor of the cella had to be relaid and enormous quantities of ivory, gold and other precious metals procured before he could even begin on the statue. The amount of ivory involved was so great that Philo of Byzantium was prompted to remark that the reason why nature had produced elephants was that Phidias might use their tusks for his effigy of Zeus.[8]

The cost of these materials and the wages for the large numbers of workmen and artists whom Phidias engaged for the preparatory work on his statue placed a heavy financial burden on the Eleans. Phidias's own fee was also considerable. But all this was a matter of concern only to the people of Elis. What interested the majority of Greeks[9] was the way in which Phidias proposed to solve the artistic problems. The principal difficulty was posed by the head and the upper part of the body, which had to appear natural both in close up, *i.e.* as seen from the gallery, and also from a distance. At first Phidias worked on the statue in his workshop, where he was better able to test the reactions of his public. It is possible therefore that there may have been a grain of truth in Lucian's anecdote, according to which Phidias was supposed to have hidden behind the door of his

workshop when the public was first allowed in to see his statue in order to hear their comments and, above all, their criticisms. When they had gone he shut himself in again and carried out modifications in accordance with the general consensus. Commenting on this anecdote Lucian made the interesting point that the artist evidently placed greater faith in the group than in the individual, even when that individual was a Phidias.[10]

The problems of perspective raised by this work must have been enormous. In his book on the Zeus

Fig. 38: The Zeus of Phidias (reconstructed by Adler).

of Phidias, Liegle relates an anecdote current in the days of antiquity from which it would seem that Phidias was a past master in this particular sphere. According to this story Phidias once entered a competition with Alcamenes, and the populace, who had been asked to judge their two works, was so enraged by the apparent lack of harmony in Phidias's statue that it was on the point of stoning the sculptor. But when the two statues were placed in position on their lofty pedestals the people saw their error, proclaimed Phidias the winner and simply laughed at Alcamenes.[11] Although this anecdote is almost certainly spurious in terms of historical truth, it was a genuine parable, which afforded the naive visitor to Olympia some idea of Phidias's genius.

The statue of Zeus needed careful maintenance and was cleaned with oil, 'for oil is good for the statue at Olympia as it prevents the ivory from being harmed by the dampness of the grove'.[12] But in the later days of the sanctuary the god appears to have been neglected. Dion Chrysostom described his effigy in the words with which Odysseus greeted his old father, speaking of its ill-kempt appearance, its burden of sad age, its general squalor and wretched garments.[13] When Dion passed this comment the Zeus of Phidias had already been reigning in Olympia for more than 500 years.

3. The Workshop of Phidias

The deep excavations carried out in 1954–5, 1956, 1957 and 1958[14] led to the discovery of the workshop of Phidias, which is mentioned by Pausanias.[15]

The first excavation took place on the site of the elongated building south of the Byzantine church (building C, 56.12 metres long by 6.50 metres wide). It was established that this building, which was used as a shed, had been erected after Phidias's time and that previously the site had been occupied by a number of work installations. Although virtually no trace was discovered of the actual installations their existence was proved beyond all possible doubt by the archaeological finds made on the site. Next the church (building A) was investigated and it was found that this had been the workshop of Phidias. Scholars had long been aware of the striking resemblance between this Byzantine church with its central nave and twin aisles and the cella of the temple of Zeus: its basic measurements were the same (32.18 metres long by 14.50 metres wide) and it had the same alignment. Moreover, the solid foundations were suggestive of high walls and this also made it seem probable that it was in this room that Phidias created his colossal statue which, according to the testimony of the poet Callimachus, stood 12.22 metres high.[16] It was not until the fifth century AD that the building was converted into a church; the old eastern entrance was then abandoned and an apse added at that end while a new entrance was made in the west. All this was discovered by the modern archaeologists, who confirmed what had long been suspected, namely that this building had originally been the workshop of Phidias. The only light in the church came from the entrance and this would certainly have been inadequate for Phidias's purposes. In fact, additional lighting was provided by small windows in the two principal walls of the chamber. Six of these have been identified and it seems probable that there were actually six groups of windows in all, three on each side. In front of the windows there was a stone scaffolding consisting of three separate platforms supported by pillars. This of course gave access to the statue, which could however be dismantled since its wooden core was made in sections. In the middle of the workshop there were two forges and an enormous bronze cauldron, which was set in a shaft and used as a water container. It was filled from a well which had been sunk inside the workshop and whose sides were faced with Poros stones. A number of bone gravers and handles were found in the workshop together with a quantity of bronze tools for fine work, including a small chasing hammer. The workshop was built some time after 440 BC and is unlikely to have been completed before 435 BC. Consequently this is the earliest date at which Phidias could have started work on his statue.[17] No pieces of clay or other waste material were found inside the workshop, which must have been thoroughly cleaned out at some

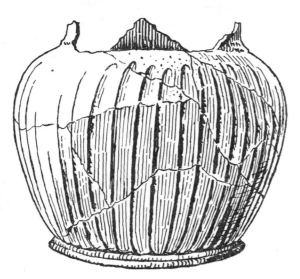

Fig. 39: Mug belonging to Phidias (view of side and base). Clay vessel with fluted surface and coated with black varnish discovered in a building outside the altis which had been converted into a Byzantine church. As a result of the deep excavations carried out in 1954–55,

1956 and 1957 it was established that originally this was in fact Phidias's workshop. The base of the mug bears the inscription: 'I am [the property] of Phidias'. This find proves that the sculptor came to Olympia himself and worked there on his statue of Zeus.

point. The refuse removed on that occasion presumably was piled on a heap to the south-east of the workshop and subsequently covered over when building G was erected there. The excavation of this building—an earlier version of building C—yielded large quantities of many different kinds of waste: slivers and flakes of bone and ebony, pieces of obsidian, some of which had been processed, traces of pale blue and red ochre, bits of plaster and even a lump of rock crystal. Deposits from the forges were also found—bronze dross and clippings and pieces of iron and lead—together with large quantities of scrap metal, e.g., pieces from bronze cauldrons, the legs of tripods, old shields and helmets, which had been collected for melting down. There were remnants of clay moulds for bronze castings, numerous fragments of glasswork, including palm leaves and three-pronged stars, and an assortment of glass ornaments, which had evidently been rejected after casting. The archaeologists also

unearthed many of the clay moulds for these ornaments, which may conceivably have been used to decorate the drapery on the ebony throne. One of the moulds still contained a star.

There was one find which caused a real sensation: a group of over sixty drapery moulds in various sizes. These had all been fashioned from soft, lightly baked clay and the largest of them had been reinforced with iron bars. It was quite evident from the variation in size that they had been used to create the drapery for one large and at least one small statue, while the fact that they were made from clay meant that the metal employed for the castings must have been very soft and flexible. Only gold, Kunze suggests, would have been flexible enough, especially when heated.[18] Certainly, all the indications are that the drapery for the statue of Zeus and for the life-size statue of the winged victory was made in these moulds.[19] The same site yielded large numbers of ceramic objects including pieces from the terracotta roof of the workshop as well as functional objects, *e.g.*, lamps, plates, kitchen utensils (cauldrons, pans and bread plates), bowls, beakers, small purse-shaped mugs, salt cellars, fluted mugs, dishes, mixing vessels, amphorae, water pitchers, lekythoi (single-handled jugs), lids of jars, crucibles and measuring beakers.[20] The major part of this functional pottery has been dated to *c.* 420 BC.

The most important find was a simple clay mug with a fluted surface which had been coated with black varnish and bore the inscription: 'I am [the property] of Phidias.' Nearly all the mouth of the mug is missing; so too is the handle. The height as it now stands is 7.7 centimetres while the diameter of both the base and the neck is 6.3 centimetres. The fluting dates the mug to the period between 440 and 430 BC.[21] This find proves beyond all doubt that Phidias actually stayed in Olympia, which means that the old controversy as to whether he created his Zeus before or after his Athene has now been solved. Phidias did not die in prison in Athens but fled to Elis, where he probably spent a period of ten years creating his great masterpiece.[22]

4. Phidias's Vision of the God

Phidias appears to have rejected the traditional image of Zeus handed down from Homeric times. According to Dion Chrysostom,[23] he refused to depict the supreme deity as a Greek national hero and commander-in-chief of the armed forces. Zeus the thunderer, it seems, was not for him. On the contrary, Chrysostom says, Phidias's Zeus was a god of peace and love; he was the father of all mankind. To some extent the words which Chrysostom places in Phidias's mouth in his 'Olympic Oration' were dictated by the spirit of his own times, *i.e.*, the *pax romana* of the early empire. But this subjective response must have been prompted by objective factors for, otherwise, Chrysostom would hardly have chosen Phidias as his spokesman. Consequently we may assume that the conception of the deity attributed to Phidias in this oration is substantially true. Amongst other things Chrysostom has him say: '…like the ruler of this peaceful Hellas that is no longer rent by civil strife our Zeus is peace-loving and gentle in all his ways. After taking counsel with my own artistic genius and with the wise and noble community of the Eleans I tried to depict him…as a gentle and exalted being with an untroubled and serene countenance. ….And now tell me whether my statue does not do justice to the god's many epithets. Of all the gods Zeus alone is called father and king, he alone [is] the protector of towns, the god of kinship, of friendship and communities, the god of suppliants and refuge and hospitality, of trade and fertility. He is called king because of his power and glory, father because he is gentle and solicitous, the protector of towns because he maintains the law and the common weal, the god of kinship because gods and men are of the one stock, the god of friendship and communities because he joins all men together and wishes them to be friends and not enemies … the god of suppliants because he listens graciously to all requests, the god of refuge [and hospitality] because men should receive guests and treat no one as a stranger, the god of trade and fertility because he dispenses the fruits [of the earth] and is the source of wealth and riches.'[24]

This vision of the supreme deity, this deeper and purer conception of the godhead, then had to be expressed in sculpture: 'The great, imposing figure is meant to portray the king and his supremacy, the air of gentleness and friendliness the father and his loving care, the exalted and serious countenance the protector of towns and the legislator, while the similarity between this and the human form is meant to symbolise the kinship between men and gods; finally, the god of friendship, of suppliants, of hospitality, of refuge and all such properties is expressed by the gentleness and fidelity which are a prominent feature of the statue, while the god of trade and fertility is depicted by the simplicity and the touch of magnanimity which informs the whole composition; the overall impression is one of love, the noblest of all conditions and the source of all good. It is this which I have tried to portray…'[25]

The Greeks, of course, anthropomorphised their gods. This was in the Homeric tradition, which

Phidias followed in all formal respects.[26] The only question is whether his vision of Zeus as the loving father and one true god was not also derived from Homer. According to popular belief it was. Dion Chrysostom says that Phidias was supposed to have found the inspiration for his statue in the passage in the *Iliad* in which Zeus promises Thetis that he will help her son Achilles: 'Zeus, as he finished, bowed his sable brows. The ambrosial locks rolled forward from the immortal head of the king, and high Olympus shook.'[27]

Certainly Homer's Zeus was an extremely human figure. When Thetis approached him to make her petition she 'put her left arm round his knees [and] raised her right hand to touch his chin.'[28] But there was another side to him, for he was also an implacable nature god, who was quite capable of destroying a whole army. Consequently, it is difficult to accept the view that Phidias drew his inspiration from Homer, for it would seem that the sculptor consciously dissociated himself from the poet's conception of the godhead. He followed him in structural but not in spiritual matters. Thus, although the Zeus of Phidias was a monumental figure and as such resembled the mighty Zeus of the *Iliad* who dwelt on Mount Olympus, he was also a spiritual being, the creator of all life and the organising principle at work in the universe.

5. The Execution of the Statue

Phidias's votive statue of Zeus was over twelve metres high. Such colossal proportions were something quite new in this genre and something which Libon, the architect of the temple of Zeus, had certainly not expected. But Phidias wanted to represent Zeus as the lord of the universe and the great father of mankind and in order to do this he had to use superhuman proportions. In actual fact, it was the head which needed to be so large, for it was in the facial expression that the artist could best express the idea of the supreme godhead. This, of course, called for a correspondingly large body[29] and also determined the posture, for with a seated figure attention is automatically focused on the head.[30] The Elean coins which were issued in AD 133 give a fairly clear impression of this head, which is still extremely noble even in miniature.[31]

Phidias was also an innovator in his choice of materials. He had already used gold and ivory for his statue of Athene at the Parthenon and he did so again in Olympia. Nothing was too good for the god. Man bowed to his will and offered his greatest treasures to him. But Phidias was the first sculptor to fashion votive statues from gold and ivory. Before his day all such effigies had been made from limestone, marble or bronze. This then was a genuine innovation. In the statue of Zeus all the naked parts of the god's body, *i.e.*, the waist, chest, arms and head, were made of ivory. The fine, smooth texture of this material created an impression in which complete naturalism was combined with the idealism appropriate to a god.[32] Gold, of course, had been associated with the deity since time immemorial. But even in his use of this material Phidias was an innovator. In the *Iliad* Zeus is described as having blue-black hair. Phidias gave him golden hair. He also replaced the thunderbolt in the god's right hand by a gold and ivory statue of the winged victory. And so, by the new uses to which he put this traditional material, Phidias showed that he had moved away from the Homeric conception of Zeus as an anthropomorphic nature god.[33]

In the final analysis, however, his reasons for choosing gold and ivory were probably of an artistic order. If his statue of the god was to possess spiritual force it had to be light and buoyant. Consequently, neither stone nor bronze could be used, for in a work of such dimensions they would have appeared cold and lifeless. Gold and ivory would have had quite a different effect. The reflected light from these surfaces would have counteracted the sense of dead weight which would otherwise have been produced by a statue of such proportions. In fact, mass would have been transformed into light, as was only fitting for this god of light, who was the guiding spirit of the universe.

Prior to Phidias no sculptor had represented Zeus wearing an olive wreath. Although this was, of course, a particularly appropriate emblem for the god of Olympia it was far more than a gesture to local tradition. We have already seen that Phidias depicted Zeus both as the guiding spirit of the universe and as the father of mankind. By virtue of this wreath he also indicated the possibility of communion between the supreme god and mortal man. Pliny says that the victors at Olympia received their wreaths at the feet of the god.[34] The crowning ceremony was, in fact, treated as a sacrament, in which men communed with the deity.[35] Later generations then extended the range of this mystic union; they came to regard it as a manifestation of divine grace, in which all members of the cult might participate. In the first century AD Apollonius of Tyana, the prophet and miracle worker who once taught in the temple of Zeus at Olympia, addressed the god in the following words: 'Greetings, good Zeus. For your goodness is so great that you even share yourself with men.'[36]

6. Public Reaction

The really impressive thing about the Zeus of Phidias was not its great size but its great dignity.[37] This we know from the reactions of contemporary observers. Polybius, for example, says that the statue made an enormous impression on Aemilius Paulus, the Roman general who visited Greece in 167 BC after having defeated the Macedonians at Pydna in the previous year. Paulus appears to have been quite overcome by Phidias's great work, which surpassed all his expectations.[38] Commenting on this account Livy said that, when Paulus encountered Zeus face to face, he must have felt strangely moved for he commanded that a larger sacrifice than usual be prepared for the god; it was almost as if he himself were about to make an offering at the Capitol in Rome.[39]

Cicero also tried to feel his way into the artist's soul by a process of retrospective empathy. He followed the Platonic line, arguing that, in creating his statues of Zeus and Athene, Phidias must first have conceived some perfect form in his own mind, which he then attempted to express in sculpture.[40] The basic principle of this system of thought is well-known: no human creation can ever compare with the god–given vision which prompted it. And yet Phidias's Zeus seems to have come so near to this vision that it was widely thought to have made its own specific contribution to received religion. This belief was recorded by Quintilian, the Spanish-born rhetor, who was active in Rome in the first century AD.[41]

Epictetus, the Stoic philosopher who lived from AD 60 to 140, regarded the Zeus of Phidias as the absolute embodiment of truth: 'The Zeus at Olympia does not frown at you, he looks you straight in the eye, as if to say: "I cannot take back what I have said, and besides it is true."'[42]

Because this statue reflected the deity so perfectly it provided ancient man with a profound religious experience. And it was because he had 'seen the god' that Phidias was able to create this overpowering work. Without the vision he could never have done so:

> Either Zeus descended to you from heaven;
> Or you, great artist, ascended and saw the god.[43]

The gap which separated Phidias from his predecessors was truly enormous. His god was so great and so powerful that he 'would not suffer any strange gods' to share his splendour. Although the old Homeric gods continued to exist, they no longer existed in their own right; they had become symbols for the primeval power of the godhead which was concentrated in Zeus. In Phidias's great work Zeus appeared both as the father of the gods and as the father of men, whom he loved and to whom he brought greater understanding through knowledge and suffering. The Chorus in Aeschylus's *Agamemnon* describes this condition precisely:

> Now Zeus is lord; and he
> Who loyally acclaims his victory
> Shall by heart's instinct find the universal key:
> Zeus, whose will has marked for man
> The sole way where wisdom lies;
> Ordered one eternal plan:
> Man must suffer to be wise.[44]

Ever since Phidias Greek culture in Olympia had been moving towards monotheism. Dion Chrysostom of Prusa, who was a contemporary of Trajan and lived some 500 years after Phidias, marked the culmination of this long development. Because of his romantic attachment to ancient Hellas he made a passionate attempt in his 'Olympic Oration' to renew the cult of Zeus and transform it into a genuine monotheistic religion that would go beyond Phidias's aspirations. This attempt to bring about a religious reform was doomed to failure for, even if it had been possible to revive the moribund belief in Olympian Zeus, it could never have been disentangled from Homeric myth.

7. The Decline of Zeus-Worship

The first stage in the decline of Zeus-worship in Olympia seemed harmless enough in itself. All that happened was that people began to criticise the enormous size of Phidias's statue. Strabo had said that if his Zeus were to stand up he would raise the roof off the temple[45] while Caecilius, the Sicilian orator and rhetor who was a contemporary of Strabo, went so far as to speak of this 'defective colossus.'[46] Pausanias was aware of these criticisms and took their authors to task: 'I know that the size of the Olympian Zeus both in height and breadth has been stated, but I cannot bestow praise on the measurers, for their recorded measurement comes far short of what anyone would infer from looking at the statue.'[47] But the derisive comments of contemporary critics were not the only hazard to which Phidias's statue was exposed. Emperor Caligula gave orders for it to be transported to Rome in AD 40.[48] The Jewish historian Flavius Josephus[49] has described Caligula's despoliation of the Greek temples. The emperor seems to have acted on the premise that all things beautiful naturally belonged in the most beautiful of all towns, Rome. He decorated his palace and gardens and his country residences throughout Italy with art treasures stolen from the Greeks. But his attempt to acquire the Zeus of Phidias was eventually baulked by his governor, Memmius Reg-

ulus, who informed him that, in the opinion of the architects, the statue would break if it were moved from its site. Had it not been for Caligula's timely death this refusal to comply with his orders would almost certainly have cost Regulus his life.

The advice tendered by the architects was not the only inhibiting factor as far as Regulus was concerned. Initially he had fully intended to dismantle the statue and had had scaffolding erected in order that this might be done. But suddenly the god let out a raucous laugh, which so terrified the workmen that they fled from the shaking scaffold. This and other supernatural phenomena, Suetonius tells us, prompted Regulus to desist from his purpose.[50]

Caligula was of course quite godless. (He did not hesitate to remove the heads of statues of gods which he had stolen from Greece and replace them with carvings of his own head.) And yet his attempted despoliation of the temple of Zeus was not as baneful in its effect as the gradual decline of religious sentiment. Once men had lost their fear of the gods, their covetousness was bound to emerge and in the secularised world of latterday Greece there were those who dared to lay hands on the effigy of the god in order to plunder it. We learn from one of Lucian's dialogues, in which Zeus confesses his powerlessness to Poseidon, that his ritual statue in Olympia had been despoiled: 'Do you think that, if the situation had been under my control, I would have allowed the desecrators to have escaped from Pisa [Olympia], when they cut off two of my locks, each of which weighed six minae [2.620 kg]?'[51] This sacrilegious act was only one of many.

But the most destructive influence was exercised by the enlightened scoffers. It was they who really undermined Zeus-worhip. It is quite evident from Lucian's biting satires that in his day the cult of Zeus, which had once been the focal point of the games, had become a pure formality, a meaningless ritual. One of Lucian's attacks on the god for example, reads: 'Oh Zeus . . . where are your crackling lightning and your roaring thunder now? Where is your fearful, lightning flash? If we disregard the barrage of words, it all appears an empty farce, a poet's pipe dream. Your much vaunted, far-ranging and ever-ready weapon has—I know not how—lost its fire and grown cold and possesses not even a tiny spark of anger against evil-doers...nobody sacrifices to you now and nobody crowns you save perhaps an occasional victor at the Olympics; and even he does not consider his actions obligatory but is simply paying tribute to an ancient custom. In short, they will soon depose you, most noble god, and cast you in the role of Cronus.'[52]

The image of Zeus which Lucian set out to destroy was Homeric. That was how he saw the Zeus of Phidias, for he even transformed the sceptre, which the god held in his left hand, into a thunderbolt. It would seem that Lucian was quite incapable of recognising Phidias's purer conception of the godhead, such was the hold which the great Homeric god of thunder had obtained over the Greek mind.

153

Olympia's Downfall

Lucian's satirical attack on Zeus-worship reopened the wound which Greek society had sustained long before his day and which was ultimately to bring about its downfall. The enlightenment had grave repercussions on this ancient culture, for the secularisation which was its inevitable concomitant eroded the metaphysical basis of social life created by Homer. Although adverse developments in the political sphere had certainly contributed to the gradual demise of Olympia the really crucial factor in this development was the waning of religious belief. The heyday of the sanctuary came in the period between the Persian wars and the outbreak of the Peloponnesian War; then mind and spirit, knowledge and belief, were still fused in a perfect entity and the cult, the contests and the art of Olympia were completely interrelated and interdependent. This brief period of only fifty years was charged with such creative power that it engendered a 'sacred spring', in which the multifarious buds of Hellenic culture blossomed forth and transformed Greece into a flowering garden of humanity. In Olympia the simple, regional festival of Zeus developed into a splendid five-day festival of pan-Hellenic importance; Libon erected his Doric temple with its severe and highly symbolic statues and reliefs; Phidias created his noble vision of the god, and men vied with one another in contests which were celebrated by Pindar. But then, in 431 BC, came the fatal blight of civil strife: the Peloponnesian War shattered the Greek cosmos.

1. The Violation of the Sacred Truce

Olympia's decline began with the violation of the sacred truce and of the sanctity of the altis. The latter eventuality had been foreseen by Pericles at the very outset of the Peloponnesian War, for he had fully expected that the enemies of the Athenian League would try to seize the money and treasuries deposited in Olympia and Delphi in order to fit out their fleet.[1] The Olympic games of 420 BC had to be held under the protection of several thousand native and allied troops because Elis, after joining forces with Athens, Argos and Mantinea, had banned Sparta from this Olympiad on the flimsiest of pretexts and the whole festival gathering went in fear of Spartan intervention.[2]

On this occasion the sacred truce and the sanctuary were merely threatened. Later they were to be violated, for at the Olympiad of 364 BC the altis became the scene of bitter fighting. The Arcadians, aided by the Pisatans, had wrested control of the sanctuary from the Eleans shortly before and organised the forthcoming Olympiad on their own account. But, in the midst of the festival, the Eleans secretly armed and attacked the occupying forces, inflicting heavy losses and penetrating into the sacred grove itself before being forced to retire.[3]

During their period of supremacy the Arcadians had not hesitated to plunder the temples at Olympia in order to pay the army. This had provoked determined resistance from the Mantineans, who insisted that the temple treasures must be held sacred lest their descendants should be cursed for all time by a legacy of sacrilege.[4] The Mantineans carried their point before the allied assembly, whereupon it was decided to make peace with the Eleans and restore the sanctuary to them, this being the most equitable course and thus the most pleasing to the gods.[5]

Two factors emerge from these violations of the sacred truce. In the first place it is quite evident that

81a/b.   Elean coins representing the Zeus of Phidias.

82. In AD 267 the outer buildings of Olympia were destroyed to provide the materials for a defensive wall in order to protect the altis from the Heruli who had invaded Hellas. The plate shows the western tower of the fortification which was constructed from Doric and Ionian fragments of the Leonidaeum.

religion was on the wane and no longer afforded a point of contact for the peoples of Greece, and in the second place Elis was no longer neutral.

2. The End of Elean Neutrality

As the custodian of Olympia Elis had been regarded as a sacred territory and as such had received guarantees of non-aggression from all the other Greek states. In return she had sworn perpetual neutrality. She renounced her traditional status quite simply because it had become untenable following the decline of the religious authority on which it had been based. As a result Elis was embroiled in internal Greek politics from the Peloponnesian War onwards. The hostile attitude which she adopted towards Sparta at the Olympiad of 420 BC had its inevitable sequel when the Spartans emerged victorious from the civil war. In 402 BC they proceeded to humble Elis. Under the leadership of King Agis they subjugated the territory, taking large numbers of slaves and herds of cattle as booty and annexing various border territories.[6] But they did not take control of the sanctuary away from the Eleans for they considered the Pisatans, the only rival claimants, unfit to exercise this office.[7]

In 365 BC the Eleans fought their unsuccessful war against the Arcadians and Pisatans. On this occasion, as we have just seen, they were obliged to cede the sanctuary to the Pisatans but regained it when their enemies fell out amongst themselves. They then struck the Olympiad of 364 BC, which had been held under Pisatan control, from the official records.

Nor was Elis spared in the wars fought by Alexander's heirs. In 312 BC Telesphorus, one of Antigonus's generals, undertook a campaign against the Eleans on his own account, in which he occupied their capital city and plundered the sanctuary at Olympia. With the proceeds from the invasion—over five hundred talents of silver—he began to recruit mercenaries; but then his freebooting enterprise was brought to a sudden halt by Ptolomaeus, another of Antigonus's generals, who restored the Eleans to liberty and returned the treasures to the sanctuary.[8] Some hundred years later the Spartan leader Machanidas planned a similar campaign against the Eleans when they were preparing to celebrate the Olympiad of 208 BC but abandoned the project when news reached him that Philip V of Macedonia was marching to the defence of Elis.[9]

A few years earlier Philip had been less charitably disposed. Between 219 and 218 BC, in the course of his war against the Aetolians, he subdued the whole of Elis and took up residence for a while in Olympia, where he doubtless occupied the attractive guesthouse built by Leonidas of Naxos. The great hardships suffered by this wealthy and populous land as a consequence of Philip's campaign prompted the historian Polybius (c. 201 to c. 120 BC), to advise the Eleans to work for the restoration of their neutral status, which they had renounced in 365 BC at the outbreak of the Arcadian war.[10] But his advice went unheeded and conditions in Elis remained unchanged until the Romans incorporated the territory into their growing empire in 146 BC.

3. Roman Despotism

The Roman conquest of Greece was not synonymous with the *pax romana*. The hundred years which elapsed before this new dispensation was first introduced in 31 BC under Emperor Augustus were given over almost entirely to civil wars, which soon spread from Rome to her subjugated provinces and Greece became a theatre of war for the warring Roman factions. Not even the holy places were secure.

As far as Olympia was concerned Sulla's reign was the most harmful. We have already seen that he used the temple treasures at Olympia, Delphi and Epidaurus to finance his war against Mithridates, king of Pontus, although he subsequently indemnified all three sanctuaries by granting them control of one half of the territory of Thebes.[11] But this was not the worst of Sulla's outrages. In the year 80 BC he transferred the games to Rome, ostensibly to divert the Roman populace after their long years of tribulation but actually in order to celebrate his

155

victories over Mithridates and the Italian tribes.[12] The only contest held in Olympia on that occasion was the stade-race for boys.[13] Curtius argues that Sulla intended to transfer the Olympic games to Rome permanently in order to establish its pre-eminence as the capital of the Graeco-Roman world.[14] But, if such plans existed, they did not survive Sulla's death in 78 BC.

By comparison with such despotism Nero's intervention in the 211th Olympiad in AD 65 appears positively harmless. We have already seen[15] that Nero had this Olympiad deferred for two years so that it should coincide with his visit to Greece. He also required the Eleans to extend the range of the festival by including contests for singers, zither players and tragedians, an innovation entirely counter to the tradition of the Olympic games. Nor was Nero content with a team of four in the chariot-race. He had to have a team of ten, and when he was thrown from his chariot and unable to complete the course he nonetheless received the victor's crown. For their enforced deference the hellanodicae all received Roman citizenship and considerable sums of money.[16] In the following year, when the emperor committed suicide, the Eleans struck the 211th Olympiad from the records and so declared Nero's victories invalid. Pausanias says that this was the only Olympiad passed over by the people of Elis in their records.[17]

But, however objectionable Roman interference in the festival programme may have been for the Elean authorities, the attempts made by certain of the Roman rulers to strip the sanctuary of its art treasures were far worse. We have seen that Caligula tried to have the statue of Zeus shipped off to Rome.[18] Nero went even further. In order to wipe out all memory of the other victors in the sacred games he decreed that their statues should be toppled and then sunk in the cesspools outside the altis.[19] Whether this decree was acted upon and, if so, to what extent is something we shall never know. But we do know—from Pausanias[20]—that Nero had a number of statues removed from the altis and taken to Rome, namely the Odysseus from Onatas's Achaean group and various votive offerings donated by Micythus.

156

However, we must not overestimate Roman usurpation in Olympia. Sulla, Caligula and Nero were probably the only rulers to exploit their power in this way and by and large it would be true to say that the *pax romana* carried Olympia forward into a new period of greatness, which began under Augustus and reached its peak under the philhellenic Emperor Hadrian.

4. The Invasion of the Heruli

Since both the Greeks and the Romans had violated the Olympic sanctuary it is scarcely surprising to find that the barbarians, who knew nothing of Greek religion and culture or of its moral requirements, should have done likewise. The incursions carried out by the Germanic peoples far beyond their own borders in the course of the third century AD were perhaps the most devastating of the many disorders which contributed to the downfall of the principality and which even appeared to herald the dissolution of the Roman empire.

In AD 267 Greece was invaded by the Heruli, a tribe from the coast of the Sea of Azov in southern Russia, where they were close neighbours of the Goths. They set out with a fleet of five hundred ships, conquered Byzantium, fought their way through the Hellespont and eventually emerged into the Aegean, where they landed on the coasts of Asia Minor and Greece. Most of the towns which they sacked were seats of classical culture. They conquered Athens, occupied Corinth, Argos and Sparta, laid waste the territory of Achaea and also seem to have descended on Olympia. Eventually the Roman fleet dispersed these raiders and forced them to retreat overland.[21]

In AD 265 the written records listing the officiants at Olympia were suddenly broken off and, since there is no good reason why the Eleans should have voluntarily discontinued this traditional practice, there is probably some connection between this fact and the invasion, which came just two years later. This assumption seems all the more plausible if we consider that a defensive wall was built around the altis at about that time, for this would certainly

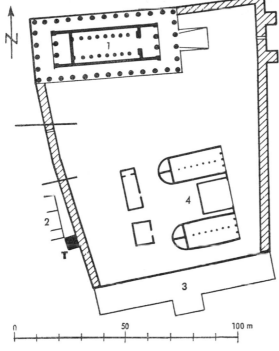

Fig. 40: Ground plan of the altis in late antiquity showing the defensive wall built to keep out the Heruli. The figures refer to: 1 The temple of Zeus, 2 The southern baths, 3 The southern colonnade, 4 The buleuterion. (T = Tower).

suggest that Olympia was endangered and may even have been attacked. Moreover, the wall was built in a great hurry. Apparently there was no time to wait for materials to be brought in from outside for the Eleans demolished the buildings on the outskirts of the sanctuary in order to make their enclosure around the inner grove, which contained the gold and ivory statue of Zeus.

These defence works, which were reinforced by towers at key points, were regarded by the nineteenth-century archaeologists as a 'Byzantine fortification' and dated to the second half of the fifth century AD, when Justinian ruled the eastern empire. Since the wall had quite evidently been built from stones and rubble of buildings belonging to the sanctuary, early archaeologists dismantled it in the hope that, by examining the individual stones, they might learn more about these buildings. But in 1954–55 Emil Kunze found that one of the towers, which had undoubtedly formed part of the original fortifications, had been overlooked by his nineteenth century predecessors. This tower, which is the only reminder of those grim days to have survived intact,[22] has now been dated with absolute certainty to the third century. Consequently, the original fortifications can only have been intended for defence against the Heruli.

5. The Secularisation of the Games

The physical decline of the sanctuary was accompanied by a weakening of religious feeling and the growing secularisation of the games. As long as the contests had had their *raison d'être* in the cult of Zeus they had constituted an act of homage. But no sooner were the liturgical contests transformed into sporting contests than voices were raised in protest against the undue importance attached to such physical exercises.

Xenophanes, the Greek philosopher from Colophon in Asia Minor, who lived from *c.* 570 to 480 BC, was one of the first to inveigh against the nationwide glorification of athletes. He stated quite bluntly that his wisdom was better than brute force and that the accomplishments of successful boxers and wrestlers and runners served no useful purpose whatsoever.[23] This criticism was to be repeated frequently and—when the sporting contests became the prerogative of professional athletes, who travelled from festival to festival, earning a handsome living in the process—it became more acrid and more derisive.[24]

The nobles and freemen participated less and less in the games, leaving the light and heavy athletic events to the members of the lowest class. We know, for example, that Alcibiades refused to measure his skill with the athletes in the stadium because many of them were men of low social standing with little or no education, while others were citizens of tiny states.[25] By and large the wealthy Greeks preferred to enter for the equestrian events, which required no active participation on their part. If the games had retained their religious significance the upper classes would scarcely have dissociated themselves in this way. As it was, however, the old ritual contests were superseded by sporting contests and the owner of a team of valuable horses was esteemed more highly than the charioteer who actually raced them. Eventually, in the late phase of the festival, all contestants had to undergo ten-months Olympic training, a requirement which could only really have been met by professional athletes. The Spartans were the first to dissociate themselves from the contests in the stadium (from 600 BC onwards) and the probable reason why they did so was in fact this growing trend towards professionalism, for at no time had Spartan wrestlers been allowed to engage trainers.[26]

With the increasing secularisation of the games the moral standards of the competitors declined. The first recorded case of bribery was in 388 BC at the 98th Olympiad and from then onwards the authorities were obliged to impose heavy fines to combat this new phenomenon.

Step by step the contests separated out from the cult until—in about 350 BC when the third stadium was built—the running track was removed from the altis and separated from it by the new western embankment. With this the 'unity of the world of mythical thought', the simple, spontaneous unity of cult and contest, devolved into two separate spheres: the sacred and the profane. The same process was repeated when the hippodrome was removed from the altis, although in this instance the effects were somewhat mitigated by the erection of a number of altars in the vicinity of the new starting gate, which were included in the monthly round of sacrifices.

Originally participation in the games had been restricted to free-born citizens of Greek descent and, consequently, to adherents of the Olympian faith. But, as this faith began to wane, other nationalities were also admitted. First came the Romans, who were invited to compete after Titus Quinctius Flamininus had proclaimed Greek liberty at the Isthmian games in 196 BC, and they were followed by the Egyptians, Lycians, Lydians and even the Phoenicians.[27] The last recorded victor was the Persian Varazdatos, a member of the royal family of the

Arsacidae and a citizen of Artaxata in Armenia. Varazdatos won the boxing at the 291st Olympiad in AD 385.[28]

6. The Waning of Religious Belief

The Greek enlightenment first questioned and then destroyed the validity of the divine myths. The city states, whose ritual observances were threatened by these attacks, tried to save their national gods by instituting proceedings against the apostles of rationalism on the grounds of 'godlessness'. Nonetheless, the new religious development, which first set in during the age of Pericles and in which the old Homeric conception of Zeus was gradually stripped of its polytheistic attributes, appeared distinctly promising. If this trend had been carried through to its logical conclusion Phidias's vision of the one, true and all-loving god would have become a reality. But, because of their particularist thinking, the city states were unable to abandon their belief in their individual gods and heroes. This, together with the great resilience of the Homeric tradition, was enough to frustrate the movements towards monotheism. Even in Olympia, where Phidias had provided such a powerful stimulus and which might well have become a stronghold of a new monotheistic cult, the movement ceased and disappeared eventually beneath a great welter of myths.

The deification of mortals also contributed to the decline in religious belief. The first Greek to be honoured as a god was the Spartan Lysander, the victor of the Peloponnesian War. He underwent his apotheosis in the temple of Hera on Samos. And then there was King Philip II of Macedonia, who erected a tholos in the altis following his victory over the Greek confederates at Chaeronea in 338 BC and placed chryselephantine statues of his own royal family in the cella. In classical Greece gold and ivory were normally reserved for statues of the gods, from which it follows that Philip was virtually intent on the deification of his dynasty.[29]

The Romans were motivated by the same spirit when they transformed the temple of the mother of the gods into a temple of the *Dea Roma* and *Divus Augustus*. Moreover, they referred to Augustus as 'the son of god and the saviour of the Hellenes' and built his statue larger than life in a blatant imitation of the Zeus of Phidias, such proportions also being the prerogative of the gods.[30] By using the Olympian cult as a means of extolling the power of the state the Romans weakened the cult still further. But religious belief reached its lowest ebb when Lucian began to scoff at Zeus-worship. The scorn which he lavished on the great god of the Olympian pantheon was blasphemous to a degree. But it was also grounded in truth: the sacrifice at the great earth altar of Zeus, which had once been the point of reference for the whole of the Greek world, had become a meaningless ritual, a mere adjunct, or *parergon* to use Lucian's own expression. The principal aspect of the Olympics was the festival of sport and even that was little better than a funfair.

7. The Banning of the Cult of Zeus and the Abolition of the Games

In AD 391 all pagan cults and, consequently, the cult of Zeus were banned by Emperor Theodosius I (379–395). It is widely held that this same emperor also abolished the Olympic festival, which had been mounted in honour of Zeus every four years ever since 776 BC, i.e., over a period of 1168 years. According to this tradition the last Olympiad held in ancient Greece was the 293rd, which was celebrated in AD 393. The Byzantine historian Georgius Cedrenus, who lived about AD 1100, presents this version in his *Historia Comparativa*.[31]

But there is another record, which is reported in two different versions of a scholium on Lucian[32] and which dates the abolition of the Olympic games to the reign of Theodosius II, the grandson of Theodosius I, who ruled the eastern empire from AD 408 to AD 450.

In one of these versions we are told that the festival was discontinued following the fire which destroyed the temple of Zeus. This probably dates the action

to AD 426 when Theodosius II ordered the destruction of all pagan temples in the eastern empire: it seems likely that the temple of Zeus was burnt down under the terms of his edict. If this were the case then the last Olympiad would presumably have been held in AD 425. This tradition is borne out by a coin, discovered in the stadium, bearing a likeness of the head of Honorius, (western emperor 395–423). Honorius was the brother of Arcadius, (eastern emperor 395–408). Phidias's statue, which was seen in Olympia by the sophist Themistius as late as 384,[33] had already been removed from its temple by 395, for at the time of Theodosius I's death in 395 it was in Constantinople in the palace of a certain Lausus.[34] Apparently the statue was brought there following the proclamation of the ban on pagan cults in 391. Consequently it escaped destruction when the temple of Zeus was burnt down. But this was only a reprieve, for in 462 Lausus's palace was destroyed in the fire which razed many of the great houses of Constantinople.[35] The Zeus of Phidias, one of the seven wonders of the world, disappeared in the flames together with many other statues.[36]

8. The Destruction of Olympia

With the banning of the pagan cults, the abolition of the Olympic games, the removal of Phidias's Zeus and the destruction of his temple the fate of the sanctuary on the Alpheus was sealed.

From 395 to 397 Alaric and his Visigoths exercised absolute control over the Peloponnese. Then, after an inconclusive battle with the west Roman army on the plateau of Pholoë to the north-east of Olympia, they withdrew to Epirus. A few decades later the Vandals under Gaiseric plundered the western coast of Greece. The old fortification works erected around the altis in the third century AD to defend the sanctuary from the Heruli were doubtless used again. Meanwhile the Greeks had become Christian and in Olympia mass was celebrated in the workshop of Phidias, which had been converted into a Byzantine basilica. This church was certainly far too large for the needs of the poor, primitive village community which had settled amidst the ruins of the sanctuary.

In 589 the Avars mounted an invasion, which is remembered to this day in the name of Navarino (from *ton Avarinen*), the Messenian port where they established a colony. Whether the small Byzantine settlement at Olympia survived this invasion we have no means of telling. The Slavs came in the wake of the Avars in the eighth century. In 782 they were defeated by Constantine Porphyrogenitus, who converted them to Christianity and persuaded them to establish settlements. It is not known whether Slavs actually settled in Olympia.

But, although Olympia was certainly not spared by the migrating tribes who penetrated into Greece, it suffered far more from the ravages of nature. In 522 and 551 two great earthquakes devastated the sanctuary and toppled the pillars of the temple of Zeus, the last surviving emblems of a proud past. The work of destruction was completed by the water. The Cladeus, whose wild course had long since had to be restrained by a dam, changed its direction as a result of the earthquakes and carried great quantities of alluvium into the sacred grove. Winter rains and cloudbursts broke up the earth on the slopes of the Hill of Cronus, sweeping it down into the valley, where it spread out over the altis and the stadium. Even the mighty Alpheus changed its course and over the years its waters washed away the major part of the hippodrome. In the end the sanctuary was completely submerged beneath a layer of alluvium, whose average depth was four metres.

Bibliography

Notes

List of Illustrations

Index

Bibliography

The abbreviation RE in the Bibliography and Notes stands for *Real-Encyclopädie der classischen Altertumswissenschaft.*

I Recent general bibliographies dealing with ancient Olympia and the Olympic games

Kerestényi, József, *Guide à la recherche scientifique sur la culture physique de l'antiquité,* Conseil Scientifique de l'Education Physique, Budapest 1966. Review of writings of 156 ancient authors on physical culture in antiquity; an extremely useful source book. In Hungarian and French.

Lázsló, István, *Olimpiai Bibliográfia,* Conseil Scientifique de l'Education Physique, Budapest 1964. Lists 752 works dealing with the ancient and the modern Olympic games.

Marouzeau–Ernst, *L'Année philologique: Bibliographie critique et analytique de l'antiquité gréco-latine,* Société d'édition 'Les Belles Lettres', Paris; published annually.

II Reports on excavations made under the auspices of the German Archaeological Institute

Adler, Friedrich and Curtius, Ernst (eds), *Olympia: Die Ergebnisse der von dem Deutschen Reich veranstalteten Ausgrabung,* Berlin 1890–97.

> 1. *Topographie und Geschichte,* by Adler, F., Curtius, E., Dörpfeld, W., Graef, P., Partsch, J. and Weil, R.
> 2. *Die Baudenkmäler,* by Adler, F., Borrmann, R., Dörpfeld, W., Graeber, F. and Graef, P.
> 3. *Die Bildwerke in Stein und Ton,* by Treu, G.
> 4. *Die Bronzen und die übrigen kleineren Funde,* by Furtwängler, A.
> 5. *Die Inschriften,* by Dittenberger, W. and Purgold, K.

Berichte über die Ausgrabungen in Olympia, Berlin 1937–67; *First Report,* Autumn 1936 and Spring 1937, by Wrede, O., von Gerkan, A., Hampe, R. and Jantzen, U.; Berlin n. d.
Second Report, Winter 1937–38, by Kunze, E. and Schleif, H.; Berlin n. d.
Third Report, Winter 1938–39, by Kunze, E. and Schleif, H., with contributions by Eilmann, R.; Berlin n. d.
Fourth Report, 1940 and 1941, by Kunze, E. and Schleif, H., with contributions by Eilmann, R. and Jantzen, U.; Berlin 1944.
Fifth Report, Winter 1941–42 and Autumn 1952, by Kunze, E., with contributions by Herrmann, H.-V. and Weber, H.: Berlin 1956.
Sixth Report, Winter 1953–54 and 1954–55, by Kunze, E., with contributions by Eckstein, F., Herrmann, H.-V., Mallwitz, A. and Walter, H.; Berlin 1958.
Seventh Report, Spring 1956–58, by Kunze, E., with contributions by Goette, E., Habicht, Ch., Mallwitz, A. and Willemsen, F.; Berlin 1961.
Eighth Report, Autumn 1958–Summer 1962, by Kunze, E., with contributions by Bartels, H. and Mallwitz, A.; Berlin 1967.

III Other works

Adler, Friedrich, *Die Baudenkmäler:* see under Adler and Curtius, *Olympia* in section II above.

Aelian, *Variae Historiae,* trans. Thomas Stanley, London 1665.

Aeschylus, *Agamemnon,* trans. Philip Vellacott, Harmondsworth 1956.

Africanus, Sextus J., in Eusebius, *Chronicon,* q.v.

Andocides, *Orations,* in *Minor Attic Orators,* trans. K. J. Maidment and J. O. Burtt, 2 vols, London and Cambridge, Mass. 1941, 1954.

Anecdotae Graecae, Siebenkees edition.

Antiphon, *Fragments,* trans. Louis Gernet in *Discours suivis des fragments d'Antiphon le Sophiste,* Paris 1923. (Greek text with French translation.)

Arend, W. (compiler), *Geschichte in Quellen:* Vol. I, *Altertum – Alter Orient, Hellas, Rom,* Munich 1965.

Aristotle: *Motion and Progression of Animals,* E. S. Forster's translation of *De Incessu Animalium;* published with *Parts of Animals,* London and Cambridge, Mass. 1937; rev. edn, 1945.

———— *Politeia (De Republica Atheniensium),* in *Fragments,* Warsaw 1961.

———— *Problems,* W. S. Hett's translation of *Problemata,* 2 vols, London and Cambridge, Mass. 1936; rev. edn, 1953.

Arrian, *Anabasis* (Expedition of Alexander), trans. Aubrey de Selincourt, Harmondsworth 1958.

Ashmole, Bernard and Yalouris, Nicholas, *Olympia: The Sculptures of the Temple of Zeus,* London 1967.

Athenaeus, *The Deipnosophists,* trans. C. B. Gullick, 7 vols, London and New York 1927–41.

Berichte über die Ausgrabungen in Olympia, 1937–67: see under section II above.

Bernhardt, Max, 'Die Olympischen Spiele auf antiken Münzen', in *Blätter für Münzfreunde,* Vol. 73, 1936, pp. 393–403.

Blümel, Carl, *Der Hermes eines Praxiteles,* Baden-Baden 1948.

Boetticher, Adolf, *Olympia: Das Fest und seine Stätte,* 2nd edn, Berlin 1886. Based on ancient accounts and the earlier German excavations.

Bulle, H., 'Der Ostgiebel des Zeustempels zu Olympia', in *Jahrbuch des Deutschen Archäologischen Instituts,* Vol. 54, 1939, pp. 137–218.

Callimachus, *Fragments,* trans. C. A. Trypanis, London and Cambridge, Mass. 1958.

Capelle, Wilhelm, *Die Vorsokratiker,* Leipzig 1935; 4th edn, Stuttgart 1953. For English version of fragments and sources, see Kathleen Freeman's translation, Oxford 1948, 2nd edn, 1949.

Cicero: *De Divinatione,* published with *De Senectute* and *De Amicitia,* trans. W. A. Falconer, London and New York 1923.

———— *Tusculan Disputations,* trans. J. E. King, London and Cambridge, Mass. 1927; rev. edn, 1945.

Clement of Alexandria: *Paedogogus,* trans. Rev. G. W. Butterworth, London and New York 1919.

———— *Protrepticus,* trans. Thomas Merton (selections), New York 1962; Rev. W. Wilson (full text), Edinburgh 1867 and 1869.

Cook, Arthur Bernard, *Zeus: A Study in Ancient Religion,* 3 vols, Cambridge 1914–40.

Coubertin, Pierre de, *Der Olympische Gedanke,* Stuttgart and Lausanne 1966; also in French. Speeches and essays edited by the Carl-Diem-Institute at the Deutsche Sporthochschule, Cologne.

Curtius, Ernst: 'Entwurf einer Geschichte von Olympia', in *Topographie und Geschichte,* pp. 16–65; see under Adler and Curtius, *Olympia* in section II above.

———— *Olympia,* Berlin 1935; with selected texts from Pindar, Pausanias and Lucian.

———— 'Olympia: Ein Vortrag', in *Die Antike,* vol. 12, 1936, pp. 229–52.

Delendas, Plato N., *The 'Nea Altis' Society for the Restoration of Olympia,* Athens 1956.

Deubner, Ludwig, *Kult und Spiel im alten Olympia,* Leipzig 1936.

Diels, Hermann, *Die Fragmente der Vorsokratiker,* 3 vols, Greek text and German translation; 6th edn, Walther Kranz (ed.), Berlin 1950. For English version of these fragments, see Kathleen Freeman's translation, Oxford 1948; 2nd edn, 1949.

Diem, Carl: *Ewiges Olympia,* Minden, Westphalia 1948. Sources of the Olympic idea.

———— *Weltgeschichte des Sports und der Leibeserziehung,* Stuttgart 1960.

———— *Olympiaden 776 v. Chr. – 1964. Eine Geschichte des Sports,* Stuttgart 1964. Taken from the *Weltgeschichte,* it deals with Olympic contests from 776 BC to 1964.

Dio Cassius, *Roman History,* trans. E. Cary, 9 vols, London and Cambridge, Mass. 1917–27.

Diodorus Siculus, *Works,* trans. C. H. Oldfather, C. L. Sherman, Russel M. Geer, 12 vols, London and New York 1933–67.

Diogenes Laertius, *Lives of Eminent Philosophers,* trans. R. D. Hicks, 2 vols, London and New York 1925.

Dion Chrysostom of Prusa, *Opera,* trans. K. Kraut, Ulm 1901; *Works,* trans. J. W. Cahoon and H. Lamar Crosby 5 vols, London and New York 1932–51.

Dionysius of Halicarnassus, *Ars Rhetorica,* Leipzig 1804.

Dittenberger, W. and Purgold, K., *Die Inschriften:* see under Adler and Curtius, *Olympia* in section II above.

Dörpfeld, Wilhelm, *Alt-Olympia,* 2 vols, Berlin 1935; contributions by Forbat, F., Goessler, P., Rüter, H., Schleif, H. and Weege, F. A history of the ancient sanctuary of Olympia and its art, based on the findings of Dörpfeld's excavations.

Drees, Ludwig, *Der Ursprung der Olympischen Spiele,* in the series *Beiträge zur Lehre und Forschung der Leibeserziehung,* vol. XIII, Schorndorf near Stuttgart 1962.

Ebert, Joachim, *Zum Pentathlon der Antike,* Berlin 1963. An enquiry into the system of determining the victor in the pentathlon and the use of jumping weights.

Epictetus, *Dissertationes* and *Encheiridion,* in *The Discourse and Manual,* trans. P. E. Matheson, Oxford 1916.

Eusebius of Caesarea: *Chronicon,* in J. P. Migne (ed.), *Patrologia Graeca,* Paris 1857; Latin version of St Jerome, A. Schoene (ed.), Berlin 1866–75; Armenian version, trans J. Karst, Leipzig 1911.

———— *Evangelica Preparatio,* trans. E. H. Gifford, Oxford 1903.

Bibliography

Fränkel (ed.), *Corpus Inscriptionum Graecarum Peloponnesi et Insularum Vicinarum*, Berlin 1902.

Gardiner, E. Norman, *Olympia: Its History and Remains*, Oxford 1925.

Hampe, Roland: 'Ein neues Beschlagblech aus Olympia', in *Archäologischer Anzeiger*, a supplement to the *Jahrbuch des Deutschen Archäologischen Instituts*, Vol. 53. 1938, cols. 359–69.

——— Review of the Sixth Report of the Excavations at Olympia, in *Gymnasium*, Vol. 68, 1961.

Heliodorus, *Aethiopica*, trans. M. Hadas, Ann Arbor, Mich. 1957.

Herodotus, *Histories*, trans. A. D. Godley, 4 vols, London and New York 1920–24.

Homer: *Iliad*, trans. E. V. Rieu, Harmondsworth 1950.

——— *Odyssey*, trans. E. V. Rieu, Harmondsworth 1946.

Horace, *Carmina*, verse trans. Edward Marsh, London 1941.

Isocrates, *Orations and Epistles*, trans. George Norton (Vols I and II) and Larue van Hook (Vol. III), London and New York 1928–45.

Jacoby, Felix, *Die Fragmente der griechischen Historiker*, Berlin and subsequently Leyden 1923 ff.

Jantzen, Ulf: 'Die Geschichte Olympias', in *Olympia in der Antike* (q.v.), pp. 16–24.

——— 'Das Zeusheiligtum', in *ibid.*, pp. 37–59.

Josephus, Flavius, *Works*, trans. William Whiston, new edn, London 1963.

Jüthner, Julius: *Über antike Turngeräte*, Vienna 1896.

——— *Die athletischen Leibesübungen der Griechen*, Vol. I in F. Brein (ed.) *Geschichte der Leibesübungen*, Vienna 1965.

——— *Philostratus über Gymnastik*, Leipzig and Berlin 1909.

Kähler, Heinz, *Das griechische Metopenbild*, Munich 1949.

Kirsten, Ernst and Kraiker, Wilhelm, *Griechenlandkunde*, 4th edn, Heidelberg 1962.

Kunze, Emil: *Neue Meisterwerke griechischer Kunst aus Olympia*, Munich 1948.

——— 'Olympia', in *Neue Deutsche Ausgrabungen im Mittelmeergebiet und im vorderen Orient*, Berlin 1959, pp. 263–310.

——— 'Terrakottaplastik: Athenagruppe', in Sixth Report, pp. 169–88: see under *Berichte...* in section II. above.

——— 'Zeusbilder in Olympia', in *Antike und Abendland*, Hamburg 1946, Vol. II, pp. 95–113.

——— 'Zu den Anfängen der griechischen Plastik', in *Athenische Mitteilungen*, Vol. 55, 1930, pp. 141–62.

Langlotz, Ernst, 'Die Bedeutung der neuen Funde in Olympia', in Helmut Berve (ed.), *Das neue Bild der Antike*: Vol. I, *Hellas*, Leipzig 1942, pp. 153–71.

Lauffer, Siegfried, *Abriß der antiken Geschichte*, Munich 1956.

Liegle, Josef, *Der Zeus des Phidias*, Berlin 1952.

Livy, *Works*, trans. B. O. Foster, F. G. Moore, E. T. Sage and A. C. Schlesinger, 14 vols, London and New York 1919–59.

Lucian, *Anacharsis, Hermotimus* and *Peregrinus*, in *Works of Lucian of Samosata*, trans. H. W. Fowler and F. G. Fowler, Oxford 1905; German trans. Theodor Fischer, Berlin und Stuttgart, 1855–1903.

Lysias, *Olympiacus*, in *Opera*, Oxford 1912.

Mallwitz, Alfred, 'Das Stadion', in Eighth Report, pp. 16–83: see under *Berichte...* in section II above.

Mallwitz, Alfred and Schiering, Wolfgang, *Die Werkstatt des Pheidias in Olympia*, Part One; published as *Olympische Forschungen*, Vol. 5, Berlin 1964.

Meyer, Ernst, 'Pisa, Pisatis', in RE XX, 2nd part, 1950, cols. 1732–55.

——— *Pausanias: Beschreibung Griechenlands*, Zürich 1954.

Mezö, Franz, *Geschichte der Olympischen Spiele*, Munich 1930.

Nilsson, Martin P.: *Geschichte der griechischen Religion*, Vol. I, Munich 1941 (2nd edn, 1955), Vol. II, Munich 1950.

——— 'Der Ursprung der Tragödie', in *Opuscula Selecta*, Vol. 2, 1951, pp. 61–145.

Oberhummer, E., 'Olympos', in RE XVIII, 1939, col. 311.

Olympia: Die Ergebnisse..., 1890–97; see under section II above.

Olympia in der Antike, exhibition in Essen, June 18 to August 28, 1960; collection of studies under same title published in association with the exhibition, Essen 1960.

Palaeologus, Cleanthis, 'The Ancient Olympics: Proclamation, the Truce, the Organisation, Arrangements for the Contests, the Events', in *Report of the Fourth Summer Session of the International Olympic Academy*, Athens 1964, pp. 61–89.

Pausanias, *Description of Greece*, trans. A. R. Shilleto, London 1886; *Description of Greece*, trans. W. H. Jones, 5 vols, London and Cambridge, Mass. 1959–61. German translation, Ernst Meyer, *Beschreibung Griechenlands*, Zürich 1954.

Philostratus the Elder: *Apollonius of Tyana*, trans. J. S. Phillimore, Oxford 1912.

——— *Imagines*, trans. Arthur Fairbanks, London and New York 1931.

Philostratus, son of Verus, *Gymnasticus*, text and German translation in Julius Jüthner, *Philostratus über Gymnastik*, Leipzig and Berlin 1909.

Phlegon of Tralles, *Fragments*, in *Fragmenta Historicorum Graecorum*, 5 vols, Paris 1841–44; German trans. in Jacoby, *Die Fragmente...*, q.v.

Pindar, *Works*, trans. L. R. Farnell, London 1930.

Plato: *Apology of Socrates*, trans. Henry Cary, London 1871; trans. John Warrington, London and New York 1963.

——— *Epistolae*, trans. J. Harward, Cambridge 1932.

Plato: *Protagoras,* published with *Laches, Meno, Euthedemus,* trans. W. R. M. Lamb, London and New York 1924.

——— *Republic,* trans. B. Jowett, Oxford 1888; trans. Paul Shorey, London and Cambridge, Mass. 1930, rev. edn, 1937.

Pliny the Elder, *Natural History,* trans. H. Rackham and W. H. S. Jones, London and Cambridge, Mass. 1960 (Vols. I–VI) and 1965 (Vol. IX).

Plutarch: *Parallel Lives,* trans. B. Perrin, 11 vols, London and New York 1914; trans. Ian Scott-Kilvert, Harmondsworth 1960 and 1965.

——— *Quaestiones Convivales,* in *Opera,* Leipzig 1774–82.

——— *Roman Questions,* trans. H. J. Rose, Oxford 1924.

Polybius, *Histories,* trans. W. R. Paton, 6 vols, London and New York 1922.

Popplow, Ulrich, *Leibesübungen und Leibeserziehung in der griechischen Antike,* Schorndorf near Stuttgart, 2nd edn 1960.

Porphyry, *De Vita Pythagorae,* Genoa 1665.

Quintilian, *Institutio Oratoriae,* trans. H. E. Buller, 4 vols, London and New York 1920–22.

Rappaport, 'Heruli', in RE VIII, 1912, cols. 1150–67.

Real-Encyclopädie der classischen Altertumswissenschaft, ed. Pauly, Stuttgart 1893 ff. Abbreviated to RE.

Robert, Carl, 'Sosipolis in Olympia', *Athenische Mitteilungen,* Vol. 18, 1893, cols. 37–45.

Rodenwaldt, Gerhart, *Olympia;* photographs Walter Hege, 2nd edition, Berlin 1937.

Rudolph, Werner, *Olympischer Kampfsport in der Antike,* Berlin 1965. Boxing, wrestling and the pankration.

Schachermeyr, Fritz, *Die ältesten Kulturen Griechenlands,* Stuttgart 1955.

Schleif, Hans, 'Der Zeusaltar von Olympia', in *Jahrbuch des Deutschen Archäologischen Instituts,* Vol. 49, 1934, pp. 139–56.

Schleif, Hans and Weber, Hans, 'Das Nymphaeum des Herodes Attikos', in *Olympische Forschungen,* Vol. 1, 1944, pp. 53–82.

Schleif, Hans and Zschietzschmann, Willy, 'Das Philippeion', in *Olympische Forschungen,* Vol. 1, 1944, pp. 1–52.

Schneider, K., 'Hippodrom', in RE VIII, 1913, cols. 1735 to 1745.

Schöbel, Heinz, *Olympia und seine Spiele,* Leipzig 1964.

Schröder, Bruno, *Der Sport im Altertum,* Berlin 1927.

Seneca, *De Beneficiis,* trans. T. Lodge, London 1899.

Sophocles, *Electra,* trans. E. F. Watling, Harmondsworth 1953.

Statius, Publius Papinius, *Thebais,* verse trans. Alexander Pope, *Works,* Vol. I, London 1740; trans. J. H. Mozley, 2 vols, London and New York 1928.

Strabo, *Geography,* trans. Horace L. Jones, 8 vols, London and New York 1917–32; German trans. A. Förbiger, Berlin and Stuttgart, 1855–1900.

Suetonius, *Lives of the Twelve Caesars,* trans. H. M. Bird, Chicago 1930.

Themistius, *Orationes,* Paris 1684.

Thiemann, Eugen, 'Die Olympischen Spiele im Altertum', in *Olympia in der Antike* (q. v.), pp. 61–71.

Thucydides, *History of the Peloponnesian War,* trans. Rex Warner, Harmondsworth 1954.

Vacano, O. W. von, *Das Problem des alten Zeustempels in Olympia,* thesis, Cologne 1937.

Virgil, *Aeneid,* trans. C. Day Lewis, London 1954.

Vitruvius, *De Architectura,* trans. Frank Granger, London and New York 1931–34.

Walter, Otto, 'Zum Westgiebel des Zeustempels von Olympia', in *Rheinisches Museum für Philologie,* New Series Vol. 94, 1951, pp. 203–13.

Weege, Fritz: 'Zu den Bildwerken des Zeustempels in Olympia', in Dörpfeld, *Alt-Olympia,* (q. v.) Vol. II, pp. 449–81.

Weniger, Ludwig: *Der Gottesdienst in Olympia,* Berlin 1884.

——— 'Der heilige Ölbaum in Olympia', in *Jahresbericht über das Wilhelm-Ernstische-Gymnasium in Weimar,* Weimar 1895.

——— 'Das Hochfest des Zeus in Olympia', in *Klio, Beiträge zur alten Geschichte:* I.'Die Ordnung der Agone', Vol. 4, 1904, pp. 125–51; III. 'Der Gottesfriede', Vol. 5, 1905, pp. 184–218.

——— 'Die monatliche Opferung in Olympia', in *Klio,* Vol. 9, 1909, pp. 291–303; and Vol. 16, 1920, pp. 1–39.

Wiesner, J., 'Olympia: Topographie und Geschichte der Monumente', in RE XVIII, 1939, cols. 71–174.

Wilamowitz-Moellendorff, Ulrich von, *Der Glaube der Hellenen,* 2 vols, 2nd edn, Darmstadt 1955.

Wolters, Paul, 'Die archaische Hera in Olympia', in *Festschrift Heinrich Wölfflin zum 70 Geburtstag,* Dresden 1935.

Wunderer, W., *Olympia,* Leipzig 1935.

Xenophon, *Works,* trans. H. G. Dakyns, London 1890; *Hellenica* published with *Anabasis* etc., trans. C. L. Brownson and O. J. Todd, 3 vols, London and New York 1921.

Ziehen, Ludwig, 'Olympia: Olympische Spiele', in RE Vol. XVII, 1936, cols. 2520–36; and RE Vol. XVIII, 1939, cols. 1–71.

Zschietzschmann, Willy, *Wettkampf und Übungsstätten in Griechenland,* Vol. I, *Das Stadion,* Schorndorf near Stuttgart 1960; Vol. II, *Palästra-Gymnasion,* Schorndorf near Stuttgart 1961.

Notes

The abbreviation RE in the Notes and Bibliography stands for *Real-Encyclopädie der classischen Altertumswissenschaft*.

Introduction

1. Strabo, *Geography*, 353.
2. See Lucian, *Peregrinus*. (Fischer III p. 5)
3. Herodotus, *Histories*, VIII, 26.
4. See Lucian, *Anacharsis*. (Fischer I, p. 211)
5. Pindar, *Olympic Odes*, VIII, 10–11 (Farnell translation p. 41).
6. Winter Olympics: 1908 London; 1920 Antwerp; 1924 Chamonix; 1928 St Moritz; 1932 Lake Placid; 1936 Garmisch; 1948 St Moritz; 1952 Oslo; 1956 Cortina; 1960 Squaw Valley; 1964 Innsbruck; 1968 Grenoble. Equestrian Olympics: 1956 Stockholm.
7. He not only used his own resources for the reconstruction of the stadium, but also persuaded the German Olympic Society and the German Sports Federation to contribute DM 200,000. Later, the German Sports Federation made a further grant of DM 40,000, and the DM 90,000 required to complete the project were provided by the central office and the Athens branch office of the German Archaeological Institute.
8. Plato N. Delendas, a high-ranking official of the Greek National Bank, pursued a similar objective. When Coubertin died, Delendas founded the *Nea Altis* society with the object of setting up a centre where athletes could compete and where 'the younger generation could be instructed in the spiritual, intellectual, artistic and physical ideals of classical culture'. See Delendas, *The 'Nea Altis' Society*, pp. 5 and 8.
9. Drees, Ludwig, *Der Ursprung der Olympischen Spiele*.

1. The Sanctity of Olympia

1. The question as to whether there actually was a town of Pisa was a matter of controversy even among the ancient Greeks, and continues to be one today. Its exact location, of course, is even more disputed. Many ancient authors used Olympia and Pisas synonyms.
2. Strabo, *Geography*, 357.
3. Pausanias, *Description of Greece*, V 10, 2.
4. Lysias, *Olympiacus*, 33, 2.
5. For the history of the Olympic cult, see Drees, op. cit., pp. 20–51.
6. Pausanias, V 10, 1.
7. Oberhummer, 'Olympos', in RE XVIII, col. 311.
8. Pausanias, V 14, 10.
9. Dörpfeld, *Alt-Olympia*, I p. 63.
10. Pindar, *Olympic Odes*, X 49–51 (Farnell p. 58).
11. 'Olympos', in RE XVIII, cols. 258–324.
12. Schachermeyr, *Die ältesten Kulturen Griechenlands*, pp. 232–3.
13. Wilamowitz-Moellendorff, *Glaube der Hellenen*, I p. 37.
14. Pausanias, V 14, 10.
15. Ibid., VI 20, 4–5.
16. Ibid., VI 20, 2–3.
17. Robert, 'Sosipolis in Olympia', *Athenische Mitteilungen*, XVIII, 1893, col. 40.
18. Nilsson, *Geschichte der griechischen Religion*, I p. 63.
19. Pausanias, V 14, 10.
20. Ibid., V 4, 2.
21. Ibid., V 13, 1–2.
22. In the north-eastern section of the circle of stones, a pre-Dorian child's grave (pithos containing bones) was found, which presumably belonged to apsidal house No. 5. (See p. 123 our text.) But was there some religious connection here with Pelops as the slaughtered child? Cf. Dörpfeld, op. cit., I pp. 94 to 95; and Drees, op. cit., pp. 68–9.
23. Pausanias, VI 20, 7; and V 16, 6.
24. Ibid., V 13, 2–3.
25. Ibid., V 14, 2.
26. Ziehen, 'Olympia', in RE XVII, col. 2521, line 62ff.
27. Ziehen, loc. cit., col. 2522; and Drees, op. cit., note 218.
28. Nilsson, *... Religion*, I pp. 174–5.
29. Mezö, *Geschichte der Olympischen Spiele*, p. 13.

2. The Cult of the Olympian Gods

1. Pausanias, V 13, 8–11.
2. Wiesner, 'Olympia', in RE XVIII, col. 146; and Schleif, 'Der Zeusaltar von Olympia', *Jahrbuch des DAI*, XLIX, 1934, pp. 139–56. Schleif discusses the altar in considerable detail, and concludes that it was rectangular in shape. He argues that the sacrificial animals were not slaughtered on the stone base, since this would have been too small (especially when a hecatomb was being offered up) and since it would have been extremely time-consuming to have led the live animals up the stone steps on to the prothysis. He suggests that the animals were tethered, and subsequently slaughtered, in the immediate vicinity of the altar, which stood in the triangle formed by the temple of Hera, the temple of Meter and the Pelopium.
3. Pausanias, V 13, 11.
4. Ibid., V 15, 9.
5. Wiesner, RE XVIII, col. 146.
6. Adler, *Die Baudenkmäler*, in *Olympia: Die Ergebnisse* series, col. 211a.
7. Pausanias, V 14, 1.
8. Pliny the Elder, *Natural History*, 10, 12.
9. Pausanias, V 14, 1.
10. Pliny the Elder, 19, 106; and 10, 75.
11. Pausanias, V 15, 9.
12. Nilsson, . . . *Religion*, I pp. 135 and 315.
13. Pausanias, V 15, 12.
14. Ibid., V 15, 11.
15. Ziehen, 'Olympische Spiele', in RE XVIII, col. 49.
16. Pausanias, V 15, 10.
17. Nilsson, . . . *Religion*, I p. 166.
18. Pausanias, V 14, 10.
19. Ibid., V 15, 4.
20. Ziehen, RE XVIII, col. 53.
21. Plutarch, *Roman Questions*, 112.
22. Pausanias, VI 20, 1.
23. Nilsson, . . . *Religion*, I p. 481, note 1.
24. Strabo, 343.
25. *Anecdotae Graecae* (Siebenkees edition p. 95).
26. Lucian, *Herodotus sive Aetion* 1; cf. also pp. 62–3 our text, and Ziehen, RE XVIII, col. 46.
27. Deubner, *Kult und Spiel im alten Olympia*, p. 5.
28. Pindar, *Olympic Odes*, VI 5 (Farnell p. 26).
29. Curtius, 'Entwurf einer Geschichte von Olympia', in *Topographie und Geschichte*, in *Olympia: Die Ergebnisse* series, col. 27b.
30. Cicero, *De Divinatione*, I 41.
31. *Greek Anthology*, App. III 31.
32. Pindar, *Olympic Odes*, VIII 1–7 (Farnell p. 41).
33. Ziehen, RE XVIII col. 61.
34. Xenophon, *Hellenica*, IV 7, 2.
35. Plutarch, *Agis*, 11.
36. Pausanias, V 15, 10.
37. Ibid., V 15, 12.
38. Weniger, *Der Gottesdienst in Olympia*, p. 20.
39. Pausanias, V 13, 2.
40. Curtius, 'Entwurf einer Geschichte', cols. 35b–36a.
41. Ibid., col. 32a.

3. Ritual Games in the Sanctuary

1. Pausanias, III 12, 1. See also Pindar's *Pythian Odes*, IX 11, 117–24 (Farnell pp. 136–7), where the poet describes the suitors' race staged by Danaos for his daughters.
2. Pausanias, V 7, 6–9.
3. Drees, op. cit., pp. 81–2.
4. Ibid., p. 82.
5. Pausanias, V 20, 6–7.
6. Ibid., V 20, 8.
7. Ibid., V 16, 2–4.
8. Ibid., V 20, 1.
9. Ibid., V 13, 4–6.
10. Curtius, 'Entwurf einer Geschichte', col. 20b.
11. Nilsson, *Der Ursprung der Tragödie*, p. 99.
12. Plutarch, *Quaestiones Convivales*, V 2, p. 675; see also Drees, op. cit., p. 66.
13. Clement of Alexandria, *Protrepticus*, II 34.
14. Africanus, Sextus J. see RE XVIII, col. 17.
15. For a fuller account of this synopsis, see Ziehen, RE XVII, cols. 2529–30.
16. Pausanias, VI 9, 5. Pausanias is in error here. It was in 495, and not 491 BC, that Gelon moved his residence to Syracuse. See Ernst Meyer's translation of Pausanias, *Beschreibung Griechenlands*, p. 625; and note re. p. 313, 2.

4. The Great Festival of Zeus

1. Pindar, *Olympic Odes*, II 1–4 (Farnell p. 10).
2. Ibid., X 24–63 (Farnell pp. 58–9.)
3. Achilles Tatius, I 18. See also Nilsson, . . . *Religion*, I p. 221.
4. Aulus Gellius, *Noctes Atticae*, I 1.
5. Pausanias, V 8, 4.
6. Ibid., V 4, 6.
7. Ibid., V 8, 6.
8. Ibid., V 8, 5.
9. Ibid., V 8, 9.
10. Phlegon of Tralles, in Jacoby, *Fragmente griechischer Historiker*, No. 257, Fragment I 2.
11. Ibid., No. 257, Fragment I 10–11.
12. Cook, *Zeus: A Study in Ancient Religion*, II p. 490.
13. *Oxford English Dictionary*, and Weniger, 'Der heilige Ölbaum', p. 3.

14. Pausanias, V 15, 3.
15. Aristotle(?), *Mirabilia,* 51; and Scholium on Aristophanes, *Plutus,* 586.
16. Weniger, 'Der heilige Ölbaum', pp. 11–12.
17. Scholium on Pindar, *Olympic Odes,* III 60. See also Ziehen, RE XVIII, col. 32. For information about the number of contests, see Palaeologus, *The Ancient Olympics,* p. 77.
18. Weniger, 'Der heilige Ölbaum', p. 3.
19. For sources, see Weniger, ibid., pp. 8–9.
20. Pindar, *Olympic Odes,* III 11–32 (Farnell pp. 17–18).
21. Pausanias, V 14, 3.
22. Ibid., V 15, 10.
23. Lucian, *Anacharsis* (Fischer 1 p. 210).
24. Ibid. (p. 211).
25. Phlegon of Tralles, in Jacoby, op. cit., No. 257, Fragment I 3.
26. Pausanias, V 20, 1.
27. Phlegon of Tralles, in Jacoby, op. cit., No. 257, Fragment I 9.
28. Strabo 357–8.
29. Gardiner, E. Norman, *Olympia: Its History and Remains,* 1925. Gardiner paints too black a picture. The Eleans wanted to take part in the battle of Plataea, but their contingent arrived too late. After the Persian Wars, they founded the city of Elis as the capital of their territory by a process of synoecism. The Elean architect Libon built the temple of Zeus in Olympia.
30. Andocides, IV 29; and Ziehen, RE XVIII, col. 33.
31. Livy, XXVII 35, 3.
32. Weniger, 'Das Hochfest des Zeus in Olympia': Part III, 'Der Gottesfriede', in *Klio,* V, 1905, pp. 198–202 passim.
33. Ibid.

5. The Competitors

1. Herodotus, V 22.
2. Philostratus, *Gymnasticus,* 25.
3. Plato, Protagoras, 312B.
4. Ziehen, RE XVIII, cols. 41–2.
5. Mezö, op. cit., p. 54, note 19.
6. Pausanias, VI 2, 2–3; Xenophon, *Hellenica,* III 2, 21; and Thucydides, *History of the Peloponnesian War,* V 49–50.
7. Plutarch, *Themistocles,* 25. The validity of Plutarch's testimony is questioned by many authorities; see Ziehen, RE XVIII, col. 36.
8. Pausanias, VI 1, 4–5.
9. Herodotus, II 160.
10. Plutarch, *Agesilaus,* 20; and Xenophon, *Agesilaus,* IX 6.
11. Pausanias, III 8, 1.

12. Ibid., VI 1, 6.
13. *Greek Anthology,* XIII 16
14. Pausanias, V 12, 5.
15. Diem, *Weltgeschichte des Sports,* pp. 240–1.
16. Lucian, *Anacharsis;* in Diem, *Ewiges Olympia,* pp. 31–2.
17. Antiphon, Fragment 128.
18. Lucian, *Harmonides* 4.
19. Pausanias, VI 7, 10.
20. Philostratus, *Gymnasticus,* 11.
21. Epictetus, *Encheiridion,* 29.
22. Philostratus the Elder, *Apollonius of Tyana,* V 43.
23. Pausanias, V 24, 9.
24. Ibid., V 21, 12–14.
25. Zschietzschmann, *Palästra-Gymnasion,* Vol. II of *Wettkampf und Übungsstätten in Griechenland,* pp. 32–6.
26. Pausanias, VI 23, 1–2.
27. Zschietzschmann, op. cit., p. 34, note 65.
28. Pausanias, VI 23, 4.
29. Ibid., VI 23, 5.
30. Ibid., VI 24, 2.
31. Ibid., VI 24, 1.
32. Philostratus, *Gymnasticus,* 11. According to Pausanias (V 21, 12–14), the boxer Heraclides was also granted a walk-over.
33. Philostratus the Elder, *Apollonius of Tyana,* V 43.
34. Pausanias, V 16, 8.
35. See p. 154 our text.
36. Pausanias, VI 21, 2.
37. Zschietzschmann, op. cit., pp. 39–56; illustrations 5–10 and note 85. See also Wiesner, RE XVIII, cols. 139–42.
38. Vitruvius, *De Architectura,* V 11.
39. Zschietzschmann, op. cit., p. 56.
40. Pausanias, VI 6, 3.
41. For further information on the bathing facilities, see *Berichte über die Ausgrabungen in Olympia;* and Kunze, 'Olympia', pp. 271-275
42. Kunze, loc. cit.
43. For further information on the southern and northern baths, see the discussion in *Olympia in der Antike,* pp. 52 and 58.
44. Pausanias, VI 15, 1.
45. Ibid., VI 14, 1.
46. Ibid., VI 14, 1–2.
47. Ziehen, RE XVIII, col. 8.
48. Pausanias, V 24, 10.
49. Xenophon, *Hellenica,* IV 1, 40; and Plutarch, *Agesilaus,* 13.
50. Pausanias, VI 24, 1.
51. Ibid., VI 23, 2.
52. Ibid., VI 13, 4. (This passage is garbled.)
53. Ibid.
54. 'Gamma' is the third letter of the Greek alphabet.

55. Lucian, *Hermotimus*, 40.
56. Pausanias, VI 1, 2.
57. Ibid.
58. Horace, *Epistolae*, I 1, 49–51.
59. Pausanias, V 21, 12–14; and p. 43 our text.
60. Ibid., VI 6, 5–6.
61. Ziehen, RE XVIII, col. 33 gives sources.
62. Ibid.
63. Pausanias, VI 20, 13; and p. 99 our text.
64. Ibid., V 24, 9.
65. Ibid., VIII 40, 1–2; and p. 83 our text.
66. Ibid., VI 9, 6.
67. Photius, Bibl. CXC; cf. Mezö, op. cit., p. 189.
68. Dionysius of Halicarnassus, *Ars Rhetorica*, VI 6; cf. Mezö, op. cit., p. 188.
69. Themistius, Oration I, *De Humanitate*, p. 13; cf. Mezö, op. cit., p. 188.
70. Pausanias, V 21, 3.
71. Ibid., V 21, 5–6.
72. Ibid., V 21, 16–17.
73. Dionysius of Halicarnassus, *Ars Rhetorica*, VI 6; Mezö, op. cit., p. 188.
74. Pausanias, VI 13, 1.
75. Ibid., VI 18, 6.
76. Ibid., VI 4, 11.
77. Herodotus, VI 103.
78. Pausanias, VI 2, 3. The campaign against Elis took place between 402 and 400 BC.
79. Curtius, 'Entwurf einer Geschichte', col. 23b.
80. Pausanias's statement (V 9, 4) that two judges were appointed by lot as from 580 BC (50th Olympiad) is incorrect, for it is contradicted by the old Olympic inscriptions. Probably the second judge was appointed when the Eleans redrafted their constitution in 470 BC.
81. Xenophon, *De Republica Lacedaemoniorum*, 18, 31.
82. Pausanias, V 9, 5.
83. Philostratus the Elder, *Apollonius of Tyana*, III 30.
84. Pausanias, VI 24, 3.
85. Ibid., VIII 48, 2; and Plutarch, *Quaestiones Convivales*, VIII 4, 1; see also p. 85 our text. The ceremony was subject to variation, for the boxer Heraclides received his olive wreath immediately after the contest; see Pausanias, V 21, 12–14; and p. 43 our text.
86. Philostratus, *Gymnasticus*, 54.
87. Mezö, op. cit., p. 54, note 74; see also p. 25 our text.
88. Pausanias, VI 3, 7.
89. Herodotus, II 160; and p. 42 our text.
90. Philostratus the Elder, *Apollonius of Tyana*, IV 29.
91. Dion Chrysostom of Prusa, *Orations*, XXXI 111.
92. Suetonius, Nero, 24; and p. 156 our text.
93. Dio Cassius, *Roman History*, 63, 14.
94. Pausanias, VII 17, 14.

6. The Spectators

1. Pausanias, VI 20, 9; see also ibid., V 13, 10.
2. Ibid., V 6, 7–8; and Philostratus, *Gymnasticus*, 17.
3. Pindar, *Olympic Odes*, VII—to Diagoras.
4. Ziehen, RE XVIII, col. 34.
5. Drees, op. cit., pp. 119–24.
6. Dion Chrysostom, *Orations*, LXVII 4; and Mezö, op. cit., p. 63.
7. Cicero, *Tusculan Disputations*, V 3, 9.
8. Lucian, *Peregrinus* (Fischer III, p. 12).
9. Epictetus, *Dissertationes*, I 6, 23–9.
10. Ibid., IV 4, 24.
11. Lucian, *Anacharsis*; in Diem, *Ewiges Olympia*, p. 35.
12. Aelian, *Variae Historiae*, XIV 18.
13. Lucian, *Peregrinus* (Fischer III, p. 18).
14. Ibid., *Anacharsis*; in Diem, *Ewiges Olympia*, p. 34.
15. Ibid., *Peregrinus* (Fischer III, p. 5).
16. Lysias, *Olympiacus*, 1–2.
17. Isocrates, *Panegyricus*, 43–4.
18. Ibid., *Archidamus*, 95.
19. Plutarch, *Themistocles*, 17.
20. Diels, *Vorsokratiker*, Fragments 7 and 8.
21. Diodorus Siculus, *Bibliotheca Historia*, XIV 109.
22. Dionysius of Halicarnassus, *De Lysia*, 29.
23. Isocrates, *Panegyricus*, 187–8.
24. Plutarch, *Alexander*, 4.
24a. Diodorus Siculus, *Bibliotheca Historia*, XVIII 8, and XVII 109.
25. Arrian, *Anabasis*, II 15.
26. Diodorus Siculus, *Bibliotheca Historia*, XVII 113, 3. See also Ziehen, RE XVIII, col. 37.
27. Pausanias, V 23, 1–2; and p. 130 our text. On the votive offering dedicated to the god in Delphi (now in Constantinople), 31 states are listed.
28. Pausanias, V 23, 4.
29. Thucydides, *Peloponnesian War*, V 18.
30. Ibid., V 47.
31. Livy, 26, 24.
32. Curtius, 'Entwurf einer Geschichte', col. 58b.
33. Thucydides, *Peloponnesian War*, III 8.
34. Livy, 27, 35.
35. Herodotus, VI 126.
36. Ibid., VI 127–30.
37. Lysias, *Olympiacus*, 2.
38. Isocrates, *Panegyricus*, 1–2.
39. Philostratus the Elder, *Apollonius of Tyana*, VI 10.
40. Lucian, *Herodotus sive Aëtion*, 1–2. The division of Herodotus's work into nine books, each named after a Muse, was undertaken in Hellenistic times.
41. See Lucian, *Herodotus sive Aëtion*, 3.
42. Plato, *Hippias Minor*, 360 D ff.
43. Philostratus the Elder, *Apollonius of Tyana*, IV 31.
44. Lucian, *Herodotus sive Aetion*, 4.
45. Aelian, *Variae Historiae*, X 7.

46. Mezö, op. cit., p. 171.
47. Philostratus the Elder, *Apollonius of Tyana*, III 29. Apollonius's journey to India was probably legendary.
48. Diogenes Laertius, *Lives of Eminent Philosophers*, I 10 and 12.
49. Ibid., I 72.
50. Philostratus the Elder, *Apollonius of Tyana*, I 2.
51. Ibid., I, 1.
52. Athenaeus, *Deipnosophists*, I p. 3 D.
53. Plato, *Epistolae*, VII (350 B).
54. Plutarch, *Lycurgus* 1.
55. Dinarchus, *Kata Demosthene*, 81.
56. Plutarch, *Lycurgus* 23; and Drees, op. cit., p. 106.
57. Diem, *Weltgeschichte des Sports*, pp. 258–9.
58. See chapter 12 below.
59. Pliny the Elder, *Natural History*, XXXV 36, 3.
60. Plutarch, *Alexander*, 4.

7. The Sequence of Events

1. Curtius, 'Entwurf einer Geschichte', cols. 63b–64a.
2. For sources and interpretations, see Ziehen, RE XVIII, cols. 10–16. For the reconstruction of the sequences, see Weniger, in *Klio*, IV, 1904, pp. 125 ff.
3. Pausanias, VI 15, 5.
4. Diodorus Siculus, *Bibliotheca Historia*, IV 73, 4; and Pausanias, V 14, 6.
5. Pindar, *Olympic Odes*, X 70–1; VII 145; III 33–4 (Farnell pp. 57, 33, 17).
6. Philostratus, *Gymnasticus*, 5.
7. Heliodorus, *Aethiopica*.
8. Pausanias, V 9, 3.
9. Xenophon, *Hellenica*, VII 4, 29. In Delphi the horse-races also took place in the morning; see quotation on pp. 71–2 our text.
10. The fifth day of the festival of Zeus was the sixteenth day of the festival month; Scholium on Pindar, *Olympic Odes*, V 8.
11. Pausanias, V 24, 9–11.
12. Ziehen, RE XVIII, col. 17.
13. Ibid., for sources.
14. Pausanias, V 22, 1.
15. Ibid., VI 13, 9.
16. Ibid., V 9, 1.
17. Aristotle, *Politeia*, VIII 4, 1.
18. Philostratus, *Gymnasticus*, 46.
19. Mezö, op. cit., p. 73 and note 38 for sources.
20. Pausanias, VI 3, 6.
21. *Greek Anthology*, XVI 1.
22. Schröder, *Der Sport im Altertum*, p. 122.
23. Pausanias, VI 12, 6.
24. An intermediate group between the boys and the men, which did not exist in Olympia.
25. Pausanias, VI 14, 2–3.
26. Ibid., VI 2, 8.
27. Ibid., VI 12, 1.
28. For sources, see Ziehen RE XVIII, cols. 22–6.
29. See table on pp. 31–2 our text.
30. Boetticher, *Olympia: Das Fest und seine Stätte*, p. 128; and Drees, op. cit., p. 86 and note 240.
31. Mezö, op. cit., pp. 138–9.
32. Schröder, op. cit., p. 138.
33. Pausanias, VI 16, 4.
34. Ibid., VI 13, 9; see also p. 69 our text.
35. Pindar, *Olympic Odes*, III 59; and Scholia on II 92 and VI 75. See also Ziehen, RE XVIII, cols. 22 ff., and p. 97 our text.
36. Ziehen, RE XVIII cols. 22–3. See also the reconstruction of the hippodrome on pp. 97–8 our text.
37. Pindar, *Pythian Odes*, V 49.
38. See pp. 78 and 107 our text.
39. Sophocles, *Electra*, 698–760.
40. Ebert, *Pentathlon*, pp. 18–20. It would seem, however, that the stade-race was the first event in the Olympic pentathlon; see Xenophon, *Hellenica*, VII 4, 29. See also p. 67 our text.
41. Pollux, *Works*, III 151; see Ebert, op. cit., p. 20.
42. Philostratus, *Gymnasticus* 3.
43. Ibid., 31.
44. For evidence, see Mezö, op. cit., p. 118. The boys' discus found at Olympia weighs 1,860 grammes.
45. Pausanias, VI 19, 4.
46. Ziehen, RE XVIII, col. 22.
47. Philostratus the Elder, *Imagines*, I 23.
48. The original bronze, which was cast shortly before 450 BC, is lost. Numerous replicas in marble, a small one in bronze and a number of cameo reproductions have been preserved, some of which bear the name Hyacinthus.
49. Thiemann, 'Olympische Spiele', in *Olympia in der Antike*, p. 66.
50. Ibid., p. 61.
51. Statius, *Thebais*, VI 673–7.
52. Diem, *Weltgeschichte des Sports*, p. 172.
53. Mezö, op. cit., p. 123; Boetticher, op. cit., p. 113; Ebert, op. cit., p. 35.
54. Thiemann, op. cit., p. 66.
55. Mezö, op. cit., p. 126 and note 1.
56. Ebert, op. cit., pp. 44–5.
57. Pausanias, V 7, 10.
58. Ibid., V 26, 3.
59. Mezö, op. cit., p. 112; and Jüthner, *Antike Turngeräte*, pp. 3–18.
60. Boetticher, op. cit., p. 107.
61. Philostratus, *Gymnasticus*, 55.
62. Aristotle, *Problemata*, 5, 8; 881, a39–b6.
63. Ebert, op. cit., pp. 46–54.
64. Ibid., pp. 35–42.

65. Ibid., p. 58.
66. Ibid., pp. 13 and 62.
67. Thiemann, op. cit., p. 66.
68. For sources, see Mezö, op. cit., p. 129.
69. Ebert (*Pentathlon*, pp. 10–13) assumes a length of five stades for the pentathlon foot-race, and bases this assumption on an inscription disovered in Anazarbus in Cilicia, which he renders as follows: '...at the festival games of the provincial diet of Asia, Demetrius gained the victory on the fifth straight after making Optatus his pace-maker for the first four'. (For original inscription, see Gough, *Anatolian Studies*, III, 1952, 127 ff., No. 1, lines 12 to 14.) Even if this rendering is correct—and there are other interpretations of this particular passage—it is by no means certain that this account refers to a foot-race held within the framework of the pentathlon. Nor is there any other reference to a five-stade race in the source material.
70. Rudolph, *Olympischer Kampfsport*, p. 58.
71. Pausanias, III 11, 9.
72. Plutarch, *Quaestiones Convivales*, IX 2, 2.
73. Photius, *Bibliotheca*, CCXLVI 409 a (*Panathenaicus* of Aristides, III 399).
74. Ebert, op. cit., pp. 63 and 2–24.
75. Cf. pp. 17–18 our text.
76. Pindar, *Olympic Odes*, I 90–8 (Farnell p. 6).
77. Plutarch, *Alcibiades*, 11; see also pp. 71 and 107 our text.
78. Ibid., 12.
79. Mezö, op. cit., pp. 156–7.
80. Pseudo-Andocides, IV 29; and Ziehen, RE XVIII, col. 18.
81. Pausanias, VI 13, 3.
82. Ziehen, RE XVIII, col. 16.
83. The length of the dolichos varied between 7 and 24 stades according to the stadium. Suidas gives the length of the Olympic dolichos as 24 stades. See Mezö, op. cit., p. 74 and note 51.
84. Pausanias, VI 13, 3.
85. Ibid., VI 13, 4. See also p. 51 our text, and RE XVIII, col. 19.
86. Statius, *Thebais*, VI 587 ff.; and Schröder, op. cit., p. 106.
87. Heliodorus, *Aethiopica*, VI 3.
88. For further details, see Mezö, op. cit., p. 69. For details of the starting gate at the Isthmian games, see Adolf Metzner's discussion in *Die Zeit*, 1965, No. 44, p. 46.
89. Plutarch, *Themistocles*, II; see also Herodotus, VIII 59, where he specifically refers to the foot-race in this connection.
90. Diem, *Weltgeschichte des Sports*, p. 163.
91. Aristotle, *Motion and Progression of Animals*, ch. 3; see also p. 75 our text.

92. Schröder, op. cit., p. 106.
93. Philostratus, *Gymnasticus*, 32.
94. Schröder, op. cit., p. 106.
95. Ibid.
96. Mezö, op. cit., pp. 73–4.
97. Pausanias, VI 13, 4.
98. Solinus, *Collectanea*, I 96.
99. Sextus Julius Africanus, on Olympiad 113 in Eusebius, *Chronicon* (Schoene I, p. 206), and Mezö, op. cit., p. 77.
100. Cf. Fränkel, *Corpus Inscriptionum Graecarum Peloponnesi et insularum vicinarum*, Berlin 1902.
101. Rudolph, op. cit., p. 37.
102. Pausanias, VI 4, 3.
103. Sextus Julius Africanus, on Olympiad 147 in Eusebius, *Chronicon* (Schoene I, p. 210), and Mezö, op. cit., p. 80.
104. Rudolph, op. cit., pp. 39–40.
105. Ibid., pp. 29 ff.
106. Seneca, *De Beneficiis*, V 3; and Philostratus, *Gymnasticus*, 9.
107. Sextus Julius Africanus, in Eusebius, *Chronicon* (Schoene I, p. 202).
108. Pausanias, VI 14, 5.
109. *Greek Anthology*, XVI 24.
110. Pausanias, VI 14, 5–6.
111. Boetticher, op. cit., p. 101 (written in 1882).
112. Plutarch, *Quaestiones Convivales*, V 2, p. 675 c. See also p. 30 our text, and Drees, op. cit., p. 66.
113. Mezö, op. cit., p. 92.
114. Schröder, op. cit., pp. 146–7.
115. Boetticher, op. cit., p. 104; and Thiemann, op. cit., p. 68.
116. Philostratus, *Gymnasticus*, 10.
117. *Greek Anthology*, XI 81.
118. Pausanias, VIII 40, 3–5. Rudolph (*Olympischer Kampfsport*, pp. 11–12) questions the truth of this account.
119. See p. 52 our text.
120. Dion Chrysostom, *Orations*, XXIX 11–12.
121. Pausanias, VI 12, 6.
123. Polybius, *Histories*, XXVII 9–10.
123. Cicero, *Tusculan Disputations*, I 46, 111.
124. Mezö, op. cit., pp. 100–1.
125. Pausanias, III 14, 10.
126. Ibid., VIII 40, 2.
127. Philostratus the Elder, *Imagines*, II 6.
128. Ibid.
129. Pausanias, VI 6, 5–6; and reference on p. 51 our text.
130. Ibid., V 21, 18.
131. Philostratus, *Gymnasticus*, 23.
132. Pausanias, V 8, 4; see also Mezö, op. cit., for a complete list.
133. See pp. 103–4 our text.

134. Ziehen, RE XVIII, col. 15, lines. 35 ff.
135. Pausanias, VI 10, 4.
136. Ibid., V 12, 8.
137. Ibid., II 11, 8, and X 34, 5.
138. Ibid., V 8, 10.
139. Philostratus, *Gymnasticus*, 7.
140. Heliodorus, *Aethiopica*, 7.
141. Maximus of Tyre, *Dissertations*, V 8; and Cook, op. cit., II p. 490.
142. Pausanias, VIII 48, 2–3.
143. Gellius, III 6.
144. Horace, *Carmina*, I 1, 3–7.
145. Gellius, III 6.
146. Drees, op. cit., pp. 85–6.
147. Pausanias, VI 2, 2; and Thucydides, *Peloponnesian War*, V 50, 4.
148. Porphyry, *Vita Pythagorae*, 15.
149. Eratosthenes, in a Scholium on Euripedes, *Hecuba* 574. See also Clement of Alexandria, *Paedagogus*, 2, 8.
150. Pausanias, V 12, 5.
151. Ibid., V 20, 1–3.
152. Rodenwaldt, *Olympia*, pp. 21–2.
153. Scholium on Pindar, *Olympic Odes*, V 8.
154. RE XVIII, cols. 27–8; and Mezö, op. cit., p. 154, note 18.
155. RE XVIII, cols. 27–8, and Mezö, op. cit., pp. 154 to 155. See also note 85 of chapter 5 our text.
156. Pausanias, V 15, 12.
157. Pindar, *Olympic Odes* X, 72–7 (Farnell p. 59).

8. The Stadium and Hippodrome

1. Sextus Julius Africanus, in Eusebius, *Chronicon* I (Schoene p. 197); and Gellius, I 1.
2. Isidore of Seville, XV 16, 3.
3. *Stadion*. The Argive *spadion* means span, distance; it is perhaps related to Latin *spatium* (space). The change of meaning is apparently due to association with *stadios* (meaning standing) and *stathme* (meaning guideline). See Menge-Güthling, *Griechisch-deutsches Hand- und Schulwörterbuch*, 10th edn, Berlin n.d.; and J. B. Hoffmann, *Etymologisches Wörterbuch des Griechischen*.
4. Pausanias, V 16, 2
5. Kunze, 'Olympia', p. 226.
6. Ibid., p. 297.
7. For bibliography on the excavation of the stadium, see Zschietzschmann, op. cit., p. 12.
8. Ibid.
9. *Eighth Report* (*Berichte über die Ausgrabungen* series), in which Alfred Mallwitz describes the excavations in the stadium between the autumn of 1958 and the summer of 1962 (pp. 16–82).

10. Kunze, 'Olympia', p. 266.
11. *Second Report*, p. 22.
12. See Langlotz, '...Neue Funde in Olympia', pp. 155–6; and *Second Report*, pp. 67–70.
13. *Second Report*, p. 67.
14. *Fourth Report*, pp. 164 ff.; and Zschietzschmann, op. cit., pp. 23 and 55.
15. *Second Report*, p. 13.
16. Kunze, 'Olympia', p. 266.
17. *Fifth Report*, p. 18; see also ibid., p. 19; *Third Report*, pp. 11–12; and *Fourth Report*, p. 2.
18. *Fifth Report*, p. 26.
19. *Eighth Report*, p. 16.
20. Ibid., pp. 29 and 32.
21. See plate 52b.
22. *Fourth Report*, p. 2, and *Fifth Report*, pp. 12–14.
23. *Fifth Report*, pp. 13–14.
24. Ibid., p. 22.
25. Ibid., pp. 14–16.
26. Ibid., pp. 16–18.
27. Ibid., pp. 18–19.
28. Ibid., p. 19.
29. Ibid.
30. *Second Report*, pp. 13–14.
31. Langlotz, op. cit., p. 155.
32. Cf. p. 133 our text.
33. Cf. Kunze, 'Terrakottaplastik: Athenagruppe': and pp. 132–3 our text.
34. Kunze assumes that the offering was made by 493 BC at the latest; see *Fifth Report*, p. 71.
35. *Fifth Report*, pp. 68–74, esp. p. 71.
36. *Eighth Report*, p. 30.
37. Ibid., pp. 16 and 32–3.
38. A detailed sketch of both sills is given in plate 9 of the *Eighth Report*. The narrowest of the twenty starting positions at the eastern end of the stadium measured 0.935 metre across, and the widest 1.350 metres across. But there were several which were more or less equal in width, and this gave a certain impression of regularity. In the west there was one very wide position which measured 1.950 metres, while the remaining nineteen ranged between 1.045 and 1.310 metres. But since the width of the individual positions in the west all differed from one another, there was less sense of regularity here.
39. See *Eighth Report*, p. 37. This changes the Olympic foot very slightly for, if 192.28 metres = 600 feet, one foot = 0.32047 metre.
40. Ibid., p. 39
41. Ibid., pp. 37–9.
42. Zschietzschmann, op. cit., pp. 34–5.
43. *Third Report*, p. 12.
44. Zschietzschmann, op. cit., p. 26.
45. *Fifth Report*, p. 25, note 10.

46. Pausanias, VI 20, 8.
47. *Fifth Report,* p. 33.
48. Kunze, 'Olympia', pp. 267–8.
49. RE XVIII, col. 39.
50. *Second Report,* p. 18.
51. RE XVIII, col. 115.
52. *Eighth Report,* pp. 69 ff.
53. Pausanias, VI 20, 8–9.
54. *Second Report,* p. 24.
55. Cf. ibid., p. 19; and p. 159 our text.
56. Drees, op. cit., pp. 80–6.
57. Pindar, *Olympic Odes,* III 33–4 (Farnell p. 18).
58. Pausanias, V 15, 5–6; and Ludwig Weniger, 'Die monatliche Opferung in Olympia', in *Klio* IX, 1909, pp. 291–303, and *Klio* XVI, 1920, pp. 1–39.
59. In his article on the hippodrome (RE VIII, col. 1739), K. Schneider rejects this hypothesis on the ground that no such barrier is represented on any vase paintings or coins. But it is difficult to see how the Greeks could have dispensed with a barrier unless the competitors were allowed to overtake on either straight.
60. Pausanias, VI 20, 15, and 21, 1.
61. Ibid., VI 20, 15.
62. Ibid., VI 16, 4; and RE VIII, col. 1742.
63. Pausanias, V 12, 6.
64. Cf. K. Schneider (RE VIII, 1913, col. 1742) and E. Meyer (in his Pausanias, 1954, p. 635, note re. p. 334, 9)—both of whom reject the manuscript—and L. Ziehen (RE XVIII, 1939, col. 23), who reserves judgement.
65. For original text, see RE XVIII, cols. 22–3.
66. According to the manuscript, the hippodrome had a circumference of 1,538.24 metres. The circumference which we have established equals 1,473.862 metres (twice the length of the *spina,* plus twice the circumference of the turning (semi-)circles. Thus, there is a discrepancy of 64.378 mettes. This is readily explained if we assume that the measurement given in the manuscript allowed for a perimeter track. Since the length of the *spina* would remain constant whatever the circumference of the hippodrome, the variable factor would, of course, be the radius of the turning (semi-)circles. Now, if we subtract from the manuscript circumference (1,538.24 metres) twice the length of the *spina* (769.12 metres), we are left with 769.12 metres as the total circumference of the two turning (semi-) circles including a perimeter track; and, since radius equals circumference divided by 2π, the radius of this enlarged turning circle = 769.12 divided by 6.2832, which equals 122.409 metres. By subtracting from this figure the radius of the turning circle proper (112.163 metres), we obtain the width of the perimeter track: *i.e.,* 122.409 minus 112.163, which equals 10.246 metres—a measurement which seems entirely reasonable for such an installation.
67. Pausanias, VI 20, 10.
68. Ibid., VI 20, 10–13.
69. Ibid, VI 20, 19.
70. Ibid., VI 20, 15.
71. Ibid.
72. Ibid., VI 20, 17.
73. Ibid., VI 20, 19.
74. Boetticher, op. cit., p. 122.
75. Homer, *Iliad,* XXIII.
76. Pausanias, VI 21, 1.

9. The Fame of the Victor

1. Pindar, *Isthmian Odes,* I 50–1 (Farnell p. 241).
2. Dion Chrysostom, XXXI 20–2.
3. Pindar, *Olympic Odes,* X 91–3 (Farnell p. 60).
3a. Ibid., *Pythian Odes,* V 122–3 (Farnell p. 119).
3b. Ibid., *Pythian Odes,* X 10 (Farnell p. 140).
4. Ibid., *Nemean Odes,* IX 6–7 (Farnell, p. 218).
5. Strabo, IV 1, 12.
6. Pausanias, VI 14, 6–7.
7. Herodotus, III 137.
8. Strabo, VI 1, 12, 263.
9. Pausanias, VI 14, 8.
10. Ibid., VI 10, 1–3.
11. Ibid., VI 9, 6–8.
12. Ibid., VI 11, 2–8.
13. Ibid., VI, 5, 4–9.
14. Ibid., VI 8, 4.
15. Curtius, 'Entwurf einer Geschichte', col. 47a.
16. Pausanias, VI 3, 14.
17. Ibid., VI 15, 2.
18. Ibid., V 5, 1 and VI 14, 11.
19. Ibid., VI 4, 8.
20. Curtius, 'Entwurf einer Geschichte', col. 49 b; and p. 130 our text.
21. Pausanias, VI 18, 7.
22. Lucian, *In Defence of His Statues,* (Fischer IV, 106).
23. Pliny the Elder, *Natural History,* XXXIV, 9, 4.
24. Kunze, *Neue Meisterwerke,* p. 26, illustrations 55–7.
25. Lucian, *Anacharsis* (Fischer I, p. 227).
26. Pausanias, VI 1, 1.
27. For further details, see Mezö, op. cit., pp. 160–1.
28. Pausanias, VI 1, 2.
29. Ibid., VI 8, 3.
30. See p. 80 our text.
31. Aelian, *Variae Historiae,* IX 2.
32. Vitruvius, *De Architectura,* IX. Introduction.
33. Diodorus Siculus, XII 82, 1 and XIII 33, 1.
34. Ibid., XIII 82, 7.
35. Suetonius, *Nero,* 25.

36. This view is advanced by Mező, op. cit., p. 158.
37. Ibid. This account is almost entirely hypothetical. Only the final statement is vouched for (cf. *Bacchylides, VI 14*).
38. Dio Cassius, *Roman History*, 63, 20.
39. Suetonius, *Nero*, 25.
40. Vitruvius, *De Architectura*, IX Introduction.
41. Athenaeus, *Deipnosophists*, VI 237; and Diem, *Weltgeschichte des Sports*, p. 267.
42. Plutarch, *Quaestiones Convivales*, II 5, 2 p. 640; and Mező, op. cit., pp. 158–9.
43. For details, see Mező, op. cit., note 15.
44. Plato, *The Apology of Socrates*, 26.
45. Plutarch, *Solon*, 23, 5.
46. Ibid.
47. Plato, *The Republic*, 425 D.
48. Dion Chrysostom, *De Gloria*, 1; and Diem, *Weltgeschichte des Sports*, p. 267.
49. The selling price quoted for one kilogramme of silver on June 13, 1967 at the Frankfort Exchange was DM 224.80.
50. Cicero, *Pro Flacco*, 13, 31.
51. According to Thucydides, he took the first, second and fourth places. See also Plutarch, *Alcibiades*, 11 to 12, where both versions are presented.
52. Isocrates, *Peri tou zeugous* (On Chariot-racing), 32–4.
53. Plutarch, *Alexander*, 3.
54. Ibid., 4.
55. For sources, see RE XI, col. 438. See p. 54 our text.
56. Pausanias, VI 13, 10.
57. Ibid., V 12, 5.
58. Curtius, 'Entwurf einer Geschichte', col. 48a.
59. Cf. plate 47 our text.

10. The Buildings in the Sanctuary

1. Jantzen, 'Zeusheiligtum', in *Olympia in der Antike*, p. 37. According to RE XVIII, cols. 108–9, it was built between 625 and 600 BC.
2. Pausanias, V 16, 1.
3. Wiesner, RE XVIII, cols. 107–8.
4. Dörpfeld, *Alt-Olympia*, I p. 27.
5. The so-called 'Steiner statuette' in the National Museum in Athens, Exhibit No. 6178a, which was dated by Kunze. See *Athenische Mitteilungen* LV, 1930, pp. 159–60 and illustration 3. See also Vacano, *Das Problem des alten Zeustempels*, pp. 44–5.
6. Jantzen, 'Zeusheiligtum', p. 37.
7. Dörpfeld, op. cit., I p. 206.
8. Pausanias, V 4, 2.
9. Ziehen, RE XVII, cols. 2531–5.
10. Pausanias, V 17, 1; and p. 131 our text.
11. Dörpfeld, op. cit., I p. 200.
11a. Kirsten and Kraiker, *Griechenlandkunde*, p. 277.
12. Roland Hampe, 'Ein neues Beschlagblech aus Olympia', col. 359.
13. Pausanias, V 20, 4–5.
14. Wiesner, RE XVIII, cols. 111–12.
15. Pausanias, V 17, 5.
16. Ibid., V 20, 1.
17. Kirsten and Kraiker, op. cit., p. 278.
18. Wiesner, RE XVIII, col. 84.
19. Pausanias, V 10, 4.
20. Ibid., V 10, 2.
21. Ibid., VI 22, 4.
22. Ibid., VI 22, 3.
23. Herodotus, IV 148.
24. For bibliography on the ancient temple of Zeus, and also for further information about its date, see Vacano, op. cit., pp. 46–7.
25. Pausanias, V 6, 4.
26. Ibid., V 10, 2–12, 8; and Curtius, 'Olympia: Ein Vortrag', in *Die Antike*, XII, 1936, pp. 234–9.
27. The measurements quoted by Pausanias were taken from the base of the foundation and not from the stylobate (which would be the normal practice today). The effect was to increase the size of the temple in all its dimensions, from which it would seem that the Olympic guide was determined to impress Pausanias. The height (68 ft) apparently included the acroterium. Cf. Boetticher, op. cit., p. 257.
28. The archaeologists were able to establish that ten of the shields were placed on the eastern side and eleven on the western. Cf. Meyer's Pausanias, p. 605, note re. p. 252, 5.
29. This was probably the curtain which King Antiochus IV of Syria removed from the temple of Jehovah in Jerusalem when he dissolved the Jewish cult. Cf. Meyer's Pausanias, p. 609, note re. p. 258, 1.
30. The function attributed to this rim has been questioned by some scholars. Cf. Meyer's Pausanias, p. 609, note re. p. 256, 6.
31. These statements are based on Wiesner, RE XVIII, cols. 84ff.
32. Kirsten und Kraiker, op. cit., p. 283.
33. Wunderer, *Olympia*, p. 58.
34. Plutarch, *Quaestiones Graecae*, 47.
35. Curtius, 'Entwurf einer Geschichte', cols. 58b–59a.
36. Deubner, *Kult und Spiel im alten Olympia*, p. 22.
37. Pindar, *Olympic Odes*, X 49–51; see also p. 33 our text.
38. Dörpfeld, op. cit., I pp. 108–17.
39. Pindar, *Olympic Odes*, V 18; see also Drees, op. cit., p. 89 for our interpretation.
40. Dörpfeld, op. cit., I p. 112.
41. Boetticher, op. cit., p. 382.
42. Wiesner, RE XVIII, col. 119.

43. Boetticher, op. cit., p. 385.
44. Wiesner, RE XVIII, col. 119.
45. Pausanias, V 20, 9.
46. Wiesner, RE XVIII, col. 120.
47. Dittenberger, *Die Inschriften,* in *Olympia: Die Ergebnisse* series, Inscription No. 366.
48. Curtius, 'Entwurf einer Geschichte', col. 59 b.
49. Virgil, *Aeneid,* VI 781–7.
50. Pausanias, VI 19, 1 and V 21, 2.
51. Curtius, 'Entwurf einer Geschichte', col. 32 b.
52. Cf. Wunderer, op. cit., p. 81.
53. For a detailed description of the treasurys of Gela based on the findings of the new excavations, see *Olympische Forschungen,* I, Berlin 1944, pp. 83–110.
54. Thucydides, *Peloponnesian War,* I 121.
55. Plutarch, *Sulla 12.*
56. Appian, *Mithridates, 54.*
57. Schleif and Zschietzschmann, 'Philippeion' in *Olympische Forschungen,* I pp. 1–52.
58. Pausanias, V 20, 9–10.
59. Dörpfeld, op. cit., I p. 121. The diameter of the circle of stones was between 31 metres and 34 metres.
60. Cf. Pausanias, VI 20, 7.
61. In their 'Philippeion' (p. 22), Schleif and Zschietzschmann argue that the entrance must have been either in the east or in the north. They rightly reject the west as a possible site since the building extended to within a few metres of the (Greek) west wall of the altis. They also reject the south on the ground that 'the rectangular enclosure with a peristyle which was built there in late Roman times' would preclude the possibility of an entrance on that side. But in fact this rectangular enclosure might very well have served as a propylaeum. This, together with internal criteria, suggests that the Philippaeum probably faced south, as has been assumed by Wiesner (RE XVIII, col.105). Note: the ground plan reproduced in our text is taken from A. Mallwitz, who shows the entrance in the east.
62. Wiesner, RE XVIII, col. 106.
63. Ibid., col. 104.
64. Jantzen, 'Geschichte Olympias', in *Olympia in der Antike,* p. 19.
65. Pausanias, V 21, 17.
66. Ibid., V 22, 1; see also p. 69 our text.
67. *E.g.,* the long base (20 metres by 4 metres) in front of the echo colonnade for the monument to Ptolemaeus II at the southern end, and to his wife Arsino at the northern end.
68. Wiesner, RE XVIII, col. 130.
69. Ibid., col. 131.
70. Kirsten and Kraiker, op. cit., p. 282.
71. Wiesner, RE XVIII, col. 131.

72. Schleif and Weber, 'Das Nymphaeum des Herodes Atticus', in *Olympische Forschungen,* I pp. 53–82. In the *Eighth Report,* Mallwitz argues that, since Pausanias makes no reference to the exedra, it must have been erected after his visit to Olympia in AD 174. But this does not necessarily follow, for Pausanias paid little attention to functional installations. Regilla was priestess of Demeter at the Olympiad held in AD 155, and died in AD 160. See also Wiesner, RE XVIII, col. 115.
73. See p. 57 our text.
74. Wiesner, RE XVIII, col. 79.
75. Pausanias, V 15, 2.
76. Jantzen, 'Zeusheiligtum', p. 51.

11. The Statues in the Sacred Grove

1. Pausanias, V 25, 2–4.
2. Ibid., V 25, 5.
3. Ibid., V 25, 8–9.
4. Ibid., V 25, 11.
5. Ibid., V 26, 5.
6. Ibid., V 21–4.
7. Ibid., V 25, 1.
8. Ibid., V 23, 1; see also p. 61 f. our text.
9. Ibid., V 24, 4.
10. RE XVIII, col. 152.
11. Pausanias, V 24, 3. In RE XVIII, col. 151, Wiesner argues that Pausanias's account is a complete fabrication; he considers that the lettering dates the inscription to the sixth century BC.
11a. Curtius, 'Entwurf einer Geschichte', col. 50 a.
12. Pausanias, V 24, 4.
13. Ibid.
14. Ibid., V 24, 8.
15. Wiesner, RE XVIII, cols. 155–6; and Wunderer, op. cit., pp. 95–6.
16. Wunderer, op. cit., p. 96.
17. Ibid., p. 90.
18. Kunze, 'Zeusbilder in Olympia', in *Antike und Abendland,* II pp. 95–113.
19. Pausanias, V 17, 1; see also p. 112 our text.
20. Vacano, op. cit., p. 9; and Jantzen, 'Zeusheiligtum'. Both consider that the head was from a relief, either a sphinx (Vacano) or a pediment (Jantzen).
20a. Pausanias, V 17 1.
21. Wolters, 'Die archaische Hera in Olympia', in *Festschrift Heinrich Wölfflin,* p. 171.
22. Kunze, 'Terrakottaplastik: Athenagruppe', in *Sixth Report,* pp. 169–88.
23. Langlotz, op. cit., pp. 169–70; Kunze, 'Zeusbilder', pp. 109–10 and *Neue Meisterwerke,* pp. 28–9.
24. Kunze, *Neue Meisterwerke,* p. 29.
25. Ibid., p. 30.

26. Liegle, *Zeus des Phidias*, p. 384.
27. For text, see Wiesner, RE XVIII, col. 155; and also *Die Inschriften*, in *Olympia: Die Ergebnisse* series, col. 380, Inscription No. 259.
28. Rodenwaldt, *Olympia*, p. 49.
29. In a letter to his brother dated January 1, 1878. For text, see Carl Blümel, *Der Hermes eines Praxiteles*, p. 8.
30. Meyer's Pausanias, p. 606, note re. p. 253, 1.
31. Bulle, 'Ostgiebel des Zeustempels', in *Jahrbuch des DAI*, LIV p. 206.
32. Ibid., p. 208.
33. Ibid., p. 137.
34. Pausanias, V 10, 6–7.
35. Meyer's Pausanias, p. 605, note re. p. 252, 6.
36. Ibid.
37. We have followed the sequence adopted at the exhibition *Olympia in der Antike*, staged in Essen in 1960. This sequence is based on Treu's reconstruction and varies considerably from that used in the Museum in Olympia.
38. Pausanias, V 10, 8.
39. Homer, *Iliad*, XIV 347 ff.
40. Pausanias, V 10, 8.
41. For bibliography, see RE XVIII, cols. 95–97 and Walter, 'Westgiebel des Zeustempels', in *Rheinisches Museum für Philologie*, new series, XCIV, pp. 203–13. (Works propounding the Pirithous version are listed on p. 203.)
42. Pausanias, V 23, 1.
43. Curtius, 'Entwurf einer Geschichte', col. 45 b.
44. Fritz Weege, 'Zu den Bildwerken des Zeus-Tempels', in Dörpfeld (ed.), *Alt-Olympia*, I p. 475.
45. By F. Dornseiff; see RE XVIII, col. 96.
46. Walter, op. cit., p. 204.
47. Pausanias, V 15, 7.
48. Walter, op. cit., pp. 205–6. See RE XVIII for the derivation of the epithet Thermius. See also Bulle, op. cit., p. 218, note 2.
49. See Scholium on Homer, *Iliad*, XII 128. Cf. RE XIX col. 132; and Walter, op. cit., col. 206.
50. Bulle, op. cit., col. 206.
51. Ibid., p. 217.
52. Pindar, *Olympic Odes*, VI 32.
53. Bulle, op. cit., p. 218.
54. Walter, op. cit., pp. 206–7.
55. Ibid., p. 206.
56. Pausanias, V 10, 9.
57. Boetticher, op. cit., p. 285.
58. Kähler, *Das griechische Metopenbild*, p. 62.
59. Pausanias, V 1, 9–10.
60. Boetticher, op. cit., p. 294.
61. Lucian, *Imagines* (Fischer IV, p. 96-7)
62. Ibid.

12. The Zeus of Phidias

1. Pausanias, V 11, 1–2.
2. Strabo 353.
3. In his *Zeus des Phidias*, Liegle describes one of these coins.
4. Dion Chrysostom, *Orations* XII 25.
5. In his *Fabularum Liber* (223), Hyginus refers to this statue as one of the seven wonders of the world. He says that it was 60 ft high—i.e., 19.20 metres—which is about one third more than it actually was.
6. Epictetus, *Dissertationes*, I 6.
7. Pausanias, V 11, 9.
8. Philo of Byzantium, 3, 2; see also Liegle, op. cit., p. 169.
9. Dion Chrysostom, *Orations*, XII 49–50.
10. Lucian, *Works* (Fischer IV p. 107).
11. Liegle, op. cit., p. 224.
12. Pausanias, V 11, 10.
13. Homer, *Odyssey*, XXIV 249–50; see also Dion Chrysostom, *Orations*, XII 85.
14. *Sixth Report*, pp. 7–10, and *Seventh Report*, pp. 5–10, 11–12 and 15–16. See also Kunze, 'Olympia', pp. 277 ff.; and Mallwitz and Schiering, *Werkstatt des Pheidias*, Part One. Mallwitz deals with the architectural development and Schiering with the archaeological findings. A second part is to be published in which Kunze will deal with the finds that have a direct bearing on the statue of Zeus (forms for drapery, moulds for glass ornaments, tools, surplus materials, etc.)
15. Pausanias, V 15, 1.
16. Callimachus, *Fragments*, I 189, Fragment No. 196. See also Mallwitz and Schiering, op. cit., Part One, p. 1, note 1. According to Callimachus, the throne was 30 ft high and the statue 5 ells higher than the throne. Taking one foot as 0.32047 metre and one ell as 0.521 metre (the standard units for Olympia), this gives a total height for the statue of 9.6141 metres plus 2.605 metres: a total of 12.2191, say 12.22, metres. Meyer in his Pausanias (p. 608, note re. p. 254, 4) and Kirsten and Kraiker (op. cit., p. 284) give 12.40 metres as the overall height. Meyer (ibid.) calculates the height of the cella at 14.33 metres.
17. Mallwitz and Schiering, op. cit., p. 272.
18. Kunze, in *Sixth Report*, pp. 8–9.
19. Emil Kunze, the leader of the expedition, asked Hans Markl, a goldsmith, to carry out practical experiments to test his theory. (See *Deutsche Goldschmiedezeitung*. January 1956, pp. 10–13.) Instead of gold, Markl used silver with a gauge of 0.22 mm; but at the first tentative blow of his hammer, the mould shattered. He then cast the silver in a matching plaster mould, removed it and fitted it into the

clay mould. (See Roland Hampe's review of *Sixth Report* in *Gymnasium* LXVIII, 1961, p. 549.) Kunze has still to publish his analysis of these experiments, and consequently no final assessment is yet possible.

20. Mallwitz and Schiering, op. cit., p. 165.
21. Ibid., pp. 169 and 179. Schiering inclines to the view that Phidias brought the jug to Olympia on a possible visit in 436 BC (ibid., p. 273).
22. Mallwitz and Schiering have tried to date these events (ibid., pp. 272–7).
23. Dion Chrysostom, *Orations,* XII 78.
24. Ibid., XII 74–6.
25. Ibid., XII 77–8.
26. Ibid., XII 57–62.
27. Ibid., XII 25–6. See also Homer, *Iliad,* I 528–30; and Strabo, 354.
28. Homer, *Iliad,* I 500–1.
29. Liegle, op. cit., p. 221
30. Ibid., p. 220.
31. Ibid., p. 226.
32. Ibid., p. 168.
33. Ibid., pp. 169–82.
34. Pliny the Elder, *Natural History,* XVI 12.
35. Liegle, op. cit., p. 287.
36. Philostratus the Elder, *Apollonius of Tyana,* IV 28.
37. Cook, op. cit., III p. 959.
38. Polybius, XXX 15.
39. Livy, XXXXV 28, 5; Plutarch *Aemilius Paulus* 28.
40. Cicero, *De Oratore,* 8–9.
41. Quintilian, *Institutio Oratoriae,* XII 10, 9.
42. Epictetus, *Dissertationes,* II 8, 26.
43. *Greek Anthology,* XVI 81.
44. Aeschylus, *Agamemnon,* 174 ff.
45. Strabo, 353; see also p. 145 our text.
46. Pseudo-Longinus, *De Sublimitate Libellus,* 36, 3.
47. Pausanias, V 11, 9.
48. Josephus, *Antiquitates Judaicae,* XIX 1, 1. See also Suetonius, *Caligula,* 22 and 58; and Dio Cassius, *Roman History,* 59, 28.
49. Josephus, XIX 1, 1.
50. Suetonius, *Caligula,* 57.
51. Lucian, *Zeus Tragedy* (Fischer, III, p. 175).
52. Ibid., pp. 45–6.

1. Thucydides, *Peloponnesian War,* I 121, 143.
2. Ibid., V 49–50. See also Xenophon, *Hellenica,* III 2, 21; and Pausanias, VI 2, 2–3.
3. Xenophon, *Hellenica,* VII 4, 28–32.
4. Ibid., VII 4, 33.
5. Ibid., VII 4, 35.
6. Ibid., III 2, 23 ff.
7. Ibid., III 2, 31.
8. Diodorus Siculus, *Bibliotheca Historiae,* XIX 87, 1–3.
9. Livy, XXVIII 7, 14–17.
10. Polybius, *Histories,* IV 73–5.
11. Plutarch, *Sulla,* 12; and Appian, *Mithridates,* 54.
12. Appian, *Bellum Civile,* I 99.
13. Sextus Julius Africanus on the 175th Olympiad, in Eusebius, *Chronicon.* See also Drees, op. cit., p. 62 and note 166.
14. Curtius, 'Entwurf einer Geschichte', col. 57 b.
15. See p. 62 our text.
16. Suetonius, *Nero,* 22–5; see also p. 55 our text.
17. Pausanias, X 36, 9.
18. See p. 152 our text.
19. Suetonius, *Nero,* 24.
20. Pausanias, V 25, 9 and V 26, 3.
21. Rappaport, 'Heruli', in RE VIII, cols. 1154–6.
22. Kunze, in *Sixth Report,* p. 5.
23. Capelle, *Die Vorsokratiker,* p. 119.
24. See Isocrates' statement on p. 62 of our text. See also Mezö, op. cit., p. 202 ff. for further discussion.
25. See p. 107 our text.
26. Ziehen, RE XVIII, cols. 43–4.
27. Ibid., col. 40.
28. Lauffer, *Abriß der antiken Geschichte,* p. 136.
29. See p. 122 our text.
30. Ibid., p. 119.
31. Cedrenus, *Historia Comparativa,* 326 D - 327 A,
32. See Scholium on Lucian, *Rhetorum Praeceptor,* 9.
33. Themistius, *Oratio,* XXVII.
34. Cedrenus, *Historia Comparativa,* 322 B-C.
35. Ibid., 348.
36. Zonarus, *Annales* (text in Cook, op. cit., III p. 970, note 2).

List of Illustrations

Colour Plates

I Olympia. The valley of the Alpheus and the altis with the Hill of Cronus in the foreground. View from the heights above Druwa.

II Architectural developments in Olympia. Table designed by the author and drawn by Anton Zell.

III Pillars of the palaestra.

IV Horseman. Detail of Conrinthian krater. c. 570 BC. Collection of Antiquities, Munich.

V Four-horse chariots. Painting on lid of amphora by the Cleophrades painter. c. 500 BC. Collection of Antiquities, Munich.

VI Scenes from the pentathlon. Red-figured mixing vessel. 5th century BC. Museo Nazionale di Villa Giulia, Rome.

VII Runners, discus thrower and judge in the palaestra. Black-figured amphora. 6th century BC. Martin-von-Wagner-Museum at the University of Würzburg.

VIII Boxers preparing for the fight. Red-figured Attic continuous-curve amphora by the Cleophrades painter. c. 500 BC. Collection of Antiquities, Munich.

IX Competitors in the foot-race and the race in armour: Red-figured amphora. 5th century BC. Collection of Antiquities, Munich.

X Two pairs of wrestlers with youth as judge and amphora as prize. Red-figured amphora by the Andokides painter. After 530 BC. Staatliche Museen, Berlin.

XI Pankration. Scenes in the palaestra. Red-figured bowl by the painter of Vulci. 5th century BC. British Museum, London.

XII Bronze head of the boxer Satyrus, who won at Olympia in 336 BC. A work by the sculptor Silanion. c. 335 BC. 28 centimetres high. Discovered in 1880. National Museum, Athens.

XIII Temple of Hera.

XIV Olympic stadium as it is today.

XV Zeus and Ganymede. Terracotta group. 110 centimetres high. c. 470 BC. Museum of Olympia.

XVI The Philippaeum.

Black and White Plates

1. Pillars of the palaestra (re-erected).

2a. Cult of the earth mother and divine child: small clay figure from Mycenae. Before 1200 BC. Louvre, Paris.

2b. Cult of the moon goddess: clay figure of goddess (Hera?) with crescent-shaped body and arms from Tiryns. Before 1200 BC. Louvre, Paris.

3a and b. Pelops's four-hourse chariot. Pelops and Hippodamia. Red-figured Attic amphora with strap handle. 425–400 BC. Museo Civico Archeologico, Arezzo.

4. Funeral scene depicting chariot-race in honour of Patroclus. Black-figured Attic mixing vessel. Fragment by Dinos. 525–500 BC. National Museum, Athens.

5. Zeus as a warrior with conical helmet and waistbelt. Bronze statuette. 700–625 BC. 21 centimetres high. Museum of Olympia.

6. Votive relief from Eleusis. Demeter (left) is handing Triptolemus ears of corn; her daughter Persephone (right) is crowning the youth. Attic. c. 450–440 BC. Discovered in 1859. 220 centimetres high.

7. Statue of girl runner. Marble. Hellenistic imitation of a 4th century bronze statuette. Vatican Museum, Rome.

8. Bases of statues of Zeus (zanes), which were paid for from the fines imposed on athletes who resorted to bribery. The terrace of treasuries was immediately behind the statues. The entrance to the stadium is still visible on the right of the picture.

9. Two youths fighting in the presence of a judge. Red-figured, Attic bell krater by the artist who painted the Munich neck amphora (2335). Second half of the 5th century BC. Collection of Antiquities in the Archaeological Institute of the University of Tübingen.

10. Charioteer. Bronze. c. 470 BC. 180 centimetres high. According to the (controversial) inscription the statue was dedicated by the tyrant Polyzalus of Gela after his victory in the chariot-race at Delphi in 474 BC. It was discovered in the sanctuary of Apollo and is now in the museum at Delphi.

...arioteer. Votive offering at Olympia. c. 800–750 BC. Charioteer in geometric style wearing a close-fitting skull cap and a wide waist-belt. In his right hand, which is pierced, he holds a fragment of thick wire, which formed part of the reins. The axle and wheels are broken. The hub of the left wheel and the stumps of four spokes have been preserved. Olive green patina. Height overall 8.7 centimetres, height of charioteer 7.9 centimetres; height of car 4.5 centimetres; width of original axle approximately 12.5 centimetres. (See reconstruction by A. Mallwitz, Fig. 7, p. 27) Museum of Olympia.

12.   Small bronze figure of horseman. Votive offering. 500–475 BC. The place of origin and the present whereabouts of this statuette are unknown.

13a.   Four-horse chariot. Painting on a black-figured vase by the Xenokles painter. Middle of 6th century BC. Museo Nazionale Archeologico, Tarquinia.

13b.   Horseman. Painting on a Chalcidian-type amphora. 6th century BC. Louvre, Paris.

14.   Preparing for the pentathlon. Painting on the inner surface of a red-figured bowl from the school of the Brygos painter. Early 5th century BC. Museum of Fine Arts, Boston.

15.   'Discobolus' of Myron. Antique marble copy of the original bronze, which was made c. 450 BC. The tree trunk would not have been included in the original. Vatican Museum, Rome.

16.   Discus thrower. Painting on the neck of a red-figured amphora. Early 5th century BC. Collection of Antiquities, Munich.

17a.   Discus thrower. Detail from a red-figured Attic calyx krater by the Cleophrades painter. c. 500 BC. Museo Nazionale Archeologico, Tarquinia.

17b.   Discus thrower. Painting on the neck of a red-figured Attic amphora. c. 490 BC. Museo Etrusco Gregoriano, Vatican, Rome.

18.   Competitors in the pentathlon throwing the discus. Painting on the inner surface of a red-figured Attic bowl probably by the Euphronios painter. Early 5th century BC. Museum of Fine Arts, Boston.

19.   Competitor in the long jump breaking up the earth of the landing pit. Painting on the inner surface of a red-figured Attic bowl. Early 5th century BC. Collection of Antiquities, Munich.

20.   Competitor in the pentathlon holding jumping weights. Painting on the inner surface of a red-figured Attic bowl by the Panaitios painter. Early 5th century BC. Museum of Fine Arts, Boston.

21.   The first stage of the preliminary swing carried out with jumping weights. Red-figured Attic amphora. c. 500–475 BC. Louvre, Paris.

22.   Jumper about to take off. Red-figured Attic beaker, attributed to the Euergides painter. 500–475 BC. Louvre, Paris.

23.   Two jumpers and judge. Painting on outer surface of a red-figured bowl, probably by the Euphronios painter. Early 5th century BC. Museum of Fine Arts, Boston.

24.   Amphora painting depicting a jumper, flute player and discus thrower. c. 510 BC. Martin-von-Wagner-Museum at the University of Würzburg.

25.   Jumping weight belonging to the Spartan Acmatidas. Greenish-grey schistose stone. Before 480 BC. Length 25 centimetres; width 6–7 centimetres; height 10 centimetres. This weight, which was found in Olympia, was for the right hand. It no doubt was one of a pair. Museum of Olympia.

26.   Javelin thrower and judge. Red-figured Attic calyx krater by the Cleophrades painter. c. 500 BC. Museo Nazionale Archeologico, Tarquinia.

27.   Javelin thrower. Red-figured Attic amphora. Early 5th century BC. Louvre, Paris.

28.   Javelin thrower. Detail from plate 26.

29.   Pentathlon scene depicting two javelin throwers, a discus thrower and a judge. Black-figured amphora. Second half of the 6th century BC. Martin-von-Wagner-Museum at the University of Würzburg.

30.   Pentathlon scene. Runner and judge shown here with a discus thrower. Black-figured neck amphora. Second half of the 6th century BC. New York.

31.   Stade-race. Group of runners. Painting on neck of black-figured amphora. 6th century BC. Collection of Antiquities, Munich.

32.   Runners, boxers and judges. Black-figured vase. c. 510 BC. Louvre, Paris.

33.   Wrestling. Red-figured wine cooler in the manner of the Phintias painter. Late 6th century BC. Museum of Fine Arts, Boston.

34.   Two wrestlers. Black-figured amphora by the BMN painter of Agrigentum. British Museum, London.

35.   Palaestra scene: pair of wrestlers practising, runner in start position and javelin thrower. Relief on the base of a statue. c. 510 BC. National Museum, Athens.

36.   Statue of seated boxer in bronze by Apollonius of Athens. 1st century BC. 128 centimetres high. Museo Nazionale delle Terme, Rome.

37.   Boxers. Painting on the shoulder of a red-figured Attic bowl attributed to the painter of London. 475–450 BC. Louvre, Paris.

38.   Heavy athletes cleaning themselves with the strigil. Painting on the inner surface of a red-figured Attic bowl. c. 460 BC. Museo Etrusco Gregoriano, Vatican, Rome.

39.   Armed runner (hoplite) with helmet, shield and greaves. Red-figured Attic amphora attributed to the painter of Berlin. 500–475 BC. Louvre, Paris.

40a.   Armed runners. Painting on the outer surface of a red-figured bowl. Early 5th century BC. Collection of Antiquities, Munich.

List of Illustrations

40b. Armed runners. Painting on the inner surface of a red-figured bowl. 5th century BC. Staatliche Museen, Berlin.

41a. A judge handing a victor his fillet of wool (taenia). Painting on the inner surface of a red-figured bowl by the Enaion painter. First half of 5th century BC. Museum of Fine Arts, Boston.

41b. A victor with the symbols of victory: olive crown, palm branches and fillet of wool. Painting on the inner surface of a red-figured bowl. Early 5th century BC. Louvre, Paris.

42. Zeus and Ganymede. Terracotta group. 110 centimetres high. Museum of Olympia.

43. Head of Ganymede (detail from plate 42). Terracotta. Museum of Olympia.

44. Gorgon mask in wheel-vane. Bronze fitting for shield. 600–550 BC. The third blade is missing. The rotating blades were supposed to resemble the serpents in Medusa's hair and the whole device was intended to petrify the enemy. Diameter of the wheel-vane approximately 80 centimetres. Diameter of the shield probably 90–100 centimetres. Museum of Olympia.

45. The end of Caeneus. Bronze fitting on chest. c. 650 BC. Height 22.5 centimetres, width 33 centimetres. Caeneus, who was invulnerable to all normal attacks, is being driven into the ground by two Centaurs with uprooted tree trunks. Although he holds a sword in each hand and has run both his adversaries through, his feet are already embedded in the earth. Museum of Olympia.

46. Bronze tripod. 900–800 BC. Height overall approximately 65 centimetres. Museum of Olympia.

47. Horse from a team of four. Solid bronze. Early 5th century. Height 22.8 centimetres. This horse was found by the early archaeologists in the eastern part of the southern colonnade. Museum of Olympia.

48a. Bronze pony. 8th century BC. Private collection, Hamburg.

48b. Bronze pony. 8th century BC. Museum of Olympia.

49. Head of griffin (front view). Bronze. 700–650 BC. Height 22 centimetres. This head was one of the first hollow castings and was used as an ornament on a bronze cauldron. Museum of Olympia.

50. Head of griffin (side view of plate 49). Bronze.

51a. Head of griffin, ornament on cauldron. Hollow bronze casting. 700–600 BC. Height 27.8 centimetres. The left ear is missing. The eyes were added after the casting. The eyeballs were made of bone, the pupils of coloured material. The head was fixed to the upper rim of the cauldron by the neck, which was 49 centimetres long. Museum of Olympia.

51b. Head of battering-ram. Bronze. c. 450 BC. The damage to the notches indicate that this votive offering had been used in battle. It is the only battering-ram to have survived from antiquity. Height 24.2 centimetres;

length 18.5 centimetres; upper width 8.8; lower width 9.8 centimetres. Museum of Olympia.

52a. Helmet of Miltiades. Corinthian. c. 500 BC. The helmet, which had been badly damaged, was found in the third layer of the southern embankment in April 1940. Present height 18.7 centimetres; depth 28 centimetres. While the actual casque was very thin the guards for the forehead, neck and cheeks were reinforced. The edge of the nasal is 7.5 millimetres thick. The inscription reads 'Miltiadēs ane(th)ēken (t)oi Di'. Museum of Olympia.

52b. Oriental helmet taken from the Persians. c. 500 BC. The helmet, which was dedicated to Olympian Zeus by the Athenians, was recovered from a 12.60-metres-deep well at the foot of the Hill of Cronus in October 1960. The earth at the bottom of the well prevented the metal from oxidising and the bronze retained its original gleam. Height 23.1 centimetres; lower diameter 20.5–20.7 centimetres; thickness of the metal at the lower rim up to 2.5 millimetres. Museum of Olympia.

53. Starting line at the eastern end of the stadium.

54. Remains of arched gateway leading into the stadium.

55. Four-horse chariot rounding the turning post. Black-figured Panathenaic amphora; Kuban group. End of 5th century BC. British Museum, London.

56. Greek poet, probably Pindar. Antique copy of an ideal portrait from end of 4th century BC. Louvre, Paris.

57. Runner in start position. Bronze statuette dedicated to Zeus by a victor. c. 480–470 BC. Height including base 10.2 centimetres. Museum of Olympia.

58. South-eastern corner of the temple of Hera.

59a. Capital of pillar from temple of Zeus.

59b. Pillars from the temple of Zeus toppled by the earthquake.

60. Model of Olympia built for the exhibition 'Olympia in der Antike', Essen 1960, by Alfred and Eva Mallwitz.

61. Early archaic head of Hera. Limestone. Early 6th century BC. Approximately 50 centimetres high. Museum of Olympia.

62a. Lion's head. Gargoyle on the temple of Zeus. First half of 5th century BC. Museum of Olympia.

62b. Bull of Regilla, marble sculpture from the exedra of Herodes Atticus. c. AD 160. Museum of Olympia.

63. Late archaic head of Athene in terracotta. c. 490 BC. Present overall height 22.4 centimetres; height of face from chin to brow 11.8 centimetres. The head was found in the embankment of the second stadium on April 2, 1940. Museum of Olympia.

64a. Nike of Paeonius. Marble statue. c. 350 BC(?). 216 centimetres high. Museum of Olympia.

64b. Nike of Paeonius (reconstruction).

65. Nike of Paeonius (detail from plate 64a).

66. The Hermes of Praxiteles (detail from plate 67).

67. The Hermes of Praxiteles with the infant Dionysus. Marble. 4th century BC. 212.5 centimetres high. Carl Blümel considers the statue to be a Roman copy of the

original (Carl Blümel, *Der Hermes eines Praxiteles*, Baden-Baden 1948).

68a.   Eastern pediment of the temple of Zeus depicting the chariot-race between Pelops and Oenomaus. Marble. 475–450 BC. Length of pediment 2680 centimetres; height at apex 330 centimetres; height of the king approximately 315 centimetres. Museum of Olympia.

68b.   Central group from the western pediment of the temple of Zeus: Apollo and the Lapithae fighting the Centaurs. Marble. 475–450 BC. Length of the pediment approximately 2680 centimetres; height at apex 330 centimetres; height of Apollo approximately 310 centimetres. Museum of Olympia.

69.   'Seer' from the eastern pediment of the temple of Zeus. Museum of Olympia.

70.   King Oenomaus from the eastern pediment of the temple of Zeus. Museum of Olympia.

71.   Head of Apollo from the western pediment of the temple of Zeus. Museum of Olympia.

72a.   Head of Deidamia, bride of Pirithous, the king of the Lapithae. Western pediment of the temple of Zeus. Museum of Olympia.

72b.   Lapith youth fighting with a Centaur. Western pediment of the temple of Zeus. Museum of Olympia.

73.   Deidamia warding off a Centaur. Western pediment of the temple of Zeus. Museum of Olympia.

74.   Lapith maiden in grip of a Centaur. Western pediment of the temple of Zeus. Museum of Olympia.

75.   Stymphalides metope from the temple of Zeus. Marble. 468–456 BC. 160 centimetres high. Louvre, Paris.

76.   Hercules carrying the vault of heaven. Detail of the Atlas metope from the temple of Zeus. Museum of Olympia.

77.   Atlas metope from the temple of Zeus. Marble. 468–456 BC. 160 centimetres high. Museum of Olympia.

78.   Augean metope from the temple of Zeus. Marble. 468–456 BC. 160 centimetres high. Museum of Olympia.

79.   Head of Athene (detail from plate 78). Museum of Olympia.

80.   Bull metope from the temple of Zeus. Marble. 468–456 BC. 160 centimetres high. Louvre, Paris.

81a.   Elean bronze coin representing the Zeus of Phidias. Weight 25.64 grammes. Staatliche Museen, Berlin.

81b.   Didrachm. Elean silver coin representing the Zeus of Phidias. Weight 12.15 grammes. Staatliche Museen, Berlin.

82.   Western tower of the defensive wall built in AD 267 to protect the altis from the Heruli.

Text Illustrations

Fig. 1:   The altis in the Bronze Age (beginning of 2nd millennium BC). Drawing reproduced from *Olympia in der Antike* by Ulf Jantzen, p. 16.

Fig. 2:   The altis in Mycenaean times (late 2nd millennium BC). Based on drawings in *Olympia in der Antike* by Ulf Jantzen, pp. 16 and 17.

Fig. 3:   The altis in protogeometric times (11th and 10th centuries BC). Drawing reproduced from *Olympia in der Antike* by Ulf Jantzen, p. 17.

Fig. 4:   The altis in geometric times (9th and 8th centuries BC). Drawing reproduced from *Olympia in der Antike* by Ulf Jantzen, p. 19.

Fig. 5:   The altis in archaic times (7th and 6th centuries BC). Drawing reproduced from *Olympia in der Antike* by Ulf Jantzen, p. 20.

Fig. 6:   Earth altar of Zeus in Pausanias's time (*c.* AD 170) Drawing based on the reconstruction by Hans Schleif in *Der Zeusaltar in Olympia*, pp. 150/151.

Fig. 7:   Small bronze sculpture of a chariot. Reconstruction by A. Mallwitz, *Seventh Report*, Fig. 84, p. 143. For description see Plate 11.

Fig. 8:   Funeral mound of Pelops (Pelopium). Based on drawing by Wilhelm Dörpfeld in *Alt-Olympia*, Vol. I, Fig. 24, p. 121.

Fig. 9:   Funeral urn (pithos grave) containing the bones of a child. Found in the Pelopium. Longitudinal section based on drawing by Wilhelm Dörpfeld in *Alt-Olympia*, Vol. I, Fig. 15, p. 94.

Fig. 10:   Propylaeum of the palaestra. Based on the reconstruction by Hans Schleif in *Die neuen Ausgrabungen in Olympia und ihre bisherigen Ergebnisse für die antike Bauforschung*, Berlin 1943, Plate 5.

Fig. 11:   Ground plan of the palaestra. Based on reconstruction by Hans Schleif, *Fourth Report*, Plate 4.

Fig. 12:   Swimming bath. In the background the old hip-bath installation. Based on the reconstruction by Hans Schleif in *Die neuen Ausgrabungen in Olympia und ihre bisherigen Ergebnisse für die antike Bauforschung*, Berlin 1943, Plate 9.

Fig. 13:   Ground plan of the old hip-bath installation. Based on the reconstruction by Hans Schleif, *Fourth Report*, Plate 13. Built in 5th century BC.

Fig. 14:   Section of the old hip-bath installation. Based on the reconstruction by Hans Schleif in *Die neuen Ausgrabungen in Olympia und ihre bisherigen Ergebnisse für die antike Bauforschung*, Plate 9.

Fig. 15:   Ground plan of new hip-bath installation. Based on the reconstruction by Hans Schleif, *Fourth Report*, Plate 16. The installation was probably built in the early 3rd century BC.

Fig. 16:   Bowl painting illustrating the pentathlon. *c.* 500 BC. Illustration taken from *Weltgeschichte des Sports*, by Carl Diem, Fig. 143, p. 178.

Fig. 17:   Discus given as votive offering by Poplius Asclepiades. Bronze. Diameter 34 centimetres; thickness 1.4 centimetres (at centre) and 0.5 centimetre (at edge). This discus has an inscription on each side. The first refers to the 255th Olympiad, the second to the

List of Illustrations

456th Olympiad. This would seem to imply that the discus was dedicated at the 255th Olympiad (AD 241) and that this was the 456th since the inauguration of the games. If this is the case and assuming that the festival was held at four-year intervals, then the first Olympiad would have taken place in 1580 BC, at a time when Mycenae was just beginning to assert her supremacy. For further information on this point see Dittenberger and Purgold, *Olympia* . . . Vol. 5, columns 351–54. The discus is now in the Museum of Olympia.

Fig. 18: Inscription on Bybon's stone. Earlier than 6th century BC. The stone is a rough-hewn limestone block measuring 33 by 68 by 39 centimetres and weighing 143.5 kilogrammes. The inscription is very old. It occupies three lines, which run from right to left, then from left to right and finally from right to left. Phoenician script, from which Greek script was evolved, ran from right to left. For further information see Dittenberger and Purgold, *Olympia* . . . vol. 5, Inscription No. 717. Museum of Olympia.

Fig. 19: Amentum (loop attachment) and methods of gripping the javelin. The drawing illustrates two different ways of throwing the javelin, using the amentum to obtain additional power.

Fig. 20: Marble seat from the archaic stadium. The seat is now in the Museum of Olympia. Above: drawing from the photograph in *Fourth Report*, Fig. 110, p. 161. Below: drawing from ibid., Plate 67. The rough-hewn base was anchored in the earth. The visible part of the seat was 29 centimetres high, 42 centimetres wide and 31 centimetres deep. The seat was the only one found in the stadium. The inscription runs from right to left and reads: 'Gorgos the Lacedaemonian foreign representative of the Eleans'.

Fig. 21: Judges' stand in the late classical stadium. Based on the reconstruction by Hans Schleif in *Die neuen Ausgrabungen in Olympia und ihre bisherigen Ergebnisse für die antike Bauforschung*, Plate 3, Berlin 1943.

Fig. 22: Reassembled altar of Demeter from the second (Roman) stadium. Height 106 centimetres; length 157 centimetres; width 103 centimetres. Drawing based on photograph in *Eighth Report*, Plate 28.

Fig. 23: Temple of Hera (section). Based on a drawing by Hans Schleif in Dörpfeld, *Alt-Olympia*, Vol. II, Plate 5.

Fig. 24: Temple of Hera (ground plan). Taken from Hans Koepf, *Baukunst in fünf Jahrtausenden*, 5th edn. Stuttgart 1967, p. 24.

Fig. 25: Front of the temple of Zeus. Reconstruction by Hans Koepf, ibid. p. 25. (Koepf places Mummius's shields above the capitals. They should be placed in the metopes. The nike on the apex of the pediment should also be depicted with extended wings).

Fig. 26: Ground plan of the temple of Zeus. Taken from E. Norman Gardiner, *Olympia. Its History and Remains*, Oxford 1925.

Fig. 27: Temple of the Mother of the Gods (Metroum) with standing figure of the *Divus Augustus*. Reconstruction by Georg Treu, *Olympia* . . ., Vol. 3, Fig. 257.

Fig. 28: The terrace of treasuries. Based on a ground plan by Ernst Curtius, ibid, Vol. 1, p. 29.

Fig. 29: Philippaeum. Reconstruction by Hans Schleif in Schleif and Zschietzschmann, 'Das Philippeion' in *Olympische Forschungen*, Vol. I, pp. 1–52; Atlas, Plate 1.

Fig. 30: Philippaeum. Ground plan, ibid.

Fig. 31: Exedra donated by Herodes Atticus. *c.* AD 160. Reconstruction by Hans Schleif in *Olympische Forschungen*, Vol. I, pp. 53–82; Atlas.

Fig. 32: Ground plan of the theokoleon after it had been extended by the Greeks. Taken from *Olympia* . . ., Vol. 2, p. 110, Fig. 64.

Fig. 33: Ground plan of the theokoleon after it had been converted by the Romans. Taken from ibid., p. 111, Fig. 65.

Fig. 34: Southern colonnade. 4th century BC. Based on a reconstruction in Jantzen, *Olympia in der Antike*, p. 51.

Fig. 35: Frieze from the eastern pediment of the temple of Zeus. Drawing based on the reconstruction by H. Bulle in Lübke and Pernice, *Die Kunst der Griechen*, 17th edn., Vienna 1948, p. 217. The frieze is now in the Museum of Olympia.

Fig. 36: Frieze from the western pediment of the temple of Zeus. Drawing based on the reconstruction by G. Treu, ibid., p. 217. The frieze is now in the Museum of Olympia.

Fig. 37: Elean copper coins from Hadrian's time (AD 133) representing the Zeus of Phidias. Drawings taken from Boetticher, *Olympia. Das Fest und seine Stätte*. 2nd ed. Berlin 1886. p. 314, Figs. 70, 71.

Fig. 38: The Zeus of Phidias. Based on the reconstruction by Friedrich Adler in Dörpfeld, *Alt-Olympia*, Vol. 2, Appendix 22. Berlin 1935.

Fig. 39: Mug belonging to Phidias (view of side and base). Drawings based on the photograph in *Seventh Report*, p. 16, Fig. 8 and p. 17, Fig. 9. The mug is in the Museum of Olympia.

Fig. 40: Ground plan of the altis in late antiquity showing the defensive wall built against the Heruli. Drawing by Alfred Mallwitz in Emil Kunze, *Olympia*, p. 274, Fig. 10. Berlin 1959.

Maps and Diagrams

Map of the Peloponnese, page 14. The map shows the distribution of population following the invasion by the Dorians and the north-western Greeks. When the Dorians conquered the eastern part of the Peloponnese many of the indigenous Achaeans fled into the mountainous terrain of Arcadia in the heart of the Peloponnese and settled there (narrow diagonal lines). Those

Achaeans who remained behind were assimilated by the Dorians (narrow vertical lines). The Dorian Spartans also conquered Messenia in the south-west of the peninsula. For every Spartan there were probably six helots, which means that this district had a mixed population (narrow vertical and narrow diagonal lines). The north-western Greeks (Graeci septentrionalium occidentaliumque partium) occupied the north-western parts of the mainland and peninsula (broad vertical lines), while the Ionians evacuated the north-western coast of the Peloponnese and finally established themselves in Attica and on Euboea without intermixing (intersecting diagonal lines). These north-western Greeks then took over the district which had been vacated by the Ionians and the plain of Elis. The new inhabitants of Elis were the Aetolians. They subjugated and assimilated the indigenous tribe of the Epei and called themselves Eleans after their new home (Elis means valley-land). They also occupied the territory of Pisatis, which extended south as far as the Alpheus and included Olympia. The Pisatis was actually a league of eight cities, all of which were situated on the northern side of the lower reaches of the Alpheus. The fact that the Pisatans, aided by the Arcadians, made repeated attempts to regain control of the Olympic sanctuary and its games would suggest that they were a mixed race consisting of Aetolians and Epei (narrow diagonal and broad vertical lines). South of the Alpheus lay Triphylia, the land of the three tribes. According to Strabo (*Works*, VIII 337) these three tribes were the Epei, the Minyae and the Eleans; according to another authority (see *RE* VII, column 186) they were the Epei, the Minyae and the Pylians. Apart from the Eleans, who were probably a minority group, these tribes were all pre-Dorian. Consequently, the district between the Alpheus and Messenia retained a genuine pre-Dorian and Achaean character (narrow diagonal lines). The religious and political development of Olympia was greatly influenced by racial considerations, the most important of which was the antithesis between the old and the new tribes.

Front endpaper: Ground plan of Olympia. A revised version of the plan by Alfred Mallwitz in *Neue Deutsche Ausgrabungen im Mittelmeergebiet und im Vorderen Orient*, Berlin 1959, Appendix I, p. 265. All modifications are by the author. The most important of these concerns the hippodrome, which has been reconstructed on the evidence of ancient authors.
Back endpaper: Map of Aegean and Magna Graecia. The names of those cities which had treasuries at Olympia are printed in italics.

Sources of Illustrations

Alinari, Florence: Cover Picture, 17b, 36, 38, 41b. Antikensammlungen, Munich: 16, 19, 31, 40a. Bildarchiv Herbert Kraft, Berlin: III, XIII, XIV, XVI, 53, 54, 59a, 59b, 82. Bildarchiv Foto Marburg: 65, 68b, 70, 71, 74, 76, 77, 78, 79. British Museum, London: XI, 34. Deutsches Archäologisches Institut, Athens: 5a/b, 25, 42, 43, 44, 45, 49, 50, 51a, 52a, 52b, 57, 62a, 63. Dr. Karl Eller, Munich: 1, 8, 58, 64a, 73. Foto Schnell, Tübingen: 9. Clemens Hartzenbusch, Junkersdorf: 60. Hirmer Fotoarchiv, Munich: I, XII, 3a/b, 4, 10, 13a, 17a, 26, 28, 55. Dr. Martin Hürlimann, Freiburg/Br.: 6, 69. C. H. Moessner, Munich: IX. Museo Nazionale di Villa Giulia, Rome: VI. Museum für Abgüsse Klassischer Bildwerke, Munich. 12. Museum of Fine Arts, Boston: 14, 18, 20, 23, 33, 41a. Museum of Olympia: XV, 11, 46, 47, 48b, 61, 64b, 66, 67. National Museum, Athens: 35, 51b, 62b, 68a, 72a, 72b. Photographic Archives of the Vatican Museum, Rome: 7, 15. Prof. Dr. Ulf Jantzen, Hamburg: 48a. Service de documentation photographique, Paris: 2a, 2b, 13b, 21, 22, 27, 37, 39, 56, 75, 80. Staatliche Museen, Antiken-Abteilung, Berlin: X, 40b. Staatliche Museen, Münzkabinett, Berlin: 81a, 81b. Uni-Dia-Verlag, Stuttgart: IV, V, VIII. Martin-von-Wagner-Museum at the University of Würzburg: VII, 24, 29. Foto Widmer, Basel: 30, 32.

Index

Academy, Olympic, 8
Accidents in games, fatal, 52, 82, 103
Achaean League, 131
Achaeans, 11, 104, 112
Achilles, 30, 44, 150
Acmatidas of Sparta (victor in pentathlon), Plate 25
Acroterium, 113
Adler, Friedrich, 21, 125, Fig. 38
Aegina, 106
Aegis, 133, 141
Aelian (orator), 106
Aemilius, Paulus (general), 151
Aeschylus, 64, 151
Aesypus (victor in boys' horse-race), 70
Aethiopica (Greek romance by Heliodorus), 84
Aetion (painter), 63
Aetolian League, 61
Aetolians, *see* Eleans
Africanus, Sextus Julius (chronicler), 81
Agamemnon (Aeschylus), 151
Agariste (daughter of Clisthenes), 61
Ageneioi (the 'unbearded'), 50, 70
Agesidamos of western Locris (victor in boys' boxing), 102
Agesilaus (king of Sparta), 42, 51, 59
Agesipolis (king of Sparta), 25
Ageus of Argos (long-distance runner), 80, 106
Agis (king of Sparta), 54, 155
Agnaptus, colonnade of, 97
Agonothetes ('games organisers'), 54; *see also* Judges
Agrarian cult, 15
Agrigentum (Akragas), BMN painter of, 180 (Plate 34)
Akoniti victory, *see* Walk-over
Akragas (Agrigentum), 106, 130
Alaric in the Peloponnese, 159
Alcamenes (sculptor), 135, 138, 147
Alcibiades, 71, 78, 107, 157
Alcimedon of Aegina (victor in boys' wrestling), 102
Alcmena (mother of Hercules), 22, 33
Alexander I of Macedonia, 41
Alexander the Great, 41, 60, 65, 85, 107, 122
Alpheus; river, 11, 12, 17, 21, 24, 34, 35, 56, 73, 78, 86, 96; river god, 136, 137

Altar: general refs., 19–20, 21–4, 35–6, 69, 97, 99, 158, Fig. 21; at Pergamum, 21; in Samos, 21; of Gē, 13; of Hera, 13, 118, Plate II; of Hestia, 13, 23, 25; of Meter, 118, Figs. 3–5; of Zeus, 13, 17, 21, 78, 86, 88, 91, 94, 96, 159, Figs. 3–6, Plate II
Altis (sacred grove), 8, 12, 16–7, 19–20, 23, 34–6, 48, 68, 94, 96–7, 104,–5 115, 118, 120, 123ff., 130, 131, 158, Figs. 1–5, 40, Plates 54, 82, II
Alytes (policeman), 79
Amazons, 141
Amphitryon (husband of Alcmena), 33
Amyclaeum (Spartan sanctuary), 61
Anacharsis (Lucian), 36, 43, 58
Anaxagoras (philosopher), 64
Anaxilas (tyrant of Rhegium), 78
Anaximenes of Chios (philosopher), 63
Andokides (painter), 179 (Plate X)
Androleus (boxer), 82
Anecdotae Graecae, 24
Anolympiad, 130
Antalcidas, peace of, 60
Antilochus (son of Nestor), 99
Antiochus IV, (king of Syria) 116
Antiphon (writer), 43
Antoninus Pius (emperor), 126
Apelles (sculptor), 42
Apene (chariot-racing with mules), 32, 70, 102
Apolline prophets, 25
Apollo, 24, 35, 73, 74, 99, Plates 68b, 71; temple of (in Delphi), 140; A. Epicurius, 140; A. Pythius, 140; A. Thermius, 138–40
Apollonius from Alexandria (boxer), 43
Apollonius of Athens (sculptor), 180 (Plate 36)
Apollonius of Tyana (philosopher), 44, 55, 63, 64, 151
Appeals against judges' decisions, 55
Apple, as victory prize, 30, 34
Apsidal houses, pre-Dorian, 123, 124, Plate II
Arcadia, 11, 140
Arcadian war, 13, 45, 67, 130–1, 154, 155
Arcadians, 13, 14, 67, 130, 154, 155
Arcadius (eastern emperor), 159
Archaesilaus of Cyrene (victor in chariot-race at Delphi), 71

Archidamus II (king of Sparta), 42
Archidamus III (king of Sparta), 59
Archilochus (poet), 64
Archippus of Mytilene (boxer), 50
Architectural developments in Olympia, Plate II
Archives, Olympic, 128
Ares (god of war), 74, 132
Argos, Argolis, Argives, 15, 25, 41, 61, 80, 89, 154
Aristides (modifier of starting gate), 99
Aristonicus of Egypt (boxer), 83
Aristotimus (tyrant of Elis), 104
Aristotle, 64, 69, 72, 75, 79, 85, 104
Armenia, participation in Olympics, 158
Armour, race in, see Hoplite race
Arrhicion of Phigalia (killed in pankration), 52, 83
Artemidorus of Tralles (victor in boys' and men's pan-
    kration), 70
Artemis (goddess), 24, 85, 140
Asclepiades, Poplius (pentathlete), 75; votive discus of,
    Fig. 17
Asopichos of Orchomenus (victor in boys' foot-race),
    102
Asylus of Croton (victor in the stade-race and diaulos), 53
Astypalaea (island and town), 103
Athenaeus (writer), 106
Athene, 16, 35; late archaic head of, 92, 132–3, Plate 63;
    protector of Hercules, 140–3, Plates 75, 78, 79; Par-
    thenon statue of, 146, 149, 150
Athenians, 37, 53, 59, 121
Athens, 32, 41, 60, 61, 89, 106–7, 149, 154
Athletics, 41–55, 66–86, 157–8
Atlas metope in temple of Zeus, 141, 142, Plates 76, 77
Atreids (Mycenaean dynasty), 15
Attica, 16, 35
Augean metope in temple of Zeus, 141, 142, Plates 78, 79
Augustus (emperor), 94; as divinity, 119, 155, Fig. 27
Aura (race horse), 69, 71, 108
Avars, Avarino, 160

Bacchylides (poet), 64, 90
Balbis (starting and finishing line): for discus, 73; for
    javelin, 76; for foot-races, see Starting and finishing
    line
Basilae (priests of Cronus), 24
Bassae, temple of Apollo Epicurius at, 140
Bastards, excluded from Olympics, 41
Bater (aid in long jump), 74
Bathing facilities, 46, 48–50, Figs. 12–15
Berecynthian mother, 119
Berlin painter, 180 (Plate 39)
Black ram (sacrificial animal offered to Pelops), 18, 28,
    77
Blümel, Carl, 181
Boetticher, Adolf, 81, 99
Boxers: skull cap of b., Fig. 16; stories about, 103–4

Boxing, 30, 43, 53, 66–7, 72, 81–3, Plates 32, 36, 37, VIII;
    boys', 69, 83; classification of contestants, 44, 50–1;
    draw for, 51; origins, 30; technique, 81–3; thongs, 82,
    Plates 32, 36, 37; training, 44, 46, 47
Boys' contests, 69–70: see also under Boxing; Chariot-
    racing; Equestrian events, Foot-race; Pankration; Stade-
    race; Wrestling
Bribery, 52–3, 131, 158, 179
Bronze age: apsidal houses, 123; altis, Fig. 1
Bronze horse (votive offering), 108
Brygos painter, 180 (Plate 14)
Buildings A, B and G, 147, Plate II
Buleuterion (council house), 25, 68, 127, 128–9, Fig. 40,
    Plate II
Bull: Cretan, 141, 143–4, Plate 80; of Regilla, 57, 126,
    Plate 62b
Burnt offering, 18, 22, 78, 86
Bybon, stone of, 74, Fig. 18
Byzantine structures in Olympia: fortifications, 157;
    church, 147, 159
Byzantium, Olympic treasury of, 120, Fig. 28

Caecilius Lucius (orator), 152
Caenus (Lapith), 138, Plate 45
Caligula (emperor), 152, 156
Callimachus (poet), 147
Callipatira (daughter of Diagoras of Rhodes), 56
Callipus of Athens (pentathlete), 53
Cassius Dio: see Dio Cassius
Cathedra (judges' stand), 93–4, Fig. 21
Cedrenus, Georgius (historian), 159
Cenotaph, 17, 99, 122
Centaurs, 116, 137–40, Plates 45, 68b, 72b–74
Chaeronea, battle of, 123, 125, 158
Chalcidean style, Plate 13b
Chamyne (epithet of Demeter), 16, 27
Chariclea (character in Heliodorus's romance), 84
Chariot-racing, 15, 27–8, 31–2; 41, 44, 54, 66–7, 70–2,
    78, 94–5, 96–100, 115, 136–7, Figs. 7, 35, Plates 3a,
    3b, 4, 13a, 55, 68a, V: see also Chariots, racing; Eque-
    strian events
Charioteer, 41, 54, 70, 85, 99, 158, Plates 10, 11
Chariots, racing, 19, 60, 70, 99, Fig. 7, Plates 3b, 11, 13a,
    55, V; four-horse, 31, 54, 60, 70, 95, Plates 3a, 13a, 47,
    55, 68a, V; two-horse, 32, 70
Charmides of Athens (father of Phidias), 145
Cheating, 52–4
Cheilon (seer), 64
Chionis of Sparta (jumper), 75
Christians, 21, 160
Chthonic deity, 13
Cicero, 24, 57, 83, 107, 151
Cimon (father of Miltiades), 54, 92, 108
Cladeus: baths of, 48–50; river, 12, 47, 160; river god,
    136, 137

Index Classification of contestants, 44, 50–1
Claudius (emperor), 119
Clay moulds, 148
Cleitomachus of Thebes (boxer), 83
Cleitostratus of Rhodes (wrestler), 81
Clement of Alexandria (father of the church), 31
Cleoetas of Athens (deviser of starting gate), 99
Cleomedes of Astypalaea (boxer), 52, 103
Cleophrades painter, 179 (Plates V, VIII), 180 (Plates 17a, 26, 28)
Cleosthenes of Pisa (co-founder of the sacred truce), 36, 64
Clisthenes (tyrant of Sicyon), 61–2
Clytidea (family of seers), 24
Clytius (seer), 137
Coins, 87, 96, 102, 107, 145, 150, 159, Fig. 37, Plates 81a/b
Colonnades: c. of Agnaptus, 97; echo c., 91, 94, 97, 124–5, 129, Plate II; south-eastern c., 125, 129, Plate II; southern c., 97, 129, Figs. 34, 40, Plate II
Colotes (maker of ceremonial table), 85
Communion with godhead, 86, 149–50, 151
Conisterium (wrestlers' preparation room), 46
Constantinople: destruction of statue of Zeus at, 117, 159; old seraglio manuscript at, 71, 97–8
Corinth, 114, 115, 131
Corinthians, 121; see also Miltiades, helmet of
Corn mother, see Demeter as grain mother
Coroebus of Elis (victor in stade-race), 34
Coryceum (boxers' training hall), 46
Coubertin, Baron Pierre de, 8
Council, Olympic, 25, 55
Cratinus of Aegira (victor in boys' wrestling), 104
Crete, 11, 14, 19, 33, 118
Creugas of Epidaurus (boxer in Nemean games), 82
Cronus (father of Zeus), 19, 23, 118; Hill of, 12, 13, 19, 23, 33, 47, 50, 53, 87, 92, 96, 111, 120, 123, 125, 160, Plate I
Croton (town), 32, 53, 102, 103
Crown, crowning ceremony, 7, 54, 68, 85–6, 151; see also Laurel wreath; Olive crown; Victors
Cult, cults: agrarian, 15–16; chthonic, 13; Eleusinian mysteries, 12, 16, 68, 179; fertility, 13, 15, 26 ff., 34, 36, 56, 88, 97, 132; hero, 17–19, 62, 78; Olympian, 14, 101; pre-Olympian, 12–19, 21, 23, 24, 26–31; vegetation 13–14, 33, 34–6, 85–6, 132; see also Funeral rites, games; Zeus, I, II
Curetes (earth spirits), 23
Curtius, Ernst, 7, 118, 156
Cybele (Magna Mater), 119
Cycnus (son of Ares), 132
Cylon (assassin of Aristotimus), 104
Cynisca of Sparta (victor in chariot-race), 42, 108, 115
Cyrene, Olympic treasury of, 120, Fig. 28
Dactyli, the five, 16, 26

Daïcles of Messenia (first receiver of olive crown), 34
Damarmenus of Eretria (guardian of Pelops's relic), 29
Dameos of Croton (sculptor), 81
Damophon (king of the Pisatans), 114
Damoxenus of Syracuse (boxer), 82
Danube (reputed home of wild olive), 35
Darius (king of Persia), 103
Death, duels to the, 30, 81; d. penalty for married women, 27, 56, 68
Deidamia (bride of Pirithous), 138, 139, Plates 72a, 73
Deification of mortals, 119, 122, 158–9
Delos, 85
Delphi: charioteer of, Plate 10; oracle of, 24, 29, 34–5, 36, 53, 104; Pythian games at, 30, 34, 43, 50, 54, 61, 66, 67, 75, 81, 85; sanctuary at, 12, 30; temple of Apollo at, 140; temple treasure at, 121, 155
Demeter, 16, 23, 27, 29, 100; altar of 50, 95–6, Fig. 21; as grain mother, 16, 26–7, Plate 6; priestess of, 27, 56, 95, 126
Demosthenes, 64
Despoliation of temples, 41, 68, 152
Diagoras of Rhodes (victor in boxing), 83, 102
Diaulos (double stade-race), 31, 48, 53, 66, 78–80, 94
Diem, Carl, 8, 47, 75, 79
Diet, athletes' training, 43
Dinos (vase painter), 179 (Plate 4)
Dio Cassius, 106
Diodorus of Sicily, 59, 60
Diogenes Laertius (philosopher), 64
Diogenes of Synope (Cynic philosopher), 64
Diognetus of Crete (boxer), 52
Diomedes (king of Thrace), 141
Dion Chrysostum (philosopher), 64, 82, 95, 101, 107, 152
Dionysius I (tyrant of Syracuse), 59–60
Dionysius of Halicarnassus (historian), 60
Dionysodorus of Thebes (Olympic victor), 60
Dionysus, 15, 23, 30, 134; as infant with Hermes, Plate 67; torso of, 119
'Discobolus' of Myron, Plate 15
Discus, 72, Fig. 17; throwing, 30, 31, 45, 72–4, 75, Fig. 16, Plates 15–18, 29, 30, VII
Divine child, 13–14, 30, Plate 2a
Documents and records: 'quoit of Iphitus', 36, 64, 113; pan-Hellenic, 61
Dodona, oracle of Zeus at, 17
Dolichos (long-distance race), 31, 66, 78–80, 94
Dolphin, sacred to Apollo, 99
Domitian (emperor), 119
Dorian migration, 11, 16, 118; see also Pre-Dorian tribes
Dörpfeld, Wilhelm, 7, 112, 118
Double stade-race, see Diaulos
Double victory (wrestling and pankration), 84
Draw for contests, 51, 79; silver urn used for, 51
Dromeus of Stymphalus (long-distance runner), 43

Drymos of Argos (long-distance runner), 80, 106
Duels to the death, *see* Death

Earth goddess, mother, 13, 15, Plate 2a
Earthquakes, 160
Ebert, Joachim, 75, 77
Echo colonnade, *see under* Colonnades
Egyptians, 42, 43, 158
Elean judges, impartiality of, 42, 55
Eleans, 11, 13–14, 18, 37, 42, 114, 131; neutrality of, 36–7, 61, 155: *see also* Elis
Electra (Sophocles), 71–2
Eleusinian: mysteries, 12, 16, 68, 179; marble, 117
Eligibilty for games, 41–2, 68
Eliothesium (storeroom for ointments), 46
Elis: city, 36–7, 43–5; coins, Fig. 37, Plate 81a/b; country, 11; etymology of name, 11; leaders, 25, 29, 37; state, 36–7, 45, 131, 154–5
Empedocles (philosopher), 64
Empedocles of Akragas, private banquet of, 78
Enagismos (sacrifices for heroes), 78
Enaion paniter, 181 (Plate 41a)
Enelysion (place struck by Zeus's thunderbolt), 17
Epei (pre-Dorian inhabitants of Elis), 11, 37, 112
Epidamnus, Olympic treasury of, 120, Fig. 28
Epidaurus (sanctuary), 80, 121, 155
Epium in Triphylia, 114
Equestrian events, 70–2; boys' horse-race, 70; four-horse chariots, 31, 54, 60, 70, 95, Plates 3a, 13a/b, 47, 55, 68a, V; two-horse chariots, 32, 70: *see also* Chariot-racing, Horse-racing; Horses
Ergoteles of Cnossus and Himera (long-distance runner), 53, 102
Eualkes (boy competitor), 51
Eubotas of Cyrene, 105
Euerigides painter, 180 (Plate 22)
Euphronios painter, 180 (Plate 23)
Eupolemus of Elis (foot-race contestant), 55
Eupolos of Thessaly (boxer), 70
Eurybiades (Spartan admiral), 79
Eurystheus (king of Mycenae), 33, 141, 143
Eurytion (Centaur), 137–8
Euthymus of Locri (pankratiast), 51
Exaenetus of Akragas (victor in stade-race), 106
Exclusion from games, 41–2, 43
Exedra (or nymphaeum) of Herodes Atticus, 57, 125–6, Fig. 31, Plate II
Exegetes (guides), 25

Fertility cults, 13, 15, 26ff., 34, 36, 56, 88, 97, 132
Festival: delegations, 78; five-day, 66–86, 90, 154; quadrennial, 24
Fines, 41, 52–3, 84, 158
Fire, sacred, 124; *see also* Burnt offerings
Flamininus, Titus Quinctius ('deliverer of Greece'), 158

Flute player, 23, 25, 74, Plate 24
Folk tales and legends, 102
Foot-race, 26–7, 31, 51, 66–8, 78–80, Plates 30–2, 35, 53, 57, VII, IX; for boys, 31, 68; for girls, 26, 28, 29, Plate 7; *see also* Diaulos; Dolichos
Four-horse chariot teams, *see* Chariots, racing
Frigidarium (cold bath), 46
Funeral games, 30–1, 67–8, 77–8, 81, 88, Plate 4; rites, 18–9, 77–8, 122, 139

Gaeum, 13, 111
Gaiseric (king of the Vandals), 159
Galba (emperor), 55
Ganymede and Zeus, 92, 133, Plates 42, 43, XV
Gardiner, E. Norman, 37
Gē (earth goddess), 12–15, 23; altar of, 13; cleft of, 12; oracle of, 12, 17, 24
Gela, Olympic treasury of, 120, Fig. 28
Gellius, Aulus (writer), 85
Gelon (tyrant of Gela and Syracuse), 102
Georgius of Leontinoi (sophist), 59
Gerkan, Armin von, 87
Germanic tribes in the Peloponnese, 159–60
Geryones (three-legged giant), 132, 141
Girls' races, *see under* Foot-race
Glaucus of Carystus (boxer), 103
Gorgon Medusa, 115, 133, Plate 44
Gorgos of Sparta, stadium seat of, 90, Fig. 20
Graces, the, 23
Grain mother, *see* Demeter
Grave, funerary memorial: *see* Hippodamia; Pelopium; Pithos; Taraxippus
Griffin motif, tripod-heads, 89, Plates 49–51a
Grotto, cave: *see* Idaean grotto
Guesthouse: Greek, *see* Leonidaeum; Roman, 128, Plate II
Gymnasium: in Elis, 43–5; in Olympia, 14, 45–8, 57, Plate II

Hadrian (emperor), 95, 97, 115, 126, 128, 144, 145
Hagesias of Syracuse (victor in mule chariot-race), 102
Halteres, *see* Jumping weights
Heliodorus, 84
Hellanodicae, *see* Judges
Hellanodiceum (judges' quarters): in Elis, 44, 45; in Olympia, 125
Helmets (finds): 89, 148; Corinthian h. of Miltiades, 92, Plate 52a; oriental (Persian booty), Plate 52b
Hera, 15, 26, 29, 31, 53, 112; altar of, 13, 118, Figs. 3–5, Plate II; early archaic head of, 131–2, Plate 61; festival of, 18, 24, 28–9; Hera-Hippodamia, 15, 27, 29; temple of (Heraeum), 20, 29, 36, 111–14, 117, 128, 131, 132, Plates II, XIII; *see also* Heraea
Heraclides of Alexandria (boxer), 43
Heraea (women's games in honour of Hera), 29; *see also* Foot-race for girls; Hera, festival of

Index

Heraeum (temple), *see under* Hera

Heralds, Elean, 36, 54; h. and trumpeters, contests for, 68–9

Hercules, 12, 16, 26–7, 29, 33–4, 35, 62, 66, 84, 87, 96, 126; double-victor in wrestling and pankration, 84; Hercules-Iasius, 16, 27, 33–4; metopes in temple of Zeus, 115, 135, 140–4, Plates 75–8, 80; statues of, 130, 132

Hercules (boxer), 52

Hermes, 74; in stade-race, 74; of Praxiteles, 113, 134–5, Plates 66, 67

Herodes Atticus, 56, 57, 125–6, Fig. 31, Plate 62b

Herodorus of Megara (trumpeter), 69

Herodotus, 42, 62–3, 114

Heroes, cult of, 17–19, 62, 78

Heruli (Germanic tribe), defence work against, 121, 156–7, 159, Fig. 40, Plate 82

Hesiod, 19, 118

Hesperides, apples of the, 141, 142, Plate 77

Hestia (goddess of hearths), 21; altar of, 13, 25, 124, Fig. 4; sanctuary of, 125

Hiero (tyrant of Syracuse), 41–2, 102

Hieronymus of Andros (pentathlete), 77

Hip-baths, 46, 49, Figs. 12–15, Plate II

Hippias of Elis (sophist), 63

Hippocleas (victor in boys' diaulos at Delphi), 101

Hippodamia, 15, 27–9, 99, 136–7, 139, Plate 3b; funeral mound of, 122; nuptial bed of, 29, 114

Hippodrome, 18, 45, 71, 96–7, 127, 158, 160; in Elis, 44; in Rome, 97; reconstruction of, 97–8; special features, 98–100, Plate 55

Hippolyta (queen of the Amazons), 141

Hippomachus of Elis (victor in boys' boxing), 69, 83

Homer, 15, 138; and religion, 19, 32, 118, 144, 149–50, 153, 154, 158; *Iliad*, 99, 150

Honorius (western emperor), 153

Hop-step-and-jump, *see* Jumping

Hoplite race (race in armour), 31, 66, 72, 80, 84, 94, 105, Plates 39, 40a/b, IX

Horace, 85

Horse-racing, ancient style of, 106, Plates 13b, IV: *see also* Equestrian events; Hippodrome; Horse-racing

Horses: age groups, 50; draw for, 52, 99; owners of, 41, 42, 68, 70, 85, 105, 108, 158; votive offerings of, 19, 108, Plates 12, 47–48b; winning, 105, 176: *see also* Chariot-racing; Equestrian events; Horse-racing

Human sacrifices, 19, 30, 32

Hyacinthus (fertility god), 73

Hyboreans, 35

Iamidae (family of seers), 24, 136

Iamus (seer), 140

Iasius, Iasion (one of the five Dactyli), 16, 17, 26–7; *see also under* Hercules

Icarius (father of Penelope), 26

Iccus of Epidaurus (boxer), 52

Iconica (realistic statuary), 105

Idaean grotto, cave: at Olympia, 118, Fig. 28, Plate II; in Crete, 23

Iliad, 99, 150

Ilithyia (earth mother), 13–14, 23, 26

Ionian games, 43

Iphitus (king of Elis, founder of the Olympic festival), 34, 36, 54, 64, 88, 111; 'quoit of', 36, 64, 113; votive statue, 115

Isidore of Seville (writer), 87

Isocrates, 59, 60, 63

Isthmian games, 30, 43, 50, 61, 81, 107

Jantzen, Ulf, 111

Javelin throwing, 30, 34, 45, 72, 75–6, Fig. 19, Plates 18, 26–29, 35

Josephus, Flavius (historian), 152

Judges (hellanodicae), 41, 42, 43, 44–5, 50–1, 52, 54–5, 66, 68, 82, 85, 86, 93–4, 104, 128, Fig. 16, Plates 9, 23, 26, 29, 30, 32, 41a; judges' stand, *see* Cathedra

Jumping, 46–7, 74–5, Fig. 16, Plates 19–25; hop-step-and-jump, 47, 75; quintuple jump, 75

Jumping weights (halteres), 74, 105, Fig. 16, Plates 20–25

Jüthner, Julius, 47, 75

Kirsten, Ernst, 114

Kraiker, Wilhelm, 114

Kunze, Emil, 7, 87

Laconicum (Spartan-type vapour bath), 46

Ladas (fastest runner), 80

Lapith, Lapithae, 116, 137–40, Plates 68b, 72a–74; *see also* Caeneus

Laurel wreath (prize at Pythian games), 30, 85

Lausus palace (Constantinople), 159

Leo of Ambracia (runner), 55

Leochares (sculptor and architect), 122

Leonidaeum (Greek guesthouse), 57, 128, 155, Plate II

Leonidas of Naxos (builder of guesthouse), 57, 128, 155

Leonidas of Rhodes (triple-victor), 80

Leontiscus of Sicily (victor in wrestling), 81

Leophron (tyrant of Rhegium), 78

Lepreum in Triphylia, 41, 114

Letho (mother of Apollo and Artemis), 85

Libations, 14, 18, 25, 35, 78

Libon of Elis (architect), 28, 114, 115, 135, 154

Lichas of Sparta (victor in chariot-race), 54

Livy (Titus Livius), 37, 151

London painter, 180 (Plate 37)

Long-distance race, *see* Dolichos

Lower classes and slaves, 16, 157

Lucian, 51, 57, 58, 62–3, 95, 104, 105, 152, 154

Lutron (cold bath), 46

Lycians, 153

Lycurgus of Sparta (co-founder of the sacred truce), 36, 64
Lycus (winning stallion), 108
Lydians, 158
Lysander (Spartan general), 104
Lysias (orator), 58, 59–60, 62, 63
Lysippus of Sicyon (sculptor), 81

Macedonia, 41, 121–3, 158
Machanidas (Spartan general), 155
Magna Mater (mother goddess), 15, 17, 26, 30, 131
Mandragones of Magnesia (pankratiast), 84
Manlius, Titus (Roman envoy), 61
Mantinea in Arcady, 61
Marathon, battle of, 92
Marcus Aurelius (emperor), 66, 126
Mardonius (Persian general), 130
Mastigophorae (whip-bearers), 55
Medusa, see Gorgon Medusa
Megacles (suitor of Agariste), 62
Megara, Olympic treasury of, 120, Fig. 28
Melancomas of Caria (boxer), 82
Memmius Regulus (Roman governor), 152
Messenia, 61, 89, 131
Messenians, 59, 134
Messina, 130
Messinans, 89, 130
Meta (turning post in hippodrome), 97
Metapontum, Olympic treasury of, 120, Fig. 28
Meter (Mother of the Gods, q.v.), Fig. 3: see also Cybele, Rhea
Metroum, see under Mother of the Gods
Mezö, Franz, 83
Micythus of Rhegium (donor of votive offerings), 130
Milo of Croton (wrestler), 81, 102–3
Miltiades, 92, 108, 121; helmet of, 92, Plate 52a
Minoan civilisation, 11, 16, 33; see also Mycenae
Minos (legendary king of Crete), 143
Minyae (older tribes), 114
Mirabilia (ascribed to Aristotle), 35
Mithridates (king of Pontus), 155–6
Morea expedition, French (1829), 7, 141, 143
Mother goddess: see Earth mother; Magna Mater
Mother of the Gods: altar of, 118, Figs. 3–5, Plate II; temple of (Metroum), 118–19, 130, 158, Figs. 27–8, Plate II
Mules, 32, 70, 102
Mummius Lucius (Roman general), 115, 131
Munich painter, 179 (Plate 9)
Mycenae, 11, 15, 16, 29, 33, 122, 143
Myron (sculptor), 73, 105
Myrtilus (Oenomaus's charioteer), 27–8, 99
Mytilene on Lesbos, 61

Nemea, Nemean games, 30, 50, 53, 70, 81, 85
Nero (emperor), 131, 156; as contestant, 55, 62, 106, 108, 115, 125; triumphal arch of, 127, Plate II

Nestor (Homeric hero), 99
Neutrality, Elean, 37, 61, 154–5
Nicanor of Stagira (Alexander's envoy), 60
Nicasylus of Rhodes (victor in boxing), 50
Nicias, peace of, 134
Nike (goddess of victory): above apex of eastern pediment, temple of Zeus, 115, Fig. 25; of Paeonius, 133–4, Plates 64a, 65, II; of Phidias (statue of Zeus), 134, 148, Figs. 37–8
Nudity, 31, 56, 62, 84, 105
Nymphaeum, see Exedra
Nyssa, see Meta

Oaths, 14, 43, 51, 68, 128
Octagon (Roman building near hippodrome), 100, Plate II
Odysseus: suitors' race, 26; in sculpture group, 156
Oenomaus (legendary king of Pisa), 15, 33; chariot-race of, 15, 27–8, 66, 99; eastern pediment, temple of Zeus, 115, 136–7, Plates 68a, 70
Olive: crown, 34–6, 85–6, Plate 41b; grove, 35, 96; tree, 12, 16, 19, 27, 33, 34–6, 85, 88, 96, Figs. 1–4
Olympian mountains, 12
Olympic games (modern), 8
Olympus, Mount, 12
Onatas (donor of group of statues), 156
Opisthodomos (rear chamber of temple), 116
Oracle, 27; at Delphi, 24, 29, 34–5, 36, 53, 104; in Libya, 105; of Gē, 12, 17, 24; of Zeus, 24–5
Orestes (in Electra), 71–2
Oxylus (legendary king of the Eleans), 11, 111

Paeonius (sculptor), 133–4, 135, Plates 64a, 65
Painters, painting, 63, 104; see also Vase painters
Palaestra, 19, 45–7, Figs. 10, 11, Plates 1, III
Palm branch, 54, 85, Plate 41b
Panaitios painter, 180 (Plate 20)
Panathenae (Athenian festival), 62
Panegyricus (Isocrates), 59
Pankratiasts, 44, 67, 81, Plate XI; stories about, 83, 84, 103–4
Pankration, 31, 40, 66, 67, 80, 83–4; boys', 32, 35, 70, 83; draw for, 51; fatal accidents in, 52, 83; origins of, 30; Spartan, 83; technique of, 52, 81, 83; training for, 44, 45, 47, 84
Panoplia (full armour), 89
Pantarches of Elis (Elean peace-maker), 104
Pantheon: (olive grove in altis), 35; (Olympian gods), 159
Paraballon (victor in diaulos), 48
Parthenon, 113, 135
Patroclus, funeral games for (Iliad), 30, 99, Plate 4
Pax romana, 43, 61, 94, 119, 155, 156
Pelopium (funeral mound of Pelops), 17-18, 77–8, 88, 122, Figs. 2–5, 8, Plate II
Peloponnese, 15, 19, 36, 118, 145

Index

Peloponnesian War (431–404 BC), 37, 41, 52, 58, 61, 121, 134, 154, 155, 158
Pelops (hero of Olympia), 17–18, 22, 27–8, 30–2, 66–7, 77–8, 96, 99, 115, 136–7, 138, Plates 3a/b, 68a; funeral mound, see Pelopium
Penelope (daughter of Icarius), 26
Peneus, river, 11
Pentathlon (five-event contest), 31, 44, 54, 66, 67, 72–7, 105, Fig. 16, Plates 14–30, VI
Peregrinus (abusive orator), 57
Pericles, 154, 158
Persephone (daughter of Demeter), 16, 23, 30, Plate 6
Persia, Persian: participation in Olympics, 158; wars, 7, 59, 92, 138, 154
Phallus, 28
Phayllus of Croton: discus, 74; jump, 75
Pherenice, see Callipatira
Pherias of Aegina (boy wrestler), 50
Phidias (sculptor): and temple of Zeus, 114–7, 145, 146; mug of, 149, Fig. 39; statue of Zeus by, 7, 11, 31, 36, 64, 115–6, 134, 145–53, 154, 159, Figs. 37–8, Plates 81a/b; tools and workshop of, 147–9, 159
Phidolas of Corinth (race horse owner), 69, 71, 108
Philanor (father of Ergoteles), 53
Philanthropus (tyrant of Elis), 117
Philip II of Macedonia, 102, 107, 121–3, 158
Philip V of Macedonia, conquest of Elis by, 61, 155
Philippaeum (round temple), 107, 121–3, 158, Figs. 29–30, Plates II, XVI
Philo of Byzantium (mathematician), 146
Philostratus Flavius, son of Verus (sophist): author of Gymnasticus, 44, 45, 66, 69, 72, 75, 79, 82, 84
Philostratus Flavius, the Elder (philosopher); author of Apollonius of Tyana, 62; Imagines, 73, 84
Phintias painter, 180 (Plate 33)
Phlegon of Tralles (historian), 34, 95
Phlegyas (discus thrower), 73
Phoenician participation in Olympics, 158
Pholoë (plateau near Olympia), 159
Photius (patriarch of Constantinople), 77
Phrixae in Triphylia, 114
Phrygia, 15
Phyllobolia ('throwing of leaves'), 85
Physcoa (loved by Dionysus), 15, 23
Piera, fountain of, 45, 68
Pilgrimage to Olympia, 37–8, 57–8
Pindar, Olympic Odes, 7, 12, 24, 33–4, 35, 42, 64, 66, 78, 83, 86, 90, 96, 101, 102, 118, 154, Plate 56
Pirithous (king of the Lapithae), 116, 137–40, Plate 73
Pisa, Pisatis, Pisatans, 11, 45, 88, 114, 123, 130, 152, 154–5
Pisatan restoration, 112, 114, 128
Pisidorus (son of Callipatira), 56
Pisistratus (tyrant of Athens), 54
Pithos grave, 124, Fig. 9
Plataea, battle of, 130; victory monument of, 61, 120

Plato, 64, 107
Pliny the Elder (C. Plinius Secundus), 22, 105,
Plutarch, 25, 30, 41, 42, 59, 60, 77, 79, 85, 107, 117, 121
Polites of Ceramos (triple victor in foot-race), 80
Polus of Agrigentum (philosopher), 63
Polybius (Greek historian), 83, 151, 155
Polycleitus (sculptor), 105
Polydamus of Scotussa (victor in pankration), 84, 104
Polymnestor of Miletus (victor in boys' stade-race), 69
Polyzalus of Gela, votive offering of, 179
Poplius Asclepiades of Corinth (victor in pentathlon), votive discus of, Fig. 17
Poseidon, 15, 28, 143, 152
Praxidamas of Aegina (victor in boxing), 104
Praxiteles (sculptor), 113, 134–5, Plates 66–67
Pre-Dorian tribes, 115; fertility cults of, 13–14, 26ff., 34, 56, 132
Pre-Olympian cults, 12–19, 21, 23, 24, 26–31
Priests, 20, 22, 23–4, 25, 35–6, 66–7; see also Theokoleon
Priestess, 13, 25; see Demeter; Pythia; Regilla
Prodicus of Ceos (philosopher), 63
Prophecies, 24–5
Propylaeum (entrance): of gymnasium, 48, Plate II; of palaestra, 47, Figs. 10–11; of Pelopium, 124, Fig. 8, Plate II
Prothysis (base of altar), 21, 78
Prytaneum (administrative centre): at Athens, 107; at Olympia, 21, 22, 78, 80, 86, 124, Fig. 5, Plate II
Psammis (Psammetichus II, pharaoh), 42, 55
Psaumis of Camarina (victor in mule-race) 102
Ptolomaeus (general), 155
Puget, Pierre (French sculptor, 17th c.), 103
Punic War, Second, 61
Pydna, battle of, 151
Pyrgus in Triphylia, 114
Pyrrhus (king of the Pisatans), 114
Pythagoras, 64, 102
Pythia (Delphic priestess), 13, 24, 34, 103
Pythian games, 30, 34, 50, 53, 61, 71, 81, 84

Quintilian, 151
Quintuple jump, see under Jumping
'Quoit of Iphitus', 36, 64, 113

Race in armour, see Hoplite race
Racecourse, length of, 70–1, 97–8; at Nemea, 70
Racing chariots, see Chariots, racing
Records, 73–4, 75, 79
Regilla (wife of Herodes Atticus, priestess of Demeter), 56, 57, 126, Plate 62b
Rhea or Meter (Mother of the Gods, q.v.), 19, 23, 118–20
Rhegium, 89
Rhexibius of Opus (victor in pankration), 104
Ritual: dance, 18; games, 26–32; killing, 30
Rodenwaldt, Gerhart, 86

Roman emperors, cult of, 119–20, 158–9
Roman structures at Olympia: altis wall, 126–7; Cladeus baths, 49; exedra, 125–6; guesthouses, 128; hypocaust, 49, 50; Leonidaeum, modifications of, 128; octagon, 100; southern baths, 50; stadia IV and V, 94–6; theokoleon, modifications of, 127, Fig. 33, Plate II
Romans, 28, 43, 55, 57, 61, 63, 107, 155–6
Rome, 28, 61, 152, 155–6
Rudolph, Werner, 80
Rules and procedures for Olympics, 45, 50–5, 80–4, 128; appeals, 55; classification of contestants, 44, 50–1; draw for contests, 51, 79, 99; eligibility, 41–2, 68; exclusion, 41–2, 43; fines, 41, 52–3, 84, 158; oaths, 14, 43, 51, 68, 128; walk-over (akoniti), 43, 44, 51, 84

Sacred grove, see Altis
Sacred road (from Elis to Olympia), 45, 129
Sacred truce, see Truce
Sacrifices, 22–4, 158
Sacrificial animals, 38; s. vessels, 37
Sacrilege, see Despoliation of temples
Sarapion of Alexandria (pankratiast), 84
Satyrus (boxer), 105, Plate XII
Scillus in Triphylia, 111, 112
Secularisation of games, 127, 157–8
Selinus, Olympic treasury of, 120, Fig. 28
Seneca, 81
Sicyon, Olympic treasury of, 120, Fig. 28
Silanion (sculptor), 105, 179
Simonides (poet), 64, 81
Skamma (landing pit), 74, Plate 19
Slavs in Peloponnese, 160
Socrates, 71–2
Solinus (chronicler), 80
Solon (Athenian statesman), 107
Songs, Olympic, 101–2; see also Bacchylides; Pindar
Sophocles, 71–2
Sosipolis (protecting spirit), 13–14, 23, 26
Sotades of Crete (long-distance runner), 53
South-eastern, southern colonnade: see under Colonnades
Sparta, 34, 54, 61, 106, 154
Spartans, 25, 36, 37, 54, 58–9, 69, 81, 83, 90, 114, 120, 131, 134
Spectators, 56–65
Spina (barrier in hippodrome), 97, 98
Stade (ground measure, at Olympia 192.28 m), 26, 70–1, 87
Stade-race, 26–7, 31, 34, 44, 51, 66, 72, 78–80, 87, 93–4, 102, Plates 30–32, 35, 53, 57; for boys, 69, 156; for girls, 26, 28–30, 35, 87, 104, 112, 114, Plate 7; in pentathlon, 31, 77, Plates 20, 30–32, 35, IX
Stadium, 19, 27, 38, 47, 87–98, 126, 158, Figs. 5, 22, Plates 53, 54, II, XIV; entrance tunnel of, 94, Plate 54; etymology of word, 87; length of, 34, 87
Start position, 105, Plate 57

Starting and finishing line, 48, 51, 79, 93, 94, Plate 53
Starting gate (hippodrome), 98–9
Statius, Publius Papinius (poet), 79
Sterope (wife of Oenomaus), 136, Plate 68a
Strabo (geographer), 7, 24, 37, 103, 145, 152
Strigil (scraper), 81, Plate 38
Stymphalides (legendary birds), 141–2, Plate 75
Suetonius, C. Tranquillus (historian), 106
Sulla (Roman politician), 121, 155–6
Swimming bath, 49–50, Fig. 12, Plate II
Sybaris, Olympic treasury of, 120, Fig. 28
Syncretism, religious, 119, 123

Taenia (fillet of wool), 85, Plate 41a/b
Tanagra in Boeotia, 89, 115
Tantalus (father of Pelops), 30
Taraxippus ('terror of horses'), 97, 99
Tarentum, 89, 120
Taurosthenes of Aegina (victor in wrestling), 106
Telesphorus (general), 155
Temple of Zeus, see under Zeus III
Thales of Miletus (philosopher), 64
Thanksgiving, service of, 86
Thasos, 104
Theagenes of Thasos (boxer and pankratiast), 51, 103–4
Thearides (brother of Dionysius of Syracuse), 60
Theatre at Olympia, 62
Thebes, 33, 35, 59, 121, 155
Theekoleos, see Priests
Themis (daughter of Gē), 13
Themistius (sophist), 75, 159
Themistocles (Athenian statesman), 42, 59, 79
Theodosius I (emperor), 96, 159
Theodosius II (eastern emperor), 21, 96, 159
Theokoleon (priests' quarters), 25, 127–8
Thermopylae, battle of, 7
Theron of Akragas (victor in four-horse chariot-race), 102
Theseus, 85, 137–9
Thessally, 12, 17, 137
Thetis (mother of Achilles), 150
Thucydides, 61, 64, 121
Tiberius (emperor), 95, 107
Timanthes of Cleonae (pankratiast), 104
Timosthenes (father of Theagenes), 103
Tisamenus of Elis (pentathlete), 77
Tisicrates of Croton (victor in stade-race), 32
Titus (emperor), 119
Trainers, 43, 44–5, 56, 68, 69, 158
Training, 43–5, 68, 84, 158; facilities for, 45–50
Trajan (emperor), 115
Treasury, treasuries, 13, 38, 72, 118, 120–1, 123, Fig. 28, Plate II
Triastes (triple victor in foot-race), 80
Triphylia, 11, 111, 112
Tropaea (symbols of victory), 89

Index Truce, sacred, 25, 36–7, 41, 43, 59, 84, 115, 154–5; violation of, 154–5

Trumpeters, 68–9, 79, 124

Two-horse chariot teams, *see* Chariots, racing

Typaeum (execution cliffs), 56

Vandals in the Peloponnese, 159

Vapour bath, 46, 49, 50, Plate II

Varazdatos (Persian boxer, last recorded victor at Olympia), 158

Vase painters: Andokides p., 179 (Plate X); Agrigentum, BMN painter of, 180 (Plate 34); Berlin p., 180 (Plate 39); Brygos p., 180 (Plate 14); Cleophrates p., 179 (Plate V, VIII), 180 (Plates 17a, 26, 28); Dinos p., 179 (Plate 4); Enaion p., 181 (Plate 41a); Euergides p., 180 (Plate 22); Euphronius p., 180 (Plates 18, 23); London p., 180 (Plate 37); Munich p., 179 (Plate 9); Panaitios p., 180 (Plate 20); Phintias p., 180 (Plate 33); Vulci p., 179 (Plate XI); Xenokles p., 180 (Plate 13a)

Vegetation cult, 13–14, 33, 34–6, 85–6, 132

Vespasian (emperor), 55

Victors, Plates 10, 18, 41a/b, 57, XII; crowning of, 16, 27, 55, 64, 68, 70, 85–6, Plate 41a/b; fame of, 53, 62–3, 69, 78, 89, 101–8; in pentathlon, 76–7; list of, 54, 55, 102; posthumous, 52, 82, 83; votive statues of, 104–5

Victory, winged, *see* Nike

Virgil, 119

Visigoths in the Peloponnese, 159

Vitruvius (architect), 45–7, 106

Votive offerings, 19, 38, 42, 74, 89, 90, 111, Figs. 7, 17, 18, Plates 10–12, 25, 51b, 52a/b, 57, 64a–65

Vulci painter, 179 (Plate XI)

Walk-over (akoniti), 43, 44, 51, 84

Water, drinking, 57, 125–6

Weapons (finds), 89

Weights, jumping, 74, 105, Plates 20–25

Weniger, Ludwig, 38

White poplar, 18, 22, 78

Winckelmann, Johann Joachim, 87

Women: at festival of Hera, 28–9; death penalty for married w. watching games, 28, 56; participation in equestrian events, 42; priestess of Demeter only married spectator, 27, 126; religious duties of w., 13–14, 18, 28–9

Woodcutter (xylcus), 18, 25

Wool, fillet of, *see* Taenia

Workshop of Phidias, 147–9, Plate II

Wrestlers: classification of, 50–1; draw for, 51; stories about, 102–3

Wrestling, 30, 31, 44, 66–7, 76, 80–1, Fig. 16, Plates 9, 18, 33–35, X; boys', 31, 69, Plate 9; in pentathlon, 31, 72, 76, Plates 33–35; rules of, 80; trainers, 69; training, 43, 44, 45, 46; upright, 76, 81

Xenokles painter, 180 (Plate 13a)

Xenophanes (philosopher), 157

Xenophon (writer), 25, 67

Xenophon of Corinth (victor in stade-race and pentathlon), 102

Xerxes (king of Persia), 7

Xyleus, *see* Woodcutter

Zagreus (pre-Dorian fertility god), 30

Zanclians (inhabitants of Messina), 89

Zanes (statues to Zeus paid for from fines), 42–3, 131, Plate 8

Zeus I In history of religion: child Z., 14, 23; consort to Magna Mater, 26, 131; decline of Z. worship, 152–3, 154, 157–8; northern god, 11, 112, 118; Olympian Z., 7, 16–18, 19, 28, 31, 33, 88, 92, 134, 146, 150, 151; pre-Dorian fertility god, 14–15; principal god, 16–19, 24, 26

Zeus II The cult: altars of, 23; festivals of, 24, 25, 33–8, 66–86, 140, 154; great altar of, 17, 21, 78, 127, Fig. 6, Plate II; hecatomb for, 78, Fig. 6; oracle of, 7, 24–5; sacrifices for, 17, 22, 24, 66–8, 78

Zeus III In art: chryselephantine statue by Phidias, 145–153, 159, Figs. 37–8, Plate 81a/b; Ganymede and Z., 92, 133, Plates 42–43, XV; statues of, 61, 130–1, 133, 136, 137, Plates 5, 8, 68a; temple of, 7, 11, 18, 36, 63, 84, 91, 96, 108, 114–17, 130, 131, 133, 159, Figs. 25, 26, 35, 36, 40, Plates 59a/b, 62a, 68a–80, II; votive offerings with inscriptions to Z., Fig. 17, Plates 25, 52a/b, 57, 62b

Zeuxis (painter), 65

Zither accompaniment, 62, 156

m-B

8/5